D0872361

The Institutional Economy

Also by David Reisman

ADAM SMITH'S SOCIOLOGICAL ECONOMICS
ALFRED MARSHALL: Progress and Politics
ALFRED MARSHALL'S MISSION
ANTHONY CROSLAND: The Mixed Economy
CONSERVATIVE CAPITALISM: The Social Economy
CROSLAND'S FUTURE: Opportunity and Outcome
THE ECONOMICS OF ALFRED MARSHALL
GALBRAITH AND MARKET CAPITALISM
MARKET AND HEALTH
THE POLITICAL ECONOMY OF HEALTH CARE
THE POLITICAL ECONOMY OF JAMES BUCHANAN
RICHARD TITMUSS: Welfare and Society
STATE AND WELFARE: Tawney, Galbraith and Adam Smith
THEORIES OF COLLECTIVE ACTION: Downs, Olson and Hirsch

The Institutional Economy

Demand and Supply

David Reisman

Edward Elgar

Cheltenham, UK • Northampton MA, USA

Published by
Edward Elgar Publishing Limited
Glensanda House
Montpellier Parade
Cheltenham
Glos GL50 1UA
UK

Edward Elgar Publishing, Inc.
136 West Street
Suite 202
Northampton
Massachusetts 01060
USA

A catalogue record for this book
is available from the British Library

Library of Congress Cataloguing in Publication Data
Reisman, David A.
    The institutional economy : demand and supply / David Reisman.
    p. cm.
    Includes bibliographical references and index.
    1. Institutional economics. I. Title.

HB99.5.R42 2002
306.3—dc21   2001051253

ISBN 1 84064 674 8

Printed and bound in Great Britain by MPG Books Ltd, Bodmin, Cornwall

Contents

1. Introduction

Institutions are rules and routines, patterns and prescriptions. The subject of this book is the rigidity that the ongoing imposes upon the new. On the one hand there is the interpersonal constraint of fellow participants in a shared and common culture. On the other hand there is the intertemporal preconditioning that is the unselected consequence of adult learning founded upon childhood socialisation. Individuals make their choices at the margin of indifference. Even so, they start from here and not afresh.

People and past are deeply conservative. The subject of this book is the freedom that is exercised by purposive beings when they make their way to fulfilment along a road that they did not build. The inference is not that organism is superior to cell, history to innovation, idiosyncrasy to conformity, the yet-to-come to the been-and-gone. Instead the conclusion is a pragmatic one – that the truth is a mix.

The final chapter states the conclusion. Arguing that institutions are multiple and that the community within limits has the option of alternatives, the chapter is at one with Lindblom when he argues that economic discourse does wrong to imprison itself in the *a priori*s of calculative rationality: 'We have come to think not of human need and aspiration but of the market system as the fixed element in the light of which we think about policy. We find it difficult to think of the market as the variable'. (Lindblom, 1982:333). Difficult it certainly is where the subtleties of demand and supply have been schooled down to the one-dimensionality of the auction sale. Even so, the economy has many facets. Assuming a single answer is not the same as formulating the relevant question.

Chapter 11, Organisational cost, shows that even the market can be used to delimit the market. It demonstrates that the minimisation of transaction costs can be used to explain the evolution and boundaries both of *quid pro quo* exchange and of the hierarchical plan. Chapter 10, Organisational order, argues that even prudent gain-seeking only takes place in the settled context of people interacting through norms and networks, of past embodied in memory and precedent. The chapter suggests that truth-telling and promise-keeping can be the social spillover not of anonymity but of contact, not of detachment but of continuity. It says that cost minimisation makes more sense when it is embedded in social capital than when it stands free from its institutional complements.

1

Chapter 9, The demand to supply, is concerned with *homo sapiens* as *homo faber*. Its theme is that intrinsic motivation and the instinct of workmanship labour alongside the cash incentive and the prospect of consumption when active men and women invest their creativity in their work. Chapter 8, Needs and wants, explores the possibility that incremental wealth might not bring incremental happiness where people have fundamental needs that goods and services by themselves cannot meet. Chapter 7, Malevolence, is a reminder that envy and malice can dispatch self-interested demand and supply on to the minus-sum battlefield of spiteful destruction. Chapter 6, Benevolence, restores the moral balance by insisting that resources in the real world are often allocated through the generosity of gifts. Not least is the *quid* likely to be separated from the *quo* where the altruists, not isolates but members, are integrated into unifying groups. Interaction strengthens sympathy by inculcating the capacity to respect. Sympathy strengthens interaction by satisfying the need to belong.

Chapter 5, People and things, explains that consumer purchases are signifiers that identify, habits that perpetuate. Conspicuous certification as well as innate serviceability, the utility is not just in the thing itself but also in the location of which the commodity serves as the symbol. Chapter 4, Society as past, makes the case that expectations are bounded by learning and cognition biased through experience. Stressing that equilibrium is the precondition for disequilibrium, selective perception the precondition for clarity of vision, it implies that rule-breaking is ill-advised where rule-following is not a prominent part of the mix.

Chapter 3, Present as past, maintains that economic interaction is inherited constitution and *de facto* agreement even as it is competitive advantage-seizing and the spontaneous new departure. Chapter 2, Economy as society, argues that demand and supply are better understood when people become the proper study, economics is made a behavioural science and abstract demonstration ceases to be an end in itself. There is a need for the 'why' to collaborate constructively with the 'how to'. There is a need for psychology, sociology and politics to flesh out the mathematics of rational choice with a solid appreciation of 'the institutions – that is to say the habits of thought' (Veblen, 1899:133).

Reductionism and the in-period have their contribution to make. So, however, does the synthesis of people and the memory of the past. The institutional economy is the accommodation of living together as well as the self-centredness of living alone, the rigidity of cultural constraint as well as the evanescence of the market-price signal. *The Institutional Economy* says that expediency matters but that rules matter too. The truth, in other words, is the mix.

2. Economy as society

The economy comprises four functionalities: consumption, production, distribution and exchange. It is in that way bound up with the use of resources. It is not *per se* committed to the market mode of allocation: while goods and services can be allocated through the flexible pricing of supply and demand, they can also be allocated through pre-capitalist expedients such as habits and conventions and by non-capitalist mechanisms such as a national plan. Nor is it *per se* committed to the physicist's quest for maximal efficiency: while unintended slippage in the transformation of inputs into outputs will always be regretted, there is no reason to expect that the resource-efficient channel will everywhere be the channel that maximises felt wellbeing or psychic welfare. The economy *per se* does not mean the market and it does not mean the economical. What it does mean is the four functionalities of consumption, production, distribution and exchange – and that is all.

A narrow economics is precise but also restrictive. A broader economics makes the study of the four functionalities into the study of interaction and leadership as well. The truth is the whole: 'Economy and society are inextricably mixed, and there is no clear and simple domain of economic knowledge separate from the broader social world.' (Furnham and Argyle, 1998:67). To stop short at the part is to deprive the science of its ability to explain: 'The human dimension in economics is now woefully inadequate', 'so much so, that economics in its present state can hardly claim to be more than a semi-social science.' (Baxter, 1988:251–2).

It is the task of the present chapter to assess the claim that an economics without a base in shared values, patterned interaction and cultural location must forever be a 'semi-social science', blinkered by its abstractions. The first section, The maximising economics, explains the neoclassical perspective. The second section, Social economics, shows that there is a competing stall. The final section, The individual, brings in ideology and the State in the light of Löwe's contention that the *flexprice* nexus is particular and historical, neither universally valid nor the natural equilibrium: 'Far from presenting a pure theory appropriate to any social conditions, so simple a law as the law of supply and demand, as soon as we take it in its exact meaning, depicts the essential features of a very concrete society: the liberal society of early capitalism.' (Löwe, 1935:59). We start from *here*. The textbooks start from *there*. Thus does the maximising economics lend intellectual support to aspirations and realities which might not be our own.

2.1   THE MAXIMISING ECONOMICS

Alfred Marshall was wise enough to insist on an open-ended definition that precommitted the discipline to no single stock of behavioural expectations: 'Political Economy or Economics is a study of mankind in the ordinary business of life; it examines that part of individual and social action which is most closely connected with the attainment and with the use of the material requisites of wellbeing. Thus it is on the one side a study of wealth; and on the other, and more important side, a part of the study of man.' (Marshall, 1890:1). Marshall proposed that the science of wealth-getting be related to the study of the multi-dimensional whole. He was wise enough not to straitjacket his definition into a single interpretation of motives or a single toolbox of techniques.

The maximising economics that owes so much to his *Principles of Economics* has incurred a far greater debt to his modelling than it has to his pragmatism. The result has been that economics since Marshall has become virtually synonymous with the core vision of self-interested objectives pursued through a rational choice of means that Becker encapsulates in the following assessment: 'The combined assumptions of maximizing behavior, market equilibrium, and stable preferences, used relentlessly and unflinchingly, form the heart of the economic approach.' (Becker, 1976:4). The precise maximand can be material goods or altruistic devotion to duty, punishment avoidance through abstention from crime or envy gratification by means of deliberate malice. High Street shopping is not the only end or goal. Even procreation itself, widely believed to be instinctual, impulsive and random, can be shown to be in keeping with the deductive axiomatics: 'The higher value of time raises the cost of children, and thereby reduces the demand for large families.' (Becker, 1993:150). Buying a car with money or approbation through turning out to vote, what is crucial is no more than this: the action must be forward-looking and intendedly calculative if it is to be classed as economic.

Hirshleifer, like Becker, sees purposive optimisation as the economist's core concern: 'Our heartland is an intellectual territory carved off by two narrowing conceptions: (1) of *man* as rational, self-interested decisionmaker, and (2) of *social interaction* as typified by market exchange.' (Hirshleifer, 1985:53). Like Becker, Hirshleifer is reluctant to separate his chosen heartland from the general theory of real-world men and women who are indifferent to the disciplinary boundaries: 'It is ultimately impossible to carve off a distinct territory for economics, bordering on but separated from other social disciplines. Economics interpenetrates them all, and is reciprocally penetrated by them. *There is only one social science.*' (Hirshleifer, 1985:53). Like Becker, Hirshleifer is arguing for the unification of law, politics, sociology and other human sciences around a single and consistent core image of what it means to be a human being when challenged by the freedom of choice. Like Becker, Hirshleifer is convinced that the core vision may reasonably be taken to be the optimising mindset of economic man that was modelled so evocatively by the classical liberals who, in the tradition of Adam Smith, found the heartland of purposive action in the heartland of priced exchange.

Hirshleifer, like Becker, is thus arguing at once for a new interdisciplinarity and for the homogenising logic of economics. On the other hand he expects even economists to look beyond the 'terribly narrow, dull, bourgeois', the 'prosaic', the 'crassly material' (Hirshleifer, 1985:53) that is the shopkeeper's stock-in-trade to model less traditional phenomena such as the selection of mate based on brains or beauty, organisational politics where power and prestige are part of the income that is being earned. On the other hand he believes that the rational response to self-perceived self-enhancement is a social fact of such significance and generality that it would appear capable of uniting a wide range of seemingly disparate observations: 'Our analytical categories – scarcity, cost, preferences, opportunities, etc. – are truly universal in applicability. Even more important is our structured organization of these concepts into the distinct yet intertwined processes of optimization on the individual decision level and equilibrium on the social level of analysis. Thus economics really does constitute the universal grammar of social science.' (Hirshleifer, 1985:53). Economics is not economics merely because (as in the case of impulse buying that contributes below potential to Darwinian self-preservation) the medium is money and the playing-field the market. Economics is economics because it is the 'universal grammar' of men and women who, committed to survival and hungry for something more, keep input per unit of output to the minimum in order to maximise their chances of attaining their objectives. Economic imperialism this certainly is. Yet is for all the cost-awareness no more the hegemony of the shop, the factory and the bank than it is the rational response of the sensitive voter or blood-donor to the tax of conscience when he fails to volunteer his share for the public good.

Becker and Hirshleifer share the broad vision of economic action which regards the whole of social science as 'increasingly indistinguishable from economics' (Hirshleifer, 1985:53), which takes as the paradigm for 'all human behavior' the rational choice ideal-type of 'maximizing behavior, market equilibrium, and stable preferences' (Becker, 1976:5, 8). Other maximisers, equally persuaded as to the plausibility of the calculative and self-seeking stance, will wish, more modestly, to restrict their expectation of consistency, transitivity and self to the material world of goods and services where utility and profit are most likely to be the key to behaviour patterns. Whether their vision is as broad as Becker and Hirshleifer or as restricted as supermarkets and shopping, what, however, gives coherence to the maximiser's predictions is a commitment to the simplified axioms which lead the deductivists to reason that theirs is an accurate simulation of real-world decision-making. Formal, abstract, symbolic, mathematical, the pared-down model is believed by the maximising economists to provide a good picture of resource-constrained action as it really is.

The maximising economics, subjective and therefore introspective, adopts the perspective of methodological individualism. Arguing that tastes and preferences are exogenous, non-rational and quintessentially personal, it demands that the explanation of pleasures and pains traded off, costs and benefits compared at the margin be factored down to the single microeconomic decision-maker who alone can have a mind. Recognising that the psyche cannot directly be observed, it proposes that revealed preferences be employed as the second-best indicator of the hidden rankings, the invisible cardinalities for which free and flexible prices may be said to be the shadow on the wall. The maximising economics has in the circumstances a pro-market bias which, rooted in the agnostic empiricist's analytical reductionism, is permeated as well with normative individualism and a moral resistance to the forced channelling of the group.

The maximising economics, manifestly because it must rely on the invisible hand to be its information-uncovering mechanism, more subtly because it has a philosophical affinity with the 'don't fence me in' of free enterprise and the minimal State, concentrates its attention on rationing by price, factor-mobility in response to incentives, competition between units, efficiency as the test of 'ought-ness' in a means-constrained world where economising is essential since the ends are without limit. Its study is the willingness to pay made equal to the willingness to *be* paid, the gravitational pull of market equilibration, the tendency for prices to clear the quantities precisely because negotiations balance supply with demand. Its primary focus being the theory of price, it makes uncompromising use of the *ceteris paribus* razor in order to trim out the fringe variables which contribute only tangentially to the thermostat of small adjustments.

Sometimes, following Walras, the maximising economics employs the fiction of an omniscient auctioneer who costlessly manages a *tâtonnement* in order, making mutually compatible the discrete choices of the self-contained isolates, to bring into being a general equilibrium where otherwise there would be kaleidoscopic discovery and never-ending search. The Walrasian auctioneer incurs no transaction costs and experiences no difficulties in the processing and interpreting of information. As mechanistic as physics and as deterministic as a socialist plan, it is his great service that, centralising the homeostasis, he protects the particles and the cells from the tyranny of small decisions that can erect an insuperable barrier between the atoms and their comparative statics. The followers of Walras tend to model the optimality of inertia in such a way as to leave little scope for the exercise of individual choice: the price vector delivered *ex machina*, there is not a lot the unique one-off can actually do except to plug in the right numbers and respond with the conditioned reflex of the dog that associates food with the sound of a bell. Equilibrium established, changelessness takes the place of conscious economising and economic action becomes an oxymoron, a contradiction in terms.

Yet competence to the utilitarian is the ultimate selling-point. A competitive market modelled *as if* a Walrasian auctioneer can be shown by a maximising economist to provide a cost-effective means of allocating fixed endowments as between a multitude of competing ends. Price signalling in the absence of imperfections like cartels can be shown to produce an optimum in the sense of Pareto, a welfare *summum bonum* where, wasteful slack successfully eliminated, no player can be made better off without another player being required to cede some resources. No economic theory will ever command an unequivocal unanimity of consensus. Competence to such a standard must, however, strongly recommend the maximising economics to the economic imperialists and to the more moderate materialists alike.

2.2 SOCIAL ECONOMICS

The maximising economics explains preference-orderings and goal-attainment in the language of atomistic individuals acting out the logic of instrumental rationality and the own-gain drive. Social economics situates the four functionalities in the bigger picture. Sceptical about the *a priori*, avid to explore alternatives in psychology and sociology, it is simultaneously a critique of the neoclassical orthodoxy and a demonstration that new wine can be poured into new bottles.

2.2.1 The Neoclassical Shortfall

The maximising economics proceeds rigorously from the assumptions of calculative rationality and self-regarding choice to the prediction of means-ends efficiency in respect of utility and profit. Its approach is axiomatic but its ambitions are positive. The economising posture, restricted in the case of guns and butter, general in the case of marriage and suicide, makes human action into the selection of the best-fitted alternative. It does so in the confident expectation that its model of competing bundles bears a strong resemblance to the real-world nexus. Its critics object that its vision is too simplified to have the explanatory power that is needed.

Conceptually speaking, the maximising economics underestimates the difficulty of defining rationality and self-seeking in such a way as to distinguish the falsifiable hypothesis from the tautologous proposition. The impulse buyer who does not count the cost may be accused of wasteful bad husbandry – or may be said cost-effectively to be reallocating scarce time to higher-valued investments. The Good Samaritan who gives freely to the destitute may be said to be ranking Alter's need-satisfaction above that of Ego – or may be accused of selfish vanity through the purchase of feel-good self-felicitation. Examples such as these are a reminder of the sense in which all action may be regarded as rational and self-seeking provided only that it is correctly interpreted.

Yet there is a rival sense in which deliberate randomness is not the same as careful evaluation, the gift not *as much* an exchange as the sale. This stricter construction is supported by popular perceptions and usages; and it also has important implications for differing rates of economic growth. Empirical evidence on the psychological propensity to over-estimate positive outcomes, on the perceived salience of an unrepresentative occurrence, on the clinging reluctance to sell on a *status quo* endowment strongly reinforces the conceptual reservations. The maximising economics should not in the circumstances be too quick to take on trust the assumptions of rationality and interest without acknowledging the possibility that a rival interpretation would call the tautology into doubt.

No less important than the positive content is the normative binding. The maximising economics, on the track of a 'universal grammar', is reluctant to treat textbook behaviour patterns as collective choices and shared values rather than as natural laws that warrant no philosophical legitimation. Aggressive initiative-taking and wit-matching competitiveness are treated as valid models of social interaction despite the need-satisfaction through good neighbourliness that the zero-sum divisiveness can so easily put at risk. Market-clearing prices and freedom of trade are taken to be more productive of felt wellbeing than are tariffs, ration books, queues, directives and other excrescences of State intervention. More being preferable to less, scarcity is permanent since desires are without limit. Tastes being intrinsic to the actor, the autonomous mind is uniquely the best judge of the idiosyncratic self's authentic interest. Intuition is non-economising and can lead to waste. The *quid pro quo* is consonant with human nature and a stimulus to purposive activity. Property-rights, inherited wealth, passive portfolios, traditional differentials are exogeneities that require no explanation despite the fact that the plasticity of the equilibrium price is closely correlated with the distribution of effective demand. The factor 'labour' is made the drudgery of toil and not the self-actualisation of human creativity that is its own reward and compensation. The maximising economics clearly takes a view of the human condition which, not a 'universal grammar' but a contingent judgement, will be the choice of many economic men and women but none the less a choice for being a popular one.

The outlook which concentrates on market efficiency gives the impression of being a self-confident ideology, a self-justifying monopoly which, like so many other churches and faiths, believes that it alone has found the high-road to Heaven. The maximising economics would arguably command more respect if it acknowledged that its core tenets – rational choice, means–ends economising, consumer sovereignty, unlimited acquisitiveness, the stigmatisation of waste – need not be eternal truths or even consensual assessments. Attracted by custom and integration at least as much as it is repelled by material poverty, it is easy to imagine a community which reacts to the economiser's values with the objection that the attitudes being espoused may be useful for the upgrading of affluence but are not for all that the attitudes which the society ranks most highly. A collectivity which puts convention and empathy above first-best allocation and production-potential growth will be sharply critical of the economisers for passing off normative prescription as positive analysis. Such a collectivity will make the point that even if the devolved and the homeostatic do in fact maximise living standards, still there are other *desiderata* which command allegiance as well. A socially responsible economics must evidently begin with social values and not top-down from the economiser's biases which the community might or might not find to its taste.

The economiser treats specific attitudes as appropriate for his quest. If the *favelas* and the *bidonvilles*, village Russia and village India, are to secure their place on the escalator that will take them up into modern Manhattan, then there is an inescapable need for flexibility, self-reliance, alertness, parsimony, prudence, dynamism, entrepreneurship, change. Even if the economiser's expectation is in practice a well-founded one, still the community might prefer different values or, most probably, a mix of values. Each mix is absolutely itself – and each mix is absolutely economic. The economy comprises the four functionalities of consumption, production, distribution and exchange. The economist, studying those activities, seeks to find out what makes most people feel best off in their own estimation. And that is all.

2.2.2. The Social Alternative

Social economics makes the study of the four functionalities into a sub-topic in the study of overlapping lifestyles and interpersonal relations. Social economics is concerned with social values and social location, with interdependent choices and patterned homogeneities. It is concerned with goods and services and with the discrete individuals who supply and demand, first and foremost through the rules which shape and the roles which stream.

The maximising economics, however supra-individual the procedures and endstates that it seeks to elucidate, builds upwards with Becker from the irreducibly separated and special: 'The economic approach to behavior builds on a theory of individual choice... It uses theory at the micro level as a powerful tool to derive implications at the group or macro level... The analysis assumes that individuals maximize welfare *as they conceive it.*' (Becker, 1993:139, 156). The canvas may be broad or narrow but the unit is forever the isolated atom and the expected search a rational one. It is a choice-theoretical approach which Thorstein Veblen was hardly alone in finding profoundly under-determined: the 'hedonistic conception of man', he wrote, makes the economic actor no more than a 'lightning calculator of pleasures and pains, who oscillates like a homogeneous globule of desire of happiness under the impulse of stimuli that shift him about the area but leave him intact' (Veblen, 1919:73). A more comprehensive account is required, Veblen believed, of the situational context which constrains the micro one-off's free-standing plans. Social economics is the alternative which fills in the blanks.

The maximising economics adopts a micro-to-macro methodology. The social alternative proceeds macro-to-micro and not bottom-up. In reversing the chain of command, it reveals its sensitivity to common predispositions, learned opinions, acquired meanings – to the social institution, in short, which, following Hamilton, may be defined as a non-ego limit which imposes a structure on present-day deliberations: 'It connotes a way of thought or action of some prevalence and permanence, which is embedded in the habits of a group or the customs of a people. In ordinary speech it is another word for procedure, convention or arrangement; in the language of books it is the singular of which the mores or the folkways are the plural. Institutions fix the confines of and impose form upon the activities of human beings.' (Hamilton, 1932:3). The social institution, Kasper and Streit say, is a man-made regularity, prescription or proscription, which is the normative scaffolding upon which all subsequent choices are able to build: 'Institutions are rules of human interaction that constrain possibly opportunistic and erratic individual behaviour, thereby making human behaviour more predictable and thus facilitating the division of labour and wealth creation. Institutions, to be effective, always imply some kind of sanction for rule violations.' (Kasper and Streit, 1998:30). Institutions are sanctioned by the community because they are shared in the community. Whether the rules of the road, the accepted language, median table-manners or taken-for-granted dress, institutions are the norms and usages to which *I* must conform precisely because *We* are *We*.

Social economics does not deny that individual agency is capable of invention, innovation, adaptation, improvement. It would make no sense to say that the Hobbesian, Marxian, Parsonian conflict between internal and external states must necessarily be resolved through the sublimation of the self into the surroundings and the renunciation of all change lest, destabilising a tried-and-tested order, it replace a going concern with a war of each against all. What social economics would, however, contend is that the bottom-up building block is condemned by the logic of internalisation, socialisation and the life in common to situate new departures within the constricting parameters of what Veblen calls 'commonplace knowledge diffused through the community': 'Each move so made is necessarily made by individuals immersed in the community and exposed to the discipline of group life as it runs in the community, since all life is necessarily group life.' (Veblen, 1914:103–104). Initiative remains possible but still membership is a fact.

The social map gives each decision-maker a setting. As Mark Granovetter puts it, defending the classic sociological perspectives against an over-inflated economics which would ill-advisedly 'erect an enormous superstructure on a narrow and fragile base', even buying and selling are Durkheimean social facts: 'Economic action (like all action) is socially situated, and cannot be explained by individual motives alone; it is embedded in ongoing networks of personal relations rather than carried out by atomized actors.' (Granovetter, 1992:270). Rousseau-like belief-systems which are reductionist to the level of free Crusoe alone have the disadvantage that they do not convey an adequate picture of externality and constraint.

Economic action, socially situated, is pushed by material incentives but also pulled by shared goals and dominant standards. Financial gain and optimising consequentialism cause the purposive marketeer to deviate from prescribed adaptations in order to seek out new and better opportunities. Social sanctions, on the other hand, threaten with criticism, ostracism, ridicule, loss of status, denial of sociability, spoiled self-esteem, the bite of conscience the radical iconoclast who violates the rules which the group, self-replicating as well as outcome-orientated, decrees ought to be obeyed for themselves. The pecuniary and the expedient whisper in one ear. Approval solicited and guilt eschewed whisper in the other. Given the push that impels the ambitious to break ranks alongside the pull that makes the unreflecting the passive playthings of unintended determinism, it would be as one-sided to say that all action is mechanistically swept along by non-ego currents as it would be to say that economics is no more than instrumental rationality in pursuit of a fuller trough. The truth, here as elsewhere, would seem to be the mix. Not least would it seem to be the mix because even the norms, like all laws, edicts, guidelines and codes, are necessarily incomplete within the fixed goalposts that assure them their force: 'Social norms offer considerable scope for skill, choice, interpretation and manipulation. For that reason, rational actors often deploy norms to achieve their ends. Yet there are limits to the flexibility of norms, otherwise there would be nothing to manipulate.' (Elster, 1989:262).

The truth would seem to be the mix, the economic actor neither the under-socialised romantic nor the over-socialised automaton. Praise and shame as well as goods and services enter actively into the goal-function. In some cases, in the view of Dennis Wrong, the goal of 'self-validation by others' will actually take precedence over the pecuniary motives that figure so prominently in the maximising textbooks: 'Factory workers are more sensitive to the attitudes of their fellow-workers than to purely economic incentives... Voters are more influenced by the preferences of their relatives and friends than by campaign debates on the "issues"... Soldiers, whatever their ideological commitment to their nation's cause, fight more bravely when their platoons are intact and they stand side by side with their "buddies".' (Wrong, 1961:189). It is emotive herding and banding as well as the calculative reappropriation of surplus value that makes the Marxian proletariat into a revolutionary class. It is interpersonal *kiasu* within the peer group and the reference group and not just the need for a meal that leads the East Asian plutocrat to order birds-nests for his business lunch. People want goods and services. They also want a positive image of themselves. Social economics takes on board the duality of the drive – and the fact that the social map gives each decision-maker a place.

Recognising social values, acknowledging social interdependence, the outcome is an anthropocentric economics that, rejecting with Marx the alienation, the reification, the mystification, the commodity fetishism of an autonomous market where exchange is separate from exchangers, insists with Etzioni that embeddedness and not unrelatedness must become the centrepiece of a general theory of transparent interactions: 'Usually collectivities are more consequential in forming the choices of individuals than the individuals themselves; collectivities are *the* decision-making unit.' (Etzioni, 1988:181). Social relations in that way join the market mechanism as the core of a two-pronged economics, a home at once to the holism of belonging and to the individualism of independence.

What is needed is a synthesis that models the dialogue between the *I* and the *We* without regard to the routinised exclusivity of professional compart-mentalisation such as artificially screens off the cells from the organism of which each is a part. In the words of J.K. Galbraith: 'The boundaries of a subject matter are conventional and artificial; none should use them as an excuse for excluding the important.' (Galbraith, 1967:26). In the words of Kenneth Boulding: 'The convergence of theoretical systems in the various disciplines may yet produce something like a general theory, a set of concepts, relationships, and references which can provide, as it were, skeletons for the unified public image of the intellectual world.' (Boulding, 1956:139). Writing in 1956, Boulding declared that the 'profound reorganization of the departmental structure of knowledge and of academic life' had already begun: 'The old departmental boundaries are crumbling in all directions... There is something abroad which might be called an interdisciplinary movement.' (Boulding, 1956:162). As premature as his diagnosis may have been, what is clear is that social economics as a perspective is strongly in favour of any movement that seeks to weave together the separate threads.

One approach to a new synthesis would be an open-minded non-disciplinarity, one that investigates whole phenomena without preconstrained expectations. A more moderate approach would recognise the need for theory to identify relevant empiricisms where the facts do not speak for themselves. It would appeal to the division of scholarly labour precisely because specialist expertise has depth that can more than compensate for any narrowness of breadth. Such an approach, inter-disciplinary and pluri-disciplinary, would seek to build bridges between existing entities but would also respect existing boundaries. Schumpeter was strongly in favour of just such an orchestra-like harmonisation of diversity.

Schumpeter, observing that economic analysis itself is made up of four separate 'fields' (theory, economic history, statistics and economic sociology), goes on to say that there is no reason why economic activity should be studied on its own: 'Economic and non-economic facts *are* related... The various social sciences *should* be related to one another.' (Schumpeter, 1954:12, 13). Economic facts to Schumpeter included the institutions of society and their historical development: 'To use a felicitous phrase: economic analysis deals with the questions how people behave at any time and what the economic effects are they produce by so behaving; economic sociology deals with the question how they came to behave as they do. If we define human behavior widely enough so that it includes not only actions and motives and propensities but also the social institutions that are relevant to economic behavior such as government, property inheritance, contract, and so on, that phrase really tells us all we need.' (Schumpeter, 1954:21). Etzioni shares the perspective. Seeing no real need for a unitary social science that transcends the distinct specialisms, he argues nonetheless for a 'cross-disciplinary bridge between exchange and structure': his ideal socio-economics, he says, would be one that that attempted 'to integrate elements of economics and of other social sciences into one theoretical system, but not to fuse them.' (Etzioni, 1988:15, 16).

Cross-disciplinarity is intended as an antidote to excessive fragmentation. The problem that it creates is, however, not dissimilar to the problem that it solves. Defining economics as rational market choice, sociology as integration and values, politics as power and leadership, it is the signal disadvantage of the marriage made in the mainstream that it perpetuates the very *a priori* that it was intended to overcome. Subjectivists would warn that uncertainty and unknowledge ride roughshod over the forecaster's predictions: 'Valuation is expectation and expectation is imagination... What is the future but the void?' (Shackle, 1972:8, 122). Marxians would insist that exploitation within structure inexorably drives the capitalist interregnum to its final destruction: 'When the proletariat demands the *negation of private property* it only lays down as a *principle for society* what society has already made a principle *for the proletariat.*' (Marx, 1844a:190). Institutionalists would advocate an economics of customs and titles, a 'proprietary economics of rights, duties, liberties, and exposures' (Commons, 1934:8): the courts of law, Commons observes sadly, 'are closer to business practices every day than are the economists' (Commons, 1950:45). By 'the economists' Commons clearly has in mind the *maximising* economists. It is the signal disadvantage of the marriage made in the mainstream that it defines as ineligible for partnership those very schools of – non-maximising – economists who are the most receptive to a wider range of social facts than are picked up by the exchange paradigm in isolation. The economy *is* social networks and the common law, not just the pleasure principle and productive throughput. It is in the circumstances rather arbitrary and perhaps also unhelpful to treat anything redolent of patterned interaction as a visitor from another discipline. The truth is the whole. Cross-disciplinarity is an acknowledgement that the economy is no different.

The spheres of experience to which the academic disciplines by convention relate are already linked together in real-world compounds that are more than the sum of their parts. Empiricism assembles data about phenomena which have more than one dimension to their reality. Maximising nonetheless implies that it is meaningful to model market pricing without also modelling much else besides. The contribution of Parsons and Smelser in *Economy and Society* is therefore an especially interesting one, since they at least recognise the need for a comprehensive conceptual scheme in order that the facts be classified without prejudice: 'Economic theory should, according to this view, be regarded as the theory of typical processes in the "economy", which is a sub-section differentiated from other sub-systems of a society. The specifically economic aspect of the theory of social systems, therefore, is a *special case* of the general theory of the social system.' (Parsons and Smelser, 1956:6).

Parsons and Smelser identify four functional imperatives that must be satisfied in all societies. The first is adaptation, the control of the environment in such a way as to increase the supply of desired objects gratifying competing wants. The second is goal attainment, the right to intervene with authority in other people's pursuit of happiness and welfare, self-defined. The third is integration, the unification of the system in terms of coinciding recurrences and behavioural regularities. The fourth is latency, pattern maintenance, the management of tension by means of common values, signs, symbols, attitudes and motives. Each element in the AGIL schema is linked to a specific sub-system in the composite matrix – to the economy, the polity, the society and the culture, respectively. Importantly, however, there are boundary solutions and overlaps which make explicit that the sub-systems are no more than intellectual simplifications, aids to reasoning which will seldom if ever be observable on their own. The economy itself well illustrates the interconnectedness: 'The whole society is in one sense part of the economy, in that all of its units, individual and collective, *participate in* the economy... But *no* concrete unit participates *only* in the economy. Hence no concrete unit is "purely economic".' (Parsons and Smelser, 1956:14). *No concrete unit is 'purely economic'*. Any attempt to isolate the element without reference to the compound is in the circumstances doomed to fail.

The economy in its purest form is about investment, technology, population deployed in such a way as to generate wealth for final utility: 'The *goal* of the economy is to provide goods and services for consumption.' (Parsons and Smelser, 1956:42). Yet there is more to performance than the material incentive alone. Executive power in the State and in the corporation influences the choice of tasks, objectives and interests to be served. Family, stratification and solidarity sanction certain outlets while stigmatising others. The central value system loosens the link between work and pay precisely because commitment and conformity become a function of meaning and image. Visiting the business, in other words, the economist is likely to be exposed to politics (consider the patriarchal paternalism of the family firm or the organisational hierarchy of the bureaucratised corporation), to society (as where roles feed back on loyalties and conflict-resolution is ensured by stable interdependencies), to culture (the case of needs and wants made expressions of belonging and identification, the social control of deviance transmitted through the moral consensus). Political, social and cultural resources will evidently be of direct relevance to the explanation of the supply-and-demand equilibria that the textbook economist has for more than a century made it his mission to investigate. Parsons and Smelser write as follows about the special status of the economy in the macrocosm of AGIL: 'The economy is that sub-system of a society which is differentiated with primary reference to the *adaptive* function of the society as a whole.' (Parsons and Smelser, 1956:20). They also make clear that the adaptive function will seldom if ever be observable on its own.

Parsons and Smelser are advocates of a more general theory. So, it must be said, are unifying theoreticians like Mises and Becker, who see in the economist's rigorous use of maximising rationality a wonder-tool for predicting human responses to a change: 'I contend that the economic approach is uniquely powerful because it can integrate a wide range of economic behavior.' (Becker, 1976:5). Sociologists such as Blau, Homans and Coleman have been persuaded by the logic of opportunity cost, diminishing marginal utility and the *quid pro quo*. Blau's illustration of a senior expert who, paid in deference and admiration, rations his advice to a junior colleague in line with competing claims is a case in point of the sociology of elasticity, downward-sloping demand and the equilibrium price: 'He will be inclined to limit the time he spends in discussions with the junior to the level at which the support he receives from his admiration still outweighs in significance the advantages foregone by taking time from other pursuits.' (Blau, 1964:90). The respect-price paid for help will in certain circumstances not be sufficient to call forth the service desired. Social exchange can evidently be as mean and grasping as its economic counterpart.

Some scholars have opted for the cross-disciplinary and even for the synthetic approach. Most have not. The stability of the separateness is itself a social fact that must be explained.

Clearly, the technical intricacy of economic theory is a barrier and a deterrent to culturally-orientated observers without sophistication in the higher mathematics. Frank Knight recommended that the useful economist, dependent on the intuitive sensitivity to meaning and effect of the psychologist and even of the novelist, should 'give up, except within recognized and rather narrow limits, the naïve project of carrying over a technique which has been successful in the one set of problems and using it to solve another set of a categorically different kind': 'The real sociology and economics must be branches of literature as much as of science ... Man's relations with his fellow man are on a totally different footing from his relations with the objects of physical nature.' (Knight, 1935:147). Perhaps entrepreneurial flair, herd-instinct shopping, the emotive bonds of company teamwork, would indeed be better understood if modelled without the maximising calculus that may be better suited to the problems of physics and engineering than it is to all but the special cases in the business of exchange. Yet we start from here. The abstract presentation is a fact of life. A barrier and a deterrent, culturally-orientated observers have preferred not to study economic problems at all.

The perceived failure of interdisciplinarity in the past has discredited the quest. Veblen, Commons and Ayres have never had more than a minority appeal, the Historical School has disappeared without any lasting influence, and Weber alone among the canons (and then in departments of sociology but not of economics) continues to be widely read and generally respected. The lack of a common paradigm robust enough to produce good results is a further reason not to abandon the limited but the trusted. Jargon creates artificial obstacles to communication that keep outside challenge at bay. Desertion and trespass threaten the sub-culture's survival and become a focus for tribal resentment. Nor should it be forgotten that professional bodies and professional ethics, chartered as they are to defend best-practice conventions, will always act to exclude, to stream and to regiment. So will the need in each professional area to publish in core journals which pay only lip-service at best to the speculations of the neighbouring disciplines.

Cumulative causation and paradigmatic self-perpetuation are only to be expected in a professional environment where academic careers and financial success are a function of approximation to the median. In the words of Mary Douglas: 'All subjects grow strongest where they are most autonomous. The centre of an intellectual discipline is defined by its capacity to settle its own theoretical problems on its own terms. Around this centre the most forceful exponents find it most worthwhile to cluster. The fringes are for the fringy. Thus a centripetal force in the institutional framework of knowledge exerts a magnetism for talent, time and funds.' (Douglas, 1982:174). No one would want the crackpots and the cranks to be put in charge of major surgery or allowed to pilot passenger aircraft. The problem is to design the filter in such a way as not to screen out the welfare-enhancing as well. It is the message of Mary Douglas that many promising insights have been ridiculed into oblivion by the perception that the cross-disciplinary is the refuge of the fringy while the mathematics of gravity and equilibrium shares in the prestige of an unimpeachable physics.

Ideology too has stood in the way of *rapprochement*. Social variables like class and cohesion are unattractive to anti-collectivists: repelled by the insistence on conduct in common and by the notion that Marxian exploitation is the hidden underside of voluntary contract, they cling to freedom of choice and efficiency given scarcity because market devolution in their mind is the negation of suffocation and conflict. Individualistic constructs like consumer sovereignty and instrumental rationality have little appeal to the holists of the integrated order: drawn to fitting in, to equity and even equality more than *laissez-faire*, to consensual outcomes ranked above productive allocation, they criticise the economist's paradigm for being not so much a description of *what is* as the prescription of a goal that ought deliberately to be striven for. On the one hand there are those who face modernity with the fear that the group is being torn asunder. On the other hand there are those who welcome wealth-creating dynamism and reject unthinking ritual which serves no real purpose. The perspectives are not the same. No single body of theory will in the circumstances be equally compatible with both.

There is a final reason for the survival of the disciplinary frontiers. This is the widespread perception that the existing specialisations are functioning well. The sheer growth and sub-division of knowledge is a major obstacle to the evolution of an integrated theory. A concentration on exchange leaves little time for the study of values. An understanding of bureaucracy crowds out an investigation into shopping. What is clear is that the links are there – that the market reflects values, that bureaucracy through the corporation has a direct link to sales. What is less clear is whether there is a pressing need to document these relationships in order to generate useful results. Too much information can be as dysfunctional as too little. In-depth understanding can be an economic waste where just-adequate understanding produces the required predictions. The academic mind is attracted by the general theory. Most people only want tools that do the job. Most people probably believe that the existing frontiers are up to the task in hand; and that there is no need to call into question a division of responsibility which has demonstrably delivered the goods.

2.3   THE INDIVIDUAL

The market for cars is the summation of the buyers and sellers. The national economy is the collective aggregate. The truth is the added-up. The maximising economist, however, theorises outward from the part. This section is concerned with that decision to begin with the micro in order to elucidate the macro to which the statistics relate.

Methodological individualism is the scientific approach which reduces a social system to the interests and understandings of its discrete human units. Thus a firm becomes not a profit-maximising black box but a network of individuals with goal-functions of their own, while the national purpose can never be other than the reconciled objectives of the separable citizens. Methodological holism would be prepared to reify the firm or the nation into a free-standing entity, to treat each collectivity as if it had an identity of its own to which interacting persons had no alternative but to adapt. Methodological individualism, arguing that the collective identity is 'never visible' precisely because no whole can have a mind, prefers instead to build up the utility of the group from the unique actions of the component subjectivities: 'The course of history is determined by the actions of individuals and by the effects of these actions.' (Mises, 1949:43, 49). Individual choice comes first. The social system only becomes apparent when the decision-making is done.

Methodological individualism, proceeding 'step by step, part by part', traces all social preference and social change back to its origins in the expectations and intentions, the beliefs and aspirations, of the primary mover: 'What counts for history is always the meaning of the men concerned: the meaning that they attach to the state of affairs they want to alter, the meaning they attach to their actions, and the meaning they attach to the effects produced by the actions.' (Mises, 1949:46, 59). Social relationships in such a scenario can only be the result, never the cause, of the individual's decision to cooperate. Economic valuation, similarly, must always be 'entirely psychical and personal', never objective or cost-based: 'Value is not intrinsic, it is not in things. It is within us; it is the way in which man reacts to the conditions of his environment.' (Mises, 1949:26, 27). The individual alone can quantify a desire. The individual alone can express a ranking.

The approach deliberately abstains from any speculation as to the meta-origins of the tastes. Not inconsistent with the idea that the social environment hands on to its members a language that they did not create, not recalcitrant to the notion that past patterns shape current choices, methodological individualism as such assigns no moral value to the priority of microscopic expectation. The reductionism as such is not at odds with sociology or history, not a clear case of what Durkheim attacked as fictionalising psychologism: 'Every time that a social phenomenon is directly explained by a psychological phenomenon, we may be sure that the explanation is false.' (Durkheim, 1895:104). All that the reductionism as such suggests is that, individuals alone being the units that can think, act and initiate, explanations at the level of the forest and not of the tree will only by accident have any grounding in real-world sensation and intent.

Mental states are, of course, forever concealed. Reliant as it must therefore be on *revealed* preferences, methodological individualism is exposed to the problem that the observations are not easy to interpret. The *quid pro quo* only quantifies the intensity of desire if the cardinal 'by how much' and the ordinal 'in what order' have first been made subject to a rational assessment. Yet the degree of maximisation is itself hidden within the same invisible mind. One could ask the actors to put into words their motivation, or even test their verbalisations by means of psychometric experiments. In the normal run of things this is not possible. The consequence is that the methodological economist is left with Pareto's 'derivations' while having to admit that Pareto's 'residues', like Mars, are not open to tourists.

Common sense suggests that people do not cross the road at random or buy exclusively on evanescent impulse. To that extent the information they share through exchange may be taken (although no one can say this with absolute confidence) to enjoy a reasonable measure of proportionality with the directions and intensities of the actor's psyche. Besides that, there is the very obvious counsel of desperation: 'Every mind is ... inscrutable to every other mind, and no common denominator of feeling seems to be possible.' (Jevons, 1871:85). However modest the conscious element in my decision-making, however great your imaginative capacity for empathy and sympathy, there must be a presumption that I at the end of the day will be in a better position to say if I prefer sprouts to spinach or want a second cup of tea at the opportunity – cost of a newspaper foregone. Methodological individualism is an approach which derives its data from the individuals who alone possess their utility-functions. The revelations collected, it imputes no ethical 'ought-ness' to the 'is-ness' which it documents.

Normative individualism, clearly, has the grander aspirations. Concerned not with data-collection but with human dignity, it is built around 'the normative presumption that the evaluations of the persons involved, their interests and values, provide the relevant criterion against which the merits or "desirability" of alternative rules are to be judged.' (Vanberg, 1994:1). Normative individualism is classical liberalism and respect for persons. It presupposes preferences expressed by the parts, but also makes them into legitimate ends that the paternalist or the dictator has no moral right to reject.

The idea that the individual alone can say what is 'good' – that beyond the thinking agent there can be no benchmark of performance and no conceivable ranking scheme – draws its authority from a range of sources in the Western tradition. Most familiarly, there is the open-door possessiveness of meritocratic advancement through earning and investing; the social Darwinism of Spencer and Sumner; the achievement-based success indicators of competitive capitalism. More generally, there is Renaissance science (which, sceptical about authority, looks to facts for clues), the Cartesian *cogito* (which, as do Leibniz and Hume, makes the mind the bedrock of impressions), the Protestant Reformation (which was critical of the Catholic monopoly and, where Calvinist, resolutely self-reliant lest the predestined mistake their trust). The romantic movement was in sympathy with the authority-defying creativity of the one-off genius. Natural law sprang to the defence of property rights and the liberties of assembly and speech. Roman law, atheism, the Enlightenment, *laissez-faire*, cosmopolitanism, mobility, democracy, the horrors of genocide and the failures of plan – all of this militated in favour of pluralism, independence, tolerance, decentralisation, equal respect, minimal interference, self-reliance, the freedoms of conscience and opinion. The same intellectual influences, needless to say, also called into question the moral status of power, totalitarianism, tyranny, organicism, *Volk*, fraternity, *dirigisme*, nationhood and the magnification of simple adding-up into the new metaphysics of the social order *sui generis*.

Normative individualism is central to the textbook economics of supply and demand. Methodology photographs the revealed preferences. Philosophy, however, declares that the chooser knows best. Philosophy, in other words, puts the burden of proof firmly on those who would deny that the best judge of his own interest will normally be the individual himself: 'As liberals, we take freedom of the individual, or perhaps the family, as our ultimate goal in judging social arrangements... Freedom has nothing to say about what an individual does with his freedom.' (Friedman, 1962:12).

The criterion of individual autonomy was authoritatively encapsulated by John Stuart Mill in his 'one very simple principle': 'The only part of the conduct of anyone, for which he is amenable to society, is that which concerns others. In the part which merely concerns himself, his independence is, of right, absolute. Over himself, over his own body and mind, the individual is sovereign.' (Mill, 1859:68–9). Mill concedes that the rule of non-interference must be relaxed where harm is caused to others. His admission that human choice has spillovers and externalities is a hostage to fortune. There is virtually no part of life in society where bystanders are unaffected by the individual's choice. To save more is to contribute to unemployment. To miss breakfast is to underperform at work. To dress shabbily is to uglify a gala. Somewhere a line must be drawn between the privacy of the smoker and the smoking chimney which pollutes the environment. Less clear is *where* the line should be drawn – or *by whom*.

An economic system can itself be the cause of spillovers and externalities. On the one hand there is system A where jobs are guaranteed, old age is provided for, pornography and hard drugs are banned – and where citizens are denied the chance to go abroad lest they waste foreign exchange and become corrupted by foreign ways. On the other hand there is system B where living standards rise, entrepreneurial latitude is protected, self-definition and variety are made the consumer's right – and where citizens feel unloved and unappreciated unless they fight their way to the top. The former bundle means the neighbourhood effects of stability – and of repression. The latter bundle brings the neighbourhood effects of affluence – and of isolation. An economic system, in other words, is not just a machine for the manufacture of goods and services. It is also a major determinant of a nation's culture in a way that forms no part of the economist's contract.

Mill made the individual not an absolute king but a constitutional monarch. The exception which circumscribes the rule is agreed-upon harm to others. Contemplating the market capitalism of his own times, Mill expressed the concern that the economic system was imposing cultural diswelfares on him which were comparable to the establishment of a pig farm in a neighbour's garden: 'I am not charmed with the ideal of life held out by those who think that the normal state of human beings is that of struggling to get on; that the trampling, crushing, elbowing, and treading on each other's heels, which form the existing type of social life, are the most desirable lot of human kind.' (Mill,

1848:748). Logically speaking, therefore, a normative individualist like Mill would have been well within his rights to demand the redesign of the economic order in such a way as to put in place an institutional alternative which delivered to him a greater utility: 'The best state for human nature is that in which, while no one is poor, no one desires to be richer, nor has any reason to fear being thrust back by the efforts of others to push themselves forward.' (Mill, 1848:749). The consumer knows best what is in his own interest. Had other consumers shared with Mill a ranking of the quality of life above the quantity of goods, the 'one very simple principle' of Mill's historic *On Liberty* could without difficulty have led to a conservative market and not to the revolutionary market which is so much a part of the economiser's world-view.

3. Present as past

Economists trained to 'let bygones be forever bygone', to 'start from here', are understandably reluctant to invoke causal influences which, variables in the past but constants in the present, can no longer be altered by any choice that the satisfaction-seeker can currently make. Economists tend to be practical people, in search with Mill for the link between value-added, exchange and command over utility, committed with Mill to the effective enhancement of material well-being: 'Writers on Political Economy profess to teach, or to investigate, the nature of Wealth, and the laws of its production and distribution: including, directly or remotely, the operation of all the causes by which the condition of mankind, or of any society of human beings, in respect to this universal object of human desire, is made prosperous or the reverse.' (Mill, 1848: 1). Living in the present, looking to the future, economists tend therefore to hand over the extinguished and the lifeless to economic history in order to concentrate their investigations on alternative pay-offs which still have a pulse.

Yet it is by no means a simple task to uncouple the 'is-ness' from the 'was-ness' in a real world never really free from its roots. Psychoanalysis encourages the uncomfortable to re-explore their childhood in order to make themselves into better-adapted adults. Psychoanalysis, in persuading the neurotic that their mental health depends on the release of repressed tensions, takes the view that growth would most definitely be stunted were events gone by deliberately to be written off merely because the record is no longer susceptible to change. The perspective of the psychoanalyst, that the present *contains* the past, that history experienced *remains* an action variable, is shared by the economist when he or she acknowledges the continuity of habit and convention.

The customary can be the personal. Individuals develop routines to guide them through the day. They shop by precedent which only innovates at the margin. They manage complexity as an unintended outcome of being 'stuck in a rut'. They cope with their mealtimes and their television viewing in the confidence that they are 'set in their ways'. Most people would go mad if they were not born middle-aged. Even reclusive hermits can become habituated into grooves.

Conditioning can be self-imposed. Importantly, it can also be a collective representation. It was the thesis of the previous chapter that individuals acculturated into communities may be expected to adhere to patterns that are shared and not only to practices that are resolutely their own. Asch, not in sympathy with the group-mind holist who 'blots out the individual in favor of massive, impersonal forces', is therefore sufficiently impressed by the reality of an H_2O that is more than the sum of its H and its O alone, to remind the ego-centred reductionist, 'blind to the sweep of social conditions', of 'the presence of a *socially structured field within the individual*': 'Group facts may be represented within the individual in an ordered way and call upon him for action oriented to group realities.' (Asch, 1952:253). Asch would not deny that the customary can be the personal. What he would add is that membership internalises its expectations and meaningful interaction requires a measure of receptiveness and conformity: 'In society we become dependent on others for understanding, feeling and the extension of the sense of reality.' (Asch, 1952:450). In society no one is alone.

It was the thesis of the previous chapter that much of individual action is in fact social patterning. The present chapter, emphasising the persistence of the patterning, extends the argument by suggesting that horizontal standardisation is but the present-day snapshot of a lateral standardisation that extends backwards into the remembered past, forwards into a continuing future. Commons writes as follows about the handed-on custom that has a supra-personal source: 'The individual with whom we are dealing is the Institutionalized Mind. Individuals begin as babies. They learn the custom of language, of cooperation with other individuals, of working towards common ends, of negotiations to eliminate conflicts of interest... Instead of isolated individuals in a state of nature they are always participants in transactions, members of a concern in which they come and go, citizens of an institution that lived before them and will live after them.' (Commons, 1934:73-4). The repetitions are not the result of one individual's rational calculus and not the outcome of an in-period optimisation process. Exogenous to the atom, inherited from unknowable forebears, the habits and the conventions are an inter-temporal constraint which makes even the most rugged of individualists into a creature of the collective – and a representation of the past.

The present chapter is devoted to the past. The first section, The conservative market, establishes what it means to interact through a pre-patterned nexus. The second section, The evolution of the optimal, shows that heuristics and prejudices remain an element in economic decision-making. The final section, Constitutions and choices, suggests that a nation which economises on its *festina lente* will be exposing itself to unnecessary risk.

3.1 THE CONSERVATIVE MARKET

Veblen had little time for the utilitarians' context-free hedonism, for their 'faulty conception of human nature', for their sequential *ab initio* that 'has neither antecedent nor consequence.' (Veblen, 1919:73). Real people, Veblen said, are less likely to be the obsessive maximisers of evanescent utility than they are the reliable replicators of an 'accepted scheme of life' such as has acquired the 'consistency of custom and prescription': 'This apparatus of ways and means available for the pursuit of whatever may be worth seeking is, substantially all, a matter of tradition out of the past, a legacy of habits of thought accumulated through the experience of past generations.' (Veblen, 1914:6–7).

Past generations did not create the instinctual imperatives, the biological propensities, the innate predispositions that are the 'prime mover' in driving on the survival of the species. It is nature and not nurture that has instilled in man 'the promptings of sex', 'the gregarious instinct', 'the parental bent', 'the proclivity to construction or acquisition', 'the sense of workmanship' and the other purposive drives which ensure the numbers and assure the subsistence. What past generations have done, Veblen argues, is to build upon the bedrock of native teleology a superstructure of rules which make a contribution of their own to man's adaptation to his material environment: 'Institutions are an outgrowth of habit. The growth of culture is a cumulative sequence of habituation, and the ways and means of it are the habitual response of human nature to exigencies that vary incontinently, cumulatively, but with something of a consistent sequence.' (Veblen, 1919:241). Unchanging nature has contributed the physiological bedrock. Past generations have added on the preconceptions and the usages. Trapped in the body and embedded in convention, the individual has the *de facto* freedom neither to survive without food nor to re-read a mystery without remembering the end: 'All facts of observation are necessarily seen in the light of the observer's habits of thought.' (Veblen, 1914:53). Being free is not the same as being unconstrained.

Institutions, durable and long-lasting, have a lifespan in excess of that of the thinking beings whose scope for immediate optimisation it is their function to circumscribe: 'Men's present habits of thought tend to persist indefinitely, except as circumstances enforce a change. These institutions which have thus been handed down, these habits of thought, points of view, mental attitudes and aptitudes, or what not, are therefore themselves a conservative factor.' (Veblen, 1899:133). They are *themselves* a conservative factor precisely because they are *themselves* a part of the life-style, familiar, accepted and self-reproducing. They are, in short, themselves 'proximate ends', themselves a part of the matrix of group practices on which group feedback will cause socialised individuals to converge: 'The accustomed ways of doing and thinking not only become an habitual matter of course, easy and obvious, but they come likewise to be sanctioned by social conventions, and so become right and proper and give rise to principles of conduct. By use and wont they are incorporated into the current scheme of common sense.' (Veblen, 1914:7). Thus does a non-deliberative, non-calculative repetitiveness become ossified into a self-sustaining structure which for the innovative as well as for the reactionary is as much a part of the economic environment as is the supply of steel.

Hayek writes that the past is all around: 'The conscious knowledge which guides the individual's actions constitutes only part of the conditions which enable him to achieve his ends. There is the fact that man's mind is itself a product of the civilization in which he has grown up and that it is unaware of much of the experience which has shaped it – experience that assists it by being embodied in the habits, conventions, language, and moral beliefs which are part of its makeup.' (Hayek, 1960:24). Just as the market is about the conscious choice of dispersed knowledge, so to Hayek is the market about the inherited endowment of a public good. As Wolf warns, the personal and the common baggage simply cannot be written off as a *ceteris paribus*: 'Those of us, economists and others, who regard ourselves as practical problem solvers, normally view the past as concluded, done, and inert. It is not.' (Wolf, 1970:783). It is not. We start from a 'here' that is also a 'there'.

The baggage must be studied because the past embodied remains an active influence. A satisfactory understanding of social adjustment evidently presupposes a visit to a volcano that is far from extinct. Least of all can time remembered safely be neglected if the *Gestalt* of the interconnected fibres is acknowledged, as Ekkehart Schlicht advises it ought to be, as a fabric more powerful than the sum of the strands: 'It is the mutual reinforcement of received habits, legitimizing views, emotions, and motivations that renders custom effective and powerful. The force and stability of custom derives mainly from its texture, rather than from its single elements. This force evaporates if single aspects are treated in isolation.' (Schlicht, 1998:107). The complex, Schlicht stresses, acquires its force from the fact that it is a whole. The whole in place, the force is such as to make the neglect of the inter-temporal bundle a misleading omission which the positive economist would do well to correct.

The positive economist should study the inherited endowment. In the words of Commons: 'We start and continue by repetition, routine, monotony – in short by custom. The intellect itself is both a repetition of action, memory, and expectation; and an imitation – or rather, duplication – of the acts, memories, and expectations of those upon whom we depend for life, liberty, and property.' (Commons, 1934:45). The positive economist should also study the transformation of the transmitted mix through its exposure to conscious choice in a skein of material situations. In the words of Veblen: 'The situation of today shapes the institutions of tomorrow through a selective, coercive process, by acting upon men's habitual view of things, and so altering or fortifying a point of view or a mental attitude handed down from the past.' (Veblen, 1899:132–3). Conservative economics expects the handed down to be a not insignificant component of the present-day's 'what is'. To say that it predicts passivity and inertia rather than inquiry and novelty is, however, to exaggerate the determinism, to deny the creativity and the free will which give to the market economy its dynamism and its openness to change.

The positive economist, sensitive both to the stability and to the malleability, ought in the circumstances to develop an alertness to the ongoing dialogue between past and present, resistance and acceleration. Schlicht has this to say about the mutual causality of institutional brakes and entrepreneurial initiatives: 'Customary ways of behaving will be moulded by economic and other incentives. At the same time, these customary ways provide the very footing for those economic and social phenomena. Just as the bed of a river channels the flow of water and is moulded by that flow in turn, custom provides the bed for economic and social processes and is shaped by them.' (Schlicht, 1998:11). The positive economist, committed to an understanding of the real world, ought therefore to devote due attention to the two-way process.

This is not to say that sunk costs will necessarily exercise as strong an influence as marginal choices. A two-way process does not mean an equal weighting. Indeed, as Wolf points out, there are reasons for expecting a 'decay rate' in the evaluation of the past that is logically the same as the 'growth rate' that grinds out a present value for the future: 'In general, the past is more supple, malleable, and reinterpretable than we are comfortable to admit. While we know that the future is uncertain, we feel quite uncomfortable to consider that the past may also be uncertain.' (Wolf, 1970:784).

Uncomfortable or not, the possibility is a real one. Selective recall and the unreliability of memory mean that even the factual record may be open to interpretation. Outcomes in the present tend to breed revisions in the historical subset that is remembered from the past. A recent occurrence increases the salience of a similar event and accelerates the attrition of a half-forgotten outlier. Reallocating the blame means that foreign policy can be reorientated without dishonouring the fallen or forcing current leaders to say they were wrong. Considerations such as these suggest that the past may have different faces depending on the lenses and screens that are used. That the past may be uncertain does not, however, mean that the positive economist can afford to pretend that the backward-looking is anything other than all around.

Economists must study the past because the traditional differentials and the national-church filters are time-hallowed social facts that have a recognisable identity even in a forward-looking present. They must also study the past because their fellow citizens will often treat the 'done thing' as an attribute of a 'going concern' which delivers utility not as the means to an end but simply because it *is*. One could, of course, criticise those fellow citizens for being so defensive when imaginativeness would suggest improvements that could enhance their felt wellbeing. It will be their reply, however, that old friends are the best friends, and that contented people have no real need to re-open search.

Michael Oakeshott, writing in the Britain of 'you've never had it so good' (if also in the year of Hungary, Poland and Suez), saw no reason to scold contented people because, not bent on adventure, newness or change for its own sake, they had no compulsion to 'sail uncharted seas' when adequate satisfaction was already available at home: 'What is esteemed is the present; and it is esteemed not on account of its connections with a remote antiquity, nor because it is recognized to be more admirable than any possible alternative, but on account of its familiarity.' (Oakeshott, 1956:168, 173). The present had shown that it could deliver satisfactory enjoyment. Where the satisfactory satisfies, the case for the efficiency maximum is that much less pressing.

Disruption is always a deprivation since it means both the abandonment of an attachment with a track record and a shock to the coherence that defines the self: 'Change is a threat to identity, and every change is an emblem of extinction.' (Oakeshott, 1956:170). The fear of loss is an important reason why the satisfied put retention above enlargement, order above excitement, safe returns above speculative gambles: 'It is a disposition appropriate to a man who is acutely aware of having something to lose which he has learned to care for.' (Oakeshott, 1956:169). The familiar is the satisfactory and it is the cared-for. It is no surprise that contented people will resist any promise of perfection unless and until the burden of proof is overwhelming that an existing defect cannot be corrected through slow and gradual adaptation.

Familiarity in the sense of Oakeshott can be seen as the risk-averter's bulwark against something worse. What must not be forgotten is that Oakeshott sees stable certainty, means to an end though caution and prudence will so often be, as a unique final product in itself. Consider familiar tasks that are their own fulfilling wage, 'activities where what is sought is present enjoyment and not a profit, a reward, a prize or a result in addition to the experience itself.' (Oakeshott, 1956:175). Consider a friend as a sharing of personality and a familiarity transcending use, as 'somebody who engages the imagination, who excites contemplation, who provokes interest, sympathy, delight and loyalty simply on account of the relationship entered into.' (Oakeshott, 1956:177). A broad constructionist in the mould of Becker and

Hirshleifer would have no difficulty in translating intrinsic satisfaction into the rational nexus of want-satisfaction through supply and demand. Thus activity performed for its own sake may be said to be paying non-pecuniary compensation such that every nurse, teacher or housewife ought immediately to be approached for surtax; while a friend for life may be regarded as a luxury consumer durable providing a stream of non-contractual benefits on the shopkeeper principle that the flow of repeat business should not short-sightedly be put at risk. A broad constructionist will have no difficulty in identifying consumer choice even in cases of 'familiarity, not usefulness' (Oakeshott, 1956:177) such as these. Other people, however, will maintain that the conservative temperament is not by definition in line with shopping implied; and that a final product must be regarded as non-negotiable save where a high threshold of discontentment has irrevocably been crossed.

Conservatism by definition means strong support for continuity and tradition, for identity and familiarity. The British socialist Tawney seemed to regard it as the highest achievement of a civilised society: 'All decent people are at heart conservatives, in the sense of desiring to conserve the human associations, loyalties, affections, pious bonds between man and man which express a man's personality and become at once a sheltering nest for his spirit and a kind of watch-tower from which he may see visions of a more spacious and bountiful land.' (Winter and Joslin, 1972:14). Conservatism is in that sense an emotive reaction against the economisers and the modernisers, the Beckers and the Hirshleifers, whom it blames for the social dislocation of *anomie* and the relentless atomisation of commerce. The world views are opposed one to the other, the intellectual divide summed up as follows by Nisbet: 'The conflict is one between two sets of diametrically opposed values: on the one hand, hierarchy, community, tradition, authority, and the sacred sense of life; on the other hand, equalitarianism, individualism, secularism, positive rights, and rationalist modes of organization and power.' (Nisbet, 1968:4). Ideas like mechanism, volition, democracy, consciousness are the perceptual capital of a progressive Enlightenment which treats freedom *from* as construction and not as nihilistic tearing down. Ideas like family, roots, security, order are the unthinking response of the group-centred 'prophets of the past' who, noting with Bonald that 'religion' is derived from *religare* which means 'to bind together', refuse to put greedy materialism above the seamless web of church-like affiliation: 'Such ideas as *status, cohesion, adjustment, function, norm, ritual, symbol,* are conservative ideas ... Each has as its referent an aspect of society that is plainly concerned with the maintenance or the *conserving* of order.' (Nisbet, 1968:7, 73–4). Conserva-tives want to *conserve*. They do not want to escape the past by means of rational manipulation. Nor do they believe that memory will ever succeed in its studied attempt to outrun itself.

The social atheism of the stand-alone microcosm fails to pick up the hold of past practices upon present-day decision-makers. No more is it in touch with the non-rational longing that extends the partnership between the generations into a hoped-for future that perpetuates an ineffaceable past. Edmund Burke was especially insistent that the chain of harmonious organism does not end where the schoolboy closes his history text. The future, a Burkean like Boulding would say, is even now a part of us: 'The transmission of culture depends a great deal on serial reciprocity, that is, A gives something to B, which creates a sense of obligation on B's part, which he releases by giving something not to A, but to C. We make grants to our children because we received grants from our parents. We make sacrifices for posterity because our ancestors made sacrifices for us. The only answer to the famous question "What has posterity ever done for me?" indeed, is that our ancestors, ourselves and our descendants are all part of a larger community of the imagination extending over time and space.' (Boulding, 1973:54). All are part of a shared civilisation. Past, present and future stand together in their defence of a common stake.

Conservatism *is*. The familiar becomes the *desired*. There is more Conservatism *coordinates*. Market negotiation is one means of reconciling the discrete. A multiperiod constitution is another.

Transient rules, like fleeting attachments, do not inspire the confidence in institutional stability that is required to ensure a convergence of expectations. Instruments like scales and saws, the wheel and the drain, are economical of scarce means precisely because, being inter-temporal, they do not need to be re-invented each time that a recognisable function is identified: 'Familiarity is the essence of tool using; and in so far as man is a tool using animal he is disposed to be conservative.' (Oakeshott, 1956:179). A tool in the sense of Oakeshott can be an old violin for which a well-trained composer writes new music or yesterday's sieve which the experienced cook employs in order to bake today's cake. A tool in the sense of Oakeshott can also be a general rule of conduct, fixed, accepted, not susceptible to perpetual re-design such as would be a waste of scarce energy and a source of enervating confusion. This is not to say that multiperiod rules will necessarily be optimally efficient or optimally just. The important thing is that their existence *per se* makes it possible for new projects to be concerted in their protective shadow: 'Routines, no doubt, are susceptible of improvement; but the more familiar they become, they more useful they are.' (Oakeshott, 1956:181). Almost any old friend is in that perspective to be ranked above no friend at all.

The multiperiod is a focus and the habitual is a beacon. The individual always puts on his left sock before his right sock and drinks tea with his tiffin. The office does business from 9 to 5 with a meal break at 1. The village respects its squatter-tenures and makes Friday its market day. The nation adopts English as its language and the dollar as its currency. Whether the practice is as private as the bedtime and the bathtime or as collective as the Gregorian calendar and the metric system, what is clear is the conservatism. Once adopted, the rigidity may be trusted to coordinate repetitions and to orchestrate expectations. Given the established way of life, it will often be not the in-period rational choice but rather the trend-dominated multi-period perpetuator that will homogenise conduct and make human action predictable.

The remembered pattern, of value to the individual who puts on his sock, is a landmark of especial importance in a society made up of multiple decision-makers. A commitment to convention will in the forest of decentralisation empower each to confer regulative externalities upon all in a manner that would not be possible were the free market to be free of the past. The alternative would be for the free market to be superseded by the State-run directive – and that an opponent of politicised serfdom such as Hayek would find at once ethically distasteful and economically repressive. Wanting experimentation but wanting regulation as well, it is no surprise that Hayek is able to put uniformity through non-rational custom above uniformity imposed at the point of a gun: 'Coercion can be reduced to a minimum only where individuals can be expected as a rule to conform voluntarily to certain principles… Freedom has never worked without deeply ingrained moral beliefs… Paradoxical as it may appear, it is probably true that a successful free society will always in a large measure be a tradition-bound society.' (Hayek, 1960:61, 62).

Acceptance is the precondition for initiative. Inherited 'oughtness' is the precondition for spontaneous departure. Rather than acting as a brake on progress, it is, Hayek says, past standards that make possible current adaptations: 'We understand one another, and get along with one another, are able to act successfully on our plans, because, most of the time, members of our civilization conform to unconscious patterns of conduct, show a regularity in their actions that is not the result of commands or coercion, often not even of any conscious adherence to known rules, but of firmly established habits and traditions. The general observance of these conventions is a necessary condition of the orderliness of the world in which we live, of our being able to find our way in it.' (Hayek, 1960:62). Hayek insists that the preconceptions and the norms are only at the margin the product of problem-solving reason: 'The intellectual process is in effect only a process of elaboration, selection, and elimination of ideas already formed.' (Hayek, 1960:35). He also insists that the handed-on tools are the 'essential conditions' for the advances that can follow: 'While it is important to discover their defects, we could not for a moment go on without constantly relying on them.' (Hayek, 1960:34). The past coordinates. Without its guidance we would be lost.

The past coordinates. Ensuring a focus, assuring a beacon, the past promotes regularities that homogenise conduct and make human action predictable. Precommitment and rule-following improve the process of communication and concentrate the search for information. They do so both in non-conflictual environments and in situations where there is an adversarial element. The former case may be exemplified by the win–win nature of the conventional money-asset or the expected national language: consider the mutually-beneficial rules of the road which, left or right, satisfactorily define the parameters of the game. The latter case may be illustrated by the win–lose dimension of the Hobbesian passenger travelling free on his neighbours' honesty or the Bad Samaritan who decides not to donate his blood: consider the tamed confrontationalism of front-line troops reciprocating each other's misfiring on a tit-for-tat basis or a 'prisoner's dilemma' in which neither criminal implicates the other because of a cooperative rule of 'honour among thieves'. As win–win as the motorists, as win–lose as the criminals, what is clear in both the former and the latter case is that it is positive-sum to have a social contract, 'rational to *have a constitution.*' (Buchanan and Tullock, 1962:81).

Tawney, convinced that all people carry about with them the chains of the past, believed that when the historian inspects the strength of the foundations, he is also explaining the survival of the edifice: 'In this sense, there is truth in the paradox that all history is the history of the present.' (Tawney, 1933:55). Time remembered is on the horizontal axis. It is a great social spillover that it serves as an invisible hand. Situated in the spot context of the act-utilitarian calculus, self-denial in the form of promise-keeping and truth-telling, not littering and not stealing, will only have an economic return where the reward for morality is immediate approbation and the sanction for defection is a rude word from an untipped waiter, a prison sentence where a law is broken. Situated in the historical flow of the rule-utilitarian perspective, the position, still means–ends consequentialist and not deontological at all, is for all that a less frenzied one. Iterated recurrences and infinite-horizon supergames mean that a reputation for reliability becomes a sound business asset and that unacceptable selfishness will invite a retaliatory response. Stable microcosms like family and corporation inculcate convention-perpetuating dispositions such as ensure that internalised norms will be policed by conscience and cultural attitudes be diffused into general regulative externalities. Time remembered is on the horizontal axis. The upshot of long-term conservatism in preference to case-by-case reappraisal is that the past *coordinates*. It does so even where the individuals in thrall to the conventions are not named, not known and not recognisable in the crowd.

3.2 THE EVOLUTION OF THE OPTIMAL

The positive view of the economy is that it is concerned with the four functionalities of production, consumption, distribution and exchange without committing itself in advance to any single teleology or over-arching purpose. The normative view of the economy is that it is concerned with the efficient allocation of scarce goods and services in a resource-constrained world where the poverty of nations means that not all wants can be satisfied that put in a claim. Inherited 'oughtness' is clearly compatible with the impartial empiricist's 'whatever is'. The relationship between established practices and the economising mission is more difficult to evaluate. This section considers the nature of that relationship.

Veblen, not attracted by the self-balancing mechanism of comparative statics, analysed economic activity in terms of 'unremitting changes and adaptations', 'new habits of work and thought', 'new principles of conduct' and not as a one-dimensional free-fall towards an endstate equilibrium price: 'A genetic inquiry into institutions will address itself to the growth of habits and conventions, as conditioned by the material environment and by the innate and persistent propensities of human nature.' (Veblen, 1914:2, 17). Resources interact with instincts. The result is 'consecutive change, realized to be self-continuing or self-propagating and to have no final term': 'The economic life history of the individual is a cumulative process of adaptation of means to ends that cumulatively change as the process goes on, both the individual and his environment being at any point the outcome of the last process.' (Veblen, 1919:37, 74-5). Iron and oil interact with hunger and thirst which interface with laws and customs. The past labours alongside the present. The product is a tomorrow which will irrevocably have moved on.

Matter is in motion. Yet it is evolution without a plan: 'Law, language, the state, money, markets, all these social structures... are to no small extent the unintended result of social development.' (Menger, 1883:147). Institutions are in that sense the collective outcomes which innumerable individuals pursuing uncoordinated objectives unexpectedly bring into being as the by-product, Mandeville-like, Smith-like, of seeking only to promote their own interest. Menger, a methodological individualist, traced back the origin of habit, like the explanation of price, to the discrete individual who makes a choice. The institutions emerge 'organically' despite the fact that the choices are made 'pragmatically'. Juxtaposing the consciously created to the surprisingly unanticipated, Menger supports his confidence in welfare – furthering evolution by pointing to the public benefits that market economists predict from private vices advancing steadily without a plan.

Optimality is by no means guaranteed where present-day choices are made in an environment that has carried over the institutional capital of the past. Veblen, using words like 'frequent' and 'spectacular' to quantify the disappointments, makes clear that material wellbeing will not necessarily be maximised through economic adaptation where habituation drags forward the vestigial traits that slow down the advance: 'Human culture in all ages presents too many imbecile usages and principles of conduct to let anyone overlook the fact that disserviceable institutions easily arise and continue to hold their place in spite of the disapproval of native common sense.' (Veblen, 1914:25, 49). Survival of the fittest need not smile upon the *economically* fit. The 'imbecile' and the 'disserviceable' digging in alongside the competitive and the effective, what natural selection does is simply to identify those conventions that are the best fitted *to survive*.

If the health and wealth of the species were the sole explanation of institutional survival, few uneconomic octogenarians would be safe from cost-benefiting euthanasia and no ballet company would enjoy the resourcing that could feed the poor. A Darwinian vision of evolution as economics clearly has to be modified to account for social institutions that contribute nothing to productivity. Even so, it is a common conviction among evolutionary thinkers that the survival of convention and the survival of survival somehow march in step. Thus do past successes become the basis for present-day upgrading as if guided by an inter-temporal invisible hand with a vested interest in life itself. As Graham Wallas stated, explaining why a reforming liberal had also to be a conservative, the human race would be driven back into caves if deprived of its systems of logic, its industrial techniques, its medical knowledge, its reading and writing, its traditions of law and liberty: 'The process of social inheritance is, as far as I know, not necessary for the existence of any wild non-human species or variety... But the most important and progressive varieties of the human race would probably, if social inheritance were in their case interrupted, die out altogether... We have become, one may say, biologically parasitic upon our social heritage.' (Wallas, 1921:17, 18, 19). Our past is not an entertainment and a luxury. Our evolution is what keeps us alive and well.

The Hobbesian says that it is rational to have a preconstraining agreement. The Darwinian says that it is economic to rely upon evolution for the content of the clauses. Hayek is a *freedom from* conservative who, optimistic both about the social contract and the evolution of the rules, is especially insistent that not just the law-courts but also the laws may be expected automatically to gravitate into a reasonably appropriate convention: 'Like all general purpose tools, rules serve because they have become adapted to the solution of recurring problem situations and thereby help to make the members of the society in which they prevail more effective in the pursuit of their aims.' (Hayek, 1975:21). More effective means betterment. Betterment is good.

Rules, Hayek says, evolve in the course of a discovery process identical to that of the economists' competitive market. That process lends legitimacy to the norms. Proven success makes it desirable for traditional restraints to be respected even if they are neither legally enforceable nor fully understood: 'The willingness to submit to such rules, not merely so long as one understands the reason for them but so long as one has no definite reasons to the contrary, is an essential condition for the gradual evolution and improvement of rules of social intercourse.' (Hayek, 1949:23). The acceptance of the past makes possible an advance into the future which is that much more of a betterment for being the product of uncontrolled forces and not of a deliberative intelligence – or of a coercive State.

Hayek puts the natural above the man-made, the serendipitous above the planned. His ranking is, admittedly, a departure from the economist's more common assumption of instrumental rationality. Criticising scientism and positivism as strongly as he criticises the socialists' hubris – 'Intelligent people will tend to overvalue intelligence' (Hayek, 1988:53) – it is, however, Hayek's view that competition is productive of functional standards but that conscious design is marginalised into incompleteness by the sheer complexity of facts and knock-ons that no single mind can ever absorb.

Yet there is a problem. Competition tends to encourage the character traits that are the most compatible with economic rivalry – attributes like initiative, diligence, frugality, alertness, the worship of success and the determination to control. It is less favourable to socially-embedded institutions like altruism, compassion, loyalty, sympathy, satiety in consumption and acceptance of status which make no tangible contribution to the culture of superiority and conquest. Concerned about the *Geist* of economism that puts winning and overtaking before self-fulfilment through skill, Sombart warned that cold reason in the service of adventurous exploration could mean a social order that fed the body but crowded out the soul: 'Everything is sacrificed to the Moloch of work; all the higher instincts of heart and mind are crushed out by devotion to business.' (Sombart, 1915:181). Competition in such a perspective brings about its own evolution and not an alternative evolution less wedded to boundless acquisition and record-breaking as a success indicator in itself.

Sombart was concerned about a selection process that competed away all but competition itself. Hayek, on the other hand, acclaimed the spirit of undertaking and speculation as an evolution into emancipation and a promise of survival. Perhaps it is; but still it would be premature to assume that enterprise and independence are structurally inevitable and not simply values and choices. There is, in other words, a real possibility that Hayek's evolution is no more than the procedures of capitalism putting in place the habits of capitalism. Non-capitalism, as Hodgson observes, need not apply: 'This is not *any* spontaneous order that Hayek has in mind. It concerns just *one* type: the

Great Society... Hayek believes that socioeconomic intervention must be pushed down a particular track precisely by the creation of institutions and "general rules" which are necessary for the formation and sustenance of the liberal utopia.' (Hodgson, 1993:183).

Hayek believes that the State ought to free up the economy even where the spontaneous order does not evolve spontaneously: 'Liberalism ... restricts deliberate control of the overall order of society to the enforcement of such general rules as are necessary for the formation of a spontaneous order, the details of which we cannot foresee.' (Hayek, 1973:32). State intervention to support free markets (for example, through privatisation) is good intervention. State intervention to correct free markets (for example, through minimum wage laws) is bad intervention. There being a fundamental asymmetry in Hayek's interventionism, 'the Hayekian argument is thus rigged.' (Hodgson, 1993:184). Hayek's underlying preferences must be treated with respect. Even so, they are *his* values and *his* choices. They are not a theory of evolution.

Optimality in evolution means best-possible adaptation. Best-possible adaptation in economics means allocation and growth. Some economists would rely on matter in motion to engender the most economical institutions. Other economists would deny that the pressure of present-day circumstances, arriving so late in the unbroken skein of events, will ever be sufficient to keep the handed-down fully up-to-date. Optimisation at the margin presupposes a permanent adjustment and not a once-for-all equilibrium: 'Sometimes we shall have to make the painful effort of unlearning what we have been taught, and of breaking intellectual and emotional habits.' (Wallas, 1921:23). Optimisation presupposes permanent watchfulness. Conservatism, however, can mean the perpetuation of the 'was efficient once'.

To reverse past choices is to incur present costs in order to produce an uncertain future. Information, always incomplete, is even more limited where the problem to be solved is itself unspecified and unclear, where the *ex ante* that is desired is so imprecise as to preclude prediction. Risk-aversion is protective of the *status quo*; and so is the fact that much of knowledge and interpretation is itself encoded in the going concern. Where an entrenched rule does 'well enough', there is an obvious incentive not to call into question a proven success like matrilineal inheritance, sharecropping, conscription, the spelling of 'night', the university term in rhythm with the harvests, the English breakfast originally intended for field-workers, right-handed handshaking, conspicuously weapon-free, and other fixed points that have time-out-of-mind satisfied the society's aspirations. A spectacular failure makes prohibitively expensive the retention of the persisting: slavery can be competed into freedom where a major slump reveals flexible hiring to be the more profitable option and a one-child edict might have to be replaced with 'Stop at Two' where selective abortion and female infanticide lead in the long-run to a gender imbalance. A moderate shortfall is less likely to shock the tolerably contented into challenging the habitual: the future is uncertain, things could get worse, and minimax is a persuasive reason not to gamble present costs on risky causes that might not in the end be cost-effective.

On the one hand there is the chance of something better: the fact that cash is superior to barter does not mean that there is not some unexplored alternative which would be more efficient still. On the other hand there is the psychological rupture and the paid-out expense: change is upsetting and transactions have costs. Given the unknowledge, inertia in the circumstances might be the better buy. Especially is this likely to be so where group size is large and the positive externality of the public good shared even with free-riders who play no active part in engineering a move to a more satisfactory plane: 'The rational individual in the economic system does not curtail his spending to prevent inflation ... because he knows, first, that his own efforts would not have a noticeable effect, and second, that he would get the benefits of any price stability that others achieved in any case.' (Olson, 1965:166).

The slippage can be sizeable where the group is the nation. Latent, loose, unmanaged, no single entrepreneur in such a club will have a private stake large enough to induce him to coordinate the joint consumption of a new rule that will be productive of a more cooperative endstate. No rent is payable to the constitutional reformer who trades in new initiatives. The consequence is that the sub-optimal, the sub-maximal might survive even where each individual taken in isolation would prefer a different equilibrium. Large numbers make it difficult to fine-tune conventions in poorly-specified areas like common land, property rights in space and access to the resources of the sea. The most efficient guidelines simply fail to evolve, essentially because no one person will derive sufficient gains from trade to try to dislodge the existing if also the second-best.

The incumbent in any case has the head start that is conferred by path dependence and cumulative causality. Some past event, as exogenous as a natural catastrophe or a technological breakthrough, as endogenous as the infinite sequential repetitions of the tit-for-tat supergame, has somehow put in place a rule. Whether optimal then, whether best-possible now, the point is that we today start from here and proceed down a road which is already a laid-out constant. The national language universally understood, the railway stock constrained by the embodied gauge, the QWERTY keyboard protected by costly capitalisation, video-cassettes shoehorned into a preordained specification, the vehicle has already been shunted on to a unique named track which history alone can account for and which survives into the present because of overheads which have little or nothing to do with its origins.

Consider the highly-structured factory, the product in one perspective not so much of economies of scale in the Industrial Revolution as of extra-economic mimicry in the half-century of battle from the Seven Years War through the French Revolution to Napoleon and Waterloo: 'The circumstances of war prompted militaristic forms of industrial organization, and the hierarchical regimentation of the soldiery has its parallel in the similar organization of the workforce.' (Hodgson, 1993:204). Discipline copied discipline. The values of the past live on in the relative eclipse of the small-scale firm or the producer cooperative. Efficient or inefficient, only the most gifted of horizontal thinkers will think to include the unfamiliar on the moving staircase that leads to the light.

One view of the historical cull is that it is predetermined by relative productivity. Natural selection in this interpretation is economically optimal expressly because means–ends competitiveness mounts the ultimate assault on the accidental, the vestigial, the out-of-date, the entrenched: 'Competition will make it necessary for people to act rationally to maintain themselves... In a society in which rational behaviour confers an advantage on the individual, rational methods will progressively be developed and spread by imitation.' (Hayek, 1979:75). A different view of the regularity that evolves into a custom is that the bubble gets locked in, the analogy becomes entrenched; and that self-reinforcing momentum is a considerable obstacle to new entry. Virgin territory might be open to optimisation, but we today start from *here*, and from *there*, and from shared memories which serve as a powerful reminder that being conservative and being economical need not pinpoint the same desired state.

3.3   CONSTITUTIONS AND CHOICES

Hayek is a theorist of optimality through evolution who believes that 'the pattern of our successful actions' is the consequence not so much of insight into cause and effect as of 'the kind of world in which we live': man's 'adaptation to the general circumstances that surround him is brought about by his observance of rules which he has not designed and often does not even know explicitly, although he is able to honour them in action.' (Hayek, 1973:12). His confidence in an inter-temporal invisible hand of which the citizens made subject to the rules are largely unaware is not shared by evaluative intellectuals like James Buchanan and his non-functionalist school. Vanberg, arguing that not all that *is* is optimally suited to survival, is especially clear on the need for agnosticism and understanding in respect of rationality and selection: 'In dealing with the issue of which rules are *appropriate* for our social and economic life, we cannot evade the task of analysing and comparing the specific working properties of alternative rules (or systems of rules) and of investigating systematically the various processes by which the individuals concerned can, and do, express their own judgement on the "appropriateness" of rules and their own evaluation of the kinds of order that different rules generate.' (Vanberg, 1986:80). Spontaneity by itself is not the proof of social benefit. Understanding and examination are needed as well.

Buchanan and his followers agree with Hayek that rule-following is the *sine qua non* without which the *bellum omnium contra omnes* would put an end to orderly acquisitiveness. They also stress that core institutions must be multiperiod constants since case-by-case adjustment can prove uneconomic and destabilising. Believing like Hayek that present-day choices must be nested within past-dominated guidelines, they would insist with him that in constitutional matters it is rational to abstain from the interest-riven piecemealism of the cost–benefit calculus that can all too easily translate coordinated compliance into a chaos of grab.

Believing like Hayek that it is rational to have a rule, what Buchanan and his followers would nonetheless suggest is that efficiency will be better tested by consent than by simple automaticity. Where the rule that evolves does not satisfy the high standards of agreement, it cannot in this perspective be called a good rule: '"Truth", in the final analysis, is tested by agreement. And if men disagree, there is no "truth".' (Buchanan, 1977:113). Endstate allocations, philosophical systems, Biblical commandments do not enter into the balance save through the civilising mediation of consensual expectation. The focus instead is on the procedure: 'As an economist, I am a specialist in contract.' (Buchanan, 1975:x). The focus is not on the hotline to God for the ideological authority of the taken-on-trust. Rather, it is on the way in which long-lived conventions, 'relatively absolute absolutes', are offered, democratically, a renewal of their lease.

The Hayekian identifies a structural imperative in robust rules which sink roots and survive. That authority he derives from the natural selection of the evolutionary process. The sceptical Buchananite, on the other hand, is confident of no legitimacy save that which is conferred by agreed-upon preference-reconciliation. The model here is the economic market that matches accommodating supply to individual demand: 'There is no uniquely perfect constitutional order "out there", waiting to be revealed and discovered through our trials and errors, no "optimal solution" toward which we might gradually approximate ... We create our future by our choices.' (Vanberg and Buchanan, 1989:190). We create our future through our shopping, voluntary and uncoerced. The selection of normative precommitment is no less an expression of our freedom of choice than is the discovery process that culminates in an apples-for-oranges swap.

Equity in such a framework is tested by compromise, fairness demonstrated by unanimity of concord. Just as the economist's apples paid for oranges received is socially efficient because it is mutually beneficial, so is the constitutionalist's ideal of consent given for commonness constrained a welfare-enhancing legitimation of the rules for the very reason that the institutional bargain is, as in economics, reflective, bilateral, voluntary and Pareto-optimal in thrust. In the case of the laws as in the case of the fruit, the normative justification is the same: no one would give his consent if he expected his decision to make him worse off in his own estimation.

If, however, the multi-party purchase of laws is to promise the same unanimity of concord as does the two-party exchange of fruit, then existing privileges, conflicts of interest, minority positions, known circumstances must first be netted out. Rational chess-players, clearly, will not reach unanimity on the rules of their game if each knows at the rule-making stage the in-period disposition of his strategic pieces. John Rawls, contemplating the impediment to equity that is represented by too much information, suggests that the requisite impartiality can, conceptually speaking, be ensured through positing a veil of ignorance so thick as to conceal the individual's in-period attributes: 'No one knows his situation in society nor his natural assets, and therefore no one is in a position to tailor principles to his advantage.' (Rawls, 1971:139). James Buchanan, concentrating not on the fiction of a hidden present but on the fact of an unknowable future, opts instead for the expectationalist's core construct of a veil of uncertainty such that no rational agent can be confident of his own assets and liabilities in a Shackle-like history-to-come that is textured from the purest surprise: 'The individual, at the time of constitutional choice, is uncertain as to his own role on particular issues in the future... He will see that the external benefits which he may secure through imposing external costs on others on certain occasions will tend to equal the external costs which others will impose on him on different occasions.' (Buchanan and Tullock, 1962:191).

Whether the blacking-out of the in-period is ensured through ignorance in the sense of Rawls or through uncertainty in the sense of Buchanan, the welcome consequence is an equitable agreement. Impartiality is the cause of unanimity. Unanimity is the proof of justice. Democratic scepticism, as David Gauthier points out, condenses all of morality into a viewpoint shared: 'We deny that justice is linked to any substantive conception of what is good, either for the individual or for society. A just society has no aim beyond those given in the preferences of its members.' (Gauthier, 1986:341). What Buchanan and his followers would add is that the code will only be non-particular and neutral where it is durably multi-period as well. It is equitable to have a constitution. It is rational to be a conservative.

Gauthier writes that it is rational first to agree to rules and then to comply with them: 'It is rational to be disposed to constrain maximizing behaviour by internalizing moral principles to govern one's choices... To choose rationally, one must choose morally.' (Gauthier, 1986:4, 15). Gauthier believes that own-utility-maximising individuals can make positive-sum gains from trade where they accept the authority of rules and forego the special pleading that would multiply divisive exceptions: 'In accepting moral constraints they do not express their concern for each other, but rather they bring about the conditions that foster such concern.' (Gauthier, 1986:338). Gauthier also believes that, while the self-regulating market is a short-term method of conflict resolution, moral obligation only delivers a comparable dose of harmony where the standards of cooperative conduct do not vary so frequently as to become in-period like exchange: 'Morality arises from market failure.' (Gauthier, 1986:84). Gauthier believes in consultation on the content of constraint. Gauthier also believes that mutual advantage presupposes multi-period rules. In both of these respects he shares common ground with other contractarians and democrats such as Buchanan and his followers.

The liberal's calculus of consent is broadly in line with the modern, and individualistic, consensus. The conservative's call for normative stability is more of a problem. Yesterday's agreement, once it has become today's constitution, effectively precommits the future to rules on which not the present but the past had agreed. The liberal who is also a conservative would appear to be viewing the world through two different windows at once.

In yesterday's veil there was unanimity of consensus on the higher rates of income tax, on organ transplants for the over-60s, on fast-track schooling for gifted teenagers. We today live subject to the rules. So as good democrats we should – except that the preferences embodied are not *our* preferences and the contract negotiated is not our own. It may be attractive to current principals to employ historical agents in order to preclude any hint of partiality. Even if the duty to convention is indeed the middle way between moral anarchy and police-State compulsion, yet the fact remains that other people made up our minds and that you and I were told to be conformists without being given a vote. The possibility must be faced that liberal conservatism in such a scenario becomes a *de facto* justification for slavery by consent.

Conventions become internalised into the personality as a consequence of childhood socialisation. A part of the social learning process, they will in such circumstances not have been chosen rationally but rather imposed. We today are asked to subscribe to what we never agreed; and know that to become what the liberals call a shopper and the conservatives call a deviant is to incur costs which may be in excess of the benefits expected. Exit in the form of emigration carries with it a transaction overhead and is hedged about with risk. Exit can be the cause of regret where Ulysses unbound steers his craft on to a rock and the self-employed former executive spends his day staring at the wall. Voice is muted by the public-good character of reform and revolution and by the private-good probability of revenge and retribution. It can lead to the tax of a spoiled reputation which the sensitive gain-seeker will regard as a loss: 'An important, and often dominant reason to respect a norm is that violating it would provide a signal about the type of person you are.' (Axelrod, 1986:1107). Taking into account the monitoring and the enforcement, the spoiled identity and the guilty conscience, what the rational individual might conclude is that loyalty to a long-lived *status quo* is in the event the cost-effective buy.

Doing something will be more attractive than doing nothing where existing rules have become intolerable and the groundswell of discontentment suggests that the disaffected will not have to act alone. In the normal run of things, however, it will probably be more convenient simply to rubber-stamp codes passed on without logic or explanation than to swim against the tide and agitate for a reappraisal of the constitution. Thus do our ancestors as well as our contemporaries have an impact on our behaviour patterns which is no less an unfreedom for having become an inalienable part of the self.

The likelihood that it was *other people* who made the agreement means that continued membership is only a weak endorsement of the specific standards. Where Pareto-superior rules can be found, needless to say, the law-breaking iconoclast who explores new avenues that could lead to a more satisfying compromise must in all fairness be regarded as a public benefactor. So, for that matter, is the open-minded pragmatist who, as Vanberg notes, does right to question the primacy of the constitutional knee-jerk where the piecemeal response is the more suitable tool: 'That there are advantages to rule-governed behaviour does, of course, not imply that just any rule may be preferable to discretionary choice. Many behavioural rules are conceivable which obviously would produce a pattern of outcomes clearly inferior to what could be realized by deciding each case on its own.' (Vanberg, 1994:52).

A new constitution would be superior to a superannuated constitution where the individual replaces self-destructive vodka with life-enhancing aerobics and follows Schlicht in storing his car keys in his pocket rather than 'in the simplest place conceivable – the ignition.' (Schlicht, 1998:136). No constitution would be superior to a superfluous constitution where a daring and fresh response leads to more variety in diet and wardrobe and the suppression of rigidities like job tenure and protected tenancies makes possible a faster rise in living standards. An *optimum optimorum* will always be preferable to the lazy conservative's unthinking gravitation to his time-honoured restricted view with the parrot-like legitimation that 'it is my seat because that is where I always sit'. Even so, it can be the free gift of *other people* – both current people and past people – that the law-breaking iconoclast and the open-minded pragmatist alike remain trapped in a rut which each knows that he could change.

Mutual reinforcement and shared expectations, time remembered and established conventions, all explain why people conserve a known constitution when it is in their power to constitute a better one. Momentum and convergence, as Kuran makes clear, have much to account for: 'Public opinion does not change perpetually. Under common circumstances, the transformations of public opinion will eventually produce an equilibrium. That is, public opinion will become self-reproducing... Once in place, a selected equilibrium will persist indefinitely, even if slightly different early circumstances would have produced a very different equilibrium.' (Kuran, 1995:18). We start from here. Here is where we stay. It does little for the sense of self-worth to enter the supermarket with a list partly penned by long-dead strangers. If competition is tough, then so *a fortiori* is the economics of conservative choice.

4. Society as past

Chapter 2 argued that choices are interdependent and social institutions a special topic in the epistemology of the shared: 'All sociological acts are based on expectations of expectations. Specifically, all interactive decision making involves the actor's knowledge of the other individuals' knowledge... All social problems result from conflicts over expectations (or knowledge) which in turn result from the lack of acceptable limits on the range of expectations.' (Boland, 1979:321). Chapter 3 showed that the past marches alongside the present since in-period rationality is circumscribed by rule-making rules and funnelled through multi-generational conventions: 'Custom is more than habit. It is the social habit which creates individual habit. We do not start as isolated individuals – we start in infancy with discipline and obedience, and we continue as members of concerns already going, so that conformity to repeated and duplicated practices – which is all that is meant by going concerns – is the only way to obtain life, liberty, and property with ease, safety, and consent.' (Commons, 1934:45). Sanctioning peers whisper meaningfully in our ear. Vividness of recollection grasps us firmly by the hand. Proud and purposive, we like to think that we are in a position to ferret out the best-possible. The truth, less flattering, is that all that we uncover will often be no more than the answer that other travellers have left behind for us to use.

Consensus and repetition tend to time-warp and bind: 'Since most of our everyday experience involves previously *solved* social problems, it would be fairly difficult to give a pure description of any social problem apart from its assumed solution.' (Boland, 1979:321). Our way of life and our framework of discourse are, far more than we appreciate, givens that we do not choose. This chapter explores the relationship between those givens and the general thrust of the economy. Section 1, Bounded rationality, considers the rule of thumb as a first approximation in the dark. Section 2, Cognitive bias, examines the ways in which influences like value-systems, endowment, representativeness and availability force scarce information into channels through which single-minded economisers would not want to see it flow. The final section, Performance and productivity, asks if interdependence and history normally deliver the product that most people most desire – or if non-ego invariance effectively stifles the creative response upon which the enhancement of felt welfare so much depends.

4.1   BOUNDED RATIONALITY

On the one hand there is the Walrasian auctioneer, costless, timeless, effortless, perfectly well-informed. On the other hand there is George Shackle, convinced that 'knowable circumstances can be those only of an immediate present', sharply critical of model-builders who supply the tranquilliser of rational expectations despite the danger that, assuming away the shadow-land of uncertainty, guesstimate and strategy, the picture that emerges is seriously at variance with the unknowledge of sequential imaginings: 'For the traveller in the dark, a bridge with a missing span is worse than merely useless.' (Shackle, 1972:37, 53). Business life, Shackle would say, means initiative, enterprise, speculation and rivalry. It does not mean the comfortable certainties of a predictable future.

On the one hand there is the crystal ball. On the other hand there is the impenetrable veil. In the middle there is the conservative compromise which situates the new in the context of the old. Bounded rationality and the cognitive bias are instrumentalities which current cohorts employ when they navigate their endeavour into the unexplored territory of a history-to-come which their action itself will help to mould and shape.

Information has a cost and processing takes time. The future cannot be observed since it does not exist. The incomplete data-set that misses out the visceral, the restricted computational capacity of the human mind, the unforeseeable iceberg that sends only its shadow before – it is the unavoidable consequence of information overload in pursuit of distant probabilities that actors' cognitions are at best fragmented and limited, that 'it is not possible to act rationally in complex situations, even when one is backed up with scientific knowledge and methods.' (Etzioni, 1988:126).

Textbook maximisation is not possible, Herbert Simon writes, where omissions, misapprehensions and discontinuities mean that no decision-maker is ever an omnicompetent calculator in full command of all facts and opportunities: 'The decision-maker's information about his environment is much less than an approximation to the real environment... In actual fact the perceived world is fantastically different from the "real" world.' (Simon, 1959:272). Textbook maximisation is not possible since the choice among alternatives is made on the basis of a sub-set only of the real-world conditions that are in some sense 'out there': 'The decision-maker's model of the world encompasses only a minute fraction of all the relevant characteristics of the real environment, and his inferences only a minute fraction of all the information that is present even in his model.' (Simon, 1959:272). The quantity is minute. Simon's point is that it could well be enough. The information flow exceeds the limits of the brain. The cost of assembling and analysing is high. Textbook maximisation not meaningfully an option, perhaps the best possible sub-optimality could well be the best-attainable selective standard in a real-world environment that the textbook deductions do not fully describe.

Simon, aware that information is not scarce but abundant, believes that a middle course is commonly selected which lies between the absolute certainties of rational choice and the radical randomness of the stab in the dark. That middle course, he maintains, is the heuristic with a track-record which empowers the habits of the past to shape the practices of the future. Hayek writes that it is in man's nature to be a pattern-perpetuating animal: 'Man is as much a rule-following animal as a purpose-seeking one.' (Hayek, 1973:1). It is the essence of Herbert Simon's message that rule-following is itself a purpose-serving stance: 'By its most common definition, economics concerns scarcity. Because human reasoning ability is scarce, one could as well argue that economists are by definition *required* to study bounded rationality.' (Conlisk, 1996:686).

Rule-following is economical since decision-making is a cost – and 'good economics requires that we entertain all costs.' (Conlisk, 1996:669). The rule of thumb at the level of perception provides the filter of prejudgement – of prejudice – without which the raw data could not meaningfully be ordered and classified: 'There are hosts of inferences that *might* be drawn from the information stored in the brain that are not drawn.' (Simon, 1959:273). The rule of thumb at the level of activity singles out the trigger threshold that, once attained, causes the economical searcher to declare 'good enough': 'One could postulate that the decision maker had formed some *aspiration* as to how good an alternative he should find. As soon as he discovered an alternative for choice meeting his level of aspiration, he would terminate the search and choose that alternative. I [call] this mode of selection satisficing.' (Simon, 1979:503). Both at the level of data collection and at that of problem-solving, in short, Simon's institutional economics does away with the fiction of full-information maximising in order to put in its place a tried-and-tested standard that has worked tolerably well in the past.

A repertoire of reactions is more constricting than would be a fresh and flexible response: 'A paradigm produces intellectual tunnel vision.' (Loasby, 1976:198). It is easy to criticise the handed-on focus for concentrating attention on the established to the detriment of the relevant; for directing investigation and entrepreneurship to conventional associations at the cost of novel departures; for screening out sunrise variables which would threaten the hegemony of the existing box of tools. A heuristic can be self-perpetuating even where the social consensus wants the welfare that the rule is blocking off. In its defence, however, a heuristic may be said to confer significant benefits that are themselves a part of the good life. Not least among these benefits is psychological reassurance.

People want challenge, stimulus and excitement. They flee from the boredom of perfect anticipation. People also want stable recurrences and comforting familiarity. They flee from the vacuum of 'I haven't a clue'. Sometimes they opt for pleasure-*seeking* through risk: they court the utility derived from gambling and sign up for dangerous sports. Sometimes they opt for pleasure-*finding* through habit: they return to the hairdresser whose cut they can predict and imitate a business leader whom they believe to be astute. People, in short, want both the thrill of mould-breaking and the tranquillity of science. Not, however, in equal proportions. Scitovsky is insistent that, in general, people dislike risk and go out of their way to remove it: 'Everyday experience shows that uncertainty is not only arousing, it is usually so much so that it is unpleasant. People generally dislike most forms of uncertainty... The expectation of the unexpected is bewildering and frightening more often than it is enjoyable.' (Scitovsky, 1976:56-7). People want a mixed mental portfolio. They also want a portfolio that is more manageable, more familiar, more conservative than not.

The heuristic, giving them a sense of security, is to that extent a source of felt welfare in itself. Whether spitting twice because that is what we do or squeezing the withers because that is what we learned, the intellectual going concern is a source of emotional support to the spirit without a home: 'The chief service rendered by a theory is the setting of minds at rest. So long as we have a satisfying conceptual structure, a model or a taxonomy which provides for the filing of all facts in a scheme of order, we are absolved from the tiresome labour of thought, and the uneasy consciousness of mystery and a threatening unknown... Theory serves deep needs of the human spirit.' (Shackle, 1967:288). Always a simplification, sometimes inadequate, occasionally misleading, anything that satisfies the deep-seated need for certainty cannot be said to be entirely without a function.

The heuristic is an expectation. An expectation reassures. The heuristic is reassuring because it is a history-driven regularity, tried and tested. The heuristic is reassuring as well because it is a common rigidity that shapes and defines the identity of the group. The twin elements of time and convergence come together in Keynes on the self-enforcing coordination that is imposed upon unknowledge by Veblen-like emulation and the herd instinct: 'Knowing that our own individual judgement is worthless, we endeavour to fall back on the judgement of the rest of the world, which is perhaps better informed. That is, we endeavour to conform with the behaviour of the majority or average.' (Keynes, 1937:214). Even the 'normal' rate of interest in the Keynesian speculative demand is the consequence not of detached quantification but of interdependent feedback: 'Any level of interest which is accepted with significant conviction to be durable will be durable.' (Keynes, 1936:203). All in the mind and all in the *minds*, interest is an expectation and an expectation reassures.

The heuristic is a beacon for travellers in the dark: 'To avoid anxiety', clearly, 'they need *some* kind of "recipe for success".' (Earl, 1986:227). Lacking reliable knowledge of potentials and probabilities, they use rules of thumb of great ingenuity in their attempt to control the overwhelming, to 'force random events into predictable patterns.' (Earl, 1986:229). Psychological reassurance is one benefit that is expected from the rules. Goal-attainment is another.

The team has a mascot to bring it good luck. The student strokes a rabbit's foot before an examination. The general consults the entrails of a chicken before mounting a *coup d'état*. The housewife does no New Year cleaning lest she sweep away the red packets of prosperity. Ritual and superstition in forms such as these are intended not just to reassure but to deliver results as well. They are matched in the business life by a range of procedures and practices which have the same function of guiding and planning – and of doing so without quick error-correction through supply and demand.

The consumer shops by precedent, intuition, 'gut reaction', the presentation of the product, the endorsement of a celebrity. The worker refuses wage cuts when the demand for the product falls because he treats existing differentials as an ethical absolute which cannot be re-thought. The retailer sets prices not by MC=MR but by constant markup and targets his marketing strategy on fashion leaders whom others will use as a reference point to copy. The producer hedges his bets by diversifying his output mix, copes with uncertainty by under-investing in fixed capital, protects his market share in preference to his short-run profits, stereotypes in favour of Chinese because they are normally good at science. Rules of thumb such as these are crucial for an understanding of how a real-world market really works. Perhaps 'archaic', perhaps 'ceremonial', the possibility must also be recognised that some at least of the rules adopted will be as tangential to goal attainment as would be the contribution of a goat on the turf to the success of Manchester in the Football League.

Some rules will have the scientific status of the goat. Others will have a more obvious payoff. It is the contention of economists convinced that satisficing *satisfies* that a selective standard ground out through competitive sequence, progressively modified in response to perceived disappointments, simply would not have survived if it had been a random rather than a cost-effective norm.

The evolutionary approach does not lend itself easily to real-world testing. Inertia having its utility, it is not clear how great the sub-rationality would have to be to shake the comfortable into a reappraisal of the merits and deficiencies. Time commitment and psychic upheaval being valid costs in themselves, it is difficult to falsify the hypothesis that actors optimise even when they are defeatist about potential. The evolution of the heuristic does not explain why different firms target different profit rates or why prices vary even within a small circumscription. It cannot say why a given firm becomes the price leader in conditions of oligopoly or why the kinked demand-curve kinks where it does. Economists who believe that satisficing *satisfies* would, however, assert that unknowables such as these detract little from their logic. A rule persists because people believe that it performs tolerably well. They would not believe that it was doing its job if, hiring by degree certificate while its competitors were hiring by aptitude test, a business was being pushed into the bankruptcy courts by a past procedure that had lost its cutting edge.

The market in the sense of Mises is dispersion and discovery in the sense of Hayek: 'The market is the social system of the division of labor under private ownership of the means of production ... The market is not a place, a thing or a collective entity. The market is a process, actuated by the interplay of the actions of the various individuals cooperating under the division of labor.' (Mises, 1949:258). On the one hand maximiser's certainty, on the other hand radical unknowledge-bounded rationality is the compromise that encodes past practices into inter-temporal external economies such that the market becomes able to scan with a focus and allocate with an expectation. Bounded rationality is in that way, as Heiner observes, not an *obiter dictum* but rather the very element that puts pattern into pricing: 'The observed regularities that economics has tried to explain on the basis of optimization would disappear if agents could actually maximize ... Uncertainty is the basic source of predictable behavior.' (Heiner, 1983:585–6). Indeed it is; and that is why the remembered routine makes so valuable a contribution to a free market process that does not want to be confused.

4.2   COGNITIVE BIAS

Economists attracted by the axiom of rationality tend to see the mind as a cross between a camera that takes a photograph of external reality and a computer that positions the stills in the place where they belong. Psychologists are less convinced that matter is to mind as jug is to mug. Experimental studies have identified a number of ways in which real-world decision-making deviates from textbook efficiency. These anomalies reflect the influence of the inter-personal context and of experience remembered. They are a reminder that the individual is not alone when he or she sets out from *here* – or from *there* which is so often so much nearer to home.

Social pressures and the communication of interpretation mean that the individual approaches the fresh occurrence with the standard labels that Durkheim calls 'collective representations' and Mary Douglas, in sympathy with Schotter's assessment that 'the institution tells all' (Schotter, 1981:139), sums up in the following words: 'Institutions survive by harnessing all information processes to the task of establishing themselves. The instituted community blocks personal curiosity, organizes public memory, and heroically imposes certainty on uncertainty.' (Douglas, 1987:102). The layout of the Zuñi pueblo mirrors the stratification of Zuñi social structure: 'Public memory is the storage system for the social order.' (Douglas, 1987:70). Once a Zuñi, always a Zuñi. A free spirit who thinks up a better design for his pueblo would in the circumstances be well advised to look elsewhere for its adoption.

Public anchoring, delivering though it does valuable benefits in the form of cohesion, stability and the economical throughput of information, has the less attractive implication for productivity and growth that the social control of cognition is likely to inhibit the recognition of novelty and improvement: 'Often when a new scientific discovery has been rejected and left to lie inert until later, it is precisely an idea which lacked formulaic interlocking with normal procedures of validation.' (Douglas, 1987:77). Intellectual reinforcers can be a major obstacle to the rational choice at variance with the handed-on opinion. As Timur Kuran explains it, the problem is that shared convictions, transmitted through time, have a persistence and a perseverance which makes them exceptionally resistant to new imaginings and even to new evidence: 'The limitations of human cognition steer one's attention away from undiscussed matters. Therefore, unexpressed ideas are less likely than ones expressed openly to enter the worldviews of later generations... Their thoughts will tend to conform to the dominant ideas of their parents' generation.' (Kuran, 1995:185, 186). Critical mass provides positive feedback for the generally accepted. The domino effect looks after its own. Thus does today's Zuñi become a free rider on the paradigms and proofs of Zuñis gone by.

Classes and categories, resemblance and differentiation, are themselves cultural constructs, learned reactions that strain the argument by analogy through an existing frame of reference that takes over the labour of thought: 'Sameness is not a quality that can be recognized in things themselves; it is conferred upon elements within a coherent scheme.' (Douglas, 1987:59). The aesthetic perception of beauty, the presentational attributes of male and female, the tolerable levels of pain, anxiety, stress and fatigue – the imputation of similarity that governs the choice of the file or box is in effect a collective property and a shared authority on relevance versus randomness. The automatic pilot in this way makes possible a saving of effort and energy – but it does so at a price. The Zuñi of tomorrow is likely to perceive his environment more or less as does the Zuñi of today. Otherwise he would be a Slovak and not a Zuñi at all.

Socialisation is a prism and a cause of selective perception. People see what they expect to see and treat the outsider phenomenon as a threat to their peace of mind. The consequence is what Kuran calls the 'magnetism of recent history', the 'magnetism of the prevailing equilibrium' – 'collective conservatism', in short, such that the range of free choices is bounded and self-censored in order that a settled cosmology be protected from the unsettling discourse of permanent revolution: 'At any particular time, therefore, a social order incorporates multitudes of decisions inherited from the past... No community keeps all of its social arrangements constantly open to change.' (Kuran, 1995:105, 107).

The *status quo* is authority. Authority is trust. Extrapolating from the familiar and making the expected moves, people give other people the confidence they need to plan their way into a continuing pattern made self-reproducing by the consistency of their adherence: 'Public opinion shows persistence because its realization in the immediate past shapes present expectations. Had the recent past been different, individuals would have formed other expectations, and their choices might have differed.' (Kuran, 1995:107). Not wishing to appear deviant and afraid of being ostracised, people conceal their misgivings and enter into a spiral of silence which even the majority of the conspirators might believe to be dubious and second-rate: 'Through preference falsification they may thus hold in place structures that they could, if only they acted together, easily change.' (Kuran, 1995:113).

Loyalty will sometimes be simulated because concealed preference is less expensive than exit, less risky than voice. Often, however, loyalty will be freely given and genuine, the product not of prudence and pretence but of a sincere conviction that numbers lend credibility, that a position magnified is a position confirmed. This appeal to the authority of the common perspective, termed by him 'the heuristic of social proof', is explained by Kuran with the following logic: 'If a great many people think in a particular way, they must know something we ourselves do not – as in the maxim "two heads are better than one". The basis of our judgement becomes that "everyone knows" what is best or right. In effect, we believe an explanation, assertion, prediction, or evaluation because most others do.' (Kuran, 1995:163). In politics we are persuaded by the orator who prefaces his contention with the reassurance of 'as you know'. In economics we grasp the meaning of a painting's price tag if told the artist was Picasso whom most people believe to be great. In finance we stampede or strike as bulls and bears lest A miss out on a 'bubble', B forget his 'bottom fishing' when the market hits its trough. Popularity breeds popularity. Success sells success. No one wants to make a mistake. Conformity is quality assurance against a bandwagon foregone.

Just as public opinion shapes public opinion in its own incumbent image, so too does the guidance of experts and authorities, socially certified, herd together the uncoordinated and the discrete behind a banner which no isolated utility-seeker would have identified for himself. A commentator who recommends soya beans on the television must know about soya beans or he would not have won the distinction of the television pulpit. The Bible, Adam Smith, Karl Marx buttress their claims with the legitimation of familiarity and of antiquity that can be even more powerful than the carrot of material self-interest. The household-name phrase 'From each according to his ability, to each according to his needs' enjoys the high standing born of respect by association in the mind of the 45 per cent of Americans who in one study proclaimed it to be a clause in their country's Constitution. The free market is known to be superior to the welfare State because it is linked ideationally with the 'American way of life' and is widely endorsed by trained economists who have made a careful study of the available alternatives. Not wishing to fall victim to propaganda or to manipulative advertising, what individuals do in cases such as these is to rely on leadership because cognitive limitations leave them no choice but the short-cut of trust.

People become attached to intellectual schemata: they discount new information once they have made up their minds. People become dependent on public opinion: they confirm their prejudices through peers who share their biases. People also become accustomed to endowments. In the case of objects, as with anchoring and sanctions, the existing weighs down the novel and significant opportunities remain unexploited because an outsider alone can maximise with an open mind.

Possession brings about an endogenous change in utility. The asset made a part of his lifestyle, the consumer develops a commitment to it stronger than the liking he had originally anticipated when *ex ante* he initially revealed his preference. The average cash value of a mug to individuals who had no mug was in one study found to be $3.50. It was all of $7.12 for existing owners, reluctant to let go and sensitive to the loss. (Kahneman, 1994:24). The (future) re-sale price is in excess of the (current) acquisition value. More surprising still, even shoppers experienced in the buying and selling of durables seem consistently to be myopic at the decision-making stage, predictably unaware of the underestimation into which the asymmetry of purchase as betterment, sale as deprivation is likely to lock them: 'People seem to be unwittingly trapped by their choices; they make choices with an unrealistic sense of their reversibility.' (Loewenstein and Adler, 1995:936).

If people had learned from experience that habituation upvalues compensation when new friends part company at last, they would have adjusted their initial offer-price in the light of the tastes that would later on have become their own. What the evidence suggests instead is that people are signally unprepared to conduct inter-temporal arbitrage in order to circumvent non-rational intransitivities at variance with economic efficiency. Error correction is imperfect – and for this the short-termism of memory must bear a significant share of the responsibility. Where the mug is traded on very soon after it was secured, the individual may well be in a position to juxtapose the utility that he imagined to the utility that he enjoyed. Not so the case where people hang on to their endowments until they have forgotten who they once were, until they have convinced themselves 'that their past views were similar to those held in the present... People will remember their past tastes as being similar to their current tastes and erroneously conclude that their tastes have not changed. Thus, feedback about taste-change might be less plentiful than one might expect based on the accumulation of experience with possession.' (Loewenstein and Adler, 1995:936).

People fail to anticipate how quickly they will become habituated to a change of state. The mug, gathering dust, evolves into a family friend. The painting ceases to be noticed once it looks like it was always there. The sofa is not returned after the trial period even if the seller pays for the transportation and the purchase price is fully refunded. Shareholders become attached to their company even when gain-seeking institutionals are known to be deserting a sinking ship. Depositors fail to switch their bank accounts even if a rival is promising a higher rate of interest. Being rich due to a lottery win is something after a time that one takes in one's stride. Being paraplegic following a car accident eventually becomes not a one-off calamity but an on-going fact of life. *Ex post* people settle in to an accustomed *status quo*. *Ex ante* 'people lack skill in the task of predicting how their tastes might change.' (Kahneman, 1994:33). *Ex ante* or *ex post*, the dice are weighted in favour of the existing endowment and of things as they stand.

Because alternatives are evaluated so frequently not in terms of the statistical payoffs but with respect to the current base, the reference point has an unwarranted salience in the making of economic choices: 'The marginal effects in perceived well-being are greater for changes close to one's reference level than for changes further away.' (Rabin, 1998:13). New levels of consumption are compared to old levels at least as much as to some absolute ceiling. This year's inflation is considered relative to last year's inflation to determine if it is a cause of concern. A teenager who looks like a criminal is more likely to be pigeon-holed as a criminal than is a pensioner who dresses like a clergyman. In the world of representativeness, it is the recollectable and the recognisable at least as often as the probable and the actuarial that will sit on the jury when an option is being assessed. That is why a man wishing to impress a woman should send her a few flowers day-by-day spaced rather than a single giant bouquet on her birthday alone.

Freshness is the ultimate *aide-mémoire*. People over-estimate the statistical probabilities when a disastrous airplane crash is prominently reported in the news. They vote for more policemen and tougher sentencing when a personal friend becomes the victim of an accident or a crime. They treat as familiar and to that extent reliable a well-publicised consumable, easily recalled from recent advertising. The availability bias clearly has the power to drive a wedge between measured frequencies on the one hand, perceived visibility on the other. Cognition becomes incomplete. Factuality becomes subjective. Over-weighting the memorable and neglecting the concealed, people tend not to pour through the information-sets before they exaggerate the expectation that occurrence means recurrence in a remembered world where hindsight and selective screening go hand in hand.

Vividness speaks. One consequence is systematic misperception with respect to sample size. Not only is occurrence frequently used as a weather vane for recurrence, people also jump to conclusions before the law of large numbers has had time to spotlight the specific sequence which stands the greatest chance of being representative and robust. The gambler generalises from a lucky streak that has survived too few plays to support a prediction of success. He also assumes that, because heads are equal to tails in a long series of tosses, therefore a coin tossed only twice will reliably fall to earth once on each side. The investor discards new evidence which calls into question an investment strategy that has performed well for him in the selection of current shares. He also places undeserved confidence in a professional adviser whose track record could be random: 'Because we underestimate the frequency of a mediocre financial analyst making lucky guesses three times in a row, we exaggerate the likelihood that an analyst is good if she is right three times in a row.' (Rabin, 1998:25). Tversky and Kahneman showed that effectiveness improved when trainee pilots had recently been criticised, deteriorated when trainee pilots had recently been praised. (Tversky and Kahneman, 1974:10). The rush to judgement is a familiar heuristic employed to make complex decision-making more structured and more manageable. It can also be a cause of new evidence filtered through inappropriate beliefs to such an extent as to damp down the economic progress that open-minded rationality would have been better placed to encourage.

The reference point in the remembered past sheds light on the sunk cost effect. Despite the economist's exhortation to 'let bygones be forever gone', people are seen to take historic, fixed costs into account when they make their present-day decisions. They throw good money after bad by using theatre tickets for which they regret that they have paid even if they thereby incur incremental travel costs that could have been avoided had they simply written off the initial waste. They show little awareness of water under the bridge when they practise deliberate gluttony at an all-you-can-eat buffet because they do not want to miss out on their 'money's worth', on an unlimited entitlement already guaranteed by the psychic pain of the overhead incurred. Maximisers will insist that the past embodied has lost its status as a decision-making variable. Ordinary people, psychologically conservative, seem not to notice and not to care.

As with sunk cost, so with opportunity cost; since here once again the bird in the hand has an especial attraction even where the next-best foregone is in truth the more economical buy. People weight an out-of-pocket loss more highly than an equivalent gain not secured. Shopping in the High Street, for example, they will spend more if an identical price is packaged as a discount foregone than they would if it were wrapped in a credit card surcharge: the cash is merely a sacrificed opportunity but the overcharge is a hand in the wallet. The capitalist does not give up on knitwear simply because swimwear has become the more profitable line. Direct cost has gone out. A specified endowment has come in. We start from *here*; and so does the capitalist. In possession of an asset, he does not want to let go.

The base point in time remembered date-stamps its image on subsequent schemata and responses to cost. It also sheds valuable light on the meaning that socialised citizens attach to equity in the economy. A lawful outlet is not gainfully exploited where the doctor dismisses a paying customer for whom no effective treatment can be prescribed. A traditionalised market does not clear where no employer wants to be stigmatised as the wage-cutter who Dutch-auctioned subsistence as if guided by a supply and demand text. Fairness is a consideration in business practices such as these. Whether for goodwill or repeat business or reputation or conscience, marketeers are driven not to deviate too far from the standards that their community has learned to accept.

Kahneman and his colleagues, studying the distribution of scarce football tickets in Vancouver, found that 68 per cent of the 191 adults surveyed believed the queue to be the most equitable mode of allocation; that 28 per cent were most in favour of a lottery; and that only 4 per cent expressed their support for the economist's rationing by price. Extending their brief to beer, the investigators also found that interviewees were willing to pay $2.65 for a bottle of beer in an elegant hotel but would refuse to pay more than $1.50 for an identical bottle in a local shop. Linking these two sets of observations were cost and cost-plus. Respondents, resistant to transactions which they took to be unfair, saw no reason for prices to be inflated beyond some historic benchmark simply because the monopolist or the price-discriminator could bully his way into all that the traffic will bear: 'It is unfair for a firm to exploit an increase in its market power to alter the terms of the reference transaction at the direct expense of a customer, tenant, or employee.' (Kahneman, Knetsch and Thaler, 1986:296). Pricing is signalling and signalling unlocks efficiency. That is the market; but the market is not all. Public opinion, hardly hostile to material advance, raises a moral objection to price rises not forced upon the supplier by the tax of input inflation. Such profit-seeking, people seem to believe, unjustifiably puts the Hobbesian *bellum* in the place of the Medieval just price.

If the buyers have an entitlement to a reference rigidity then so too, in the assessment of Kahneman's Canadians, do the sellers: 'It is acceptable for a firm to maintain its profit at the reference level by raising prices or rents or by cutting wages as necessary.' (Kahneman, Knetsch and Thaler, 1986:296). Customers will not withhold present business or pass future orders to rival suppliers where their regular partner, deserving no punishment, has adjusted nominal values exclusively in order to protect a baseline rate of profit against a rise in input cost. Nor will they react adversely if the firm retains for itself most or all of the profit increment engendered by a reduction in input price. Asymmetrical though it undoubtedly is, the injustice which the survey showed the public to resent was essentially the quick adaptation to an excess of demand over supply which has no underlying justification in an inflation of cost.

Inflated-cost stock may equitably be sold at a higher price. Old stock cannot be as to do so would be to cream off a windfall surplus. Existing snow shovels may not reasonably be marked up merely because demand has gone up as the result of a blizzard. It will be argued by maximisers that the neglect of the opportunity cost is to deny the firm the profits that flexible pricing would have made its reward for alertness. Conservatives take a different view. Not denying that people want novelty and initiative, conservatives say that people want loyalty and decency as well. People want a satisfying standard of living. They also want to be treated *fairly*. To deny that their motivation is a mix, non-rational and not just acquisitive, is to underestimate the sophistication of the economic problem.

The way in which information is presented is a further influence on the decision that will be made. Where belief A settles in before belief B arrives, people will become protective of existing satisfiers, resistant to advertising which markets a different brand and experience which questions an established conjecture. Where commodities A, B and C are presented as a triad, shoppers will be attracted by the least-confrontational compromise of the middle ground even if their first-ranked choice thereby becomes B in A, B, C but C in A, C, B. Where a consumable Lancaster-like has a multiplicity of characteristics, revealed orderings will differ depending on whether the most salient feature of a car is size, safety, comfort, colour, of a watch image, appearance, reliability or price. Agenda order is a problem, *à la carte* a set of permutations, multidimensionality a universe of invitations. Coherence, consistency and transivity are evidently not for all seasons in a psychological economics where market signals may be conflicting and contradictory depending on the way in which information is edited and alternatives framed.

Preferences are difficult to interpret where a context rewritten leads to an appraisal reversed. Especially evocative is the evidence collected by Tversky and Kahneman on social attitudes to two (hypothetical) medical programmes. The first offered the prospect of certainly saving 200 lives. The second promised a one-in-three chance of saving 600 lives. Seen in terms of the mathematical expectation the respondents in the survey ought rationally to have been indifferent between the two choices. Because the subjective reaction to loss is more extreme than is the felt reaction to gain they were not. Fully 72 per cent of the respondents opted for the first programme. Only 28 per cent preferred the second. (Tversky and Kahneman, 1981:453).

The respondents in the survey, not ignorant or impulsive but quasi-rational, had to decide simultaneously on their attitude to lives and their tolerance of risk. The way in which they framed the perceived probabilities clearly had an impact on the outcomes that resulted from their choices. In the case in question, it is possible that 400 human beings unnecessarily lost their lives because of the utility bias.

The phenomenon is a general one. Workers unwilling to countenance cuts in their money wages will be more accepting of price rises that do not deprive them of a nominal endowment: the reason is not money illusion but the attachment to an established value. Two nations wanting to disarm will each rank the loss in its own weaponry above the gain secured when an enemy destroys his missiles: loss aversion being the stronger force, the treaty is not signed and the concessions are not made. In both cases the disproportionality of loss condemns the parties to a sub-optimality – inflation in the former scenario, armaments in the latter – that they do not want. Re-framing the choices to reinforce the improvements would contribute actively to a reconsideration of the rankings. So, for that matter, would a less conservative attachment to reference points that endorse destinations no longer on the map.

Choices have consequences. Some are current – an apple is eaten, its core discarded. Some are delayed – a cream-cake on the lips, a size 36 on the hips. Economists, skilled in the discounting of investment goods, are less experienced in the decomposition of the utility stream that accrues to a consumer durable such as lifetime good health. The consequence is that they fail to account for the inter-temporal inconsistencies which arise when the individual, the votary of long-term utility but of immediate gratification as well, reveals a preference in the present-day which is manifestly at odds with the utility function that governs his history-to-come.

Impatient and greedy, people tend to over-weight rapid returns relative to long-run pay-offs. Wanting to be slim tomorrow, they nonetheless eat curry puffs today. They want to avoid emphysema but they also want to smoke. They want a world-class garden but they also want days out with friends. They want a medical practice but they also want an exemption from time-consuming studies. The problem in all of this is not a radical lack of foresight so much as the conflicting demands of the multiple self. Even if people want to maximise a utility function, there is more than one utility function in which they can invest their hopes.

People are aware of the cognitive bias which twists rational choice when current preferences co-exist with future ideals. Recognising *akrasia* – weakness of will – to be a threat to the *maximum maximorum*, they therefore rely on self-control and self-precommitment to ensure that downstream desires are not crowded out by earlier utilities to an extent that will later be a cause of regret. They position their alarm-clock as far as possible from the bed. They keep no alcohol or chocolates in their home. They purchase prepaid holidays where they would otherwise feel guilty about spending money on themselves. They make contracts with high cancellation penalties where they would otherwise be torn in two by indecision. Acting as conservatives who want to insulate long-term resources from short-run depletion, people in cases such as these try to bind their weaker selves precisely as the sane Ulysses precommitted the deluded Ulysses in order to protect himself from the Sirens' song.

The private sector, understanding the conflict, markets rules that reconcile the time horizons. Clinics sell aversion therapies and 'fat farms' sell weight-watching. Chocolates are seldom packaged in giant cartons and spirits seldom made the subject of 2-for-1 offers. Life assurance as contractual savings works against the temptation to put the immediacy of youth above the needfulness of old age. The principal–agent nexus in the healthcare industry absolves the parent from the risk that a choice made for a child will go badly wrong: 'Clearly, in this situation a rational consumer would want the physician to make the choice and furthermore, he would not want to know that a choice existed!' (Thaler, 1980:53). The private sector, it is clear, markets much that can contain current anxiety and later regret through the voluntary restriction of choice-sets on the part of a planning self that, frightened of myopia, seeks to share the responsibility of choice.

The private sector can supply the freedom of choosing not to choose. The State sector can do so as well. Aware that people take an 'it can't happen to me' view of diswelfares like illness and divorce, the State legislates against contra-statistical optimism by means of seat belts and national savings made compulsory, new building prohibited in established flood-plains. Aware that people lack confidence in their own fallen selves, the State taxes tobacco but subsidises milk, keeps out subversive publications and bans addictive drugs, sets wages and prices in such a way as to prevent divisive leap-frogging from depleting the public good of growth without inflation. It is easy to conflate such interventionism with authentic paternalism that treats rational voters as if they were madmen or children. A more consensual perspective would bring in the divided self and the time dimension: the enforcing State is seen here as the passive servant hired by the individual who wants not to smoke. Without the State the individual would have had to rely on inter-generational institutions like marriage and children to ensure he drove safely on the road – or on professional bodyguards paid to protect the sane Ulysses from the deluded Ulysses when he approaches the casino or the betting shop with a time frame that he will live to regret.

Always assuming, of course, that the real Ulysses can without difficulty be identified. Capitalists will say that the better Ulysses is the Ulysses who saves and invests, not the Ulysses who squanders and indulges. Conservatives will say that there is constitutional common sense in co-determining the time periods lest the last, unconsulted, be given the least. The capitalists and the conservatives are entitled to their meta-logic and their moral values. Doubters, however, will still raise questions about their blend. Why should current preferences bind future ones when people over time might change their mind? Does not such stabilisation make it more difficult for the individual to develop new tastes and to learn from doing? Why is Ulysses alive to be ranked above Ulysses dead when Ulysses himself was in two minds about security versus song? The dual self introduces a cognitive bias. Precommitment is one solution. It is also a problem in itself.

4.3   PERFORMANCE AND PRODUCTIVITY

The first section of this chapter showed that mental economies can be reaped through the repetition of a satisfactory routine: 'If rationality is scarce, good decisions are costly. There is a tradeoff between effort devoted to deliberation and effort devoted to other activities.' (Conlisk, 1996:682). The second section continued the theme of the economical heuristic by demonstrating that there is always a saving in computational capacity where decision-making is the non-calculative consequence of the knee-jerk reaction: 'If the choice context repeats itself, it is unnecessary for an individual to go through complex decision processes in the same way, and to the same degree, and with the same information and exploratory costs, on each occasion.' (Leibenstein, 1976:88). The first section suggested that a history-honed cut-off can be better than a stab in the dark. The second section showed that a psychological skewness can be at once a self-perpetuating rigidity and an insight into the reality that is yet to come. Information being scarce, the contribution to performance and productivity of systematically avoiding the new should not be neglected merely because the reproduction of fixed points differs from the textbook picture of human behaviour as rational choice.

The maximising textbook assumes stable profit functions and utility functions, preferences that are coherent, consistent, transitive and clear, a past that is understood and accurately evaluated, a future that can be moulded through means–ends purposiveness in the service of measurable probabilities. The vision is one of assessment and knowledge, options and constraints. It is not a window on to norms, routines, paradigms, habits, frameworks, traditions, schemata that theorists of inter-temporal anchoring and of interpersonal influence believe to be the more common procedures that are employed by ordinary people when confronted with economic challenges: 'The orthodox economic model of consumer behavior is, in essence, a model of robot-like experts. As such, it does a poor job of predicting the behavior of the average consumer.' (Thaler, 1980:58). Rational expectation does a poor job because, normative and not positive, it does not inquire into the systematic, schematic regularities that are produced by decision-making constancies like bounded rationality in the sense of Simon and cognitive bias in the sense of Tversky. Deduction replaced by induction, what emerges is a better forecast of the cause–effect relationship as those prospects are actually perceived by men and women whose choices – and whose mistakes – are not random but subject to a long-term rule.

Thus people are known to welcome low prices and to treat marginal add-ons as different purchases: this means that they will predictably spend more on a car, a house or a holiday if the choice is framed as an inexpensive basic model that can be complemented with optional extras than they will if the entire sequence is collapsed into a single, globally-priced package. They treat the £100 that lies between 0 and £100 as more significant (and more deserving of careful analysis) than they do the £100 that lies between £1000 and £1100: the reference points are different even though the absolute value is the same. People put a first prize of £100 above a second prize of £150 which is to them an unpleasant reminder of the coveted reward they narrowly missed because they failed to make the grade. They treat thick coins as more valuable than thin ones and hold on longer to gold-coloured currency which is felt somehow to be worth something more. Chinese gamblers are more likely to select the number 6. Western tenants are more resistant to room 13. In all of these cases the individual makes choices with the aid of selective standards that would not pass muster in the Age of Reason. People are a pill; but we start from here. A good grasp of the heuristics and even the delusions allows the observer to predict future reactions that he would not have recognised had he put patterned non-rationality on a par with the genuine unknowables of impulse, intuition, gut reaction and personal idiosyncrasy that even the subjectively-aware would have to regard as *ex machina* anomalies and Acts of God.

People selectively recall the peak pleasure in a series and also the end utility: a singer knowing that should save up his extreme highs for the finale of his concert. Recognition improves sales: the firm should go in for publicity stunts that keep the product name in the public eye. Agreement introduces regret: the seller should press for early acceptance since customers do not like later on to admit to a mistake. Certainty counts: intermediaries should take advantage of the disutility of the undetermined to cap the pay-off to low-risk investments well below their statistical mean. The step function locks in: the monopolistic competitor should exploit the market dominance that he enjoys up to the satisficing cut-off – power that he would never have noticed had he built his business on the continuous responses of a downward-sloping demand curve. What it all adds up to is clearly this: knowing the heuristic is good business for an economic agent who wants to predict.

Signalling is knowledge. *Ab initio* is anxiety. In that sense it is rational to have a constitution if only because it is a threat to the individual's peace of mind to sense that he is all at sea.

The very awareness that a choice exists, the very perception that a decision must be made and that it might be wrong, is a source of psychic cost such as will frequently exceed any reasonable gain in the utility expected. Given that fear of the unknown is normally a diswelfare in itself, it is the great attraction of a rule that, restricting the choice-set and shortening the search, it enables the individual to economise on economising which he knows to be onerous. Ignorance too is a constitution. Choosing not to choose is protective precommitment that can raise the individual's wellbeing in his own estimation above the level it would have attained if he had been free to shop around. That is an argument in favour of marriage partners selected exclusively by grandparents and a lifetime prohibition of divorce.

People are more strongly repelled by possible losses than they are attracted by equivalent gains. Individuals disproportionately retentive of existing endowments will find solace in learned routines that shelter them from something worse. A doctor shares responsibility by insisting on a second opinion and by using the standard procedure. A solider refuses to trade assignments lest he suffer guilt if a friend is killed. A Keynesian speculates on the normal rate since past experience is the best hedge he has. Even a just-acceptable *status quo* may be tolerated because of fear of disappointment should a big step up sour into a big step down. The doctor fails to cure his patient. The soldier loses his own life. The Keynesian never discovers the best-paying bond. It is easy to complain that minimax is here depriving the cautious and the pusillanimous of a gain that they would ideally have preferred. The point is that these social actors see maximisation under uncertainty in quite a different light. They believe that an adequate berth is the best refuge. They maximise their utility by staying put.

Some heuristics will contribute actively to productive efficiency. Financial markets, for example, make good use of the *as if* calculative that has evolved in a competitive environment where optimisation at speed is the *sine qua non* for survival. Not all institutions, however, can realistically be described as non-deliberative responses that optimise the output on which the nation feeds. Some bounded rationality, some cognitive bias, must inevitably be seen as the sacrifice of flashes of insight to the comfort blanket of the quiet life.

People's level of risk aversion is non-rational and can be excessive. Thus the firm can plunge extensive investment into safety equipment at work and spend heavily on consumer protection. Its purpose is to prevent any degradation in the standard of health. Laudable as that charter must be, the fact remains that resources committed to defence are inevitably resources not spendable on improvement. Popular usage validates the practice. We say that the firm has a *duty* not to harm the public but only an *option* to bring about a betterment. We in that way deprive ourselves of the wellbeing to which research and experimentation might – or might not – have led had we as a community been prepared for a more audacious mix.

Households as well as firms can err on the side of the excessive. They buy more health insurance than, statistically speaking, they will ever need since imagined illness itself fills them with dread. They demand zero user charges and the cradle-to-grave guarantee since to cost-benefit the doctoring of a parent or a child is to feel mean about oneself. Over-insured and under-deterred, they are in a position to ignore the marginal cost of treatment and in that way to impose the deadweight of medical care inflation upon their community. The framing bias complements the risk of loss with the ironies of language. If told that 10 per cent of the patients die as the consequence of an operation, the consumer is less likely to sign the consent form than he would if told that 90 per cent of the patients do well and recover. In order to invest prudently in keeping down the cost of care, doctors should therefore wear black gowns instead of white and refer to the family members exclusively as the 'surviving relatives'.

The fear of loss can frighten out ambition that could have added to the national wealth: in two minds about a rise in income that is accompanied by a possible impairment of health or earning capacity, some people at least will be prepared to content themselves with an unchanging level of consumption. It can lead to an unintegrated bundle of convictions: this is the illogical portfolio of the citizen who calls simultaneously for higher public spending (to protect him from thieves) and a lower tax-take (to free him from the State). It can also be the cause of an ossification of belief that defends an established hypothesis against the fine-tuning of feedback and revision.

The fear of *intellectual* loss can mean that the first belief to acquire equilibrium status will have an insider's head start when called into question by the interloper of surprise. An employer, convinced that racial stereotyping is a good guide to frequency when in truth it is another name for misjudged probabilities and misperceived correlations, will expect bad work from a black and discount evidence which his basepoint cannot accommodate. A shopper, using brand-name recognition and upward-sloping expense as his quality-heuristic, builds a bulwark around the less-efficient, frustrates price competition, and turns down cost-effective generics with physical charac-teristics of equal relevance. A ministry, filtering facts through man-made communication channels and the vested interest of organisational self-respect, makes unfounded assumptions that lead directly to policy disasters like the Bay of Pigs landing in 1961 – in Galbraith's opinion, 'a textbook case of bureaucratic self-deception': 'Organization needed to believe that Fidel Castro was toppling on the edge. Communism was an international conspiracy; hence it could have no popular local roots; hence the Cuban people would welcome the efforts to overthrow it. Intelligence was made to confirm these beliefs. If it didn't it was, by definition, defective information.' (Galbraith, 1969:17). The racist deprives himself of the most productive input. The snob squanders money on unreliable certification. The Cold War ministry screens and scans with an embodied projection that eternalises the threat from Stalin and his bomb. In cases such as these a deeply-flawed rule of thumb might actually produce results inferior to those that would have been the consequence of a present without a past – of an economics that starts from here.

A high dose of history can lead to error reinforcement and not to error self-correction. Especially will this be so where a hypothesis is vague ('Democracy is incompatible with African culture') and predictability intrinsically problematic. The danger here is that people will think that they know more than they do and therefore fail to seek out better data or healthier heuristics. A high dose of history can also lead to material under-performance in a market such as that for labour where reference-level demarcations evolve into *status quo* entitlements and the employee's right to retain his job makes it more difficult for the employer to dismiss and restructure. Money wages become sticky downward because framing resists the loss of endowment. Conservative expectations then have the uneconomic effect of creating involuntary unemployment for reasons which must not be confused with the aggregative alternative of a deficiency in total demand. A high dose of history can lead without question to a shortfall from productive potential.

Even so, the fact that there *can* be a shortfall does not mean that there *will* be a shortfall. Bounded rationality gives oligopolists the stability they need to plan ahead for product development. It also ensures that customers can expect to find unsold stocks when they come in to shop. Cognitive bias produces a generous supply of service in lottery-like occupations such as the bar and the theatre because of what Adam Smith himself saw not as objective life chances but as 'the natural confidence which every man has more or less, not only in his own abilities, but in his own good fortune.' (Smith, 1776:I, 119). It also causes optimists when their business goes bottom-up to rationalise away their failure as the fox did the grapes and thereupon to seek out a new and more productive opportunity. Bounded rationality and cognitive bias, in short, can be a reason for advance even as they can be a cause of slippage and loss.

5. People and things

Berthold Brecht said it in German: 'Man leistet etwas, damit man sich etwas leistet.' Adam Smith said it in English: 'The consumptibility ... of goods, is the great cause of human industry.' (Smith, 1763:199). Adam Smith believed that demand was the *primum mobile*, supply first and foremost the accommodating response: 'Consumption is the sole end and purpose of all production... The interest of the producer ought to be attended to, only so far as it may be necessary for promoting that of the consumer.' (Smith, 1776:II, 179). Alfred Marshall shared his view that the absorption of final utility is the *sine qua non* for the realisation of economic value added: 'Consumption is the end of production.' (Marshall, 1890:56). So did John Maynard Keynes: 'Consumption ... is the sole end and object of all economic activity.' (Keynes, 1936:104). Take but demand away and the process of production would cease since it would no longer have any purpose. No purpose – nor even an identity: 'Without consumption, the object does not complete itself as a product: a house left unoccupied is no house.' (Sahlins, 1976:169). Use value makes the circular flow go round. Exchange value converts a piece of cloth into a business suit.

People demand things. This chapter is concerned with the purchase of final satisfactions and the subjective significance of the choice. Not denying that food is essential for survival and that clothing keeps out the cold, its focus, following the thrust of the previous chapters, is not the isolated but the socialised individual, not consumption without time remembered but shopping situated in a historical skein. Headed People and things, the chapter deals, in accord with Fukuyama, first with Signals and symbols, then with Habits and customs: 'Our present desires are conditioned by our social milieu, which in turn is the product of the entirety of our historical past.' (Fukuyama, 1992:63). An Englishman should take this lesson to heart when next he buys a bowler hat or drinks a cup of tea.

The final section of this chapter is entitled The freedom of choice. The Stoics and the Cynics, Catholic scholastics like Chrysostom and Augustine, Puritan ascetics like Luther and Calvin, all expressed moral doubts about the feeding frenzy in the veil of restraint. Their reservations about a demand-led rise in the wealth of nations were not shared by the libertarian free marketeers who contended that the lawful protection of neighbours and bystanders are the only grounds on which the sovereignty of the consumer in the decentralised exchange economy can legitimately be infringed. The final section reconciles the position of the strict moralists who said that indulgence is Hell with the position of the strict moralists who said that tolerance is Heaven. It does so by means of sociology. It is the thesis of this section that goods and services are social tokens, messages traded in an interpersonal context that has a past as well as a present. Society constrains economy and is itself stamped by events. What we buy is in that sense a free choice that is to some extent an unfree one too.

We reveal preferences. That much we know. What we do not know is *whose* preferences we are revealing – or *why*. It is the thesis of the final section, and of the chapter as a whole, that it would be a step in the right direction to find out.

5.1   SIGNALS AND SYMBOLS

Language is always and everywhere a social fact. External to the individual, not susceptible to significant modification through a simple act of the will, endowed with legitimate authority, able to back coercion with consensus, it is a set of never-rational noises which are selected by their consumers exclusively because of the communication they facilitate within the speech community. The fact that the user is unlikely to have access to any competing code does not negate the strength of the interpersonal pressures: 'Air is no less heavy because we do not detect its weight.' (Durkheim, 1895:5).

English and French are social facts, non-personal constants that ego employs in order to share his vision. Goods and services fall into the same category of meaningful instrumentalities: 'Wants are culture products, to be judged by culture canons and understood and controlled through culture categories. Even our food and clothing, in all their concrete content, and by far the larger part of their money cost, represent social and aesthetic and not biological values.' (Knight, 1935:95). No one would deny that food and clothing (in contrast to the grunts and squiggles of English or French) have an intrinsic capacity to deliver what Leibenstein terms 'functional' utility: 'Functional demand refers to that part of the demand for a commodity resulting from the commodity's inherent qualities.' (Leibenstein, 1950:51). What Knight is saying is that 'by far the larger part' of consumer expenditure falls into the cultural and not the intrinsic category. Economists, he clearly believes, are ill-advised who explain utility in terms of individual hedonism and isolated preferences while leaving 'by far the greater part' to the marketing community which makes its money from cracking the code.

As people spend, so they speak – so they reveal information about who they are and how they would like others to classify them. In English they can make the noise 'I am very, very rich'. In consumption they can purchase a penthouse in Park Lane. In the one case as in the other they are advertising their characteristics and expressing something about themselves. As Douglas and Isherwood write: 'Forget that commodities are good for eating, clothing, and shelter; forget their usefulness and try instead the idea that commodities are good for thinking; treat them as a non-verbal medium for the human creative faculty.' (Douglas and Isherwood, 1979:62).

Goods and services are signifiers and images: 'Consumption, in so far as it is meaningful, is *a systematic act of the manipulation of signs ... In order to become object of consumption, the object must become sign.*' (Baudrillard, 1988:22). The object transmits the coordinates of social values, absolute status and comparative standing. It will be useful to examine each of these three databanks in turn.

5.1.1 Social Values

Douglas and Isherwood regard tastes and preferences as rooted and anchored in the cultural whole: 'Consumption decisions are a vital source of the culture of the time... Consumption is that very sphere in which culture is generated... In the end you should see the consumer's choices as moral judgements about everything: about what a man is, what a woman is, how a man ought to treat his aged parents, how much of a start he ought to give his children, how he expects to grow old.' (Douglas and Isherwood, 1979:292). Consumables are props in a social drama, bats and balls in a social game. Few people make a conscious choice of their drama or game. Once in, however, they are acculturated by learned expectations into the self-defining conformity that Baudrillard makes the essence of 'the imperative fetish of social valorization': 'In the United States 90 per cent of the population experience no other desire than to possess what others possess.' (Baudrillard, 1988:11). In the United States, Baudrillard calculates with a formula that he does not disclose, 90 per cent of the consumers are choosing social relationships flagged up by signs even as they plan their menus or buy a car.

Baudrillard is sceptical about isolated pleasure-seeking in the nineteenth-century sense of the searcher after satisfaction who is his own best judge: 'The liberty and sovereignty of the consumer are nothing more than a mystification.' (Baudrillard, 1988:39). Searching for egoistic predilection and ending up with community consensus instead, Baudrillard reaches the conclusion that the revelation of private preference is in its essence the felt desire for a well-integrated collectivity: 'The freedom to possess ... is a moral one. It is even the ultimate in morality, since the consumer is simultaneously reconciled with himself and with the group. He becomes the perfect social being.' (Baudrillard, 1988:13).

The idea that the shopper is 'the perfect social being', his shopping trolley 'the ultimate in morality', will not have an intuitive appeal to the Oxford Street graduate hacking his way through the summer sales. In a society which assigns pride of place to the standard of living, however, there is undeniably a certain logic in saying that so many of the referents, so much of the interpretation, will be bound up with badges and uniforms purchased rather than with role-playing not paid for in cash. Galbraith in that sense might be underestimating the true need that is satisfied by a marginal trinket. It is acceptance as well as transport that the suburbanite is buying when he goes by car and not by bus. The car to the economist might be a luxury durable with a high income elasticity. Acceptance to the 'perfect social being' is what makes the world go round.

An English breakfast is a breakfast which an Englishman usually eats. Chopsticks are cultural artefacts which the Chinese prefer because they were brought up Chinese. A 'MacDonald's' and a 'Coke' is what we want after school because it is what *we* want after school. Dress is a social regularity to which socialised actors conform: 'A man would be ridiculous who should appear in public with a suit of clothes quite different from those which are commonly worn, though the new dress should in itself be ever so graceful or convenient.' (Smith, 1759:281). Decoration is a self-publicising focus upon which sensitive neighbours converge: 'There seems to be an absurdity ... in ornamenting a house after a quite different manner from that which custom and fashion have prescribed.' (Smith, 1759:284). Society is the done thing. The done thing, 'the ultimate in morality', is what makes the world go round.

Durkheim was absolutely clear in his own mind that consumer goods can have the collective character of the external and the constrained: 'If I do not submit to the conventions of society, if in my dress I do not conform to the customs observed in my country and in my class, the ridicule I provoke, the social isolation in which I am kept, produce ... the same effects as a punishment in the strict sense of the word.' (Durkheim, 1895:2–3). The channelling and the shepherding are the product of conditioned reflexes (ego cannot imagine things to be any different), self-stigmatisation (ego if deviant suffers from a guilty conscience), public opinion (ego is eager to avoid censure and to earn fellowship) and economic sanctions (ego is eager to escape unemployment and to win advancement). The result is the reinforcement and the perpetuation of a tried-and-tested set of group standards and common signifiers: 'We can no more choose the style of our houses than of our clothing – at least, both are equally obligatory ... The type of habitation imposed upon us is merely the way in which our contemporaries and our ancestors have been accustomed to construct their houses.' (Durkheim, 1895:11, 12). Social currents, Durkheim argues, are embodied in observed choices. The individual is the entrepreneur who actually pays money for the good. There is even so no reason to be confident that his revealed utility function can be traced back no further than to his own love of port or attachment to a song.

The rule is a general one, that social facts are social values, however much they correspond to the personal sentiments of the one-off intermediary: 'Such reality is still objective, for I did not create them; I merely inherited them through my education.' (Durkheim, 1895:1). Consumption is a sub-case of the rule, one well illustrated by the Middle Easterner's resistance even to the tastiest of pork, the patriot's commitment even to a jerry-built anthem, the Amerindian Arunta's refusal to defile a totem in which is invested 'a particle of divinity', 'the soul of the group', 'the collective and anonymous force of the clan': 'If he has eaten the flesh of an animal which, though perfectly healthy, is forbidden to him, he will feel himself sick, and may die of it... The soldier who falls while defending his flag does not believe that he sacrifices himself for a bit of cloth.' (Durkheim, 1912:221, 228, 264). The decencies among the Arunta had the force of ceremony and ritual. The form is different when the Englishman chooses a pub evening with his mates and buys a hat rather than a turban that would fit just as well. The form is different. The didactics are less far apart.

Douglas and Isherwood emphasise the extent to which consumer goods are core markers in the cultural matrix. It is their contention that a social construction of reality is needed to decode the messages which are embedded in the non-verbal communication process. A *social* construction of reality – and that means the sociological basis in the sense of Durkheim at least as much as the semiological superstructure in the sense of Saussure: 'Consumption goods are most definitely not mere messages; they constitute the very system itself. Take them out of human intercourse and you have dismantled the whole thing.' (Douglas and Isherwood, 1979:72). Goods supply information about conventions and context. It is the task of the socially-aware economist to read himself in to the clues and the hints.

5.1.2 Absolute Status

Individual choices reflect social patterns. One consequence, turning from the macrocosm to the component, is that they help to pigeon-hole the consumer, to situate on the social map his specific status and functional role.

Consider the school blazer, the club tie, the military uniform. Consider the judge's wig, the monk's robe, the king's crown. In all of these cases it is the status that is selected, not the symbol *per se*. Buying the role, the consumer is condemned to buy the symbol which is its Siamese twin. Even an ugly crown, the king will reason, is better than no kingship. Forced into shoes that are too tight and obliged to dye his hair green, the fashion victim will be as one with the king on the utility that comes from the lifestyle of which the consumable is but the badge.

Consumer goods in such a perspective are also investment goods, inputs into a production function of which the end-product is the self. Goffman has been especially clear on the manner in which 'sign vehicles' such as a car, a hobby, a church, a wedding ring, a crucifix, a favourite dish can all convey signals to assessors which allow an actor to be sorted and filed using the heuristic of resemblance: 'They can rely on what the individual says about himself, or on documentary evidence he provides as to who and what he is.' (Goffman, 1959:13). The symbols have a stability and a persistence which enable the actor to put money into self-definition in the reasonable expectation that memories will be a good guide for hopes: 'Viewed as signs, objects have the peculiar character of *objectivity*, that is, they tend to evoke similar responses from the same person over time and from different people. Relative to other signs such as emotions, or ideas, objects seem to possess a unique concreteness and permanence.' (Csikszentmihalyi and Rochberg-Halton, 1981:14). That being the case, people who want to make the most of their image should take care to make consumption a part of their capital.

Clothes make the man – the reason why a male executive never cross-dresses in a skirt and a female executive often power-dresses in a suit. Vestment is the oldest form of investment. The link between signal and substance will not be lost on the job applicant. Keen to make a good first impression, he will rationally put resources into those costumes which will 'serve as a passport to the consideration of an employer who is filling a position.' (Marshall, 1919:638). Asking his clothing to write him a reference, he cannot, of course, afford the mistake of a spokesman who will let him down. A taxi-driver or welder would work against his own cause if he turned up for interview dressed in Bond Street Armani: the association of ideas being so different from that which is expected, his discordant eccentricities would contribute little to his claim that he is the template that the firm has in mind. A doctor or a lawyer, on the other hand, will have good grounds to flaunt the golf club, the Mercedes and the weekend retreat: a professional without demonstrated successes is unlikely to win the public's trust since, clearly, 'such confidence could not safely be reposed in people of a very mean or low condition.' (Smith, 1776:I, 118). The lesson which Smith draws about 'front' put on display for gain is not in the circumstances an unexpected one: 'A man, we say, should look like his trade and profession.' (Smith, 1759:292).

Goffman, like Smith, is concerned with the image presented in the course of symbolic interaction: 'When an individual projects a definition of the situation and thereby makes an implicit or explicit claim to be a person of a particular kind, he automatically exerts a moral demand upon the others, obliging them to value and treat him in the manner that persons of his kind have a right to expect.' (Goffman, 1959:24). The individual sells an impression of himself on the personality market. Props and costumes increase the likelihood that the product he is marketing will be disposed of with the level of return that he expects.

Goffman uses dramaturgical concepts like props and costumes to model the presentation of self as if it were a theatrical performance. His approximation of revealed biography to stagecraft and show is, admittedly, an analogy that misses out a crucial difference: whereas the dead Hamlet is really a live Shakespearean, the doctor and the lawyer are not pretending but instead living out their lives. If it were true that 'all the world's a stage', then it would have to be true that all the men and women are tricksters and con-artists as well. Reality is more mixed.

Thus some social actors employ consumables which tell no more than the truth about their social location. The duke dresses in tweed and buys in a grouse-beater for his hunt. The clergyman wears a cassock and rejects as 'unseemly' the *Quick-Rich Chronicle*. Other social actors, of course, are less scrupulous about their selection of insignia. A buys a small diamond to conceal her true status as a bus-conductor. B wears the livery of a butler to steal the family's paintings. C warns her 'audience' against tobacco and bad language while herself, 'backstage' in the teachers' room, smoking and swearing with the 'cast'. D puts money into hair-dye because a ballet dancer is not expected to go grey. E, 'a near-sighted plumber, to protect the impression of rough strength that is *de rigeur* in his profession, feels it necessary to sweep his spectacles into his pocket when the housewife's approach changes his work into a performance.' (Goffman, 1959:63). The equestrian manipulates nothing when he buys a horse and the snake-catcher makes no false claims when he carries a bag. The same cannot be said of the bus-conductor who passes herself off in Versace and the near-sighted plumber who demands that his clients call him Butch.

The king who consumes a throne is telling no more than the truth about himself. The faithful wife who reveals and provokes is sending out mixed messages and causing noise on the line. People are the problem; and not all advertised associations really live up to the high standards of the heuristic. Things at least are less likely to let the observer down. Consumer goods are cues and hints. They are *status* symbols in the most literal sense – since they are symbols of status which pinpoint the location of the self.

5.1.3 Comparative Standing

The status symbol *per se* is no more than the signifier of a real or a pretended role. The term is nonetheless employed with the supplementary connotation of a *success* symbol; and here it explicitly conveys information of a relative and not just of an absolute nature.

The teleology of economics is often derived from the physical deprivations of hunger and cold. The civilising mission of the economist is called into question by the never-ending pursuit of social scarcities which are desired not so much for themselves as for their capacity to confirm the 'relative ability to pay': 'So far as regards those members and classes of the community who are chiefly concerned in the accumulation of wealth, the incentive of subsistence or of physical comfort never plays a considerable part... The dominant incentive was from the outset the invidious distinction attaching to wealth.' (Veblen, 1899:36). Once a minimum threshold of bodily wellbeing has been reached, Thorstein Veblen hypothesised, the consumer thereafter values commodities preponderantly in terms of the contribution to self-esteem and competitive hallmarking that will be made by pecuniary prowess put conspicuously on display: 'With the exception of the instinct of self-preservation, the propensity for emulation is probably the strongest and most alert and persistent of the economic motives proper.' (Veblen, 1899:85). The Joneses try to own more than we do. We try to spend more than the Joneses can. To speak of 'keeping up' in the economics of beggar-my-neighbour ostentation is to understate the divisiveness of the zero-sum rivalry. The truth is more confrontational and more win-or-lose. Conspicuous consumption is red in tooth and claw.

Keynes divides human needs into two categories – 'those needs which are absolute in the sense that we feel them whatever the situation of our fellow human beings may be, and those which are relative in the sense that we feel them only if their satisfaction lifts us above, makes us feel superior to, our fellows.' (Keynes, 1930:326). Veblen, writing as he does about affluent consumers, no longer hungry or cold, tends to direct his attention to the latter and not the former set of imperatives. It is in that way that he is able to account for the expenditure of money on things that are in themselves 'ugly', 'grotesque', 'intolerable', 'unsightly', 'odious': 'Wasted effort' and 'misspent ingenuity' though they undoubtedly are, they more than compensate for their failure to constitute 'a pleasing composition of form, lines and color' through their capacity to deliver 'a gratification of our sense of costliness masquerading under the name of beauty.' (Veblen, 1899:95, 110). Gold jewellery is valued for its relative expense more than for its craftsmanship. A dog is preferred to a cat, a fat wife to a slim one, as the better proof of differential eating. An idle footman, active in conspicuous leisure, is a demonstration that his master can afford the waste. A racehorse (unlike a cart-horse) is at once unproductive, expensive and an emotional release: 'The utility of the fast horse lies largely in his efficiency as a means of emulation; it gratifies the owner's sense of aggression and dominance to have his own horse outstrip his neighbor's.' (Veblen, 1899:104). In instances such as these it is not Leibenstein's 'functional' utility that determines the choice. The designer labels and the Old Master originals are symbols and signs. Economists familiar only with the cloth embodied and the paint expended will not be in a position to pick up the clues.

Among the new rich of Newport cigars were lit with hundred-dollar bills to prove that the status-seeker had gone beyond the tradesman economics of penny-minding husbandry. Among the Kwakiutl Indians of the American North-West the status-seeker made his rivals into his witnesses at an expensive *potlatch* while neighbours felt shamed who could not match the costliness of the feast. What was value-creating in both of these instances was clearly the expressive dimension and not *per se* the Havanas and the balls. Among the self-made and among the Kwakiutl, it was the display of wealth as the proof of success that set the alarm-clock for 5 and drove the reputation-seeker to labour in the service of the cultural peg: 'In order to gain and to hold the esteem of men it is not sufficient merely to possess wealth or power. The wealth or power must be put in evidence, for esteem is awarded only on evidence.' (Veblen, 1899:42).

People demand certificates when what they really crave is approbation. To the extent that things are demanded not because of what they *are* but because of what they *represent*, an economical option would evidently be to dispense altogether with the manufactured 'please-like-mes' and to deal directly in the sympathy and fellow-feeling for which the symbols of success will often be no more than an offer to trade. Morris's *Nowhere* is a post-economic utopia in which Jack talks to Jill without the deadweight of Patek Philippe having simultaneously to talk to Mouton Cadet. Morris starts from Woodstock. We, however, start from *here*. Things are an appeal for love. In an acquisitive society, belonging is gatekeepered by economic achievement put conspicuously on display.

Adam Smith was in no doubt that the ambitious upward mobility that powers the *perpetuum mobile* of economic growth was to be derived 'chiefly' from the recognition accorded to the successful for whom the shadows were too lonely to be accepted as a home: 'It is chiefly from this regard to the sentiments of mankind, that we pursue riches and avoid poverty... The rich man glories in his riches, because he feels that they naturally draw upon him the attention of the world... The poor man, on the contrary, is ashamed of his poverty.' (Smith, 1759:70, 71). In respect of consumer goods above the threshold of bodily needs, Smith writes, 'it is the vanity, not the ease, or the pleasure, which interests us' (Smith, 1759:71): 'With the greater part of rich people, the chief enjoyment of riches consists in the parade of riches.' (Smith, 1776:I, 192).

Smith's economic sociology of symbolic differentiation makes much of the demand for relative advancement: 'Place, that great object which divides the wives of aldermen, is the end of half the labours of human life; and is the cause of all the tumult and bustle, all the rapine and injustice, which avarice and ambition have introduced into this world.' (Smith, 1759:80). People want place – and they want to prove that they have place by means of its habitual attributes. To consume in the status it is, however, necessary first to earn in the status. Even the most generous bank manager, the most liberal credit card, will not enable a hospital auxiliary to live forever surrounded by the success symbols of a famous surgeon.

To look the part it is necessary first to obtain the part. It is in terms of a hierarchy of cultural symbols hanging upon the stratification of economic success that Smith is able to explain the socio-biological 'desire of bettering our condition' – 'a desire which, though generally calm and dispassionate, comes with us from the womb, and never leaves us till we go into the grave': 'An augmentation of fortune is the means by which the greater part of men propose and wish to better their condition.' (Smith, 1776:I, 362–3). People desire place. The wealth of the nation is an unintended outcome of their self-regarding wish to jump the queue.

The wealth of nations is an unintended outcome. So is an unexpected pool of unhappiness and frustration. Success symbols are the prizes awarded to the winners. Unsuccess symbols are what is left for the also-rans who tried and failed. Seen in terms of social values and absolute status, Marks and Spencer and Majorca have the power to increase the individual's felt satisfaction. Comparative status complicates the prediction – since the very fact that Marks is not Harrod's and Majorca not Mustique inevitably debases the perceived value even of an intrinsically satisfying asset. The subject of this section is Signals and symbols. Tokens of dishonour in the form of second-class tickets are a sobering reminder that not all of wealth will be wellbeing where a fallacy of composition eats away at the utility of things condemned by economic sociology to be consumed by people who keep their eyes and ears open.

Fred Hirsch is especially sensitive to the win–lose mindset and the zero-sum society. Hirsch warns that 'what each of us can achieve, all cannot' in the over-crowded area of invidious positionality: the consequence can only be that 'the race gets longer for the same prize' since, by definition, 'if everyone stands on tiptoe, no one sees better.' (Hirsch, 1977:5, 67). The status insecurities of the rat race society, Hirsch observes, mean an economic waste of scarce resources squandered on never-ending check-mating. They also mean social division and even social unrest. It contributes nothing to social solidarity for top people to out-consume other people where out-ranked people will feel conspicuously deprived as a result.

Robert Frank has continued the theme of value derived from relativity, inter-dependence, frame of reference and limited access. Like Hirsch, he is anxious about arms race escalation in the defensive consumption of winner-take-all investments such as anabolic steroids bought by competing athletes or expensive clothing purchased by rival job-seekers: 'To land a job, for example, an applicant is well advised to "look good". But what, exactly, does that mean?... To look good means simply to look better than most other applicants. One way to do so is to spend more than others on clothing. Since the same incentives clearly apply to all applicants, however, an escalating standoff inevitably ensues.' (Frank and Cook, 1995:14). Like Hirsch, he is concerned lest there be a minus-sum de-selection of activities and consumables which would yield a higher sum total of contentment in society than would a foreign education acquired soley for 'been-to' prestige or cosmetic surgery (a medical risk at the best of times) intended purely to improve the odds in the marriage-stakes. Illustrations would include cleaner air, purer drinking water, more medical research, 'freedom from traffic congestion, time with family and friends, vacation time, and a variety of favorable job characteristics. In each of the examples discussed, the evidence suggests that subjective well-being will be higher in the society with a greater balance of inconspicuous consumption.' (Frank, 1999:90).

The evidence suggests it. The invisible hand does not bring it about. All cannot jump one and the same queue. *One*, however, *can*. It is a prospect which drives a wedge between the interest of the individual and the interest of the group: 'My claim ... is that the conflict between individual and group is the single most important explanation of the imbalance in our current consumption patterns.' (Frank, 1999:158). The world would be a much simpler place if goods and services were not also signs and symbols. The fact is, however, that we start from *here* – where *here* is Leibenstein's 'bandwagon effect' that makes us seek acceptance through conformity, Leibenstein's 'snob effect' that makes us seek distinction through standing out and, of course, Ackerman's inference that even the economist's non-satiety might only be another name for the Durkheimean's collective representations: 'Far from human nature being inherently insatiable, it is possible that competition, emulation, and socially learned behavior in general may be the primary sources of apparently insatiable desires.' (Ackerman, 1997:663). People and things in that perspective are not so much active subjects, passive objects, as the legitimated joint products of the social life that they share.

5.2 HABITS AND CUSTOMS

Consumption is disciplined by social pressures, squeezed into habitual associations, made emulative through invidious comparison. These three dimensions of goods and services as signifiers and images were discussed in the previous section. They are validated by Douglas and Isherwood in the following statement on shopping choices as cultural markers: 'Man is a social being. We can never explain demand by looking only at the physical properties of goods. Man needs goods for communicating with others and for making sense of what is going on around him.' (Douglas and Isherwood, 1979:95).

The consumer participates in the economic market not as a *tabula rasa* but as a socialised agency. The group signs, the group symbols are a part of the psyche and an element in the self. Yet it is in the nature of human webs to have an inter-temporal stability that transcends the spot, the current, the here-and-now. The consumer is in that sense a social actor not just in a novel present but in an embodied past which is too comfortable with us to pack up and move away.

This section is concerned with the past. Made one by the perception that we start from *here* but that *here* starts from *there*, it is divided into three parts: The social memory, The ratchet effect, and The economics of addiction.

5.2.1   The Social Memory

Just as the economy is embedded in the society, so the present is rooted in the past. 'Most human behavior, and especially complex human behavior, is learned behavior. The motives, attitudes, and frames of reference, and also the principles of perceptual organization which influence the behavior of human adults, are dependent on past experiences.' (Katona, 1951:43). The remembered past situates the unfamiliar stimulus. This is not to deny the possibility of rational choice and marginal utility on the one hand, impulse buying and the momentary whim on the other, only to assert that, in between the two polar freedoms of calculation and emotion, there is the unfreedom of selective recall and the conditioned response.

Thus the consumer will often, saving time and effort, decide not to compare prices and quantities, to experiment with different shopping days, to try out new recipes necessitating new shopping lists. Conservative as a consumer because all change involves a risk and because any new departure can be a blind alley, the individual might find it both economical and reassuring to repeat the habitual patterns and the customary routines on the basis that familiar associations have not yet been known to disappoint. The disadvantage is the opportunity foregone because it is excluded from the scan, the untried brand left undiscovered because past-pass-through has been made the hedge against surprise. The advantage is the peace of mind. Where it is inertia that makes the choice, at least the self-image has some protection against loss of face by virtue of a heuristic not expected to make too many mistakes.

The longer the track record, the stronger the imperative: 'In general, the longer the habituation, the more unbroken the habit and the more nearly it coincides with previous habitual forms of the life process, the more persistently will the given habit assert itself.' (Veblen, 1899:83). As with a habit such as the time of the 'elevenses' at work, so with a habit such as the composition of the family budget: 'A standard of living is of the nature of habit.' (Veblen, 1899:82). The habits of today are the habits of tomorrow. Returning after an absence of 20 years, the economist finds that Jill still shampoos her hair on Tuesday and that Jack still snacks on cream crackers with jam because that's what his family did.

The prediction of a past-coloured future is of considerable relevance to the microeconomics of consumer choice. Consider the menu for 'Christmas dinner' or 'Sunday lunch', the convention in England that the sweet course follows the meal, the acceptance in Hungary that a cold sugary soup may be eaten first, the customary shape of a wedding cake, the use of a credit card (and therewith of consumer debt) to pay for a purchase, the fact that, 'at the time of his marriage, a young man ... buys life insurance, usually not because of a rational weighing of risks or a desire to save, but because it is the thing to do, ... the same way as others act.' (Katona, 1951:110). In cases such as these it is time remembered that defines the done thing, the present that gives in to pressures and passes on the inheritance.

George Katona writes as follows about the economic non-rationalities that can be the consequence of precedence and routine: 'It is possible that no genuine decisions are ever made with respect to certain regular expenditures. The patterns may be set by our parents or friends and be taken over by us without deliberation. Or certain spending and saving patterns may be customary in our culture and our habitual behavior may be group-determined.' (Katona, 1951:68). The prediction will be of little comfort to manipulative advertisers. Hungry for a consumerhood that is vulnerable, malleable and confused, what they will find instead is the entrenched resistance of unambitious shoppers, set in their ways. Free market economists will express concerns of their own about the potential threat to allocative efficiency. Noting that the standard response can artificially segment the menu, they will object that the consequent rigidities can make even near-perfect competition into a sequence of niche monopolies. If it's summertime it must be Benidorm. If it's hiring time it must be a white suburban. If it's dinner-time it must be steak and chips. Consumers take refuge in their ruts. Even aggressive competition might not be enough to draw them out again.

Habit is not the whole of economics. Least of all will it be so in restless capitalism, where entrepreneurial profits are not to be made through passive replication. Supply-side innovation re-channels lifestyles through new products such as the car, the television and the computer. Fads and fashions appeal to banding and conformity but they do so in order to market novelty. Conspicuous consumption, estimating success through acquisition, ensures that more will constantly be sought for show lest the individual appear a failure to his peers. The prediction of a past-coloured future is clearly not the whole of microeconomic choice. The crucial point is that it is a part. Even the breach has a baseline. Habit impacts on choice. *Here* starts from *there*.

Consuming is interpersonal communication even as it is private utility: 'All consumption activity is a ritual presentation and sharing of goods classified as appropriate to particular social categories which themselves get defined and graded in the process.' (Douglas and Isherwood, 1979:26). The ritual is social: other people holding a stake, you and I are not fully free to consume as we choose. The ritual is historical: the past shapes it, the present modifies it, the future inherits it – and you and I simply come and go. Interpersonal and inter-temporal both, the consumption ritual is *social* memory and not just private habit.

Invisible internalisation, making traditional associations our own, is, in Pierre Bourdieu's words, 'an enchanted experience of culture which implies forgetting the acquisition. The "eye" is the product of history reproduced by education.' (Bourdieu, 1984:3). The 'eye', it would appear, sees what it has been trained to see in a society which 'has a biography that it wishes to protect. Consumption then becomes a function of 'educational capital', a series of responses which perpetuate the competence that has been accumulated over time.

As with perception, so with situation: 'Individuals do not move about in social space in a random way.' (Bourdieu, 1984:110). Never asking to be born into the English middle classes and not into the French aristocracy, the passive victims of past trajectories which nurtured and socialised them where they fell, they were exposed at an early and impressionable age to 'the tastes and distastes, sympathies and aversions, fantasies and phobias which, more than declared opinions, forge the unconscious unity of a class.' (Bourdieu, 1984:77). Manners, bearing and pronunciation are all class-correlated trademarks of location on the scale. So are the objects of consumption: 'A group's whole life-style can be read off from the style it adopts in furnishing or clothing.' (Bourdieu, 1984:77). The group is the irreducible message-sender. The individual in the pattern will only pass on the sign.

Society and history come together in ideas and once again in structures. What should not be forgotten is that things themselves can be an important bridge between the interpersonal and the inter-temporal: 'Every material inheritance is, strictly speaking, also a cultural inheritance. Family heirlooms not only bear material witness to the age and continuity of the lineage and so consecrate its social identity, which is inseparable from permanence over time; they also contribute in a practical way to its spiritual reproduction, that is, to transmitting the values, virtues and competences which are the basis of legitimate membership in bourgeois dynasties.' (Bourdieu, 1984:76-7). Grandfather's investments ensure the good fortune of the descendants he never met. Grandfather's piano and books and pictures, on the other hand, make the home into a museum that reminds the successive generations of the team members who have gone before. In that sense it would be true to say that consumables themselves form part of the durable stock that makes up the social memory.

5.2.2 The Ratchet Effect

Competitive ostentation is a time-dominated phenomenon. Looking backward, the consumer must identify yesterday's excellence in order to quantify the pecuniary strength that he must today in public exceed. Looking forward, the consumer must recognise that today's luxury can become tomorrow's necessity once the success-symbol has been generalised by imitation from discretion into prescription. The ratchet effect demonstrates how costly it is to stay in the same place.

Journeyman printers, Veblen found, were inclined perpetually to increase their outlay on rounds of drinks. They had to do so since, a highly mobile grade of labour, they were continually being thrown in with new colleagues who wanted to know what value the market put on an unfamiliar face. The printers could not spend less on drinks – yesterday's gift had already become ossified into today's expectation. The printers had to spend more – the alternative being a public declaration that the self that started out with such high hopes had ended up too mediocre to push upward the base level of drunkenness: 'The next step is to make this standard of decency the point of departure for a new move in advance in the same direction – for there is no merit in simple spiritless conformity to a standard of dissipation that is lived up to as a matter of course by everyone in the trade.' (Veblen, 1899:74).

The reference dissipation is the dissipation of the past. It constitutes the rock-solid minimum below which the dissipation of the present cannot be allowed to fall. Even so, drunkenness being decency, it can never be more than a short-run resting place in the ascent to even greater heights. The present-day printer is condemned by his occupational and geographical mobility to become perpetually more dissipated. Without that investment in escalating drunkenness he would stand little chance of winning, for however brief a spell, the reputation of being the market leader among printers in the competition through expensive dissipation to put economic success conspicuously on display.

The recognition that the future includes the past generates significant predictions in the macroeconomic areas of savings and consumption. The Keynesian 'fundamental psychological law' is often taken to be a timeless expectation that, current income determining current consumption, spending rises when earning rises and falls when earning falls. Keynes himself undoubtedly made use of such a simplification. What is important is that he also recognised that it missed out the conservative dimension that a realistic economics could not afford to neglect: 'A man's habitual standard of life usually has the first claim on his income, and he is apt to save the difference... A rising income will often be accompanied by increased saving, and a falling income by decreased saving.' (Keynes, 1936:97). At least in the short-run, Keynes wrote, a man is the creature of habit whose future includes his past.

James Duesenberry, convinced that both sociology and psychology were of high relevance to economics, was impressed both by the ratchet in the sense of Veblen and by habit in the sense of Keynes. The result was the *relative* income hypothesis, where previous peaks have a causal impact on current expenditures: 'Consumption is dependent on current income relative to past income as well as on the absolute level of current income.' (Duesenberry, 1949:86). Today is tomorrow's past: 'Attitudes toward future consumption depend on current consumption standards.' (Duesenberry, 1949:34). Today is tomorrow's rock-solid minimum.

Consumption rises when income rises: Duesenberry's Americans have no attachment to a tribal standard of tradition which they find difficult to leave behind. Consumption, however, does not fall when income falls: the fear of standing lost has in Duesenberry's vision so strong a hold on the mobility-seeker's imagination that he would rather go into debt than confess to his failure. Yesterday's peak, it would appear, exerts a powerfully conservative force which protects living standards from short-run adversity. Good times remembered are in that sense a built-in macroeconomic stabiliser precisely because they serve as a ratchet to prevent consumption levels from slipping back in the cyclical downturn: 'It is notoriously just as difficult to recede from a "high" standard of living as it is to lower a standard which is already relatively low'. (Veblen, 1899:81) The Keynesian State might run a budget deficit in order to prevent a passing slump from gravitating into a demand-deficient depression. So, analogously, might a Duesenberry-type consumer spend himself not into the paradox of thrift but into crippling dissaving that neighbours and colleagues cannot see in order to avoid the trauma of selling the house or taking the children out of boarding-school.

In the long run the unthinkable will have to be thought should what seemed at first to be a downswing turn out to be a trend. The problem is the short run, when habits remain Virginia Water but incomes are pushed down into Coronation Street. Veblen writes as follows about the tyranny of the life we know: 'The failure to consume in due quantity and quality becomes a mark of inferiority and demerit.' (Veblen, 1899:64). Duesenberry has this to say about the purchase of self-esteem: 'Income is one of the principal status criteria. Prestige goes to successful people and success in our society is closely correlated with income.' (Duesenberry, 1949: 30). In the long run a fall from grace will force a downward revision. In the short run, however, the constancy is real, the irreversibility a fact – and the habit encoded into the previous peak a significant brake on the response to decline.

Duesenberry's relative income hypothesis explains current preferences in terms of past choices. The fact that the expectation is an asymmetrical one – consumption rises when income rises but saving buffer-stocks the fluctuation when income falls – is a confirmation that the theory predicts something other than *status quo* inertia and a frightened reluctance to move on from the familiar. Duesenberry's consumer is quick to buy a more expensive car when he is given a promotion. Simply, he is slow to trade down to a cheaper model when his wages are cut.

Duesenberry's asymmetry is consistent with the endowment effect, discussed in Chapter 4, which Kahneman and Tversky treat as a guest who does not go: 'A salient characteristic of attitudes to change in welfare is that losses loom larger than gains. The aggravation that one experiences in losing a sum of money appears to be greater than the pleasure associated with gaining the same amount.' (Kahneman and Tversky, 1979: 229). The discovery that people charge more to surrender a possession than they would give to acquire it is an intransitivity which, fully consistent with Bernoulli and Marshall on the diminishing marginal utility of income, is also in line with Duesenberry on the belt-tightening that never was.

The *status quo* is the basis for evaluation: 'The marginal utility of consumption at different points in time depends not on absolute levels of consumption, but on consumption relative to some standard or point of reference.' (Loewenstein and Prelec, 1992:595). A recessionary downturn is for that reason perceived as a threat to endowment: 'Consumers are likely to frame drops in disposable income, or negative departures from expected gains, as losses.' (Loewenstein and Prelec, 1992:593). Framing and reference points make a present peak appear an asset to be protected and conserved. Thus does the psychometric evidence collected by Loewenstein and Prelec support the Veblenite conjecture of James Duesenberry, that a rise in consumption is more immediate, a fall in consumption a shock to the spirit that it makes good sense to delay.

Yet it is sociology rather than psychology that in the last analysis forms the core of Duesenberry's own explanation of the ratchet effect. Consumption, Duesenberry writes, is other people: 'A real understanding of the problem of consumer behavior must begin with a full recognition of the social character of consumption patterns.' (Duesenberry, 1949:19). Physical needs adequately met, Duesenberry continues, consumption is other people most of all: 'It seems quite possible that after some minimum income is reached, the frequency and strength of impulses to increase expenditures for one individual depend entirely on the ratio of his expenditures to the expenditures of those with whom he associates.' (Duesenberry, 1949:32). Duesenberry says 'entirely' because he does not see intrinsic utility as much more than a footnote marginality. People want things. Even more do they want 'the activities which make up the life of our culture.' (Duesenberry, 1949:20). Central to those rituals in a society which makes business its business is the display of consumer goods.

Acquisition to Duesenberry is all but a synonym for the defence of the self when subjected to the assault of a friend with a new house or car: 'The response is likely to be a feeling of dissatisfaction with one's own house or car. If this feeling is produced often enough it will lead to action which eliminates it, that is, to an increase in expenditure.' (Duesenberry, 1949:27). The same line of reasoning lies behind the anxious conservatism of the ratchet effect. People know what they are consuming and what the members of their peer group are consuming. Not wanting to feel inferior, they therefore keep their consumption constant even when their ability to pay for it is put seriously at risk.

The Duesenberry hypothesis makes current consumption relative in the dual sense that it is relative to previous peak consumption and relative to relevant other people. Indifferent to the leads although sensitive to the lags, what it does not do is to make current consumption relative to that imagined future consumption that dwells and drives within the mind. Milton Friedman adds the missing time period. It is his contention that averaged, multi-period ('permanent') consumption is a stable, predictable function not of measured (current) earnings but of expected, long-run ('permanent') income.

A trainee dentist who expects one day to be a highly-paid professional will not in such a long-horizoned world compel his bride-to-be to set up house with him in the shabby room behind a pub that is all that his wages can buy. Instead he will live above his means when he is young, postponing repayment and accumulation until later in his earnings-cycle when he expects *ex ante* that he will have matured into affluence. Over the years he will absorb the transitory variations in his purchasing potential through loans and mortgages at first, savings accounts and privatisation shares later on. The house in Weybridge and the membership in the golf club will, however, be relatively absolute absolutes, smoothed out over time: 'The transitory components of a consumer unit's income have no effect on his consumption except as they are translated into effects lasting beyond his horizon. His consumption is determined by longer-range income considerations plus transitory factors affecting consumption directly.' (Friedman, 1957:221). His consumption is planned long term if also shocked in-period by surprise. His consumption is not immediately governed by what he is earning today.

Friedman's expectational economics is less explicitly linked than is the ratchet effect of Duesenberry to the habits and customs that are the subject of this section. What is implied is, however, somewhat more historical than that which is stated. Expectations are not free-standing, intrinsically personal and resolutely unanchored. An entry-level accountant predicting his probable earnings cycle will rely on the cross-section of the practising cohorts because his own private time-series is yet to come. A newly-qualified dentist thinking out his permanent lifestyle will extrapolate from an older colleague who runs a Jaguar and another who owns a time-share. In the one case as in the other, the economics is in the future but it is in the record as well. This is not to say that the *ex post* is not littered with the unforeseeable, only that people formulate their expectations on the basis of the past that they know.

5.2.3   The Economics of Addiction

Addiction exists where an increase in the current consumption of a good leads to an increase in the same individual's future consumption of the good: 'A good is addictive if and only if consumption of the good at different moments in time are complements.' (Becker and Murphy, 1988:65). Alcohol, tobacco and drugs are illustrations of addictive substances: past consumption raises the average utility of present consumption and shifts the demand curve outward to the right. So are regular church attendance, ingrained work routines, the median choice of clothing in the sense of Veblen, the irreversible living standard in the sense of Duesenberry, even the moral sentiments without non-ego sanctions in the sense of the Golden Rule: 'If individuals are habitual, and if they were cooperative in the past, they might continue to be cooperative even if they could gain an advantage from uncooperative behavior.' (Becker, 1996:17). So is a one-off trauma that, forcing through the set-up costs without the cushion of calm deliberation, deprives the traveller of the option to go back: 'He accumulates sufficient capital while under stress to remain hooked afterward.' (Becker and Murphy, 1988:67). So is the love of good music in the sense of Alfred Marshall.

Alfred Marshall writes as follows about the addictive properties of learning by listening: 'The more good music a man hears, the stronger is his taste for it likely to become.' (Marshall, 1890:79). Marshall's point is that the tendency to diminishing marginal utility can be reversed by an 'alteration in the character or tastes of the man himself' precisely because time itself makes the horizontal axis its home: 'In such cases our observations range over some period of time; and the man is not the same at the beginning as at the end of it.' (Marshall, 1890:79). The man himself has become hooked. The man himself has become addicted. The present *is* because of the past that *was*.

Neoclassical economists tend to study individual maximisation in a present that remembers no past. Gary Becker is an exception but a neoclassicist nonetheless. He is an exception because, a pioneer in the area of human capital, he extends the theory of utility to bring in both the 'social capital' of other people – 'the influence of past actions by peers and others in an individual's social network and control system' – and the 'personal capital' of time remembered – 'the relevant past consumption and other personal experiences that affect current and future utilities.' (Becker, 1996:4). He is a neoclassicist, however, because he consistently maintains that even interaction and habit, interdependent preferences and time-dominated influences, can be situated within the microeconomist's standard analytic of marginal cost and marginal benefit: 'Widespread and/or persistent human behavior can be explained by a generalized calculus of utility-maximizing behavior… The economist continues to search for differences in prices or incomes to explain any differences or changes in behavior.' (Stigler and Becker, 1977:25). Even the economics of addiction is the expectation of rational choice.

Thus social contacts influence the demand for complements: a teenager joining a gang buys the rewards of acceptance, approbation and recognition through his use of the 'F-word' and his decision to smoke. A moral code can be tempted into obsolescence by authoritative intervention to cut the price of crime: the Medieval Church sold indulgences for sin and public officials with patronage are given full pardons for larceny. Present-orientated individuals will slip more easily into unhealthful choice-sets since, living for today, they apply a high rate of discount to substantially delayed disutilities. Future-orientated individuals will invest to advantage in consumption capital through their commitment to a daily swim and the education of their children in the marketable assets of punctuality and probity. Pleasing others or pleasing one's conscience, what is clear from all of this is that a choice can unquestionably satisfy the neoclassicist's test of consistency and transitivity even where the utility is inter-temporal and the effects are cumulative.

Empirical evidence supports Becker's hypothesis that dependence can have an elasticity of demand. Becker, Grossman and Murphy found that a 10 per cent rise in the price of cigarettes led to a 3 per cent decrease in consumption where the rise was believed to be transitory – but to a 4 per cent decrease after a period of one year, to a 7.5 per cent decrease several years after that, where it was perceived to be a permanent change. (Becker, Grossman and Murphy, 1994:86). Expectations as well as current values clearly enter into the calculation. The result is a general one: whereas myopic addicts do react exclusively to price changes in the recent past, fully-rational addicts are seen to alter present outlays in line with anticipated rises and falls. That multi-period alertness affords some protection against the monopolist drug dealer who, aware of price inelasticity, fixes his charge for new clients low enough for long enough for them to become 'locked in'. By then they might have come to care less about the consequences. It is in the nature of a consumable such as drugs or alcohol that far-sightedness itself can be impaired by the choice. Even so, Becker is quick to make whims and mood swings the exception, rational response to prices and incomes the rule.

Ultimate ends are often said to be inexplicable exogeneities, impenetrable mysteries condemned forever to the *de gustibus non est disputandum*. Acknowledging that he cannot say why Jack's favourite season is autumn or why Jill likes roast duck, Becker nonetheless proposes a compromise that leaves open the door to theory. Some things are underlying constants: consider the propensity to fall in love and want to marry. Some things are contingent and variable: the specific partner that one marries depends on network capital such as neighbourhood or school, the specific age on the cultural capital that legitimises the exploitation of opportunity. Food, health and shelter are metapreferences. Beefsteaks, aspirins and yurts are social facts. Becker's compromise demonstrates that basic needs interface with demand-side skills (with consumption capital analogous to the supply side's on-the-job training) to make us the people that we are. Economic reasoning, here as elsewhere, is the key.

Thus an investment-through-listening in music appreciation may be said to reduce the 'price' of good music as listeners will become more adept at absorbing the utility. The commodity being cheaper, it will also be rational for experienced listeners, musically better educated, to invest still more in music capital. What is shown by this example of a downward-sloping demand curve is that it is possible to model even stable preferences through 'the extension of the capital concept to investment in the capacity to consume more efficiently.' (Stigler and Becker, 1977:34).

Tastes do not change capriciously but neither are they invariant: 'Preferences both influence economic outcomes and are in turn influenced by the economy.' (Becker, 1996:18). The economist's invocation of economics is a clear reminder of the continuity between the economic determinism of Smith and Marx and the structural logic that underlies Becker's interpretation of how market capitalism breeds and forms the consumption and character that make market capitalism an economic success.

Economic growth presupposes not just technology and law but also functional proclivities such as deferred gratification. Economic growth, importantly, plays an active part in the production of the choices that are required for sustained expansion: 'The endogeneity of preferences implies that growth and preferences are related also because economic outcomes help form tastes. In particular, workers in economically advanced countries tend to come to work on time and value promptness not only because time is more valuable in richer countries but also because people develop a habit for promptness after living in a society that puts a premium on being prompt.' (Becker, 1996:19). An airline pilot will be led by economic self-interest to avoid an addiction to drunkenness. A small shopkeeper will be encouraged by competition to be assiduous and self-reliant. The State can come between the market and the mindset that is functional: welfare transfers can weaken independence and old-age pensions can be a threat to inter-generational thrift. The market itself is less likely to prove a bent reed.

If tastes are endogenous, then changes in wellbeing are difficult to document. If advertising alters preferences, what is the true measure of the utility differential? If people are unhappy with their addictions but cannot afford to return to an earlier *status quo*, in what sense are they sovereign and in what sense are they trapped? Does the endowment effect not discourage arbitrage by making the consumer a less than impartial judge of the time-hallowed bird in the hand that, objectively speaking, has no feathers and cannot sing? Welfare comparisons are a tough university. It is no surprise that so many who have visited it have failed to obtain their license.

Economic growth is the story of *different* people consuming *different* things at *different* times. It is undeniably a description of change. Whether economic growth is a betterment or an improvement as well must be a good deal less clear. Talcott Parsons summarises in the following words the conundrum of an evolutionary process in which the subject matter refuses to remain inert: 'The satisfaction of known wants supplies the only possible norm in terms of which the desirability or efficiency of an economic process can be judged. Once ends themselves come to vary as a function of the process of their attainment, the standard no longer exists; the argument becomes circular.' (Parsons, 1931:132–3). Addiction to new tastes, the depreciation of old ones – the evaluation lacks an objective basis.

Becker is aware of the problem but sees no reason to write off the sequence: 'Initial preferences should have no priority over final preferences in welfare analysis when policies change preferences.' (Becker, 1996:20). New habits replace old ones. Yet there is no reason to think that the old state is somehow more 'authentic' than is the new one; or that the initial addiction to crime was somehow 'better' than is the final addiction to God. Addiction is about habits and customs. Keeping an open mind about welfare, the social scientist should not lose sight of the habits and customs that make even consumption a topic in time-lagged choice.

5.3 THE FREEDOM OF CHOICE

The sellers know who we are. Double-glazing is targeted at homeowners with discretionary income. Baby food is aimed at young adults with current or planned-for babies. Advertisements for the Latin Bible appear in *The Tablet* and not in *The Canadian Sikh*. Leaflets for intensely metallic musical evenings are handed to youth culture and not to the over-75s. Stereotyping pays. The marketeers too are budget-constrained.

It would be a mistake to infer from the classification and grouping that puts teeth into the sales effort that the freedom of choice is in reality the unfreedom of the conditioned reflex. Homeowners refuse double-glazing outright. Bible buyers buy Bible B in preference to Bible C which others find the better buy. Both in selecting the product and in rejecting the brand, the individual has an autonomy which is greater than that envisaged by Galbraith when, reversing demand-led supply into producer sovereignty, he states that the mature corporation 'has means for managing what the consumer buys at the prices which it controls.' (Galbraith, 1967:217). Galbraith is exaggerating the extent to which the individual may be said to be lacking in any genuine freedom of choice that cannot be factored down to the free choice of the other-determined buttons that the consumer has been pre-programmed to press. Even so, as the first two sections of this chapter have suggested, there are grounds for thinking that private decisions are made in a situational setting of which human action is at once the cause and the effect: 'Consumerism and the science of marketing that caters to it refers to desires that have literally been *created* by man himself, and which will give way to others in the future.' (Fukuyama, 1992:63). We start from here. And from *them*. And from *there*.

This concluding section is concerned with ego's autonomy while subject to the influence of the *them* and the *there*. The third part deals with past practices, the second with social pressures. The first part shows how difficult it is to make generalisations in a whirlwind of combinations where commodities have multiple characteristics and where the social milieu is not always the same.

5.3.1 The Kaleidoscope of Choice

Kelvin Lancaster sees the commodity as a multi-attribute bundle: 'In general ... even a single good will possess more than one characteristic, so that the simplest consumption activity will be characterized by joint outputs. Furthermore, the same characteristic (for example, aesthetic properties) may be included among the joint outputs of many consumption activities so that goods which are apparently unrelated in certain of their characteristics may be related in others.' (Lancaster, 1966a:13). Lancaster is convinced that not goods *per se* but rather their differentiated features and unique qualities must be seen as the true source of consumer satisfaction. Those characteristics can be combined and recombined in a multiplicity of ways by a multiplicity of individual units – not one of them any more 'representative' of the pool than is the mix which they match and call a thing.

Goods in Lancaster's perspective are an input in a happiness production-function. The household buys in the inputs as if it were a business and does so in such proportions as to maximise the output, the return – the utility – that it expects from the endowment at its disposal: 'The consumer obtains his optimum bundle of characteristics by purchasing a collection of goods so chosen as to possess *in toto* the desired characteristics.' (Lancaster, 1975:155). People want attributes – 'the goods playing the role of intermediaries rather than being either primary resources or ultimate objects of consumption.' (Lancaster, 1975:156). They do not want hermetically-sealed categories divided by engineers into industries as if guided by an inflexible Plan that cannot possibly know better than the individual how to weight the durability, the colour, the method of finance, the convenience, the feel, the name, the image, the familiarity, the price, the urgency, the running cost that all enter into the portfolio of characteristics from which the prudent investor wishes to maximise his personal and private satisfaction, self-perceived.

A 'meal' is the chance of nutrition and the stilling of painful hunger. It is also the pleasures of flavour and smell, an opportunity for the public display of wealth, a social occasion with family and friends, a speculative investment in business contacts, an aesthetic experience in which beauty is presented on a plate. A 'house' is not just sleeping space but shared co-habitation, safety standards, size and shape, an address that conveys a message as precise as Knightsbridge or Brixton. A 'job' is not just the sale of labour but intercourse with colleagues, a forum for creativity, information about other openings, a hierarchy of authority, a predeterminant of leisure: 'A taxi driver may spend less of his budget on taking weekend drives than the social norm; yet traditional theory would find no connection between his consumption and his occupation.' (Lancaster, 1966b:48). A good, in short, is not an unambiguous gratifier but rather a spectrum of possibilities. The demand for commodities is not a final demand. Instead it is a derived demand, a demand for the properties which each good as seen by the consumer is in a position to supply.

The traditional theory conceives of commodities as complements (cars, petrol), substitutes (butter, margarine) and unrelated pairings (bread, diamonds). The characteristics approach, concentrating as it does on the flux of multidimensionality, makes the task of classification that much more difficult. Gold-tipped shoes and an opera ticket, unconnected where the utilities are defined to be walking and music, are at once complements (style is *de rigeur* where the purpose of the evening is self-advertisement) and substitutes (expensive shoes can proclaim success so loudly that the top-up of the opera visit might not be needed at all). Fresh fruit produces good health – so does on-street jogging, a supportive work environment and the closure of a local airport to minimise the risk of a crash. A car yields status – so does an invitation to the Vatican, a Rolex, a Rembrandt original, blood donorship at the place of work, voluntary service in the church and community. The most unexpected things can evidently go easily together once the similarities and the differences are defined in terms of prominent expectations and not of chemistry and physics.

Characteristics can be traded off, both in terms of objective services like transport and in terms of the logic of signs that makes a washing-machine interchangeable with a portable laptop because of the purchasing power that it certifies. Characteristics can also be addictive, in the important sense that one purchase in isolation will often be insufficient to deliver the sought-after utility. A 'fitted kitchen' is an arrangement with an identity of its own. A 'millionaire's lifestyle' is a whole in excess of the sum of its parts. Just as the Roman Pantheon was a pandaemonium of many Gods, so the fitted kitchen is a syncretism of cooker, squeezer, freezer, refrigerator and microwave; while the millionaire's lifestyle makes him a figure of fun so long as he chooses no more than the yacht without the restaurant meals, the Riviera winters and the trophy wife which convention if not technology have made the standard co-consumables. The truth, as Baudrillard emphasises, is not the single purchase but rather the bundle to which it contributes: 'Like a chain that connects not ordinary objects but *signifieds*, each object can signify the other in a more complex super-object, and lead the consumer to a series of more complex choices.' (Baudrillard, 1988:31). Preparing a meal is not a higgledy-piggledy Sunday stroll that is attracted first by some treacle and then ambles on to buy a knife. More will be needed than random travelling partners if the end is to be attained. Much that will be chosen will have the character of indivisibility, inseparability and fixed coefficients. It will not have the character of the freedom to break free.

The heteronomy of characteristics complicates the map. The choice of peer group and of reference group gives the kaleidoscope a further shock. People use other people to validate their confidence in their own aspirations and accomplishments: 'To the extent that objective, non-social means are not available, people evaluate their opinions and abilities by comparison respectively with the opinions and abilities of others.' (Festinger, 1954:124). The gain is the reassurance. The loss is the regress – since people still have to choose the precise neighbours, the specific role models, to whom they will appeal for advice and legitimation.

The choice of the peers influences the tastes that will be validated: Weber's

Calvinists and Veblen's journeyman printers will not speak with one voice on drunkeness versus thrift. The choice of the comparators shapes the preferences that will be formed: taking normative standards from film stars will throw up different results from hairstyles copied from tax inspectors. External referents once selected, people clearly have less chance to be deviant than they would were their success indicators to be theirs and theirs alone. Even so, it should not be forgotten that there is a considerable range of peer groups and reference groups; and that 'choosing the right pond' – the phrase comes from Robert Frank – is itself a creative act that at least allows the individual to have a say on the brainwashers who will wash his brains.

Individuals often have multiple peer groups and reference groups, both at one point of time and at different stages in their life-cycle. The similarity that they pick out as being the most salient forms for them the baseline for invidious comparison, the membership that frames the relative income hypothesis: 'Suppose, for example, that we are talking to a Negro businessman in the United States about equality of opportunity. As a Negro comparing himself with white businessmen, he is likely to feel relatively deprived; as a businessman comparing himself with unskilled Negroes, he is likely to feel relatively gratified.' (Runciman, 1966:30). Runciman's Negro is clearly a businessman with a serious status problem: not only does he have to decide if his relative accomplishment should be framed *within* his group or *because* of his group, he also has to impose some consistency upon the co-existing affiliations which ensure that he will on one and the same day be called 'sir' because he is rich and 'boy' because he is black. His confusion would be alleviated if he were able to ring-fence the phrase 'people like us' in such a way, comparing like with like and with nothing else, as to make unambiguous identification the guarantor of the impartiality of justice. Inconveniently, Runciman's Negro has relevant attributes that associate him with more than a single category. Over-located rather than unlocated, ranking the multiple ponds at least allows the businessman – and the Negro – the discretion to select a self-image that seems to make sense to one 'sir', to one 'boy' alone.

The choice of face-to-face peers and of benchmark ideal comparators has important implications for people and things. Desiring acceptance and confirmation, people will gravitate to groups which share their perceptions and will conform to the consumption patterns which release the scarce social resource of merited approval. Wanting to feel good about themselves, people will face a natural temptation to select those affiliations in terms of which they come off best and to reject those associations that mark them out, however successful in an absolute sense, as relatively second-rate. Sometimes they will resist the temptation: 'A college student ... does not compare himself to inmates of an institution for the feeble-minded to evaluate his own intelligence.' (Festinger, 1954:127). Sometimes they will not: an executive working to the dictates of Duesenberry's relative earnings hypothesis has the option of being a big fish in a small pond which he can exercise to win an easy promotion. Choosing the group he chooses the station. In that sense at least the individual has the freedom to say where he thinks he belongs.

5.3.2 People and Freedom

The first section of this chapter drew attention to the interpersonal constraint. Its theme was the signifier (that the shop-floor will wear overalls, that top management will wear a suit) and the convention (that the teenager is bought a car, that the girl and not the boy is dressed in pink). Its text was taken from Veblen: 'Only individuals with an aberrant temperament can in the long run retain their self-esteem in the face of the disesteem of their fellows.' (Veblen, 1899:38). Its conclusion was that the economics of consumer choice should put observed regularities in their social context rather than treating revealed preference as a forbidden exogeneity that requires no further probe.

Demand theory need not be incompatible with social content. To say that one more apple is ranked above one more pear is simply to record an empirical observation. The downward-sloping utility curve only means that the consumer gets a smaller increment of satisfaction from the fifth cup of tea than he does from the first. The indifference curve traces out different combinations that deliver constant gratification. Formal and abstract, nonetheless there is little in these constructs that is incompatible with social interdependence.

Demand theory formulates propositions which make so much sense as to have the feel of a tautology. The preferred choice could be the one that targets intrinsic satisfaction from the thing itself, inertial satisfaction from the failure to search out a cheaper substitute, self-affirming satisfaction from other people who approve of the choice. Demand theory does not look behind the concrete manifestations to disentangle competing causalities such as these. A more socially-informed economics fills in the blanks.

Thus invidious comparison is a feature of a relatively open, unstratified, materialistic, acquisitive society such as Duesenberry's America. The invocation to 'be the first in your crowd' is an appeal which accounts for relatively less of the variance in a traditional society where rigid prescription limits the scope for visible display. The axiom of monotonicity, again, is a reflection of a culture that has become accustomed to a rise. A culture built around replication and acceptance will not be so confident that more is preferable to less if the social externality is change. Even 'rationality' and 'maximisation' have themselves an ideological dimension. People in some societies will have been educated into obsessive cost-consciousness and the high value of value but in others they will have been encouraged to seek self-mastery, moderation and knowledge. Desperately, one could say that what the non-economical are really doing is simply maximising the services of non-maximisation. It is most unlikely that the forest monk, meditating in order to free himself from the very single-mindedness that makes the gain-seeker into a captain of industry, would accept so simplified an explanation of his life.

People differ but so do their cultures. It is the task of a socially-informed economics, going behind the ordinal rankings and the price/quantity cardinalities, to make a useful contribution to the theory of freedom by demystifying consumption into those choices which are as ego-authentic as the atom's desire to put Bach before Beethoven, those choices which rubber-stamp a cultural artefact as if a ritual fetish in a tribal society. The truth will be a mix – some imitation, fashion and communication co-existing side by side with A who likes black dogs because they are the dogs that he likes and B who wears a hat lest he feel too hot in the sun. The truth will be a mix. Not, however, a constant mix. No discussion of the freedom of choice in the market exchange of commodities can ever be complete that does not disaggregate the preferences revealed into those which are collective and those which are personal.

5.3.3   Past and Freedom

The second section of this chapter showed the significance of the inter-temporal mould. The argument there was that much that is called economics is in truth economic history. The bride's family pays for the wedding because the bride's family has always paid for the wedding. Fasting is observed in Ramadan because fasting has always been observed in Ramadan. Jack smokes a pipe because Jack has always smoked a pipe. Jill goes to mahjong because Jill has always gone to mahjong. Sometimes collective and sometimes personal, the crucial point is that the choice is by no means new. The present day spends the money. The lagged response, however, severely restricts the scan.

Conservatism abridges the shopping list. Less, importantly, can also be more where the signposting is not an infringement of freedom so much as the precondition for it. The heuristic in the sense of Simon and morality in the sense of Durkheim both illustrate the extent to which inflexible constants can liberate the consumer from choice overload that is worse.

Thus the rule of thumb saves the time and effort that would have been gambled on search. Brand loyalty may not optimise but at least it guarantees the tried-and-tested. The repeat purchase blocks out the never-known exploration but it does deliver familiarity which is itself a satisfaction. Particularly in a Lancaster-type world of subsets and nuances, the information-economising contribution of a habit or rule should not be underestimated. No one can remember all the attributes of all the commodities or open-mindedly absorb all new knowledge about all new consumables. The routine targets the data collection on the particular characteristics that will have the highest pay-off. Where there are a number of paths to the same utility, the investment in patterning may be the only way in which radical indecision can effectively be prevented.

The normative standard too can be a valuable beacon in a sea of confusion: 'The rule, because it teaches us to restrain and master ourselves, is a means of emancipation and of freedom', 'the condition of happiness and of moral health.' (Durkheim, 1925:44, 49). Limitation, inhibition, specificity, finitude, discipline all protect the individual from the malady of ungoverned appetite that can lead so easily to frustration, disappointment and the sense of futility: 'The way to be happy is to set proximate and realizable goals... Pessimism always accompanies unlimited aspirations.' (Durkheim, 1925:40, 49). The Don Juan, Durkheim established, is abnormally prone to suicide because he lacks a single, fixed object of attachment and obligation: 'New hopes constantly awake, only to be deceived, leaving a trail of weariness and disillusionment behind them.' (Durkheim, 1897:271). The rule-less consumer, Durkheim added, is, like the bachelor, statistically at risk of taking his life: 'To pursue a goal which is by definition unattainable is to condemn oneself to a state of perpetual unhappiness... The more one has, the more one wants, since satisfactions received only stimulate instead of filling needs... Unlimited desires are insatiable by definition and insatiability is rightly considered a sign of morbidity.' (Durkheim, 1897:247,248). Goal-less passions add up to the permissiveness of *anomie*. *Anomie* irrespective of prosperity can lead to self-destruction. Moral conditioning carried over from the past restricts the range of choices open to the consumer. The circumscription of freedom, on the other hand, is also likely to keep him alive.

Galbraith writes as follows about authenticity and individualism: 'If the individual's wants are to be urgent they must be original with himself. They cannot be urgent if they must be contrived for him.' (Galbraith, 1958:131). The position taken in this chapter on People and things has been a different one. Not denying the existence of personal predilections and intrinsic satisfactions, the chapter has argued that other people and historical continuity interact with the self to such an extent as to make the ego-to-alter and the alter-to-ego extremely difficult to distinguish. The point is well made by Katona, who believes that experience is the source or modifier of much that is elliptically called individual: 'Economic behavior is learned behavior in the sense that it develops and changes with experience. Learning is inter-communication. In addition to the learner, there must always be stimuli from the environment: a teacher, a book, an event, a newspaper, or even an advertisement. It makes no sense whatsoever to distinguish between wants, desires, or behavior that we have acquired spontaneously and not spontaneously.' (Katona, 1964:54–5). Childhood socialisation teaches the individual to cook his meat and use a knife and fork. Adult socialisation trains the individual to wear leather shoes and look like his trade and profession. Somewhere in social space there is the irreducible self that wants air-conditioning to keep the temperature down. It is the message of this chapter on People and things that it is by no means easy to isolate that irreducible self in such a way as to separate it conclusively from interdependence and from the common past.

6.   Benevolence

Consumption is an other-regarding activity. It involves the collaboration of other people, present-day spectators who function as ego's externality and embodied cohorts whose legacy is the convention. Consumption in that sense is relativities and not just absolutes. A's Cartier yields satisfaction that is diminished by B's Calvin Klein. A's kilt yields satisfaction that is enhanced by B's bagpipe. Invidious comparison or passive conformity, what is clear is that consumption is standing and esteem even as it is nutrition, temperature-control and transportation.

Consumption is an other-regarding activity – and that is why people will frequently take steps to alter the choice-sets of their partners and fellows. In the case of benevolence they will do so because, warm-hearted and caring, they in the words of Smith obtain satisfaction from the satisfaction of others: 'How selfish soever man may be supposed, there are evidently some principles in his nature, which interest him in the fortune of others, and render their happiness necessary to him, though he derives nothing from it, except the pleasure of seeing it.' (Smith, 1759:3). In the case of malevolence they will do so because, driven by envy and defensive of place, they in the words of Hume hunger for the utility that only another's fall can supply: 'Envy is excited by some present enjoyment of another, which by comparison diminishes our idea of our own... A superiority naturally seems to overshade us, and presents us a disagreeable comparison.' (Hume, 1739–40:II, 162). Benevolence and malevolence, in short, cause people not just to compare and conform but also to transfer resources, to become involved.

The subject of the previous chapter was looking and ranking. The subject of the present chapter and of the next one is looking, ranking and getting involved. An inquiry into A's resources regarded as B's consumable, the present chapter on Benevolence builds on David Collard's important conclusion that 'human beings are not entirely selfish, even in their economic dealings' (Collard, 1978:3). The discussion is divided into three sections. Section 1, Altruism and interest, defines the two polar positions and draws attention to the significant degree of intellectual overlap. Section 2, The gift relationship, identifies the sense of duty and the feeling of sympathy as the two main sources of the propensity to care. Section 3, Gifts and groups, says that sacrifice can have a function but that sometimes sheer decency simply gets in the way.

6.1 ALTRUISM AND INTEREST

Market capitalism as an economic system would not be viable in the absence
of self-interested calculativeness and the self-seeking search for advantage.
Supply and demand would be immobilised in the intractable indeterminacy of
an eternal 'after you' the moment that the buyers and the sellers decided to
love their neighbour as they loved themselves. Robin Matthews explains
clearly what pure and universal love would mean for a community that wanted
simultaneously to allocate and expand: 'I am selling you a house. Your utility
ranks equally with mine, both in my eyes and in yours. So the price is a matter
of indifference to both of us. £10,000 more to me, £10,000 more to you – there
is nothing in it. As a result, no market signals emerge.' (Matthews, 1981:291).

Private gain is the *sine qua non* that delivers the goods. Adam Smith,
appealing to common knowledge for the confirmation that 'we are not ready
to suspect any person of being deficient in selfishness' (Smith, 1759:446),
extended to it an economist's welcome on the pragmatic grounds that contract,
rights, reciprocity and fair dealing made a reliable contribution to the sustained
rise in the wealth of nations: 'It is not from the benevolence of the butcher, the
brewer, or the baker, that we expect our dinner, but from their regard to their
own interest. We address ourselves, not to their humanity but to their self-love,
and never talk to them of our own necessities but of their advantages.' (Smith,
1776:I, 18).

We address ourselves not to their fellow-feeling but to their egoism.
Detached and unsentimental, we simply try an offer which will release in our
favour all the latent power of the tradesman's *quid pro quo*: 'Give me that
which I want, and you shall have this which you want, is the meaning of every
such offer... It is in this manner that we obtain from one another the far
greater part of those good offices which we stand in need of.' (Smith, 1776:I,
18). The good offices are delivered expeditiously. The mutuality of the
bargain gives a guarantee of justice. Benevolence to the true free-trader is
evidently no more than the icing on a cake in which, as James Buchanan
observes, the active ingredient is the payment for service: 'I do not know the
fruit salesman personally, and I have no particular interest in his well-being.
He reciprocates this attitude... Yet the two of us are able to complete an
exchange expeditiously, an exchange that both of us accept as "just".'
(Buchanan, 1975:17). Given the efficacy combined with the equity in a
democratic nexus, 'bi-laterally voluntary and informed' (Friedman, 1962:13),
no one but a beggar, it would appear, would intendedly address himself to
benevolence when his dinner and his dignity would more dependably be
defended by exchange.

Edgeworth made the complementarity of gain the hard core of economic theory: 'The first principle of Economics is that every agent is actuated only by self-interest.' (Edgeworth, 1881:16). What Edgeworth also recognised is that real-world self-interest is seldom observed save in a compound: 'Between the two extremes Pure Egoistic and Pure Universalistic there may be an indefinite number of impure methods; wherein the happiness of others as compared by the agent (in a calm moment) with his own, neither counts for nothing, not yet "counts for one", but *counts for a fraction.*' (Edgeworth, 1881:16). On that middle ground, Edgeworth suggested, the agent might be thought of as incorporating other people's utility-functions, suitably weighted, into his own. Private gain remains the *sine qua non*. Motivation, even so, is a bundle of drives; and other people are a fact.

Kenneth Boulding was especially insistent that other people cannot reasonably be netted out. The emotional independence of the closed-door monad is, Boulding argued, likely only 'between people who are quite ignorant of each other and have no relationships. The moment people enter into relationships they tend to develop either benevolence or malevolence to some degree.' (Boulding, 1981:119). Like Edgeworth, Boulding saw that economic interest is only one point in a gamut of desiderata: 'Selfishness is merely the zero point on a scale of benevolence and malevolence and, hence, is likely to be very rare.' (Boulding, 1981:119). Like Edgeworth, Boulding believed that the bread-and-butter impulsion is best understood if integrated with the other elements that make up the self: 'I came to see the social system as a total pattern – of which economics is only a part.' (Boulding, 1981:v).

Economics, Boulding accepts, has an especial concern with resource allocation in conditions of scarcity. That, indeed, is precisely the reason why it should be open to tribute exacted through the fear of threat and, most of all, to the gift or grant that redistributes demand for supply in a way that price theory alone cannot explain. Even alms given to a beggar has implications for economic theory which the neoclassicist's focus on buying and selling can all too easily obscure: 'This focus is unfortunate, for not only is the one-way transfer a significant element in social life, but it is an element whose importance has been growing rapidly in the twentieth century. Today, for instance, according to various possible definitions, we could say that from about 20 to almost 50 percent of the U.S. economy is organized by grants rather than by exchange.' (Boulding, 1981:1). The possibility that love, loyalty and devotion can explain as much of resource allocation in the United States as can the pecuniary *quid pro quo* is a salutary reminder that altruism too, and not just self-interest, is an influence on the wealth of households dwelling for all time on the middle ground.

Self-love is at one pole. Self-abnegation is at the other. Egoism means putting one's own welfare first. Altruism means making sacrifices in order that others might thrive: 'In general terms we class an action as altruistic when its outcome is primarily beneficial to someone else, and when its performance is dictated by the desire to help another person. Faced with a choice between personal convenience or advantage and furthering someone else's goals, the individual deliberately chooses the latter.' (Wright, 1971:127). A deliberate choice must be made. The action is primarily of benefit to someone else: 'When a person (or animal) increases the fitness of another at the expense of his own fitness, he can be said to have performed an act of *altruism.*' (Wilson, 1975:117). Even so, the *sine qua non* for an action to be called other-regarding is not the consequentialism *per se* but rather the deontology which certifies as ethically purposive and not merely an unintended accident the transfer of time, of energy, of money, of life itself.

Nagel is insistent that a prudential concern with the instrumentality of means and ends must be complemented by affect, involvement and the desire to make a difference if an intervention is properly to be termed an altruistic one: 'I cannot be motivated simply by the knowledge that an act of mine will have certain consequences for the interests of others; I must care what happens to them if this knowledge is to be effective.' (Nagel, 1970:28). Service to others is a necessary but not a sufficient condition. For an observed choice properly to be called an altruistic one, something more is needed than the bare fact of reallocation. That something is perception, understanding and fellow-feeling that verges on commitment: 'Altruism ... depends on a recognition of the reality of other persons, and on the equivalent capacity to regard oneself as merely one individual among many.' (Nagel, 1970:3).

Altruism can be the noble self-sacrifice of the soldier who volunteers for a suicide mission or the mundane small service of the bystander who informs a motorist that his tyre is flat. Altruism can be as current as the decision not to jump the queue, as long-horizoned as the choice to put money into the education of a child. Altruism can be activity – the case of soup kitchens, unemployment benefits or foreign aid. Altruism can be abstention – consider the smoker who refrains from polluting a crowded carriage or the decorator who refuses cheap carpets hand-knotted by indentured children. Altruism, it is clear, can present itself in a variety of forms. Always, however, it must satisfy the dual standard of intentionality and transfer. Altruism may be defined as '*any* behaviour motivated merely by the belief that someone else will benefit or avoid harm by it.' (Nagel, 1970:16n). The *quid* without the *quo*, the butcher, the brewer and the baker would go out of business if they made the unilaterality of altruism too frequently the basis for their business plan.

Self-interest and benevolence are two polar types. The definitional problem is that they are opposites which can also be regarded as convergent. Altruism, after all, presupposes the opportunity to make a deliberate choice. No one who is rational would deliberately make a choice that left him worse off in his own estimation.

The Good Samaritan chose to share his resources in preference to spending them exclusively on himself. Reacting to need but aware of the opportunity cost, it may be assumed that he expected more satisfaction if he delivered the gift than he would have enjoyed if he had played the Bad Hobbesian by means of self-centred consumption. Negatively speaking, the Samaritan can be regarded as having hired the man robbed on the road to Jericho in order to protect his self-image from a guilty conscience. Positively speaking, the Samaritan can be seen as having converted the victim of distress into an outlet for his desire to feel needed and an asset which confirmed to him that he knew what was right. The butcher's charity is not the same as the butcher's sale. Crucially, where he puts the welfare of another above his own private profit, it cannot be denied that he is making a decision to maximise his own utility *through* the choice that he is making to maximise the utility of his neighbour. His altruism is altruism. Yet it is egoism as well.

The interpenetration of utility functions means that A is happy because B is happy and has therefore a selfish interest in an endowment shared. Becker captures the economiser's vision of the externality internalised in his description of the benevolent donor as an other-sensitive marginalist. The economic altruist, Becker writes, 'would eat with his fingers only when its value to him exceeds the value of the disgust suffered by the other, or would read in bed late at night only when its value exceeds the value of the loss of sleep suffered by the other.' (Becker, 1981:6). The wellbeing of the other being an argument in ego's own welfare function, to be a Good Samaritan is *de facto* to be a sensible shopper. Put in this way, feel-good is a goal like wealth, private vices engender public virtues, economising is everywhere and pure benevolence does not exist.

Hobbesian interest is win–lose. Smithian interest is win–win. The supply of altruism as a demand for reward is, as Sen points out, unambiguously a win–win game in which interest places both St. Anthony and the beggar on a higher plane of utility: 'The awareness of the increase in the welfare of the other person then makes this person directly better off.' (Sen, 1977:92). Blau, like Becker, uses the language of marginalism to explain the shopkeeper's rectitude and the shoplifter's self-control: 'Men who forego the advantages made possible by cheating do not act contrary to their self-interest *if* the peace of mind and social approval they obtain for their honesty is more rewarding to them than the gains they could make by cheating.' (Blau, 1964:268). Even Durkheim, unprepared as he is to treat the moral code as if a commercial tradeable, nonetheless concedes that the individual feels more at ease when his fellows feel more at ease as well: 'We are vitally hurt by everything that diminishes the vitality of the beings to whom we are attached; being attached to them, it is to a part of ourselves that we are attached.' (Durkheim, 1925:215). We are attached to ourselves because we are attached to them. Our vitality rises because their vitality goes up. The situation is strictly win–win. If a bottle of whisky makes us sleep better at night, so too does a gift of blankets to help the homeless sleeping rough.

Anthony Culyer uses the language of interest to explain why an integrated nation will opt for free-on-demand health: 'The state of health of others is itself an object of interest to all . . . One individual is not affected merely by the possibility of another passing some disease on to him . . . but also, and much more importantly, by the state of health of the other in itself. Individuals are affected by others' health status for the simple reason that *most of them care.*' (Culyer, 1976:89). Culyer accounts for the National Health with reference to the caring externality and the interdependence of utility. It is an appeal to interest which is none the less *self*-ish for not being commercial.

Titmuss, writing of the gift of blood, confirms that there is a reward for ego even when it is alter's life that must be saved: 'The self is realized with the help of anonymous others.' (Titmuss, 1970:239). Team-playing donors, spending their blood, have never been in any doubt that they were securing an entitlement to self-esteem in return: 'To "love" themselves they recognized the need to "love" strangers.' (Titmuss, 1970:269). It is the duty of the National Health and of the Transfusion Service to give citizens the opportunity they need to practice 'creative altruism', to find an outlet for their 'social and . . . biological need to help.' (Titmuss, 1970:239, 274).

People who are fulfilling themselves, as Lutz and Lux observe, cannot realistically be seen as people who are making a sacrifice: 'When those at the higher end of the need hierarchy help those at the lower, they are in fact promoting their own growth . . . The rich give the poor enough to take them out of their poverty, and the poor give the rich the opportunity to serve.' (Lutz and Lux, 1979:167). The lower need for food adequately met, people move up to a higher need for contact and community which other people alone can assist them to satisfy. The return gift is not pecuniary reciprocation but it is value in exchange nonetheless.

Self-love may be found even in benevolence. Titmuss himself conceded the impurity: 'No donor type can, of course, be said to be characterized by complete, disinterested, spontaneous altruism. There must be some sense of obligation, approval and interest; some awareness of need and of the purposes of the blood gift; perhaps some organized group rivalry in generosity . . . and some expectation and assurance that a return gift may be needed and received at some future time.' (Titmuss, 1970: 101). Altruism may be interpreted as a special case of interest. Altruism and interest may be seen as coexisting drives within a motivational mix. Altruism is defined as intended loss. Interest is defined as intended gain. What this section has suggested is that the definitional problem is a maze within a minefield which the butcher, the brewer and the baker, concentrating on their dinner and busy maximising their wealth, did right to avoid. No doubt they did – but *we* start from here.

6.2 THE GIFT RELATIONSHIP

Altruism is the unilateral transfer: 'Altruistic behavior is behavior that promotes the welfare of others without conscious regard for one's own self-interests.' (Hoffman, 1981:124). Altruists give without contracted return in the certain knowledge that the resources alienated could have been invested in a paying sale. Their deeds reveal that they made a choice to put the gain of another above the cost to oneself. What their actions cannot explain is the state of mind that triggered off the self-denial. Intentions and motives being by their very nature hidden and unobservable, it is not easy to establish the precise causes that unleash the donations to charity and repress the slacking and the cheating at work. This section nonetheless speculates that duty and sympathy are the interlocking sources of legitimation which put the 'ought to be' into the gift. Underlying both are the social bonds and the remembered practices that, as in the other chapters in this book, make economics into a sub-discipline in the general theory of the life in common.

6.2.1 Duty

The sharing of resources can be the consequence of externally-imposed obligation. Where there is a normative standard, the believer is bound by the rule. An altruistic rule elicits an altruistic response. A thicket of altruistic rules engenders a society that does not automatically merchant or cost.

Karl Marx made his normative standard 'from each according to his ability, to each according to his needs.' (Marx, 1875:566). The appeal to the authority of his name has often been used to make voluntary overtime a valued privilege and famine relief the chance to do what one must. Far more influential has, however, been the Old Testament's 'love your neighbour as a man like yourself' (*Leviticus* 19:18) that to St. Paul represented the summit of human striving. The core commandments and injunctions, St. Paul told the Romans, 'are all summed up in the one rule, "Love your neighbour as yourself". Love cannot wrong a neighbour; therefore the whole law is summed up in love.' (*Romans* 13:9–10). It is summed up in love: 'If I have no love, I am nothing . . . In a word, there are three things that last forever: faith, hope, and love; but the greatest of them all is love.' (*1 Corinthians* 13:3, 13). It is summed up in love – and it is summed up in money: 'God loves a cheerful giver.' (*2 Corinthians*

9:8). If Marx was concerned that the needy should not be left out in allocation, so too was the even more widely read St. Paul.

St. Paul taught that we are all parts, one of another. Not an individualist but an organicist, it was his message that rights come with duties attached: 'A body is not one single organ, but many... The eye cannot say to the hand, "I do not need you"; nor the head to the feet... Quite the contrary... If one organ suffers, they all suffer together. If one flourishes, they all rejoice together.' (*1 Corinthians* 12:15, 21–22, 26). So much at least is sociology. Where St. Paul's teaching goes beyond the Parsonian functionalism is that he appeals explicitly to the Author of Nature who alone is in a position to issue a binding instruction: 'Do you not know that your body is a shrine of the indwelling Holy Spirit, and the Spirit is God's gift to you? You do not belong to yourselves; you were bought at a price.' (*1 Corinthians* 6:19–20). People who hold a property in themselves have the freedom to pursue their self-defined objectives. People who believe with St. Paul that God alone owns the leases and the freeholds have a God-given duty which the maximising individual is not at liberty to neglect.

Jesus too invokes the authority of God to support his proposition that the economic problem can be solved as certainly as the 5000 at Bethsaida were fed with only five loaves and two fishes but that the moral problem remains the greater challenge to imperfect man who wants to emulate the caring interventionism of the Invisible Hand: 'If you lend only where you expect to be repaid, what credit is that to you? Even sinners lend to each other to be repaid in full. But you must love your enemies and do good; and lend without expecting any return... Be compassionate as your Father is compassionate.' (*Luke* 6:34–5, 36). Jesus is reassuring to the lilies and the ravens for whom God will provide. He is hard on the camel attempting to pass through the eye of the needle with the rich man who misguidedly plans for the Kingdom of Heaven: 'No servant can be the slave of two masters... You cannot serve God and Money.' (*Luke* 16:13). Jesus is articulating a duty to love and to care. He is legitimating his call for altruism through an appeal to the Great Architect who alone has the blueprint and knows the nature of the temple that he wishes his collaborators to erect.

Jesus couches his theory of duty in the non-discriminatory language of the Golden Rule: 'Give to everyone who asks you; when a man takes what is yours, do not demand it back. Treat others as you would like them to treat you.' (*Luke* 6:30–1). His emphasis on equal respect and equal involvement looks forward to the 'single categorical imperative' which Immanuel Kant formulated in the following command: 'Act only on that maxim through which you can at the same time will that it should become a universal law.' (Kant, 1785:88). Each of us does as he would be done by and expects that others will supply the like consideration in return. Each of us wants to be accepted for his common humanity and not judged by his productive performance: 'Man, and in general every rational being, *exists* as an end in himself, *not merely as a means* for arbitrary use by this or that will.' (Kant, 1785:95). Each of us wants to be offered the supreme gift of equal dignity. Each of us is prepared to supply the duty of equal care in return.

Kantian men and women make a free gift of their truth-telling and their promise-keeping. They donate a kidney where a fellow human being would otherwise lose his life and turn out to vote even if they could easily ride free on the non-economic commitment of the uncompromisingly cooperative. Kantian men and women choose to buy products made with minimal damage to the ozone layer and minimal over-cropping through slash-and-burn. Protective of future generations as well as of the here-and-now, what such men and women are proclaiming is that there is more to human character than that 'narrowness, meanness, and a selfish disposition, averse to all social pleasure and enjoyment' (Smith, 1776:II, 188) which to Adam Smith was one of the less attractive features of a nation that relied upon commerce for its wealth.

Outcome-orientated interest is not explicitly the reason why good Kantians, non-consequentialists, always pay their tax and abstain from litter. Implicitly, however, the sensitivity to cost and the estimation of benefit are by no means absent even from the strict Kantian model in which opportunistic selfishness is made the first sad step on the road to the *bellum*. Kant himself gave the quasi-commercial example of the liar, forever afraid of being repaid 'in like coin': 'I can indeed will to lie, but I can by no means will a universal law of lying; for by such a law there could properly be no promises at all.' (Kant, 1785:71). The liar, by abstaining from his lies, is in effect making an investment in insurance such as would cover him against the damage caused by the duplicity of others. He is opting *de facto* for a social contract, a multi-period constitutional settlement which protects him from the dishonesty of others even as it protects others from being conned by his wiles. The future is unknown and unknowable. The 'single categorical imperative' has the great attraction that the Kantian absolute makes the uncertainties of life very much easier to manage.

The future is unknown and unknowable. So, in the 'original position' situated behind the 'thick veil of ignorance', is the Rawlsian present. Rawls employs a thought experiment in which rational actors are denied all information on their individual coordinates to derive the prediction that frightened loss-averters, unable to recognise their personal interests, will define to be just that allocation of resources that maximises the welfare not of the average citizen but of the most deprived: 'Social and economic inequalities are to be arranged so that they are both (a) to the greatest benefit of the least advantaged and (b) attached to offices and positions open to all under conditions of fair equality of opportunity.' (Rawls, 1971:83). Interest leads to redistribution since minimax in combination with impartiality breeds a consensus that is favourable to self-protection. Thus does the pursuit of mutual advantage engender a society that agrees on altruism as a duty that delivers a gain.

Even Titmuss was prepared to acknowledge that the duty to give and the belief in reciprocation were seen by blood-donors as somehow connected despite the absence of a legal contract, a monetary consideration, a binding guarantee or a face-to-face sanction: 'In not asking for or expecting any payment of money these donors signified their belief in the willingness of other men to act altruistically in the future... By expressing confidence in the behaviour of future unknown strangers they were thus denying the Hobbesian thesis that men are devoid of any distinctively moral sense.' (Titmuss, 1970:269). Recognising that even the Blood Samaritan might one day himself be dependent on others for the gift of life, Kenneth Arrow was able to identify the generalised exchange implicit in a skein of obligations 'such that each performs duties for the other in a way calculated to enhance the satisfaction of all': 'One may be thought of as giving blood in the vague expectation that one may need it later on. More generally, perhaps, one gives good things, such as blood, in exchange for a generalized obligation on the part of fellow men to help in other circumstances if needed.' (Arrow, 1972:348, 349). Altruism in such a perspective is analogous to buying a round of drinks in a sequence of drinking sessions. Duty in such a perspective is like precautionary saving against a non-specified rainy day.

Implicit exchange may be detected in the benevolence of Titmuss's donor, just as it may be detected in Rawls's leveller, Kant's truth-teller and Jesus's Samaritan whose prize will be awarded in Heaven and whose default would be front-page news in Hell. It is difficult to separate duty from interest without recalling the terminological minefield of Section 1. Falling back on common sense, however, the Briton who needs blood will be given blood even if he has no personal record of donation. Titmuss to that extent had the street-smart definition of altruism on his side when he argued that the Briton who rises to his duty is making a genuine gift that is more than the sum of the transfusions which he wishes to pre-pay.

6.2.2 Sympathy

Adam Smith, influenced by Newton on gravity without direction and Mandeville on order without design, wrote that man is 'led by an invisible hand to promote an end which was no part of his intention... By pursuing his own interest he frequently promotes that of the society more effectually than when he really intends to promote it.' (Smith, 1776:I, 477–8). Interest performs. Justice ensured, the pleasure-pain principle is all that is required to ensure that self-seeking citizens will contribute to one another's wellbeing as if conscious of the circular flow: 'Society may subsist among different men, as among different merchants, from a sense of its utility, without any mutual love or affection.' (Smith, 1759:124).

Emotive attachment is not needed to protect the going concern. It is not needed – but it nonetheless exists: 'Man', Adam Smith said, 'has a natural love for society, and desires that the union of mankind should be preserved for its own sake, and though he himself was to derive no benefit from it.' (Smith, 1759:127). Society is arrangement and arrangement is participant's surplus: 'The orderly and flourishing state of society is agreeable to him, and he takes delight in contemplating it.' (Smith, 1759:127). Society is fitness and function, harmony and aesthetics: 'The contemplation of them pleases us', so much so that even the butcher, the brewer and the baker will want to do what they can 'to put into motion so beautiful and so orderly a machine.' (Smith, 1759:265, 267). Society, above all else, is other people. The sensitive individual by means of socialised imagination is able to empathise himself into the wants and needs of his fellows. Entering into their mental states, learning to feel as they feel, the congruence of the passions – the *sym*pathy between the units – means that discrete monads share their mental states and society becomes a part of the self.

Sympathy is an emotive response which the psychopath cannot experience but the bulk of the community can. Putting himself into the position of another, bringing home to himself how he would feel if he were in the other's shoes, the sensitive individual is being an egoist, in the literal sense that he is extrapolating and generalising from the self's own desires and perceptions. Yet he is being an altruist as well, to the extent that the exchange of places 'in fancy' enables him to conjure up a universe of sensations that would never have been his own had he remained a young white man and not become an old black woman in his mind: 'When I condole with you for the loss of your only son, in order to enter into your grief, I do not consider what I, a person of such character and profession, should suffer, if I had a son, and if that son was unfortunately to die; but I consider what I should suffer if I was really you; and I not only change circumstances with you, but I change persons and characters. My grief, therefore, is entirely upon your account, and not in the least upon my own. It is not, therefore, in the least selfish.' (Smith, 1759:4, 466).

The first step is the exchange of places 'in fancy'. The second step is the reappraisal of expenditure patterns in the light of the internalised distress. The butcher spends time helping the confused to cross the road because he can sense in his heart what it must mean to be febrile. The brewer donates money for hurricane victims because he can picture clearly what a person would feel who had lost his home. The baker puts his energy into a sponsored swim because he can imagine vividly the misery of a refugee on the run from a war. It is easy to conclude, as Sen would do, that the butcher, the brewer and the baker in cases such as these are acting not from benevolence but from their regard to their own interest: 'Behaviour based on sympathy is in an important sense egoistic, for one is oneself pleased at others' pleasure and pained at others' pain, and the pursuit of one's own utility may thus be helped by sympathetic action.' (Sen, 1977:92). What is interesting is that Adam Smith, writing about caring, reached quite a different verdict: 'Sympathy ... cannot, in any sense, be regarded as a selfish principle.' (Smith, 1759:465). Sympathy, Smith reasoned, is all about you. Being all about you, it is not at all about me.

Since time, money and energy are being used to buy peace of mind when they could have been allocated to private consumption or personal saving, the philanthropic transfer can certainly be seen as no more than one utility ranked above another utility for the purpose of self-indulgence. In a sense it can. Yet there is a difference. Egoistic self-interest means that ego pays and ego eats. Altruistic self-interest means that ego pays and alter eats. In the former case only one party enjoys the psychic gratification. In the latter case both parties do so. A reluctance to make a distinction between self-interest and self-self-interest in effect 'robs the concept of self-interest of any distinguishable content.' (Hirshleifer, 1985:55). A willingness to accept that sympathy with alter is not the same as sympathy with ego, reinstating the falsifiable hypothesis, at least clears a path through the minefield of definition.

Sympathy means that the relief of the poor becomes an argument in the utility-set of the rich. Enhancing life chances, alleviating grief, sharing thus 'enlivens joy by presenting another source of satisfaction.' (Smith, 1759:11). Sympathy also means that the donor himself has the reassuring confirmation that he has conformed to the normative benchmark enforced by 'the impartial and well-informed spectator.' (Smith, 1759:429). To deliver the normal quantity of altruism is to make oneself 'that thing which, though it should be praised by nobody, is, however, the natural and proper object of praise.' (Smith, 1759:166). To default on the expected quantity of benevolence is to make oneself 'in some measure the object of his own hatred and abhorrence': 'When the happiness or misery of others depends in any respect upon our conduct, we dare not, as self-love might suggest to us, prefer the interest of one to that of many. The man within immediately calls to us, that we value ourselves too much and other people too little, and that, by doing so, we render ourselves the proper object of the contempt and indignation of our brethren.' (Smith, 1759:121–2, 194). Torn between praiseworthiness on the one hand, contempt and indignation on the other, it was Adam Smith's contention that most people, desirous of sympathy for themselves, reliably supply the quantity of gifts that the sounding-board spectator reasonably defines to be the norm.

Adam Smith made the *impartial* spectator the sole arbiter of propriety in situation. Charles Cooley appealed more directly to the *real* spectator, the felt-and-seen other whose 'kindliness and deference' is so highly valued, whose 'coldness or contempt' (Cooley, 1902:208) is so greatly feared. In the Cooley case as in the Smith case it is long-term learning, socialised imagination and the non-ego assessment that dictate to the receptive self what gifts should be supplied and to whom: 'Our ideals of personal character are built up out of thoughts and sentiments developed by intercourse, and very largely by imagining how our selves would appear in the minds of persons we look up to.' (Cooley, 1902:242). In the Cooley case as in the Smith case it is self-approbation as others' approbation that makes even strong adults existentially dependent: 'The self that is the most importunate is a reflection, largely, from the minds of others.' (Cooley, 1902:246). I am myself because you are my mirror. It is not a thought on which the rugged individualist will wish to dwell.

Cooley like Smith makes much of the 'impressionable social self', of 'social self-feeling': 'Self-respect means that one's reflected self is up to the social standard.' (Cooley, 1902:204, 208, 270). Cooley like Smith denies that gifting on the basis of empathetic identification within the framework of fair play and the institutions that guide can ever be a selfish action: 'Selfishness as a mental trait is always some sort of narrowness, littleness, or defect: an inadequacy of imagination. The perfectly balanced and vigorous mind can hardly be selfish, because it cannot be oblivious to any important social situation, either in immediate intercourse or in more permanent relations.' (Cooley, 1902:207). Cooley like Smith, in short, was a believer in the power of the larger society that surrounds the mind: 'Persons have power over us through some hold upon our imaginations.' (Cooley, 1902:207). The search for sympathy is evidently a topic in social control.

Smith and Cooley both saw the self in situation as a relative entity: 'The individual self is felt only in relation to other individuals.' (Cooley, 1902:210). The Smithian self is for all that the stronger craft. In the Smithian case the insecure ego, putty in the hands of the impartial spectator, will nonetheless stand up to the crowd where the man in the street is ill-informed. Cooley's self, on the other hand, is forever dependent on early corroboration and personal support from the real spectator whose opinions and perceptions all but make him the person that he is: 'A self-idea of this sort seems to have three principal elements: the imagination of our appearance to the other person, the imagination of his judgement of that appearance, and some sort of self-feeling, such as pride or mortification... We always imagine, and in imagining share, the judgements of the other mind... A social self of this sort might be called the reflected or looking-glass self.' (Cooley, 1902:184–5). Estelle could not comb her hair without the image mirrored in the eyes of Inez. Garcin knew that he had been a coward because Inez told him that he had been a coward. Cooley's comment on the tyranny of the other is as follows: 'A sensitive man, in the presence of an impressive personality, tends to become, for the time, his interpretation of what the other thinks he is.' (Cooley, 1902:206). Sartre's comment on the eternal redefinition of Inez by Estelle, of Garcin by Inez, of Estelle by Garcin, of Estelle by Inez, of Garcin by Estelle in a sealed-off space from which there is no escape is more succinct but also more harrowing: 'Hell is other people.' (Sartre, 1946:166).

Whether the sounding board is the impartial spectator in the sense of Smith or the real spectator in the sense of Cooley, what is clear is the search for sympathy which to both authors means a precommitment of self-definition. Altruism is one of the ways in which the end of sympathy is effectively secured. Ego feels better because alter feels better. Ego feels better because the spectator approves of the relief. Sympathy is the motive. Sympathy is the reward. The gift relationship is the visible manifestation.

6.3   GIFTS AND GROUPS

Adam Smith emphasised that normative constraint is context-dependent: 'Those general rules of conduct, when they have been fixed in our mind by habitual reflection, are of great use in correcting the misrepresentations of self-love concerning what is fit and proper to be done in our particular situation.' (Smith, 1759:226). So did Charles Cooley: the 'highest self is a social self, in that it is a product of constructive imagination working with the materials which social experience supplies.' (Cooley, 1902:242). What both authors stressed is that self-control is powerfully influenced by other people and self-restraint copied from the habitual standard of conduct. Even the gift relationship is not simply altruism unfettered, freely expressed. It is also a symbolic expression of who we are and of the traditions that we have made our own.

Thus my gift to you is limited by the duty I have learned and by the sympathy to which I aspire. Even the Best Samaritan knows he is expected first to look after himself, then his family, then his friends, and only then 'the great empire of China' (Smith, 1759:192) which is so remote, so distant, so far removed. The very content of the gift is an indicator of what a given culture has come to call appropriate in the circumstances and in the setting. British people do not donate a second wife to an oldest son, or share a pipe of opium with colleagues after work, or maximise a child's utility by allowing it to do without education. British people do not – and other people do: 'There is hardly a principle that, cherished under one social climate, is not violated in another.' (Asch, 1952:376). The principle is a shared and a remembered one.

The altruist without a context would want to help but not know what to do.

The relativism and the environmentalism clearly make the whole concept of benevolence into a minefield of circularities. A wants alcohol and an abortion *but* B gives A soup and a book on hard work *because* B fears that C, D and E will withdraw their fellowship from B *if* B gives A the gift that will optimise A's satisfaction in A's own eyes. No doubt a gift relationship is here being committed in public. Who, however, is the donor and who is the beneficiary?

Schwartz draws attention to the isolating and the segregating which is a characteristic of the unilateral transfer that has a context: 'Those to whom we give gifts are in some way different from those to whom no token of regard is given. The gift exchange, then, is a way of dramatizing group boundaries.' (Schwartz, 1967:10). Of course there are people who go without their dinner because of their commitment to common humanity in 'the great empire of China'. Even more numerous, however, are the altruists who give birthday presents to their children, care for an aged relative in the home, volunteer for a clan-based vendetta, sign up for military service in time of war. Gifts are a group fact. They cement the social bonds and strengthen the ties of reciprocity that constitute the invisible line separating 'us' from 'them'.

Mauss emphasises the group-based nature of the gift: 'It is not individuals but collectivities that impose obligations of exchange and contract upon each other.' (Mauss, 1950:5). In treating giving and accepting as a special topic in 'allegiance and commonality' (Mauss, 1950:13), Mauss is revealing that he shares with Durkheim the belief that 'ought-ness' is other people: 'There are no genuinely moral ends except collective ones. There is no truly moral force save that involved in attachment to a group.' (Durkheim, 1925:87). The gift in such a perspective is shaped by the collectivity's conventions and is an investment in the acceptance and integration that are yet to come. Even Santa Claus lacks the discretion to define 'naughty' and 'nice' by his own personal standard. Instead he is compelled by his very status as a judge to favour with his Christmas presents those children who have scrupulously made their advance payment of helpfulness, tidyness, politeness and cheerfulness as laid down in the social contract which their parents too have signed.

The gift is a group fact. As such, it must satisfy two conditions. First, it must make a useful contribution to the smooth functioning of the ongoing whole. Second, it must interact with other institutions in such a way as to ensure its own future. It will be useful to examine each of these conditions in turn.

6.3.1 Function

Duty is normative constraint. Sympathy is emotive attachment. The former is in the mind. The latter is in the heart. Both are fully compatible with the evolutionary perspective which sees altruism as the *sine qua non*.

Darwin in *The Origin of Species* said that the self-sacrifice of the member could be the precondition for the survival of the group. The antelope that gives the warning signal puts its own existence at risk but invests in the biological continuity of its herd. The parent who rescues a child from a blazing building endangers a donor life but protects the blood dynasty and the genetic inheritance. The aged tribesman who makes his way into the jungle lays down his life but frees up food for the productive. In cases such as these the collectivity is strengthened because the unit part refuses to put narrow advantage first.

There is clearly an element of selfishness in any sacrifice made to maximise the numbers of one's own descendants. Donating a kidney to rescue one's kindred is not the same as donating bone marrow to save an unknown other. Wilson, visiting the definitional minefield, is right to comment that a loss that is also a gain is not what most people understand by a transfer: 'The theory of group selection has taken most of the good will out of altruism. When altruism is conceived as the mechanism by which DNA multiplies itself through a network of relatives, spirituality becomes just one more Darwinian enabling device.' (Wilson, 1975:120). The words 'just one more' convey the fallen message that the benevolence is compounded with multi-generational interest. The words 'enabling device' suggest even so that the world does not stop short at the shopping trolley. Natural selection favours the cooperative. Their chances of successful adaptation being relatively higher, it then stands to reason that over time there will be a cumulative expansion in the descendants of the other-regarding as compared with the descendants of the narrow and selfish.

Marshall, influenced by Darwin, writes as follows on the functionality of the gift: 'The struggle for existence causes in the long run those races of men to survive in which the individual is most willing to sacrifice himself for the benefit of those around him; and which are consequently the best adapted collectively to make use of their environment.' (Marshall, 1890:202) . Parents work and save in order to give the next generation a better start in life. Employers invest in on-the-job training despite the fact that, the skills being 'the property of the workman himself', 'the virtue of those who have aided him must remain for the greater part its own reward.' (Marshall, 1890:470). Traders and brokers make verbal contracts on the basis of 'my word is my bond': without their generalised confidence the fast-paced Cotton and Stock Exchanges would effectively be uneconomic. Salaried managers maximise the shareholders' profits and not their own bureaucratic utilities: without their silent self-restraint the separation of ownership from control could never have taken place. Marshall, in short, looked forward to an exchange economy in which self-preservation would be promoted by a healthy concern for others as well as by the entrepreneurial gain-seeking which contributed in a more familiar fashion to the advancement of the wealth of nations.

Marshall predicted and welcomed the evolution of a mixed ethos. The fact that he made an increase in the supply of the *quid* without the *quo* the 'supreme aim' of the economist demonstrates how much he was in tune with Fred Hirsch's assertion of complementarity, that 'the Good Samaritan remedies a market failure' (Hirsch, 1977:79): 'No doubt men, even now, are capable of much more unselfish service than they generally render; and the supreme aim of the economist is to discover how this latent social asset can be developed most quickly, and turned to account most wisely.' (Marshall, 1890:8). Marshall believed that the under-developed social asset of altruism should be exploited to the best possible social advantage. He also believed that the economist *qua* economist should take a professional interest in the functionality of the unilateral resource.

Kropotkin agreed on the functionality but was not satisfied by the middle way. Entitling his book *Mutual Aid* and not *Principles of Economics*, Kropotkin planned for a social order where, capitalism and State having given way to convention and anarchism, it was cooperation in the sense of Godwin and not competitiveness in the sense of Bastiat that would prove itself the better guardian of economic welfare: 'Under *any* circumstances sociability is the greatest advantage in the struggle for life.' (Kropotkin, 1902:57). Kropotkin, rejecting both the 'crushing powers of the centralized State' and the 'mutual hatred and pitiless struggle' of the pro-market maximisers, put his faith in affectual belonging and not in conflictual strife: 'The need of mutual aid and support ... claims its right to be, as it always has been, the chief leader towards further progress.' (Kropotkin, 1902:292).

Kropotkin, like Darwin and Marshall, believed that evolution had a tendency to favour benevolence. Benevolence, he believed, was functional for the survival of the species. Kropotkin favoured complete unselfishness whereas Darwin and Marshall associated healthy development with a mix. Still, however, all three authors were at one in the recognition that some altruism at least is the *sine qua non*.

Gift supply is of particular value in that penumbra of ambiguity where time is on the horizontal axis, information is incomplete, the future is uncertain, contracts are under-specified, enforceability is problematic and action is sequential. The butcher, the brewer and the baker, making spot trades as perfect competitors, have no reason to deliver a unilateralism that fulfils no function. The politician speculating on a 'log-rolling' exchange of favours, the prisoner wondering if his confederate will confess or collude, the working wife investing in a student husband who, she hopes, will not subsequently upgrade – social actors like these live in a less easily modelled world where a tradition of benevolence at least introduces some fixed points into the void.

The archetype is the Kula. Malinowski when he studied the nature of exchange among the Trobriand Islanders found that alongside the normal economic trades there existed a circular flow of non-utilitarian symbols which through patterned gifting served to keep in good repair the bonds of community and of trust: 'This partnership is a lifelong relationship, it implies various mutual duties and privileges, and constitutes a type of inter-tribal relationship on an enormous scale.' (Malinowski, 1922:92). The objects themselves are 'meaningless and quite useless' (Malinowski, 1922:92): there is not a great deal a Trobriander can do with red necklaces or white shell armbands, especially since he is expected soon to pass them on. What is more significant is the socialised reciprocity for which the trinkets stand. Prepared to give without demanding an immediate return, the Trobrianders were expressing their confidence in an ongoing structure of rights and duties which would protect their interests when their own turn came round.

What Malinowski observed in the Western Pacific was not pure communism but an implicit contract that brought about social peace. Sahlins would regard this as just another case where Mauss on barter swaps was triumphant over Hobbes on brute force: 'For the war of every man against every man, Mauss substitutes the exchange of everything between everybody... As against war, exchange... The primitive analogue of social contract is not the State, but the gift.' (Sahlins, 1972:168–9). Malinowski's Kula shows clearly how gift giving and gift receiving keep strong and robust the moral ties that reinforce the material flow: 'If friends make gifts, gifts make friends.' (Sahlins, 1972:186). It is more difficult to lie or steal or over-charge or misrepresent where the victim is not an outsider but a member of a common Kula whose hospitality one has shared.

Tribesmen purchase fellowship through the mutual aid and mutual debt, the mutual helpfulness and mutual dependence of a Kula that all accept will know no final round. The monetised and the modern are no different in the conscious strategies they employ, the non-calculative patterns they repeat, that *de facto* buy them into alliances in a sequence over time. This is true at the level of dyadic reciprocity, of the stable group, and of the generalised other as well.

Thus, in the dyadic case, a neighbour extends a dinner invitation in the expectation of a counter gift. Jill sends Jack a birthday card because Jack sends Jill the equivalent in exchange. The parent cares for the child when young because the child will later care for the parent when old. The dyadic case is face-to-face interaction. People repay those who have underwritten and affirmed and helped in the past.

The stable group is different from the dyad in that, like the Kula, the structure *sui generis* has a continuity of its own. Transfers in the face of such persistence look forward and backward at least as much as at the self. Boulding gives the example of the time-dominated family, where A enjoys B's kindness and then passes on the benevolence to C: 'Even in modern societies ... serial reciprocity is by no means an insignificant phenomenon. It is very important, for instance, in the relations of the generations. The debt we owe to our parents is not often repaid to them but to our children instead, who in turn pay the debt they owe us to their children.' (Boulding, 1981:32). Morally speaking, the commitments are tit-for-tat. In the legalistic sense, the nexus is under-defined. The transfers are separated and non-contractual. The reciprocation is deferred and imprecise. The beneficiaries are recognisably not – yet – the donors who have borne the cost.

The generalised other involves an extension of the stable group to embrace the unknown stranger who is despite his irremediable anonymity for all that one of us. Today's Earl has an ancestral hall where portraits remind him what his forebears have done for his name. Today's Englishman has a similar if also a multiparty bond with Shakespeare who gave the world *Hamlet* and Popper who showed that not all swans are white. We are, as Boulding explains it, but one small link in the unfinished and unbroken chain: 'We inherit ... from the society around us cathedrals, literature, pictures, music, the great achievements of the past that are part of our heritage. The principle of serial reciprocity comes into play here, for those who are aware of this inheritance acquire a sense of community with the past and hence also with the future; they become concerned not only with conserving but also with increasing the inheritance that is passed on to the next generation.' (Boulding, 1981:39). Today's Earl knows that posterity will not thank him for over-grazing a commons that was given to him in trust. Today's Englishman knows that every Pinter improves the quality of the fabric and every polluter runs down the stock that is ours and not his to use up.

Ongoing structures make good Kantians, willing to do what is right for the generalised other, prepared to abstain from self-seeking exploitation that would take advantage of the other's vulnerability. Embedded social altruists avoid the premature depletion of oil, coal and gas so that future generations will have as much and as good of their irreplaceable scarce resources. Autonomy expressed through the offer of equal respect leads the present cohort to honour the budget deficit and the pension plans that were handed on without consultation by the past. The confidence that future strangers will continue the cooperation that current strangers have inherited inspires blood donors to do their part because they go in faith: 'In not asking for or expecting any payment of money these donors signified their belief in the willingness of other men to act altruistically in the future.' (Titmuss, 1970:269). Titmuss in his study of sociability transfused with blood argued that the alternative to voluntary donorship was inadequate supply, a high price and the stranger gift of hepatitis or syphilis passed on free by Skid Row blood sellers who knew no life but 'ooze for booze'. Blood sellers, concealing a history of drugs or AIDS in order to maximise their revenues, were not giving a Pareto-optimal answer to the Kantians' question 'What would happen if everyone behaved that way?' Blood altruists, Titmuss concluded, were more likely than were blood merchants to deliver a product that was functional for the physical health of the patient even as it was functional for the moral health of the group.

6.3.2   Dysfunction

Altruism is attractive and selfishness is mean. It would be an appealing result if it could be shown that economic adaptation is better favoured by social duty and social sympathy than it is by the butcher, the brewer and the baker in the service of the invisible hand. Ethics being the Good Life while gain-seeking is only lunch, the temptation must be a strong one to predict that the Good Samaritan will also be the best economist. Such an inference, sadly enough, is too general and too confident to pick up the multiple turnings of the economic middle mix. Altruism in some circumstances is as self-evidently functional as a phone call to the police when a neighbour's house is being ransacked by thieves. Altruism in other circumstances, however, is less obviously the best means to the attainment of the collectivity's end.

Altruism in respect of one group can, for one thing, mean betrayal in respect of another. A sensitive employer offers a Kantian wage when he could easily pay his unskilled labour what its marginal product is really worth – but he in consequence of the supra-competitive remuneration creates fewer new jobs for young entrants, the unemployed, the excluded and the desperately deprived. A forward-looking union decides against the blackmail of a strike lest short-sighted acquisitiveness deprive future cohorts of work – but its passive complacency towards cheap labour then retards the adoption of labour-saving machinery that would in the long run have meant higher living-standards for all classes of society. A conscientious doctor clings without deviation to the professional code that protects his patient from the pathologies of unequal knowledge – but the unintended outcomes of his self-insurance through convention are the higher charges and the resistance to improvement that are the anti-social by-products of the corporate monopoly. Altruism in cases like these allows one group to give expression to its sense of moral commitment. It also deprives the surrounding 'group of groups' of economic wellbeing such as might have represented the greater net benefit.

Altruism is always problematic once the knock-on ramifications have been taken into account. The poor if guaranteed a citizen's minimum income might decide not to train, to re-train, to limit family size, to search for work. Criminals spared the deterrent of punishment by a permissive society that weights the present so highly as to crowd out the future might see no disincentive to a long-run increase in the supply of misery. Salaried managers ranking the interests of society above the goals of the profit-recipients put money into emission control and the sponsorship of the arts which the shareholders might wish to see invested in business-expanding plant. Generous parents saving obsessively for their children's future might be a cause of slow growth in a consumption-starved present-day, of graduate unemployment in a machine-poor nation that needs industrial investment but has enough of skills. Altruism in some circumstances will push outwards the consumption possibility frontier. In others, however, it will rein in the expansion of wellbeing to an extent that will cause sincere philanthropists to call for an early return to the butcher, the brewer and the baker who did without benevolence but got the job done.

Wellbeing is private, personal and subjective. The gift relationship, on the other hand, refracts the beneficiary's sensations through the donor's own frame of reference. It is easy to assume that the person who is targeted for a gift will necessarily be pleased with the result. To the extent that he is not – to the extent that the life-holder finds the intervention meddlesome, ill-informed and unwelcome – the uninvited altruism will be seen by the person whose pain is the focus as dysfunctional to his attempt to retain his dignity and his independence: 'For the most part he must live his own life; others are not in a position to live it for him, nor is he in a position to lead theirs. Sometimes, indeed, attempts at positive assistance will themselves constitute objectionable interference, if the activity is one in which autonomy, spontaneity, and originality are important. People who are painting, or writing poetry, or making love, will usually be ungrateful for assistance.' (Nagel, 1970:129). The gift of food to a starving man will usually be appreciated even if it is accompanied by a compulsory sermon. The gift of a subsidised education provided that the supplicant abandons drama in favour of computing is a more difficult case. Wanting education but wanting drama more, the student who refuses the grant might actually end up on a higher plane of wellbeing, self-perceived, than he would have reached had he surrendered his goal-setting autonomy to a sacrificing Samaritan with a strong line in solipsism.

Solipsism is a philosophical position which, denying the reality of knowledge of any other person but oneself, makes Ego's own experiences the sole basis for the meanings that Ego ascribes to Alter. An acceptance of the first-person psychology of the solipsist standpoint necessarily suggests that Ego is relieving not Alter's headache but Ego's own. Ego may be said to be extrapolating from one consciousness to another consciousness on the assumption that pleasure and pain do not require extensive personalisation before a species gift can be made. To the extent that the variance is limited, Ego's assumption may be said to be a reasonable one. To the extent that Alter's conceptions are not intelligible to Ego, there is, however, a real risk that the gift will be dysfunctional if Alter and not Ego is indeed the being of whom the welfare is the *raison d'être* for the transfer.

Economic inefficiency is a further reason why an overdose of benevolence can do serious harm. Titmuss, arguing from blood, said that cost and waste fall, quantity and quality rise, where a country looks to the Good Samaritan for its effective supply. Roberts and Wolkoff, on the other hand, maintain that a self-correcting blood market provides the better guarantee that operations will not have to be postponed or non-price rationing rules introduced: 'A more effective approach would be to allow individuals to capture more tangible personal benefits in exchange for donating blood. Approaches based on increasing the personal reward for giving are likely to increase supply and allow collectors to be more selective in the blood they use.' (Roberts and Wolkoff, 1988:177). Poor remuneration is an incentive only to the down-and-out: in such a situation an appeal to community spirit and universal commitment is functional precisely because the pecuniary reward is inadequate to correct the shortage. Market-clearing compensation would bring in a better class of seller: paid in money, in theatre tickets, in tax rebates, in education vouchers, in blood insurance itself, high-quality bleeders will rush to match supply to demand if the blood buyers meet their price. Roberts and Wolkoff state that voluntary donorship in the sense of Titmuss only corrects a market failure that a failure to trust the market has itself created. They recommend a return to the wisdom of the butcher, the brewer and the baker lest patients, untreated, die for lack of blood.

The externality of contamination is a blood-borne threat. One solution is ethics: consider Titmuss's contention that non-commercial donors are the more likely to reveal a medical history that could jeopardise the recovery of the beneficiary. Another solution is profits. Blood businesses could be required in law to screen all blood: testing imposes cost but it also protects against cross-infection. Blood businesses could be made fully liable for the diswelfares they pass on: 'Because neither hospitals nor blood banks and their supply sources are legally responsible for contaminated blood', Johnson writes of a Wild West blood market that knows no regulator, 'they have no incentive to pay higher prices to obtain a better quality of blood.' (Johnson, 1982:103). Where legal rules are lax and spillovers lie where they fall, social rules in the sense of Titmuss might well be the best game in town. Where, however, legal institutions provide an appropriate constitution for procurement, there altruism could safely be returned to the world of morality and not made a second-rate make-do chosen because supply and demand have produced precisely the outcomes that an exemption from prosecution and an indifference to internalisation would lead the economist to expect.

Benevolence is often invoked because the business alternative has not been given an open road. Blood for transfusion is one case where the efficiency of the gift can, conceptually speaking, be equalled or even exceeded by the performance of a gain-seeking market given the freedom to maximise within enabling rules. It is not the only case. Corneas could be pre-sold by utilitarian cornea-holders who want to spend on themselves: 'The most feasible method for establishing a market in cadaveric organs would be to structure it as a futures market – that is, the right to harvest a person's organs upon death must be purchased from him while he is alive and well.' (Hansmann, 1989:62). One kidney could be alienated by a two-kidney merchant who knows that the risk of death is higher on the roads: 'Any individual who would agree to sell would evidently rather have the money than have the slightly greater chance of avoiding the death or illness that would result from keeping the kidney.' (Hansmann, 1989:73). Babies could be bred for adoption by women who see no reason why they should not sell their bodies in this way rather than some other. Votes in national elections could become commercial tradeables that the impoverished could exchange for the money that would contribute so much more to their utility.

Benevolence is often invoked in cases like these despite the fact that business too has the power to do good. The result is a division of labour which sceptics will call the tyranny of the *status quo*. Hair and sperm can be bought and sold as business assets. Heart and liver must remain stranger-gifts through the donor card. Miners and divers can gamble with their lives for a danger differential. Kidney merchants are told that the needs of the patient suffering painful dialysis because a matching organ may not be bought for money must not be taken into account. Hansmann, approximating the kidney to Adam Smith's meat, beer and bread, sees no reason for life-saving trades to be blocked off because social taboos and remembered ruts prevent demand and supply from entering into a mutually-satisfying compact. There is an inference, he writes, 'that such transactions are efficient in the economic sense – that is, that the organ is worth more to the recipient than it is to the donor – and thus that there will commonly be a price that will make both donor and recipient better off even in the absence of altruism.' (Hansmann, 1989:72). If such transactions are welfare enhancing, there is a strong sense that they should be allowed. There is also a strong sense that deep-seated convention and unthinking inertia should not be permitted to come between business and its power to do good.

This is not to say that the gift of blood or the gift of candour will never be the more functional option, only that benevolence will sometimes be the better buy but at other times the second choice that does not maximise the return. Here as elsewhere, it is likely, the truth is the open mind and the desired pragmatism that of Jevons when he wrote as follows about the most suitable tool for the job in hand: 'We can lay down no hard and fast rules, but must treat every case in detail upon its merits.' (Jevons, 1882:vii). Even the gift relationship, where it is less effective than the next-best foregone, might have to be rejected by an economising community that judges the Good Samaritan not by his motivation but by the outcomes that he delivers. The victim robbed on that famous road to Jericho had, economically speaking, only himself to blame. Rather than waiting for the *ex machina* of an altruist, he should have privatised his own welfare and carried a knife.

7. Malevolence

Economic man is concerned with profit-seeking and consumption. Malevolent man concentrates his attention on the crippling of his fellows. Economic man labours for personal uplift and advancement: Ego's utility is a function of Ego's own progress. Malevolent man is focused on debasement and disadvantage: Ego's satisfaction is heightened by Alter's definitive fall. Economic man, 'splendidly neutral to others', is concerned '*only* with the bundle of goods and services he is to receive.' (Collard, 1978:6). Malevolent man, involved and alert, is hungry at best for the acquisitive transfers of deception and malversation, at worst for the destructive creativity of arson, murder, mutilation and disfigurement.

Economic man wants Ego to go up. Malevolent man wants Alter to go down. The third ideal type is altruistic man, caring and kind. David Collard, attracted as he is by the self-denial that puts resources into the collection box, is prepared nonetheless to come down in favour of economic man where the alternative to detachment would be not the gift relationship of St. Anthony but the misanthropy of Hitler's genocide and the paranoia of Stalin's purges: 'To be sure, economic man is incapable of sympathy, benevolence or love. But he is also incapable of envy, malevolence or hatred... Self-interest, it may therefore be argued, is a neutral or middle assumption and certainly morally more attractive than envy, malice or hatred.' (Collard, 1978:6). Stranded in the minimax between Titmuss and Hobbes, the butcher, the brewer and the baker have at least this to be said in their favour, that they keep the peace. In a world where Alter's cattle can be stolen or poisoned in order that Ego's herd might appear the more significant, the businessman's indifference to another's suffering becomes somewhat less of a chilly dystopia than it would be were the alternative to Economic Man necessarily the Good Samaritan and not the Machiavellian Iago with an axe to grind.

The economics of malevolence is the subject of this chapter. Its worst-case scenario is taken from Adam Smith: 'Such, it seems, is the natural insolence of man, that he almost always disdains to use the good instrument, except when he cannot or dare not use the bad one.' (Smith, 1776:II, 321). Section 1, The destruction motive, considers the psychological and biological underpinnings of envy, malice or hatred. Section 2, Market and malevolence, returns to the invisible hand to ask if gain-seeking capitalism can itself be held responsible for the hard-heartedness and the insensitivity. Section 3, The political economy of other people, assesses the social institutions that are built upon the foundations of love and war, of Chapter 6 and Chapter 7.

7.1   THE DESTRUCTION MOTIVE

The thrust is affectual, the threat a symbolic one. It is in the nature of the destruction motive that it seeks first and foremost to eliminate, only secondarily to redistribute and reallocate. Assassination ranked above theft, the distinctive utility is therefore the pure harvest of *Schadenfreude* that is the compensation paid to the second string for the identity spoiled through not being the best. The first part of this section explores the origins of the impulse to pull down. The second part examines the link, however loose, between the desire to cause hurt and the wish to be fair.

7.1.1   The Seeds of Destruction

The destruction motive may have its roots in the biologically-based struggle for food or sexual partners. Conspicuous aggression ('picking a fight') might in that sense be a success symbol like an expensive car, a message conveyed to a female making a choice that one protector is better placed than another to provide for her and her children. Sexual inadequacy ('penis envy') may be a related force in accounting for the neurotic resentments, even the castration fantasies, that Freudians ascribe to women who wish they were men, the old who think that the young have more fun. The selfish gene measures its performance by the number of its offspring: Solomon's judgement is absolutely at one with the Darwinian expectation that the lioness will not devour her own cub and the real mother will always prefer a live descendant to a half-share in a posterity wiped out. The selfish gene also knows that one bucket going down may be the *sine qua non* for another bucket coming up: where middle-class children have an educational head start only so long as less-privileged children do not share their grammar and their public schools, the parents of the haves will fight tooth-and-claw to circumscribe the life-chances of would-be competitors with an eye on a limited supply of executive opportunities. Limited endowments make unattainable the across-the-board diffusion of what the civilised Locke, justifying appropriation, called 'enough, and as good left in common for others.' (Locke, 1690:288). Economics and business, concerned as they are with scarce resources upon which survival itself depends, must at least in the short-run be front-line outlets for the release of age-old instincts.

Intra-family relationships too can shape the anxieties that find their expression in the destruction motive. The son and the father may see each other as rivals for the mother's love: consider the Oedipus complex and its representation in the killing of Laius at the crossroads. The daughter may be jealous of the mother who shares with her the father's affection: Clytemnestra and Aegisthus lost their lives because Electra could not compromise on revenge. The siblings may spend their formative childhood in perpetual fear that parental support will be redistributed to a competitor: the slaying of Abel by Cain, the betrayal of Joseph by his brothers, illustrate the kind of hostility that adults can spend the rest of their lives in defusing – or in acting out.

The phenomenon is a time-dominated trend, that destruction as well as construction has its origins in the home. The children of today are evidently also the children of tomorrow. The child's resentment of another child's superiority, the child's experience of early bullying and sustained mockery, the child's weakness and defencelessness *vis-à-vis* the parent's absolute discretion – a past remembered in cases such as these can inspire the achievement-starved to pull themselves up but it can also encourage the chronically insecure to get even for history's slights by means of smashing and putting down. Childhood in many respects may be regarded as a consumer durable that lasts a lifetime. An obsession with pecking order, the first strike fight for rank, the nightmare vision of humiliation on the way, all are instances where reflexes conditioned in early life may mark out the top-flight executive as a maladjusted candidate for the psychoanalyst's chair.

Later in life as well as early on in life, the destruction motive can be fostered by low self-esteem and a self-poisoning self-hatred which, wavering between the masochism of suicide and the sadism of homicide, ultimately converts Ego's shame and guilt into a malicious assault on Alter for having been directly responsible for Ego's failure, self-perceived. The Jews are scape-goated for pound-of-flesh pricing, outsiders' assiduity and synagogue favouritism such as somehow keep out go-ahead true *bumiputras*. The capitalists are blamed for retaining the value surplus when the truth is that their indolence in their villas is matched by the wasted lives of the lumps of labour used up in their mills. The rich are accused of witchcraft and black magic by the poor who complain that they at least were decent enough to play by the rules. Economic analysis will be able to make a detached assessment of the business practices that are the explicit grounds for the assault. The destruction motive is less intellectual. Taking a still photograph of the unequal outcomes, the destruction motive tends to victimise success and to stigmatise deviance for no less emotive a reason, more the heart than the head, that they are seen as a lion in a path that is not the lion's own.

Because *it is*, therefore *I am not I*. In the case of the destruction motive, this perception in itself can be enough to bring about a radical levelling down. Rage and indignation at once result from self-pity and lead on to self-righteousness. Importantly, however, for that vindictiveness to be translated into aggression, there must be a fundamental lack of self-confidence accompanying the anguished discovery that others have run faster in the race. The fit runner resolves to train harder in order to win in a subsequent round. Only the embittered loser blinds a fellow painter or cuts off the hand of a famous musician.

Destruction is annihilation in preference to appropriation. It has to be such. Were Ego to be dispossessed, were Ego's assets to be transferred into the property of Alter, Alter would then acquire the responsibility for keeping the beautiful body beautiful and the encyclopaedic mind absolutely up to date. To do what is needed would be tiring and stressful – and even then there would be no guarantee of success. Thence the attraction of targeting the high flyers and cutting them down to the size of the average. If Ego can't have it, reasons Ego, then no else should have it either. The shop is looted and the shopkeeper closes down. Inconvenient as it is to have no shop at all, at least the Chinese, the Indian and the Korean will no longer be in a position to make money out of us.

7.1.2   Destruction and Justice

The destruction motive is a topic in psychological illness. The self-critical and the over-sensitive, obsessive about comparison and threatened by excellence, launch an attack on the brightest flowers because they win a disproportionate share of scarce social approbation. The destruction motive is not a topic in philosophical justification. Malevolence is about one person's joy at another person's loss. It is not about enhancing the stock of equity in the society.

Few people, however, are prepared to confess to repressed anxieties: they prefer to use verbal rationalisations which make them appear moral crusaders against unjust institutions rather than to admit that they have been reduced to the level of jealous neurotics by Shakespeare's 'green-eyed monster which doth mock the meat it feeds on'. Most people, moreover, lack the intellectual *finesse* that is required to distinguish between laudable resentment when conduct is unjust and self-punishing rancour when another does well: they run together the destruction motive and the justice motive, effectively because the two different mindsets are by no means easy to separate out in the darkness of the subjectivity. Whatever the reasons, as John Rawls points out, the overlap between the moral and the immoral is a social fact: 'The appeal to justice is often a mask for envy. What is said to be resentment may really be rancor.' (Rawls, 1971:540). The motives are different. Superficially, however, they look alike.

Great care must evidently be taken to distinguish the destruction motive from the justice motive in the rhetoric of which the pulling down is so commonly clothed. When we say that a person is 'too big for his boots', we are implying that he is guilty of arrogance, vanity, bragging, showing off – of hubris, in other words, that is well deserving of Nemesis in the form of social control. What we do not say is that 'the bigger they are, the harder they fall' – that it is *our* boots and not *their* boots that we are thinking about, that we will feel a sense of relief once the source of our second-rateness has been struck down by the lightning that always prefers the taller trees. We say equity. We mean vandalism. Our rhetoric is not what it seems.

One concept can be unfairly employed to legitimise another. The fact that it can be misapplied does not, however, mean that it has no proper application. Sometimes we say equity because we mean vandalism. Sometimes, less insidiously, we say equity because we mean equity. Where it is justice that we are making our highest-ranked objective, any levelling that we propose will not be the demolition of construction as an end in itself so much as the negation of the negation that is represented by unfairness. Such a positive-minded negation is no more an instance of the destruction motive than would be the intervention of the surgeon to cut out a diseased appendix. The operative incentive is here not the destruction motive but the justice motive. The case can be made on one of two levels: endstates and procedures.

At the level of *endstates*, the focus could be on a 'deduction' from value-added seized whenever the idle rentier or the absentee landowner opts to reap where he never sowed. It could also be on the stock of assets. Plato in *The Laws* advises that the dispersion in wealth holdings be capped at 4:1: a greater inequality would be unmerited in terms of talents and dysfunctional for the sense of community that to Plato is more valuable than material affluence. St. Paul, strong on fellowship and committed to service – 'We must be regarded as Christ's subordinates and as stewards of the secrets of God' (1 *Corinthians* 4:1-2) – emphasised that God's will was to be done on earth as well as in Heaven and that consuming without producing was a betrayal of trust: 'The man who will not work shall not eat.' (2 *Thessalonians* 2:10). Karl Marx, more recently, was sharply critical of profit-recipients who alienate the surplus value generated exclusively by labour power: 'Capital... consists in living labour serving accumulated labour as a means for maintaining and increasing the exchange value of the latter... It is indeed just this noble reproductive power which the worker surrenders to the capitalist in exchange for the means of subsistence received. He has, therefore, lost them for himself.' (Marx, 1842:266). Plato, St. Paul and Karl Marx all had a clear perception of the outcomes that *ought not to be*. In preaching justice, they were clear in their own minds that they were not preaching spite.

At the level of *procedures*, the proponent of justice will ask not if the prizes are excessive but if the race is fair. This is why Buchanan, as was explained in

Chapter 3.3, would legitimate destinations in terms of rules and rules in terms of consent: 'A "fair rule" is one that is agreed to by the players in advance of play itself, before the particularized positions of the players come to be identified. Note carefully what this definition says: a rule is fair if players agree to it. It does not say that players agree because a rule is fair.' (Buchanan, 1986:126). A normative framework agreed to in the ignorance of endstate that precedes the contest is, Buchanan says, the sole test of whether the final outcomes can appeal for legitimation to the baseline consensus of precommitment and meta-contract.

We as a community might deny that a result is acceptable if there has been a violation in the condition of equal starting points and abstention from sabotage that is the obligation entered into by each gamesman when he pits himself against his fellows: 'In the race for wealth, and honours, and preferments, he may run as hard as he can, and strain every nerve and every muscle, in order to outstrip all his competitors. But if he should justle, or throw down any of them, the indulgence of the spectators is entirely at the end. It is a violation of fair play, which they cannot admit of.' (Smith, 1759:120). We as a community might insist that a result is acceptable even if as unachieved as the luck of a lottery so long as all the contestants were given an equal opportunity to become unequal and all had decided in advance that the winners were to be allowed to retain their gains: 'The equality before the law which freedom requires leads to material inequality ... Equality before the law and material equality are therefore not only different but are in conflict with each other.' (Hayek, 1960:87). Importantly, however, we as a community, having decided on our constitution, must tolerate the outcomes and not begrudge the successes. The rules being fair, the possession too is fair. The fact that the same prize is coveted by all the players is not a reason *ex post* to share out the rewards. Unless, of course, that is what we promised each other *ex ante* that we would do.

The justice motive is not the same as the destruction motive. At the endstate level the outcomes may be deemed to be out of line with respected evaluatory standards. At the procedural level the rules may be held not to have been validated by agreement or followed in practice. Where an injustice is identified on either of these levels, there destructive action to root out the abuse is evidence not of ill-will unleashed but of the constructive desire to correct a flaw.

Destructive action need not be the consequence of malevolence intended. Sometimes, however, it will be. Then verbal aggression in forms such as sarcasm and criticism will act in combination with physical expropriation and institutional appeasement to level down the gifted in order to equalise up the mediocre. Fernandez, citing Seneca's *Epistle to Lucilius* - 'The less the success, the less the envy' (V, 42); 'Envy is a pernicious dart directed at the best' (VIII, 74) – is in no doubt as to what this means: 'To punish the best is always more feasible than to produce the best. The easiest electoral promise to fulfil is to satisfy the envious by punishing the envied.' (Fernandez de la Mora, 1987:96).

The superior person could be seen as an ally and an exemplar. Instead he is made an enemy and victimised for sport: 'Emulation moves to lift oneself, envy to break other people. The envious one does not find dominant the desire to be more, but rather to make the other less; there is no will to improve, but rather to level all.' (Fernandez de la Mora, 1987:68). Discontentment could be a spur to productivity. In the case of envy it is negative and nothing else: 'It does not incite to create, but to cancel out, not to establish hierarchies but uniformities; envy does not move toward anything positive.' (Fernandez de la Mora, 1987:83).

Envy, Fernandez writes, 'is the pain we feel at the happiness of others, a happiness that is seen as superior to ours, that we desire, that is inaccessible and cannot be assimilated.' (Fernandez de la Mora, 1987:123). Their happiness is the cause of the pain. The destruction of that happiness is an obvious response to the imputation of a pleasure deficit. Obvious or not, Fernandez states, it is an avenue which must not be explored: 'In order to cure envy, the envied does not need to be generous – he must be miserable. This is the only thing we cannot ask from humans who are intrinsically and essentially made for happiness.' (Fernandez de la Mora, 1987:117). The envious person will invoke justice to provide legitimation for his destructiveness. He will do so in vain. Having no right to that which he desires, his appeal to a justice motive will be no more than an exercise in injustice which fails to conceal the underlying frustration that is the true cause of the humbling, the debunking, the cutting down.

7.2   MARKET AND MALEVOLENCE

There is a sense in which it is true to say that the modernisation of traditional *stasis* into the acquisitive individualism of market capitalism is an institutional development that is likely on balance to keep divisive negativities well in check. There is a countervailing sense in which the evolution into the market economy is believed to throw up such obstacles to peaceable utility-seeking as to make recrudescent malevolence yet another, Schumpeter-like, of the market order's self-threatening contradictions. This section asks if the universalisation of upgrading will commonly be accompanied by the equalisation of misery when a society steers its course from ascription to achievement, from status to contract.

The market economy is dependent for its success upon differential reward payable for differential contribution. Handicaps imposed on talent and effort are clearly incompatible with its incentive structure; while the persecution of the non-normal and the exceptional leads to a clustering around the mean which is a discouragement to the innovativeness, the novelty, the 'creative destruction' that is the very essence of the profit-seeking dynamic. The market economy is the world of anonymous competitiveness, ambitious materialism, negotiated exchange, value for money. A world in which sustained performance means rising living-standards whereas envying destructiveness means stagnation or something worse, tolerant acknowledgement may reasonably be expected to be the rule of the day, spiteful tearing down to wither away because it lacks a social function.

Affluence means an improvement in the quantity and quality of the goods and services that fall within the choice-set of the representative consumer. Absolute deprivation is not the same as relative standing, and Adam Smith was therefore right to make a clear distinction between neediness and jealousy when he wrote as follows about social distance and social disharmony: 'The affluence of the rich excites the indignation of the poor, who are often both driven by want, and prompted by envy, to invade his possessions.' (Smith: 1776:II, 232). Smith's message is in his 'and'. It is not a comforting diagnosis. That said, absolute upgrading does alleviate the 'want' of all those of the poverty-stricken who manage to secure a place on the escalator of economic growth. Economic growth in that way serves as an important safety-valve for invidious comparison which in a less prosperous community might have caused the hungry to storm the palace.

Meritocratic capitalism relies upon an open road to squeeze the greatest efficiency from its labour pool. Conservatives might have mixed feelings about the maximisation of life-chances diffused throughout the population as a whole. Not so the capitalists: desperate for profits, they call for good education even for the present-day's have-nots in order to ensure that gifts, talents and natural endowments will be freed to find their most lucrative outlets. This is not to deny that there can and will be envy on the part of those left behind. The point is simply that there are likely to be fewer chips on fewer shoulders than would be the case in a pre-capitalist or a command society where the excluded, held back, know that they don't stand a chance.

The market economy, again, may be able to neutralise the destructiveness of malevolence to the extent that the flaunting of conspicuous consumption gives way to secrecy and private enjoyment. Designer labels are an invitation to envy. Bank balances, share portfolios, fine wines consumed in the home, a Matisse original on the bedroom wall, all come within the protective rubric of 'out of sight, out of mind'. Comparison is most of all divisive where the differences are put on show. History is the antidote to the poison where the evolution of capitalism entails a transition from the self-publicised to the unseen, the quiet and the confidential.

Non-capitalist man knows enough to conceal his wealth rather than using it for display: 'In Haiti, G.E. Simpson found that a peasant will seek to disguise his true economic position by purchasing several smaller fields rather than one large piece of land. For the same reason he will not wear good clothes. He does this intentionally to protect himself against the envious black magic of his neighbours.' (Schoeck, 1969:47). The under-developed peasant under-reports his economic success lest visible truth-telling attract to him the Evil Eye. The vanguard capitalist American, Galbraith would argue, can hardly be said to be a world away in his tendency increasingly to dispense with the blatant boast: 'With the decline of ostentation, or its vulgarization, wealth and hence inequality were no longer flagrantly advertised. Being less advertised they were less noticed and less resented.' (Galbraith, 1958:102). The British experience, Anthony Crosland reported in the rampant consumerism of the post-war boom, had been the same: 'Ostentation is becoming vulgar; rich men tend to disclaim their wealth; and a general modesty in consumption becomes the fashion. This naturally reinforces the trend towards equality in outward style of life.' (Crosland, 1956:214). It is arguably the seen distance and not the statistical difference that causes the greater envy on the part of the disappointed. The verdict of Galbraith and Crosland is therefore a welcome one, that the evolution of the market economy is such that it is favourable to the hidden inequality and not to the exaggerated frivolities of Veblen's *nouveaux riches*.

Mass production results in mass consumption. Consumer credit and rising incomes facilitate the inclusion but it is economies of scale that are at the core of the convergence. Thus do e-mail messages, Internet chat-rooms and boy-band recordings produce a common identity and a common culture which reduce the felt gap that separates the status groups.

New substitutes contribute still further to the perceived levelling: 'Bourbon is almost as palatable as Scotch, South African as Spanish sherry, and tinned as fresh asparagus.' (Crosland, 1956:213). Big has a car. Little has a car. Big holidays abroad. Little holidays abroad. The makes and the resorts are not the same. The genus, on the other hand, is recognisably a single one. The likelihood that Little will accuse Big of enjoying the greener grass will presumably be much reduced by the knowledge that both Britons have consumables as well as consumption in common.

Lifestyle homogenisation is an unintended consequence of long production runs reinforced by close but less costly substitutes. With the perceived levelling is likely to come a greater sympathy. It is easier to empathise with a person who shares one's way of life than with a person who is seen as an alien and even a thing. The most optimistic scenario is this: as A's happiness comes to figure with greater frequency in B's utility-function, so benevolence is more likely to come into play and the unproductive passions be challenged by the commensalism and the comradeship that are promoted by the community of consumption in unison. That is the most optimistic scenario. The discussion now turning from the tendency of the market economy to keep malevolent impulses in check to the tendency of capitalism's evolution to cut away at the system's own supports, what will be apparent in the remainder of this section is that there can be more antagonistic scenarios as well.

There is a tendency under market capitalism for reference groups to become wider and self-location to be less a function of birth. Felt social proximity and a perceived reduction in man-made disparities are the likely consequence of the move from ascription to selling, of non-selective comprehensive education, of the universalisation of advertising appeals. The equalisation of opportunities and starts brings the marshal's baton within the dreaming range of the ambitious private. With the greater freedom to succeed goes, however, the greater freedom to fail – and the greater likelihood that Ego will feel envious of Alter who made the grade that Ego found too steep.

Envy is a group-related manifestation. As Choi puts it: 'Envy is most strongly exhibited among people belonging to the same community, and, within that community, among individuals regarded as similar in standing; it is less likely among individuals regarded as members of different classes or different communities.' (Choi, 1993:132). We are less likely to be envious of the king in all his pomp than we are of a fellow fisherman whose catch is good: the neighbour is one of us whereas the king, non-comparable, is bred to be blood and birth apart. Our envy is directed towards our own people and not towards a far-off set with whom we have nothing in common: 'In short, the stronger the sense of group, the stronger the sense of envy.' (Choi, 1993:132). Distance protects: 'A poet is not apt to envy a philosopher, or a poet of a different age.' (Hume, 1739–40:II, 163). Closeness, on the hand, unlocks Pandora's Box.

Distance defuses the tensions. Helmut Schoeck is right to make this statement about the fish-and-fowl society in which the greengrocer's wife is debunked as Lady Muck but the Marchioness of Tewkesbury is followed avidly in the tabloid Sundays: 'In some situations, the best means of protection against the envy of neighbour, colleague or voter is to drive, say, a Rolls-Royce instead of a car only slightly better than his, or, if Brighton is his resort, to choose a world cruise rather than a holiday in Sicily. In other words, overwhelming and astounding inequality, especially when it has an element of the unattainable, arouses far less envy than minimal inequality, which inevitably causes the envious man to think: '"I might almost be in his place".' (Schoeck, 1969:62).

Distance defuses the tensions. Closeness, on the other hand, makes the relativities more of a corrosive: 'Envy develops among equals or those who are almost equal.' (Schoeck, 1969:220). That is why the very success of market capitalist evolution might be a cause of concern to all those who believe that there is more to the relationship between the butcher, the brewer and the baker than peaceable exchanging alone. A common idiom and the career open to the talents widen the reference groups into which each is able to imagine himself. Similarity is promoted and self-presentation democratised. Yet the outcome despite the convergence need not be the non-conflictual utopia of the social democrats and the libertarians alike. Instead it can be resentment and animosity for the very reason that the market order will have succeeded so well in breaking down the social walls that once divided the nation into stable and structured pools.

Market can unleash malevolence to the extent that the open society makes the reference group every person on every street. It can do so as well for the simple reason that change is a hurricane and not a state of rest. The ups and downs of unceasing experimentation generate a status problem for the dot.com technopreneurs, the futures traders, the wheeler-dealers at the coal face of speculative capitalism. That status problem is to deliver not just success but conspicuous proof of success. Veblen's Newport lives on in the world of the *nouveaux riches* which is also the arena where so much of economic progress is engendered.

David Hume, friend and contemporary of Adam Smith, saw scarcity as a function of inter-temporal and interpersonal comparison: 'So little are men govern'd by reason in their sentiments and opinions, that they always judge more of objects by comparison than from their intrinsic worth and value.' (Hume, 1739–40:II, 158). The memory of the historic self gives present peaks and troughs a context: 'Thus the prospect of past pain is agreeable, when we are satisfied with our present condition; as on the other hand our past pleasures give us uneasiness, when we enjoy nothing at present equal to them.' (Hume, 1739–40:II, 161). The basepoint of another's felicity makes our own felicity appear more vivid or more muted through the contrast: 'Objects appear greater or less by a comparison with others ... The misery of another gives us a more lively idea of our happiness, and his happiness of our misery. The former, therefore, produces delight; and the latter uneasiness.' (Hume, 1739–40:II, 160–1). Veblen is not of direct relevance to our own past success recalled. Other people, however, are the more mordant relativity. Hume, reluctant to give economic scarcity an objective meaning, illustrated the propensity to juxtapose with the case of a rich man who 'feels the felicity of his condition better by opposing it to that of a beggar.' (Hume, 1739–40:II, 110). He *feels* his condition because he *sees* his condition. Mental states aside, social actors are obliged to look their parts for their relative position to deliver the requisite utility. Veblen's Newport lives on in competitive capitalism where success is not success if it is not put on show.

Galbraith and Crosland anticipate a domestication of luxury and a decline in public display. Hume and Newport reinstate the imperatives of judgement and grading. Veblen may be *passé* in the relatively administered world of civil servants, hospital pharmacists and university teachers. Not so at the cutting edge of money-making endeavour. The rich in Newport bought villas in Tuscany to show that they were not lagging behind. Present-day profit-seekers will be under analogous pressure not to be so self-deprecating and modest as to miss out on the esteem that is their due. Envy can be the motive. Envy can be the endstate. Destructiveness can be the unintended outcome.

Acceptance keeps the leapfrogging and the jealousies within the finite boundaries that are, Durkheim says, the *sine qua non* for social cohesion: 'What is needed if social order is to reign is that the mass of men be content with their lot. But what is needed for them to be content, is not that they have more or less, but that they be convinced that they have no right to more.' (Durkheim, 1928:200). Justice may or may not be the precondition for tolerance. That is not the issue. The issue is a practical one: how best can the pebble be kept out of the shoe before the irritation begins to inflict real damage on the individual and his social fellows?

One solution, historically speaking, has been the non-rational authority of religious commandment. The Old Testament imposes an injunction on wishful thinking that puts the stability of the tribe at risk: 'You shall not covet your neighbour's house; you shall not covet your neighbour's wife, his slave, his slave-girl, his ox, his ass, or anything that belongs to him.' (*Exodus* 20:16–17). The New Testament preaches Christian charity, neighbourly love and the duty of the Good Samaritan to supply fellowship without stint. The Schoolmen had it that envy was one of the seven 'deadly sins'. The hymn book proclaimed that, the rich man in his castle, the poor man at the gate, '*God* made them high and lowly, and ordered their estate'. Confucianism emphasises personal contentment, inner tranquillity, acceptance of hierarchy, harmonious adjustment. If malevolence is a social problem, then religion, historically speaking, has sought to keep the communion from degenerating into a brawl.

Too much religion, admittedly, can produce a stoicism that is resistant to change, an asceticism which associates consumption with guilt, a traditionalism that makes caste privilege the norm. Too much religion can damp down the ambitiousness and the dissatisfaction which is path-breaking capitalism's most valuable factor of production. The point is simply that too little moral constitutionalism can also have a braking effect on the process of change. Where negative attitudes are a threat to social stability, there even Marx's 'opium of the people' (Marx, 1844b:44) may well be a functional support. That is why the scientism, the secularism, the calculativeness, the acquisitiveness, the individualism of the free market economy must be feared as potentially harmful to the moral capital which keeps the Hobbesian demons in their box.

7.3 THE POLITICAL ECONOMY OF OTHER PEOPLE

On the one hand there is the altruistic desire to help. On the other hand there is the envious urge to destroy. Situated between the life-force and the death-wish is the State.

The government cannot create either Eros or Thanatos *de novo*. What it can do is to respond, to reinforce and to balance. Altruism is one outcome. Policies that contribute to mutual support will be considered in the second part of this section. It is not the only possibility. The new Hobbesianism in which politics prunes back the successes who are blamed for other people's inadequacies makes the first part of this section the story of an equality of misery that cannot reasonably be described as an equality of joy.

7.3.1 Malevolence

The destruction motive can find expression in the nationalisation without compensation of factories, mansions and art-collections. It can lie behind the enforced conversion of intelligence-tested schooling into comprehensive schooling despite the minority stake of the above-average child. It can be the reason for the punitive taxation of capital gains and for confiscatory death-duties that challenge the continuity of family-perpetuating inheritance. In cases such as these the envious could be saying to their State that they are relying on politics to knock down a nail that is sticking up.

The politics of malevolence must not be confused with the politics of equity. Of course it can be justice that balances welfare transfers to the poor with progressive tax rates that impose a disproportionate burden on high-income earners. Of course it can be justice that demands the termination of independent schooling on the grounds that Eton and Harrow unfairly give the privileged child a head start in life's race. Of course it can be justice that enjoins the middle classes to be means-tested out of the child benefits and the prescription rebates for which those who have won prizes in the lottery of life will stand in no real need. What appears on the surface to be the destruction motive might not, in short, be the destruction motive at all. Instead it might be the morally-minded attempt of a justice-furthering collectivity to concentrate what it can do on those whom the consensus identifies as the most deserving of support.

The politics of malevolence bears an undoubted resemblance to the politics of equity. Importantly, however, the will to destroy is an entity in itself, a negative force that is the polar opposite to the fair-minded righting of a previous wrong. Anthony Crosland was one socialist who did not hesitate to acknowledge the psychic benefits that are generated by the trimming down of the taller trees: 'It is sometimes said that one is doing something disgraceful, and merely pandering to the selfish clamour of the mob, by taking account of social envy and resentment. This is not so. These feelings exist, amongst people not morally inferior to those who administer such high-minded rebukes; and they are quite natural.' (Crosland, 1956:135).

Envy and resentment 'exist'. The feelings are 'quite natural'. The people are 'not morally inferior'. Crosland was able in the circumstances to recommend a socially restorative policy of levelling down 'if spirits are to be kept high' (Crosland, 1949:11) and the masses not to be discouraged by excessive achievement. Envy, Crosland believed, 'is a social fact of cardinal importance; and since it makes society less peaceful and contented, it is wrong not to try and adjust affairs in such a way as to minimise the provocation to it.' (Crosland, 1956:136). There is little in the way of public finance that can be expected, Crosland says, from a wealth tax, an unearned income surcharge or a 98 per cent marginal rate. The gain will be realised not through the transfer but through the destruction. The endstate will be a 'spirit of contentment and cooperation amongst the workers' (Crosland, 1949:10) that in Crosland's view made entirely justifiable the socialist economics of deliberate distress.

We close down the private hospitals: more patients must then be treated by the State. We prohibit academic certification: the costs of doing business rise because employers must conduct their own aptitude and intelligence screens. We hunt with the pack to avoid drawing attention to excellence: imitating and copying, we are too dependent, too inhibited, to take new initiatives. We wield the fiscal weapon as if vandalising a neighbour's car: the consequence is less assiduity, less saving, less risk-taking and a slower rate of economic growth. We sabotage outsiders through 'Kauft nicht bei Juden' and employ verbal humiliation to force British Asians to study less hard: we in the long run cause the butcher and the brewer to close down and limit the baker to a narrow and repetitive range of cakes. It can be a source of considerable satisfaction to trip up a competitor whose success feels like a libel or to teach a flamboyant innovator that 'pride goeth before a fall'. As with all economic choices, however, what must be remembered even by the martyred, the paranoid, the victimised, the victimising and the deeply insulted is that the utility is not purchased without a concomitant cost.

The purchase of the malevolent option might be deemed the cost-effective choice. Where it is, State and society will be in agreement that the higher level of final satisfaction well warrants the cutting off the nose to spite the face that is a part of the price. The Jewish professors sent to the gas chambers, the Kampala retailers rusticated initially to Southall and then on to Knightsbridge, our nation will breathe a sigh of relief at having purged itself of resented non-conformists who had made themselves a focus for envy. Economics being economics, however, our nation cannot rationally refuse to count the potential amenity foregone. Eminent scientists are in Auschwitz and Belsen. Valued entrepreneurs are in Southall and Knightsbridge. We as a nation must have lost *something* as a result.

Where the benefit exceeds the cost, the malevolent option will be the utility-maximising choice. Where the cost exceeds the benefit, the destroying asset will be left on the shelf. Where the cost exceeds the benefit, thinking citizens in the triangle delimited by exchange, altruism and annihilation will endorse as healthy some or all of those tendencies and policies that protect the mix of markets and gifts from the depredation of fanatics prepared to go down with the ship.

Acceptance, tolerance, equal respect, enhanced self-respect are all intellectual developments which help to contain the indignation that rankles. Envy poisons the peace of mind as surely as the bee sting kills the bee. Individuals who learn to sublimate their destructive urges will find a reward in stoicism and tranquillity which can exceed the delight they would have experienced at the misfortune and decline of a deviant peer who has failed to under-perform.

Emotional detachment is in a sense the most valuable of all the recommendations that can be made to neutralise the self-destroying determination of the envious to get even. The discovery process of the free market throws up economic endstates which are influenced by luck or randomness at least as much as they are proportioned to ability and achievement. To expect the prizes to gravitate mechanistically to the productivities is to expect the impossible from a tombola of accidents that knows no final term.

Crucially, however, for succeeding endstates to be accepted as tolerable, there must not be procedural inequities that could give rise to the suspicion that Alter had access to 'ill-gotten gains' because Ego, dispossessed, 'never had a chance'. Enforceable rights, equal opportunities, possibly even a welfare State to level up the absolutely impoverished must evidently go hand in hand with any meaningful detachment save that of the most resigned of fatalists. Without good procedures, wins and losses can become exaggerated into discontentment and frustration. Given fair rules, the disappointed will no longer have any reason to blame the victors for their own lack of success.

Equity ensured, game-playing and rivalry can be a cause of mutual respect. Competition need not be the same as competitiveness; and losing athletes are known to be among the most appreciative of a fellow contender's prowess. Particularly will this be so where the sport is enjoyable in itself and where 'personal best' forms an important part of the prize. As with the ludic nature of tournament athletics, so with the intrinsic satisfaction of economic activity. Outlets for creativity, workmanship and self-realisation reduce the salience of the workmate's rent of ability. Team responsibility in place of the production line gives the worker a professional pride in a task recognisably completed. Power-sharing and consultation foster feelings of belonging and self-worth which an authoritarian boss can so easily make into a confrontational struggle for revenge and psychic compensation. Even without the extra-economic detachment of a monk or a guru, it is clear, the residual jealousies that are so resistant to the excellence of elites can be confined to the backwaters and the footnotes simply by making the most of those tendencies and policies that draw upon job satisfaction and the healthy exercise of faculties.

Maslow, taking issue with the misanthropy of the Social Darwinians on life as gladiatorial slaughter and with 'Fall of Man' Christianity on the ubiquity of sin, denies that human nature is inherently evil: 'Destructiveness, sadism, cruelty, malice, etc. seem so far to be not intrinsic but rather they seem to be violent reactions *against* frustration of our intrinsic needs, emotions and capacities.' (Maslow, 1962:3). Physical survival ensured, Maslow argues, the higher needs for creativity, integration, security, respect, approbation become the more pressing imperatives that the economy must seek to satisfy. Denied that satisfaction, stunted development makes the one-dimensional easy prey for demagogues who manipulate the distress into an attack on another's happiness. Offered, however, full *freedom to*, it is individualism itself, positive and constructive, that constitutes the best defence against anger, hatred, hostility and dominance. The human personality has a hierarchy of aspirations that it must fulfil. The best defence against malevolence, Maslow clearly believes, is to ensure that the higher needs are not neglected in favour of a constraining materialism that stands in the way of personal growth.

7.3.2   Benevolence

The State can give in to democratic demands for a politics of malevolence. It can also introduce countervailing policies to shrink the destructiveness that threatens social harmony. Some of those policies (considered in the previous subsection) attack the bedrock evil directly. Others do so through the liberation of outlets for the altruistic and the other-regarding sentiments. This subsection suggests ways in which public policy can increase the ratio of benevolence to malevolence in the nation's stock of attitudinal capital by means of an appeal to the sense of community and the latent pressure to do good.

However strong the altruistic groundswell, businesses will be reluctant to make their sacrifice unless and until they know that their competitors will be subject to a similar handicap. The policy-option of small-group conservatism is one way of protecting social institutions that are productive of confidence.

Organisations which survive for long periods develop robust internal rules and procedures. Elinor Ostrom cites evidence from the Philippines, Japan, Spain, Switzerland and California to show that non-formal standards dating back 100 or even 1000 years have stood the test of time despite political upheaval, drought, famine and the sheer randomness of economic mutation: 'Given the temptations involved, the high levels of conformance to the rules in all these cases have been remarkable.' (Ostrom, 1990:59). People had the chance to over-fish (depleting the food stock) and to over-graze (causing soil erosion and producing a dust-bowl). In a position to steal water in the dry season or to fell timber despite the ecological consequences, what is striking is that people in stable networks with a long-term identity are observed to make a credible commitment – 'I will if you will' – to other-regarding attitudes in defence of common-pool resources. It is a commitment to trustworthiness and duty which a sensible State will do well to weight carefully before it privatises the village commons or re-settles the population in high-wage industrial districts.

Conservatism hands on the practices. The small group monitors the deviations, anarchically develops its tit-for-tat, informally imposes its sanctions for the infraction of a social norm. The result is self-denial and voluntary service as the direct consequence of conventions and precedents enforced by the principals themselves: 'Because of the repeated situations involved in most organized processes, individuals can use contingent strategies in which cooperation will have a greater chance of evolving and surviving. Individuals frequently are willing to forgo immediate returns in order to gain larger joint benefits when they observe many others following the same strategy.' (Ostrom, 1990:39). Because the rules have a history, we know that head-enders should not take more than their fair share of scarce irrigation. Because the club is transparent, we recognise who is not present to drain a marsh or raise a barn. People are powerful. The past is powerful. Mutual aid in support of shared benefits is the win-win result.

Precedents have benefits, but they also have costs. Even in the case of small-group conservatism, failure and expense constitute an ever-present threat to joint exploitation: 'One cannot view communal property in these settings as the primordial remains of earlier institutions evolved in a land of plenty. If the transactions costs involved in managing communal property had been excessive, compared with private-property institutions, the villagers would have had many opportunities to devise different land-tenure arrangements.' (Ostrom, 1990:61). On the one hand there is the snowball momentum of the length of time: we reason 'if it ain't broke, don't fix it' and carry on as before because of a low discount rate that values continuity. On the other hand there is the financial overhead of doing the uneconomic: rational maximisation suggests that a new rule should be put in the place of an old one where the evidence confirms that the going concern has an absolute disadvantage. Even a believer in the ethical *de facto* would have to accept that no rule is safe forever from the encroachment of supply and demand merely because it is old – or because it is ours.

Common-pool resources, Ostrom states openly, are less productive than their profit-orientated counterparts: 'CPR situations are rarely as powerful in driving participants – even survivors – toward efficiency as are competitive markets. Nor is there any single variable, such as market price, that can be used as the foundation for making rational choices in a CPR environment.' (Ostrom, 1990:207). Taken literally, and assuming that reliable data is readily accessible, the Swiss mountain village ought to be packing its bags. In reality there are reasons for thinking that institutions that separate the *quid* from the *quo* have a reasonable shelf-life even where supply and demand *ceteris paribus* would deliver a higher rate of return.

Some public goods, for one thing, have private good properties as well. It is in the nature of a closed community that the social sanctions of disapproval and ostracism can act to insulate the collectivity from diswelfares like duplicity, litter and pollution. Such sanctions have the character of a tax or price. In the limit they have the character of a prohibition: a doctor or architect pooling secretarial and other overheads with professional associates will find himself excluded altogether from the partnership where his long-distance phone calls and his failure to contribute to the coffee fund makes his office more costly than his business rivals. Also, in the outside market, the label of rectitude can be an economic investment. No one in a trading sequence that has a past and a future can afford to deplete to zero the reputation and the trust upon which his standing and his livelihood must inevitably depend.

Joint-use institutions can be protected by interdependence, interest and time remembered. They can also be protected by a citizen-following State which recognises that mutual agreement and social capital will sometimes not be enough to promulgate the set of rules that the separate units most want to see. Where the group is large and the individual unit but a drop in the ocean, spontaneity lets the community down and formal law rather than informal institutions can be the only way of generating predictable coordination in line with the unanimity of consensus.

State control is superior to self-control where discreteness releases the free riders who see no economic reason to do their part. People who cannot be excluded from the benefit will not find it attractive to contribute to the cost. It is in acknowledgement of this threat to the gift relationship that Mancur Olson, stating that the prudent calculator 'has no incentive to sacrifice any more than he is forced to sacrifice' (Olson, 1965:11), makes a recommendation for democratic coercion as the Pareto-optimal choice. I will give my vote if you give your vote. I will pay my tax if you pay your tax. I will join the union if you join the union. I will refrain from first-strike use of my nuclear arsenal if you like me agree to mutual security through sensors and observers. Strategy and secrecy give way to statutes and regulations; and the reason here is an electorate-following leadership that knows when automaticity is likely to fall short. Compulsion by consent is not the same as the dominance of a Leviathan. Generally acceptable and the response to a demand, across-the-board binding gives the devolved and the decentralised the freedom to donate the *quid* without the *quo* that is in their own estimation the highest-valued choice.

The State as coordinator ensures that small-scale unilateralism will be forthcoming as expected. The State as choice-maker can do much more. In some cases the individual units have no wish or incentive to participate at all in social gift-giving. In such circumstances the State can prime the pump of altruism by imposing rules on the game which *ex post facto* but not *ex ante* will be perceived as the cause of welfare enhancement.

Corporate philanthropy is a case in point. Managers in the private sector are paid to maximise the profits and therewith the dividends of their shareholding capitalists. Managers are not paid to maximise their own utility by making voluntary gifts out of money that is not their own in a competitive environment where selfish rivals will then be better placed to attack their market share. Managers have no moral right to sponsor an adventure playground or to donate beds for a leprosy hospice. The State, on the other hand, has a democratic mandate to impose good rules. As Baumol puts it, writing about the controls that universalise the duty to care: 'The invisible hand does not work by inducing business firms to promote the goals of society as a matter of conscience and good will. Rather, when the rules are designed properly it gives management no other option.' (Baumol, 1975:49). It is not to the benevolence of the executives and the bureaucrats that the nation looks for the institutionalisation of altruism but rather to the rewards and penalties that the politicians use to condition the giving reflex.

The State can force businesses to conduct themselves *as if* altruistic. It can do this by means of quotas guaranteeing employment for under-represented minorities, health and safety regulations to minimise workplace accidents, tax concessions granted for non-noxious emissions. In each case the *quid* is only superficially separate from the *quo*: the police and the law courts stand behind the rules of the game and impose a man-made incentive structure that is not the natural order of the invisible hand. Yet time is on the horizontal axis. Initially an imposition, the behaviour pattern might evolve into a habit and an expectation. In such circumstances the pump-priming function would no longer be needed to ensure the desire for the gift; and the State could confine itself to the coordinative function which confirms to the generous that their altruism will not be a waste.

Laws can channel impulses in the direction of other-regarding customs. So can a considered refocusing of the social environment. Childhood socialisation in schools where informal pressures reinforce self-policing guidelines gives the adult a conditioned dis-ease when he defaults on an externality which he knows to be an obligation. Regional policy to perpetuate stable localities can protect on-going networks and make the empathetic interchange of position that much easier to effect. Family policy to reinforce inter-generational responsibility can contribute to the national pool of trust and trustworthiness. The State, in other words, has genuine tools at its disposal that can concentrate the forces of learning by doing on the public interest in a healthy supply of gifts.

Titmuss gives the instance of a nationalised blood bank working in collaboration with a National Health Service: 'Voluntary blood donor systems ... represent one practical and concrete demonstration of fellowship relationships, institutionally based in Britain in the National Health Service and the National Blood Transfusion Service. It is one example of how such relationships between free and equal individuals may be facilitated and encouraged by certain instruments of social policy.' (Titmuss, 1970:273). Market capitalism restricts the individual's freedom to love a stranger as a member of a group. Nationalisation of the allocative mechanism expands the individual's freedom to act out his communitarian inclinations. Titmuss writes that integrated citizens get positive satisfaction from the knowledge that they are contributing to the welfare of unknown others: 'Socialism is also about giving.' (Titmuss, 1970:212). A British blood donor, like a British haemophiliac, would not wish to emigrate.

Participation itself gives the donor the welcome feeling of cohesion and community that the exchange nexus can never deliver. More involved with others, less single-minded about wealth, the individual is freed for self-actualisation because, in the submission of Maslow, he had been able to transcend the duality between the self and the other that had been leaving the *homo economicus* narrow, avaricious and under-developed: 'Duty became pleasure, and pleasure merged with duty. The distinction between work and play became shadowy. How could selfish hedonism be opposed to altruism, when altruism became selfishly pleasurable?' (Maslow, 1962:140). The strongest egos are in that sense the most egoless.

Only, however, if the social environment allows the self to mature. Titmuss, in sympathy with Maslow on growth, warned that gifts like blood would remain unsupplied so long as the institutional set-up was not conducive to the satisfaction of the higher aspirations. There must be an acceptance that the free gift will not later be sold at a profit. There must be an expectation that future cohorts, unseen and unmonitored, will be equally prepared to do their share. There must be an assurance that the donor's own transfusion will not be made contingent on a record of personal subscription. Able to ride free on the outcomes of others, the altruistic donor must be in a position proudly to declare that his preference is for commitment and that economising makes him feel unfulfilled. He is empowered to make this declaration, Titmuss writes, because the National Health Service has given him the open road that he requires: 'The most unsordid act of British social policy in the twentieth century has allowed and encouraged sentiments of altruism, reciprocity and social duty to express themselves; to be made explicit and identifiable in measurable patterns of behaviour by all social groups and classes.' (Titmuss, 1970:254–5). The Good Samaritan is the ideal, the model and the exemplar. His lead only becomes operational, however, where it is complemented by empowering social institutions that allow the self to mature.

Empowering social institutions encourage the gift relationship to blossom. The absence of a supportive political economy means a positive threat to society. Some people would say that in the absence of stranger gifts the value neutralism of exchange subject to law will provide the suffient cement. Not so Richard Titmuss: 'If the bonds of community giving are broken the result is not a state of value neutralism. The vacuum is likely to be filled by hostility and social conflict.' (Titmuss, 1970:224). To Titmuss at least the choice lay between doing good and doing harm. To Titmuss at least, there was no third way between the benevolence of the previous chapter and the malevolence of the present one.

8. Needs and wants

Needs, non-discretionary, are the province of the required, the necessary and the indispensable. Wants, non-prescriptive, are the realm of the desired, the longed-for and the craved. Both are plus-points, positive utilities and not unwelcome diswelfares. Both are success indicators that make possible a reasoned appraisal of goal attainment. The two terms clearly have much in common. Even so, they are two quite separate terms. The former constant, the latter contingent, the meaning of needs and wants is not the same.

Textbook microeconomics, like classical individualism, has traditionally shown a reluctance to test a revealed preference for a good standard of spelling and a strong healthy pulse. Its traditional stance has been that the decision-taker alone can know what is expected to maximise his felt wellbeing, and that a tolerant society does right to allow the rational to shape their lives: 'Underlying most arguments against the free market is a lack of belief in freedom itself.' (Friedman, 1962:15). Such an agnosticism neither affirms nor denies the possibility of non-reducibles lying hidden beneath the choices. What it does say is that only the individual can identify a locus of satisfaction or rank one course of action above another. Pushpin is as good as poetry and gin as good as tea if that is the way the individual perceives his options. Wants in such a perspective might indeed be the surface manifestation of a non-visible buried need. They might be or they might not be. All that can be known is the want. The need itself is no more than the inelasticity of demand. The arbiter is the statistician. The philosopher arrives *post festum* or, better still, stays at home.

The neoclassical economics, arguing that the individual is the best judge of his own best interest, chooses not to evaluate a want or to establish if it is as good as a need. Other schools, less cautious, begin with the core and work outward to the wrapping. Their point of departure is not tastes expressed in the market but rather the social, the psychological and the biological endowments which personal biography has to reconcile with the shopping list. The point of departure, in other words, is nothing less than the richness of human nature, driven organically to evolve and develop. A person, as Veblen writes, 'is not simply a bundle of desires that are to be saturated by being placed in the path of forces of the environment, but rather a coherent structure of propensities and habits which seek realization and expression in an unfolding economy.' (Veblen, 1919:73). There is more to a person than hunger and thirst in the

here-and-now. It is the task of the economist to explore the full range of needs
– and to study the way in which the individual grows and changes over time.

The subject of this chapter is the fullness and the mutation. Speaking
optimistically, it is improvement, betterment and upgrading as well. It would
certainly be the ultimate legitimation of the sustained rise in the gross national
product if it could be shown to satisfy underlying needs and not simply the
evanescent wants that even Socrates would share with a pig.

This chapter is divided into three parts. The first section, Happiness and
wealth, considers the relationship between material affluence and self-
reported felicity. The verdict of history is a surprising one to an economist
trained to believe that growth narrows the felt deficiency of supply relative to
demand: 'The average level of subjective well-being within a country remains
remarkably stable even in the face of manyfold increases in material-goods
consumption.' (Frank, 1999:180). Richer consumers appear not to be deriving
proportionate pleasure from their unprecedented abundance: 'Happiness with
life appears to be increasing in the United States. This rise is so small,
however, that it seems extra income is not contributing dramatically to the
quality of people's lives.' (Oswald, 1997:1818). Hunters and gatherers,
Sahlins writes, 'seem neither harassed nor anxious': 'This was ... the original
affluent society. By common understanding an affluent society is one in which
all the people's wants are easily satisfied.' (Sahlins, 1968:85–6). Our own
position is far less attractive: 'We stand sentenced to life at hard labor.'
(Sahlins, 1968:86). Scarcity economics, unable to see what it means to chase
a mirage through a darkness of unappreciated plenty, has much to answer for:
'Scarcity is the particular obsession of a business economy, the calculable
condition of all who participate in it. The market makes freely available a
dazzling array of products, all these "good things" within a man's reach – but
never his grasp, for one never has enough to buy everything. To live in a
market economy is to live out a double tragedy, beginning in inadequacy and
ending in deprivation.' (Sahlins, 1968:86).

The second part of this chapter, The hierarchy of needs, turns to the
fundamental imperatives that must be met if the individual is to be
emancipated from stunting and released into health. Its inference is that
self-actualisation and self-esteem, not only a good feed and a sound sleep,
must be made arguments in any theory of the production function that takes a
balance of fulfilments as its mixed maximand. Frank Knight was especially
clear on the need to interpret economic life as multi-faceted striving and not
as want-satisfaction, narrowly defined: 'It is simply contrary to fact than men
act in order to live. The opposite is much nearer the truth, that they live in
order to act; they care to preserve their lives in the biological sense in order to
achieve the *kind* of life they consider worthwhile.' (Knight, 1935:26). Men
have an image of wholeness, Maslow argues, such that they feel unsatisfied

when they are forced to terminate their personal unfolding at the foundation level of physical survival: 'The human being is simultaneously that which he is and that which he yearns to be.' (Maslow, 1962:26). Lutz and Lux, translating developmental psychology into humanistic economics, are convinced that the example of Midas shows all too graphically the low level of contentment that can obtain when the obsession with gain causes people to lose sight of their higher nature: 'From the perspective of the hierarchy of needs, the single-minded and exclusive pursuit of money past the point of security not only fails to facilitate growth but impedes it.' (Lutz and Lux, 1988:15).

The third and final section is entitled Anthropocentric economics. Drawing together the themes from the first two sections, it shows how heterodox thinkers have sought to write and teach an encompassing economics that brings out 'the environmental conditions that are conducive to the full development of man's potentialities'. (Fromm, 1973:260). Consumption can mean passivity: 'The attitude inherent in consumerism is that of swallowing the whole world. The consumer is the eternal suckling crying for the bottle.' (Fromm, 1976:36). Possession can mean de-personalisation: 'Modern consumers may identify themselves by the formula: *I am = what I have and what I consume.*' (Fromm, 1976:36). An economics that concentrates on *having* to the neglect of *being* and *becoming* is, Fromm like Maslow would maintain, a thing-centred economics that fails to incorporate the full range of dimensions that make up the broader economic problem.

Economics, Knight suggests, is about activity and search: 'Life is not fundamentally a striving for ends, for satisfactions, but rather for bases for further striving... We do things to prove that we can, and to find out whether we like to.' (Knight, 1935:23, 101). Economics, Jevons says, is about better desires evolving once physiological imperatives have been met: 'The satisfaction of a lower want ... permits the higher want to manifest itself.' (Jevons, 1871:24). Economics, in short, is about a wide range of drives and motives. It is the task of an anthropocentric economics to ensure that all the dimensions are incorporated into the account.

8.1   HAPPINESS AND WEALTH

People want to be happy. In that self-conscious aspiration, Mill writes, resides the sole piece of proof that happiness is itself a desirable objective: 'No reason can be given why the general happiness is desirable, except that each person, so far as he believes it to be attainable, desires his own happiness.' (Mill, 1861:234). To an epistemological sceptic like Mill, perception is the sole test of existence: 'The only proof that a sound is audible, is that people hear it.'

(Mill, 1861:234). Mill applied the same subjective standard to the utilitarian maximand of pleasure: 'The sole evidence it is possible to produce that anything is desirable, is that people do actually desire it.' (Mill, 1861:234). No higher ethical legitimation is provided. That is because, to Mill, no higher ethical justification can be found. People desire happiness. There is nothing more to say.

People want to be happy. Inaccessible as their state of mind will always be to outsiders (and sometimes even to themselves), still it is possible to hazard a guess as to the objective benefits that they promise themselves from the subjective state. Happy people, free from the debilitating negativities of depression, stress, anxiety, hopelessness, are in a strong position to experience the positive emotions of satisfaction, joy, wellbeing. The inner peace which they experience, the bliss, the oneness, is clearly a strong selling point in itself to the unhappy, trapped as they see it in a self-denying struggle to make ends meet and persuaded on a daily basis that things and circumstances are spiralling out of control.

Happiness is an end in itself. It is also a psychological state which empowers the contented more successfully to attain the goals that will keep them contented. Happy people tend to have more energy, more creativity, better recall. They are likely to be more trusting, more tolerant, more helpful to others. Happy people will be less vulnerable to suicide, less at risk from alcohol dependency, less exposed to involuntary loneliness imposed by marital break-up. Happy people, less bored, less boring, are more sociable and more likely to have friends. Happy people, calm enough to plan long-term, are better placed to make good use of money-earning opportunities. Happy to begin with, happier later on, happy people, where rational and self-observant, will evidently be right to value happiness both as an end in itself and as the means to a still higher state of wellbeing, self-perceived.

The Medieval idea of Paradise reserved happiness for the after-life that succeeded the veil of tears. Renaissance humanism located the Good Society not in Heaven but on earth. The Industrial Revolution made the continuing rise in the standard of living the core expectation in an age of acquisition. By the time of Adam Smith, in other words, the association of enjoyment and elation with *economic* wellbeing had become so firmly established as to be unchallengeable. There will always be those who say that the passivity of television soaps makes them gloomy, that microwaved pizzas neither nourish nor provoke. Happiness being entirely in the mind, their self-diagnosis of mental distress can never be refuted through a simple Pollyannaing of objective indicators: 'If someone says they are very satisfied with, say, their mud hut on stilts, then we must assume that they *are*.' (Argyle, 1987:3). The caveat entered, the fact remains: a politician who came down in favour of mud huts and against electric washing machines would rapidly be made an ex-politician by a popular consensus which works all week for the nosebag and the togs.

Objective indicators may be reasonable proxies. Thus unfocused vandalism and paralysing drug dependency may be taken to shadow the incidence of dead-end dissatisfaction; while falls in mortality and morbidity, the installation of central heating and the expansion in per capita housing-space, may be treated as material comfort in step with the felt quality of life. Statistical aggregates may undoubtedly be a basis for inference. What must not be forgotten is that raw numbers can never be the state of mind itself. To find out what people happen actually to be feeling, there is no alternative but to ask.

It is possible but not definite that increasing prosperity is an index of increasing happiness. A recourse to self-reporting enables the observer to trace out the perceptions that link the happiness to the wealth. Welcome as must be any effort to use self-rating in place of telephones per 1000 households or comprehensive connection to the electricity grid, the evidence must nonetheless be acknowledged to include a certain measure of bias. One distortion relates to self-delusion in preference to admission of error: people who have devoted their lives to the production of a higher standard of living are prone to pronounce themselves happier because they want to believe that the hard work invested, the quiet life foregone, have indeed paid off as they had hoped. Another distortion relates to the diminishing disutility of toil-and-trouble supplied: even if rising consumption itself yields no greater satisfaction, still it might be perceived as somehow more attractive where growth means saving, saving means investment, and investment means the mechanisation (analogous to the use of labour-saving consumer durables in the home) of exhausting physical exertion in the increasingly outdated sense of Marx on monotonous and actively unpleasant work. There is a benchmark problem: where per capita income has *recently* risen, people are liable to report a higher level of happiness than they would have experienced had the unaccustomed been given time to ossify into the unchanging. There is a *ceteris paribus* effect: thus a rise in income might be correlated with a rise in happiness for the exogenous reason that both are correlated with more social status and more job satisfaction brought about by a proportionate increase in white-collar employment, while inter-temporal comparisons are made more difficult by the fact that local communities decay and noise levels rise at the very time that living standards improve. There is a 'mirage of rising expectations' problem: 'The increase in output itself makes for an escalation in human aspirations, and thus negates the expected positive impact on welfare.' (Easterlin, 1974:90). What all of this suggests is that the evidence, self-reported, on the causal link between measured affluence and felt well-being ought to be treated as indicative but not as the last word.

That said, surveys of self-perceived happiness (the randomised samples approached by means either of self-administered questionnaires or of verbal replies in structured interviews) have been conducted in a number of countries. Such evidence documents the manner in which people rate their own feelings within the context of their own frame of reference. It shows that, irrespective of differences in culture and language, happiness is a universal concept, not tied to a single nation or specific outlook on life. The evidence makes possible cautious comparisons over time and (between countries) in space. It also demonstrates a remarkably high degree of consistency. Rich and hedonistic like the United States, more traditional and more collectivist like the less-developed countries, the dispersion of the evaluations and the midpoint of the scales tend to indicate a high degree of convergence in the globalised human nature.

One finding suggests a reliable correlation between greater happiness and greater affluence. Veenhoven, concluding that values and attitudes are not a major predictor, homes in on the primacy of per capita income – and of the associated consumption which contributes so much to the satisfaction-with-life index: 'The better the living conditions the country provides, the happier its citizens are on average. Economic prosperity is one of the strongest predictors of happiness.' (Veenhoven, 1993:49). Summarising the investigations, Veenhoven reports that 75 per cent of the population of north-western Europe calls itself 'happy' or 'fairly happy' whereas many countries in the Third World throw up results as low as 25 per cent. In the Dominican Republic fully 84 per cent of the respondents in one study saw themselves as 'unhappy'. The differences in outlook, Veenhoven states, are rooted in economics. Philosophy contributes little to the bias or to the skew: 'The differences in happiness between nations can be largely explained by variation in living conditions. There is thus a good alternative to the cultural-outlook explanation.' (Veenhoven, 1993:77).

Prosperity is the predictor. Yet it must not be thought that the happiness it makes possible is simply another name for the hypermarket and the mega-mall. Economics may be the cause, but there is much nonetheless that follows in the wake of the market. Rich countries tend to have press freedom and non-coercive governments: the improvement in self-respect, the conviction that one is the master of one's own fate, makes a positive contribution to felt welfare. Rich countries tend to offer a more democratic distribution of opportunities: the reduction in seen social distance (together, conceivably, with the fall in violent crime which the alleviation of poverty is capable of delivering) contributes too to the sense of wellbeing. As Veenhoven writes: 'Happiness is highest in the countries that provide most material comfort, social equality, political freedom and access to knowledge.

Together these input indicators explain 77 per cent of the variance in average happiness.' (Veenhoven, 1993:79). Sometimes the separable characteristics will not be cross-correlated: thus interest groups in a democracy can have a negative feedback on economic growth, while widening reference groups can make the equalisation a cause of unhappiness. Even so, there is much evidence that the positive features will tend to be self-reinforcing and that happiness can be approximated across borders by output, growth and the GNP.

Cross-country comparisons are bullish about plenty. The evidence from the time-series is more problematic. Examining such subjectivities as had been measured for the United States in the post-war decades, Easterlin found little or no proof that the 62 per cent rise in per capita incomes had had any real effect on felt felicity: 'By 1970 the proportion "very happy" is just about the same as in 1947. If one views the period as a whole, there is a noticeable swing, but little indication of any net trend up or down.' (Easterlin, 1974:110). The association was just as weak in Japan, where per capita income increased five-fold. Average level of happiness, it would appear, remained constant throughout an economic boom that *inter alia* witnessed the revolutionary proliferation of consumer durables like cars, fridge-freezers and the portable tape-deck. Poor countries like India and Brazil were able to benefit from economic growth to boost happiness through the satisfaction of subsistence needs. Richer countries, however, had apparently fallen victim to the diminishing marginal utility of income and moved into a no-win range: 'The importance of marginal increments of all production is low and declining. The effect of increasing affluence is to minimize the importance of economic goals.' (Galbraith, 1958:143). It is curious in the circumstances that happiness-seekers despite the flatness of the curve remained committed nonetheless to the fuller basket.

Always assuming that the sample data does in fact mean what it says, Easterlin is able to resolve the paradox. He does so, as does Duesenberry, with reference to culture, conformity, and the relativities of the pecking order. Thus Easterlin writes as follows about economic status as a shared and meaningful signifier: 'In judging their happiness, people tend to compare their actual situation with a reference standard or norm, derived from their prior and ongoing social experience.' (Easterlin, 1974:118). People tend to treat the accustomed and the recognisable as their benchmark and their reference point. Having less than the norm, they strive to raise their incomes in order, catching up with the Joneses, to fit in with the familiar.

Catching up is one reason why the dissatisfied might expect greater happiness from greater prosperity: 'Judgements of personal well-being are made by comparing one's objective status with a subjective living level norm, which is significantly influenced by the average level of living of the society as a whole.' (Easterlin, 1995:36). The demonstration effect and the done thing are in that sense a cause of never-ending dissatisfaction in a dynamic economy. If, clearly, the social norm rises, then each is obliged to work harder and to earn more merely to win the same *quantum* of approbation that he was accorded before the 'average level of living' moved on – and moved up. When social norms and disposable incomes rise across the board, there is no solid prediction that the happiness of *each* will rise when each moves along the time-series at the median pace of the *all*. All that can be predicted is that the happiness of each would actually fall if the peers raced on ahead while Ego, even if advancing absolutely, still lagged relatively behind.

Where relative standing is unaffected, Easterlin writes, there is no reason to expect a rise in national happiness to be the consequence of a rise in national wealth. What one can do, all cannot: 'The farther he is above the average, the happier he is; the farther below, the sadder. Moreover, if the frame of reference is always the current national situation, then an increase in the income in which all share proportionately would not alter the national level of happiness. A classical example of the fallacy of composition would apply: An increase in the income of any one individual would increase his happiness, but increasing the income of everyone would leave happiness unchanged.' (Easterlin, 1974:112). Seen as a problem of macro-social policy, a richer nation need not be a happier nation. Clearly, 'if everyone stands on tiptoe, no one sees better.' (Hirsch, 1977:5). Situated in the winner–loser context of the micro-social contest, however, the correlation between happiness and wealth is a stronger one. It is well documented by the evidence: 'Those in the highest status group were happier, on the average, than those in the lowest status group.' (Easterlin, 1974:100). Queue jumping within a cross-section or a hierarchy raises the self-rated satisfaction of those who move up: 'I am inclined to interpret the data as primarily showing a causal connection running from income to happiness.' (Easterlin, 1974:104). Only for those, of course, who take home the prizes.

Marx evokes the perception of decreasing contentment brought on by relative immiseration in the following terms: 'A house may be large or small; so long as the surrounding houses are equally small it satisfies all social demands for a dwelling. But if a palace arises beside the little house, the little house shrinks into a hut... The dweller in the relatively small house will feel more and more uncomfortable, dissatisfied and cramped within its four walls.' (Marx, 1842:268). The dweller's floor space is totally unaffected by the proximity of the palace. The dweller's wellbeing, however, varies inversely with the introduction of a first-class compartment which makes him feel that he is embarassingly second-rate: 'Happiness, or subjective well-being, varies directly with one's own income and inversely with the incomes of others.' (Easterlin, 1995:36).

Taken literally, the lesson from interdependent utility-functions and zero-sum emulation is a stark one indeed. If all incomes rise at the same rate, the contribution of rising wealth to rising happiness will be small or even negligible. If, however, Ego's income rises in consequence of a leap-frogging in position, then Alter's welfare falls in consequence of the relative loss in place. It is a physical impossibility that each member of the community should live in a palace while every neighbour lives in a hut. Taken literally, what this means is that the consumption opportunities brought within the choice-set by material upgrading may only loosely be correlated with the satisfactions of the 'good life', self-perceived. Perhaps there will be no correlation at all.

John Stuart Mill, writing in the Dickensian London of *Hard Times* and in the year of Marx's *Communist Manifesto*, was able to defend the 'dismal science' of the classical Ricardians against the charge that the inescapable stationary state would condemn the society to widespread misery. Growth, Mill wrote in 1848, was hardly the *sine qua non* for happiness where it was other people's approbation that was at the margin the scarce utility that was being purchased: 'I know not why it should be a matter of congratulation that persons who are already richer than any one needs to be, should have doubled their means of consuming things which give little or no pleasure except as representative of wealth.' (Mill, 1848:749). Distribution and re-distribution retained an unavoidable urgency in a Britain where so many were poor. Growth, however, was different: 'It is only in the backward countries of the world that increased production is still an important object.' (Mill, 1848:749). Once the material aspirations had become synonymous with envy and invidious comparison, there a state of satiety may be pronounced and qualitative development be made the successor to more and more.

Keynes in 1930 fully endorsed Mill's prediction that the state of plenty was a prospect that the unemployed of Jarrow would never see but that Jarrow's grandchildren would one day live to experience: 'I draw the conclusion that, assuming no important wars and no important increase in population, the *economic problem* may be solved, or be at least within sight of solution, within a hundred years. This means that the economic problem is not – if we look into the future – *the permanent problem of the human race*.' (Keynes, 1930:326). In the past the economic problem had been one of survival given scarcity. In the present it was 'the enormous anomaly of unemployment in a world full of wants.' (Keynes, 1930:322). In the post-economic future the challenge would be a different one – to use the new-found 'freedom from pressing economic cares' to turn abundance and leisure to personal advantage, 'to live wisely and agreeably and well'. (Keynes, 1930:328).

In the short-run the economics of rewards and penalties remained a functional necessity for a society that had to define performance in the currency of wealth: 'Avarice and usury and precaution must be our gods for a little longer still. For only they can lead us out of the tunnel of economic necessity into daylight.' (Keynes, 1930:331). In the long-run the obsession with wealth-getting at the expense of other, non-economic, needs would rightly be seen as an abnormal, a pathological condition. It would be regarded as 'a somewhat disgusting morbidity' (Keynes, 1930:329) that must be handed over to the psychiatrist for his expert cure.

Economic prosperity can and will mean the general satisfaction, for all social classes, of the basic physiological needs. Social standing will be more of a problem. Absolute subsistence will be the reasonable expectation of our grandchildren. The craving for relative advancement, on the other hand, is insatiable and without equilibrium. Keynes for his own part could find little to say in favour of zero-sum jealousies such as put the society at risk from a 'general "nervous breakdown".' (Keynes, 1930:327). He certainly was unprepared to impute economic purposiveness to a cat chasing its tail.

Greater affluence need not mean greater happiness: once people become accustomed to the more sophisticated plateau, only new services and settings will deliver the requisite stimulus, the desired excitement. Habit embodies living-standards ratcheted-in from the past: while the wake-up of novelty and the winner-take-all of place make possible a rise in aspirations that smashes the stasis of endowment, the idea that a fall rather than a rise will be the greater source of satisfaction is seldom one for which market capitalism mobilises any significant consensus. Considerations such as these, always simply suggestions and never solid facts, inevitably reopen the debate about mental contentment and material prosperity. Seneca says: 'It is the mind, and not the sum, that makes any person rich... No one can be poor that has enough, nor rich, that covets more than he has.' Hamlet says: 'There is nothing either good or bad but thinking makes it so.' Economists like to reason that more wealth means more happiness. What Seneca and Hamlet would argue is that happiness is first and foremost a thing of the mind. Happy people are people who have made up their mind to feel happy. The number of jackets worn once or twice, the number of car journeys made where the bus will do, the number of pills swallowed to relieve the symptoms of a rat race that was itself a choice, may not after all be the most efficient input into a production function intended to supply the output of feeling good.

Most people in affluent societies think they are 'short of money'. Wishing to spend more, they complain that their happiness is being held down because their ends are infinite but their means are in scarce supply. Sahlins takes rather a different view of what it costs to be at ease. Refusing to accept that a renunciation of acquisitiveness is in some sense a suppression of self, Sahlins draws attention to 'a Zen road to affluence, departing from premises somewhat different from our own: that human material wants are finite and few, and technical means unchanging but on the whole adequate. Adopting the Zen strategy, a people can enjoy an unparalleled material plenty – with a low standard of living.' (Sahlins, 1972:2). It is no real sacrifice to do without the satisfaction of desires that are more obviously cultural constructs than they are universal imperatives: 'The "economic problem" is easily solvable by Palaeolithic techniques. But then, it was not until culture neared the height of its material achievements that it created a shrine to the unattainable: *Infinite Needs.*' (Sahlins, 1972:39). Associating happiness with an increase in supply rather than with a diminution in demand, it is the tragedy of market capitalism's 'uneconomic man' that he can never find peace for the simple reason that his restless economic order has made scarcity its axial principle. It has done so 'in a manner completely unparalleled and to a degree nowhere else approximated.' (Sahlins, 1972:4, 13). Hunters and gatherers have fewer possessions than does the 'uneconomic man'. Poorer in the net worth sense, they are also richer in the sense that their life is built around self-sensed abundance whereas the 'uneconomic man' is never free from the treadmill obsession that never grants him rest.

Sahlins describes the confidence of the hunters and gatherers in a generally beneficent natural environment with which they feel at harmony. They are prone to feasting and prodigality rather than to husbanding and hoarding because they have no folk-fear of food supplies forever poised on the brink of exhaustion. They work no more than 21–35 hours per week – ' 'Hunters keep banker's hours' – since they prefer to devote time not needed for subsistence to recreation, conversation and general social interaction: 'The amount of work (per capita) increases with the evolution of culture, and the amount of leisure decreases.' (Sahlins, 1972:34, 35). Careless with the possessions they have, likely to regard additional property as a burden and an encumbrance, they deliberately under-employ their productive potential since the economic value of the under-exploited capacity is to them so low. They are weak on economic calculus but strong on want-satisfaction. They do not feel poor. The owner of the respectable dwelling next door to the palace will not be in a position to say as much: 'Poverty is not a certain small amount of goods, nor is it just a relation between means and ends; above all it is a relation between people. Poverty is a social status. As such it is the invention of civilization.' (Sahlins, 1972:37).

Noble Nomads, neither pulled by hunger nor pushed by peril, treat their work as play: 'Their wanderings, rather than anxious, take on all the qualities of a picnic outing on the Thames.' (Sahlins, 1972:30). Deprived moderns are in a less attractive position. Acculturated into rising expectations and socialised into competitive consumption, their material prosperity may be high but nonetheless not in a position to buy them the sense of arrival for which they yearn. The gain is the standing: 'With the greater part of rich people, the chief enjoyment of riches consists in the parade of riches.' (Smith, 1776:I, 192). The loss is 'the composure of the mind': 'In ease of body and peace of mind, all the different ranks of life are nearly upon a level, and the beggar, who suns himself by the side of the highway, possesses that security which kings are fighting for.' (Smith, 1759:265, 360). Adam Smith, growth economist as he was, recognised that there was much in the Stoic ideal of acceptance, security and permanence that could not but recommend it to the consistent utilitarian: 'Happiness consists in tranquillity and enjoyment. Without tranquillity there can be no enjoyment; and where there is perfect tranquillity there is scarce anything which is not capable of amusing.' (Smith, 1759:209).

Tranquillity is the end. Sometimes it will be the personal best that comes from the equilibrium of *enough*. Never one to decry the benefits of economic growth, Smith at least was clear in his own mind that the majority of fickle history's unfortunate victims had in truth brought their downfall upon themselves. Myopic, misguided, avaricious, they had allowed themselves to become ensnared through 'not knowing when they were well, when it was proper for them to sit still and to be contented.' (Smith, 1759:211). We today, valuing tranquillity and composure, would be well advised not to repeat the same sad mistake of believing that things above all else can set us free.

8.2 THE HIERARCHY OF NEEDS

Needs have an objective existence that cannot be factored down to individual inclinations or to cultural expectations. Universals and irreducibles, their 'ought-ness' derives from their 'is-ness' and only tangentially from the endorsements of the sages. Not to satisfy the want for a second chocolate is to experience a frustration of the pleasure potential. Not to eat any food at all is to cease to be. The second chocolate is a preference. The food *per se* is a precondition. Only the most relativistic of subjectivists would suggest that the urgency of the promptings is in the two cases the same.

Needs are human prerequisites and parts of the machine. To refuse a need is evidently to inflict 'serious harm' on the human essence, to act against 'the objective interests of the individuals involved.' (Doyal and Gough, 1991:39). A need in the circumstances is not only distinct from a want but also logically deserving of a lexicographic priority. *Homo sapiens* is a creature in whose nature it is to solve intellectual problems and to think things out. *Homo faber* is a being that is led by invisible instinct to produce and to reproduce. The *sapiens* and the *faber* have got to be given the freedom to become themselves.

To clip their wings is to mutilate them into a constraint that can only be viewed as unimaginative and shallow, 'abnormal and unnatural'. (Doyal and Gough, 1991:39).

What mankind wants will often be what mankind needs: consider the want for sleep which acknowledges the need for rest, the demand for an appendectomy which delivers the continuation of life. Sometimes, however, the revealed preference will demonstrably be at odds with the structural absolute: thus the factory operative may end up unfulfilled but well-paid, the cut-throat entrepreneur successful but lonely. Sometimes congruent and sometimes divergent, the relationship between the wanted and the needed is described in the following manner by Doyal and Gough: 'You can need what you want, and want or not want what you need. What you cannot consistently do is not need what is required in order to avoid serious harm – whatever you may want.' (Doyal and Gough, 1991:42). Needs, human prerequisites, are logically deserving of a lexic priority. To validate a want that rides roughshod over 'what is required' is evidently not an admirable exercise of tolerance so much as a deplorable denial of support.

Maslow's humanistic psychology takes as its starting point the uncompromising bedrock of general human need: 'We have, each of us, an essential biologically based inner nature, which is to some degree "natural", intrinsic, given, and in a certain limited sense, unchangeable.' (Maslow, 1962:3). Good health, physical and mental, presupposes tension-reduction through the satisfaction of those species-absolutes which, transcending the unique idiosyncrasies of the one-off psyche, unite separable individuals in a single human race. Maslow makes it his cause to promote full humanness, self-expression, 'the development of the biologically based nature of man'. (Maslow, 1962:vi). The alternative to need-satisfaction, he writes, is nothing less than the physical deficiencies identified through low birthweight, tuberculosis and premature death, the mental deficits that come to the surface as anxiety, guilt, frustration, shame, despair, self-disgust and other cries of psychic pain. Malfunction, whether the diseased body or the neurotic spirit is, Maslow writes, the ineluctable consequence of the need left ungratified. It is 'born out of being deprived of certain satisfactions which I called needs in the same sense that water and amino acids and calcium are needs, namely that their absence produces illness'. (Maslow, 1962:26). Illness is a bad thing. Prevention and cure then speak with a single voice in support of a pathology rectified, an under-provision put right.

Maslow is a theorist of needs who is unprepared to reduce all potentialities to taste. Importantly, he is also a developmental thinker who makes growth through stages the core of his message: 'The single holistic principle that binds together the multiplicity of human motives is the tendency for a new and higher need to emerge as the lower need fulfils itself by being sufficiently gratified.' (Maslow, 1962:55). A comparative statics approach would be that the removal of an irritant restores the quiescence of the state of rest. Maslow's approach, process-orientated and not homeostatic, sees in the elimination of an annoyance not so much the cessation of a lower tension as the opportunity to wrestle with an ever-higher aspiration. An equilibrium is in that sense a disequilibrium as well, not an end but a new beginning, not a finality that closes doors but a continuity that unleashes capacities.

It unleashes – and it upgrades. Maslow's theory is a life-cycle account of how the relief of a lower need releases individual self-search for a voyage of discovery that progresses stepwise through a hierachy of imperatives. The higher builds on the lower need. No one, clearly, can be an adult who has not first lived through the status of the child: 'Man's higher nature rests upon man's lower nature, needing it as a foundation and collapsing without this foundation. That is, for all the mass of mankind, man's higher nature is inconceivable without a satisfied lower nature as a base.' (Maslow, 1962:173). First things come first: 'Our godlike qualities rest upon and need our animal qualities.' (Maslow, 1962:174). They rest upon and need. They do not replace.

Maslow believes that the impressionable child grows into a well-balanced adult as a consequence of passing step by step up a five-stage hierarchy of needs. One set of needs satisfied, the person does not sink into inertia but rather proceeds serially to deal with the next – and higher – set of needs in the sequence: 'Need gratifications lead to only temporary happiness which in turn tends to be succeeded by another and (hopefully) higher discontent.' (Maslow, 1954:xv). Creative dissatisfaction is endemic to the human condition: there is no 'happily ever after', no Paradise regained, no Garden of Eden, no successful revolution that ushers in the utopia, in what is in essence a theory not of perfection but of progress. Maslow's theory of need-satisfaction is in that sense a theory of improvement but also one of change: '*Being* a human being – in the sense of being born to the human species – must be defined also in terms of *becoming* a human being.' (Maslow, 1954:xviii). Economics, non-developmental, makes the mistake of stopping short at the first of the five sets of needs. Its quest is a socially useful one: even if man does not live by bread alone, still, without bread, he would not live at all. Simply, its fixation with the lower needs means that the economy might in the end fail to satisfy the higher needs which, not luxuries but necessities, constitute nothing less than 'a series of increasing degrees of psychological health.' (Maslow, 1954:67). Bodily needs come first – but they are not the end.

The lowest of the five sets of needs is physiological in nature. Human beings, like all living creatures, have a need for food, for shelter, for sleep, for the opportunity to reproduce. Survival is the *sine qua non*. Scarce physical resources are the original constraint.

Physiological needs satisfied, the individual is then free, moving bottom-up, to advance to a second, and more specifically human, bundle of imperatives. These needs relate to safety and security, to anxiety modulated and fear allayed. Just as people aspire to something more and something better, so there is a latent terror that their realisable hopes will be dashed by a destructive force that takes away even their existing endowments. Real or imagined, the threat of attack opens up a perceived gap between the *status quo* and the ideal which it is in man's nature to need to reduce. One consequence, historically speaking, has been the call for a Hobbesian *Führer* to choke off the incursive aggressions of murder and theft. A related response, also of a political nature, has been the constitutional separation of powers, annual parliaments and/or referenda, a bill of rights, an upper house with a property qualification, a balanced budget amendment, the earmarking of taxes, a money-supply rule. In modern times the gratification of the need for protection has increasingly taken the economically-related form of precautionary savings, health insurance, job tenure and the Welfare State.

The third set of needs relates to integration, belonging, togetherness, communication, community, fellow-feeling and rootedness. It relates, in other words, to man's innate gregariousness and to the warmth of human contact which makes so meaningful the membership of a family, a neighbourhood, a circle of friends, even of the nation as a whole. Strongly resistant to isolation and exile, the individual because of this third set of needs is impelled to conform lest the penalty for innovation be the pariah stigma of the rejected misfit. It is clearly because of its methodological reductionism as well as its stage-one fixedness that Maslow is out of sympathy with the neoclassical economics. Like Freudian psychoanalysis, he believes, it too quickly takes the fragmentation as a matter of course: 'The atomistic way of thinking is a form of mild psychopathology, or is at least one aspect of the syndrome of cognitive immaturity. The holistic way of thinking and seeing seems to come quite naturally and automatically to healthier, self-actualizing people.' (Maslow, 1954:xi). The psychopath, self-sufficient, is stranded at a low level of personal evolution. Able to hunt his food and even to hoard his money, even so there is a social need for embracing human relationships which, neglected and unexpressed, leaves the outsider only partially himself.

The fourth set of needs, proceeding upward from the non-calculative love of the third, has to do with esteem. People when they work have a need for something that is qualitatively different from the cash they are paid. They have a need to find a non-ego purposiveness in the activity they perform, a need to affirm their own identity through the execution of a task that is not random, not senseless and not harmful. The relevance of labour is here being defined in terms of the end that is being served. The 'striving toward health' is deemed to be on course where the product supplied is literacy lessons in the slums or a well-cooked meal that gives the family strength. No analogous welfare enhancement can, however, be the psychic reward of the operative taught to limit the useful life of his product or of the sales executive who must conceal the dangerous side-effects if he is to take home his bonus. People need purposiveness in their lives. A commodity which fails to deliver that purposiveness leaves its suppliers in a state of apathy, emptiness and even self-loathing.

The fifth and highest set of needs relates to the nirvana of self-actualisation, to the self-realisation that is the enlightened reward for the full utilisation of potential. Individuals, Maslow argues, have a need to unfold their essence, to become all that they are capable of being. In the case of work, and accepting that people differ innately in their endowments of talent, what this would suggest is that appropriate openings for the exercise of creativity are essential if the personality is to mature. Job satisfaction and non-alienating labour are evidently the precondition for the healthy development of the mental faculties. Activity rather than passivity, growth rather than repression, then reinforce the sense of self-respect that makes the fully-rounded feel good about themselves. The wholeness of the individual negates the negation of arrested development and reduces the incidence of disappointment and hopelessness in the nation as a whole. The stultified person, flat, frozen and controlled, is cautious, inhibited and also unhappy: 'Real guilt comes from not being true to yourself, to your own fate in life, to your own intrinsic nature.' (Maslow, 1962:121). The more actualised person, on the other hand, is more harmonious and more joyous within himself, better placed therefore to demand love, to supply trust, such as open up the self-accepting to the humanity and the worth of their fellow creatures: *'The pursuit and the gratification of the higher needs have desirable civic and social consequences...* People living at the level of self-actualization are, in fact, found simultaneously to love mankind most and to be the most developed idiosyncratically.' (Maslow, 1962: 99–100). Self-love at the lowest level of need is in conflict with the bonds of community. By the highest level the unit and the matrix will evolve into a synthesis. Socially as well as psychologically, it would appear, the progression through the hierarchy delivers a wholeness that must always be a rarity until man, well-fed, raises his eyes from his plate.

Hunger and thirst must be satisfied first. Taking that prepotency as its model, Maslow's ordering has the character of a truism. Richard III said 'My kingdom for a horse': since his very survival depended on reliable transport, his perception was correct that the horse and the kingdom were not complements and that the need for the horse had inevitably to be given the higher priority. The street mugger says 'your money or your life': knowing as she does that consumers without a life are not in a strong position to spend their money, her appeal is to the strict criterion that necessities must be demanded first and that no rational person will assign the dictionary-order primacy to marginal luxuries instead. The Engel Curve is an empirical demonstration that, food enjoying the low price and income elasticity of the *sine qua non*, the percentage of income devoted to that first-ranked essential has a tendency to fall as the household's income rises. Richer consumers (empowered to buy more through a fall in the price of food or a rise in their money incomes) are most unlikely to plunge the increment into bread and dripping simply because it is cheap. What they are more likely to do is to demand something different, something that they could not have contemplated unless and until the demand for necessities had been adequately met.

The neoclassical economist will accept with Richard III, the street mugger and the Engel Curve that there is a logical distinction between the essential and the discretionary in the ranking of options. He is less likely to accept with Maslow that there is a hierarchy in respect of safety and security, then integration, then esteem, then self-actualisation. Maslow posits an individual (and, in aggregate, a collective) evolution from the bodily to the socio-psychological needs. The neoclassical economist will be less than comfortable with a historical trajectory which seems to leave the 'Midas-eared Mammonisms' of Carlyle's 'dismal science' stranded, Engel-like, at a stage of material development which the more mature present will increasingly treat as a conquest and a foundation upon which it can build.

An important objection will relate to Maslow's suggestion that the lower needs are easily satisfied, that they are early on succeeded by higher needs only indirectly gratified through the consumption of goods and services: 'Only so much food can be eaten, but love, respect, and cognitive satisfactions are almost unlimited.' (Maslow, 1954:100). Here the materially-minded economist will seek to defend commodities against the charge of infantilism and retrogression by pointing out that there is more to family budgets than food alone. The stilling of hunger and thirst must obviously be regarded as the basis and the foundation. Yet the next step up from food and drink need not be 'love, respect, and cognitive satisfactions'. Instead it might be a car, a home computer and a holiday in India. Maslow is confident that there is a single hierarchy, and that it involves a movement from the material to the non-economic. An alternative interpretation of the layers of need would be that there is more than one hierarchy. On the one hand the material scale that rises up from a loaf of bread to a home cinema and a stamp collection, on the other hand the socio-psychological scale that begins with a loaf of bread and ends up with *Gemeinschaft* – it will be the contention of the convinced economist that economic growth can indeed proceed up the material scale without any ineluctable pressure to take the socio-psychological route instead.

Carl Menger, like Maslow a lexicographic thinker postulating a hierarchy of needs, demonstrates the extent to which the committed ordinalist can confine his incrementalism to the material sector alone. Menger is in no doubt that needs have an objective character that cannot be downgraded from requirement to whim: 'An imperfect satisfaction of needs leads to the stunting of our nature. Failure to satisfy them brings about our destruction. But to satisfy our needs is to live and prosper.' (Menger, 1871:77). Menger, like Maslow, states that needs must be satisfied, and that important needs will without reservation be satisfied first by any economic person who grasps what is good: 'It is evident that satisfaction of his need for food, up to a certain degree of completeness, has a decidedly higher importance to this individual than satisfaction of his need for tobacco.' (Menger, 1871:127). Diminishing importance extends to things: food comes before tobacco. Diminishing importance relates to units: the first plateful sustains life, the second yields mere pleasure, the third is over-eating, gluttony and a threat to health. It is Menger's hypothesis that at some point the need-satisfaction from the last unit of an indispensable commodity like food will be equal to the need-satisfaction that is produced by the last cigarette smoked. Like Maslow, the theory is one of progression and priority. Unlike Maslow, however, it is a theory of material needs alone. Food is chosen before tobacco. The socio-psychological scale is not chosen at all.

Maslow is convinced both that the socio-psychological scale exists and that people will at some stage become converted to its impulsion. His model is the growth of the self-centred child into the caring parent who gets more pleasure from the giving of sweets than from the consumption of sweets by himself: 'To some extent, the higher the need the less selfish it must be. Hunger is highly egocentric; the only way to satisfy it is to satisfy oneself. But the search for love and respect necessarily involves other people.' (Maslow, 1954:100). The problem here is that not all people will accept that it is in their nature to evolve into belongingness. Wanting love and respect but wanting independence too, they might feel that as much integration as they need is delivered by market interdependence and the complementarity of interest. In such a case the seamless web would be the consequence of economic exchange and the attachment to others the by-product of the lowest-level gratifications.

Rank-orderings can differ: risk-lovers such as war correspondents put self-actualisation before safety and security since a long life without excitement seems to them like no life at all. Rank-orderings can be in conflict: loners like visionary hermits are unwilling to put integration before creative freedom lest too little self-ownership deprive them of the initiator's self-respect. The 'pleasure principle' is difficult to fit into the schema: people consciously opt out of exercise classes, trade-union meetings, cod-liver oil and other worthy disutilities that fail to entice while surrendering knowingly to high-tar cigarettes, addictive psychotropics, cholesterol-enhancing fats and other goods and services that cater to desires and urges incompatible with the five-part schema. It is hard to tell an addict that his craving is not a need, or to convince a smoker that self-poisoning only satisfies a negative, or to persuade a monk that his celibacy is a violation of the natural sexual need, or to get across to the gourmet that his taste buds must forever play second fiddle to his vitamins and his calories. Considerations such as these raise doubts as to the extent to which Abraham Maslow's world-view, however constructive and liberating in itself, accurately picks up the heterogeneity and the dispersion that too is a characteristic of the human zoo.

The sequential approach is itself a problem: whereas the growth of a child is visibly a developmental process, the sum total of human needs in society will normally have to be satisfied all at once. The insistence that the higher needs are in essence 'instinctoid and biological, precisely as biological as the need for food' (Maslow, 1954:101) has the uncomfortable implication that moral philosophy is redundant where the charitable donation is no more than the satisfaction of the blood donor's personal need to give. There is also a question about interdependence in a Veblenite world where so much of individual identity is bound up with self-presentation and relative standing. Clearly, where the satisfaction of physiological needs is *simultaneously* the satisfaction of a need to belong and to be esteemed, it is difficult to separate the nutrients from the symbols in the case of food, the shelter from the role-playing in the case of housing. Each of Maslow's needs, in other words, has a cultural as well as a biological dimension. Maslow, concentrating as he does on the minimum standard, objectively defined, may in the circumstances be pyramiding his sequentialism, like the Freudians and the neoclassicals, upon an innate individualism which assigns insufficient importance to traditions and conditions, mutability and variation.

The psychology is there but the sociology is not. Peter Townsend adds the missing element when he says that human needs are 'the conditions of life which ordinarily define membership of society.' (Townsend, 1979:915). Townsend finds it unhelpful to begin his thought experiment with Robinson Crusoe. Maslow's first stage, Townsend would say, is, in the real world, inseparable from Maslow's third stage of belonging and Maslow's fourth stage of esteem: 'People's needs, even for food, are conditioned by the society in which they live and to which they belong.' (Townsend, 1979:38). Even tea, nutritionally worthless, can be a necessity of life. An Englishman feels ashamed of his poverty if he cannot afford to buy himself a cup of tea. Friends visiting him expect him to offer them a cup of tea. Stage one is here the same as stage four. Eating is not just chemical reactions but a repertory of patterned responses.

Townsend is in no doubt that society comes first and that the five-stage Maslovian is in truth a situated being: 'Needs arise by virtue of the kind of society to which individuals belong. Society imposes expectations, through its occupational, educational, economic, and other systems, and it also creates wants, through its organization and customs.' (Townsend, 1979:50). Psychology in the sense of Maslow has a physiological constancy in time and space. Sociology, however, is the study of needs and wants that are forever subject to redefinition by the very people who acknowledge the externality of the constraint.

Sociology reintroduced, one implication concerns the relationship between earning and spending. It is possible to answer the question 'Who is he?' in terms of the occupational function that marks him off from others: we give him identity and location by stating that he is a miner, a fisherman, a sales assistant, a managing director. Equally common is the response which labels him and packages him on the basis of his outgoings and his self-presentation: computer games and jeans say he is young, dreadlocks and Reggae say he is black, good food and wine say he is French. Work defines but so too does consumption. Work is active. Consumption is passive. Both are topics in social status and social role. Maslow's lowest stage is not just about hunger and thirst. Carefully considered, it is about the ins and the outs as well.

Consumerism in the circumstances is more than absorption alone. Bocock defines the goal-seeking and the aspiration in the following manner: 'Consumerism, that is the active ideology that the meaning of life is to be found in buying things and pre-packaged experiences, pervades modern capitalism. The ideology of consumerism serves both to legitimate capitalism and to motivate people to become consumers in fantasy and in reality.' (Bocock, 1993:50). Bocock is referring explicitly to the goods and services. What is hidden beneath the supposed final utilities is likely to be other people. Mass production, mass consumption – Gramsci's 'Fordism' – throws up a way of life and not just a bundle of things. Status groups build their common lifestyles around the same role-models and the same presentation rituals. Consumerism is sociology and not just psychology. Where the needs, Townsend-like, are social and not individual, it is much harder to call with Sahlins for a simpler way of living. Consumerism is what we are and what we want. Affirmation and admission and not merely personal frivolity, it is a social fact that tells the truth about how we live.

That is why it would be a mistake too quickly to attack the capitalist system for an over-inflation of Maslow's lowest level of need. Many critics have blamed the profit motive for image creation, manipulative advertising, surrogate gratifications, disposable fashions, exchange value placed above use value, obedient consumers made the servants of the shareholders and the property owners. There must be some truth in the reservations. Business makes its dividends and its capital gains from a high-wage, low-savings, high-growth economy, and not from the Stoics and the Galbraithians who want to call a halt. Yet there are reasons nonetheless for thinking that market and Maslow are in the end complements and not antitheses.

One reason is bound up with the *ceteris paribus*. Capitalism, historically speaking, has been the economic basis for human rights, political democracy, gender equality, rational choice, the liberation of the sense of self. Capitalism, moreover, has been the source of rising productivity and full employment – the material precondition for Maslow's multidimensional unfolding. It is not consumerism alone that gives legitimacy to the capitalist system. The stability and the sufficiency are strong arguments too.

Besides that, business cannot be criticised for trying to sell. Money-making is what it does. If consumerism has indeed breached a line, then consumers themselves must bear much of the responsibility simply because they agreed to buy. A redefinition of social needs that slows down the expansion of sales is a valid choice in a society that believes *having* to be fully compatible with *being* but that acknowledges other needs and wants as well. What is not a valid choice, saying that it was the commercials that made us obese and the dream merchants who tricked us into cosmetic surgery, is to blame business for its own success. The capitalists are the agents. Social values are the principals. It is the task of the buyers to pass on to the sellers the kind of mix that they want.

The acknowledgement of the social dimension returns the discussion to the distinction between needs and wants. So long as a need is derived unambiguously from the nature of the beast, its status as a fact and not a value is a straightforward matter of the dictionary definition. It is in man's nature to stay alive: thence the need for non-contaminated food, basic sanitation, adequately-remunerated employment, safety at work. It is in man's nature to use his mind: thence the need for education as 'drawing out', for labour that is creative and not repetitive, for self-expression that in the limit results in universal suffrage. Life expectancy on the one hand, cognitive advancement on the other – the need for physical security from sectarian bigotry, the need for personal unfolding through adult literacy, may in the one case as in the other be established with the aid of a good dictionary and a biology text.

The body is the necessary constant. By itself, however, it is not a sufficient condition. Few people would say that aggressive instincts and the destructive-ness of envy, even if irreducibly a part of the package, should be allowed to complete the course that extends from the tension of disequilibrium through conquest and mayhem to the peacefulness of release. The drive to protect one's young, most people would say, has a legitimacy and an acceptability that is more difficult to extend to the Hobbesian dystopia – 'Each person seeks mastery over a world of slaves' (Buchanan, 1975:92) – which led the misanthropic Buchanan to warn that superabundance is no reason to expect that conflict will wither away: 'Social strife might arise in paradise.' (Buchanan, 1975:23). The body by itself is believed by the Freudians to harbour a death wish and by the Darwinians to impel men in the direction of maximal impregnation and maximal progeny. The body is believed to have these needs – but that does not mean that most people will necessarily believe that human nature should be allowed to run its course.

Thus it is that Doyal and Gough make need contingent not just on goal attainment *per se* but also on society's valuation of the fulfilment and the strategy: 'The coherence of the distinction between needs and wants – and of the belief that it can be made in any sort of objective way – is predicated on some *agreement* about what serious harm itself is. But for this agreement to exist – for us to be able to recognise the harm – there must also be a consensus about the human condition when it is normal, flourishing and unharmed.' (Doyal and Gough, 1991:42). There must be *agreement* as to the presence of malfunction. There must be *consensus* as to the nature of health. There must, in short, be normative identification and not simply an appeal to a broken bone such as, proffering no value-vision of 'the good', contributes nothing to the motivator of the 'ought-to-be': 'Serious harm itself is explicitly or implicitly understood as the significantly impaired pursuit of goals which are deemed of value by individuals.' (Doyal and Gough, 1991:50).

Needs in such a perspective come perilously close to being needs precisely because they are value-stamped as wants. As close as they may come, however, a vital distinction remains. The validator in the case of a need is a *shared* outlook. It is not a private and piecemeal fancy. John has a want for a doctor to put right his broken bone. John's co-culturalists transform his want into a need by deeming it 'of value' that a perceived deviation should be restored to the norm. This is not to say that the body has no imperatives, only that no imperative can be a need – as opposed to a non-need or even a negative need – which is not *believed* to be a need by the cultural community that frames the choice.

The agnosticism that sets loose the co-culturalists is encapsulated by James Buchanan in the following appeal to consultation: 'Values are widely acknowledged to be derived from individuals, and there are no absolutes. God has been dead for a century.' (Buchanan, 1986:51). Applied to human needs, the agnosticism that looks to shared attitudes for the requisite confirmation is not necessarily a substitution of cultural relativism for the universal absolutes that Doyal and Gough endorse so strongly when they say of people and places that 'we all have the same needs.' (Doyal and Gough, 1991:9). All that is suggested by the agnostic position is that a need only becomes a need when there is agreement on its nature.

In some cases the agreement will be non-problematic: few people who believe in human potential will regard the cure for a life-threatening disease as anything other than a need. In other cases it will be more difficult to generalise from one set of collective preferences to another. Believers in autonomy will make civil and political liberty a right that is needed. Believers in leadership, on the other hand, will call romanticised hubris a threat to solidarity that is needed even more. Country A, attracted by safety and security, imposes restrictions on workplace hazards, environmental pollution and trouble-free dismissals. Country B, hungry for opportunity, favours the privatisation of industry, de-regulated markets and floating exchange rates that beckon and thrill. Where different needs are identified at different times in different places, it will clearly not be an easy task to spotlight the universals that are other than the fenced-off specificities of culture and tradition. This is not to say that no constant is ever other than a social fact, only that comparative investigation is likely to show a variance in need which militates against the notion that needs are as standard as the colour of blood.

8.3   ANTHROPOCENTRIC ECONOMICS

The first section of this chapter, reflecting the commitment even of the higher deciles to an increasing material standard, examined evidence to the effect that more wealth might not prove successful in purchasing a higher level of happiness. The second section, dealing with human needs above and beyond the individual's wants, tracked the new agenda that might emerge once the bodily basics had, physiologically speaking, adequately been met. The present section juxtaposes the maximising consumer of Section 1 to the self-unfolding multi-dimensionalist of Section 2. Its title – and its recommendation – is an Anthropocentric economics such as makes *both* the material *and* the socio-psychological imperative the joint maximand of a productive system that treats its human input as something qualitatively superior to capital and land.

No human-centred theory of need-satisfaction can afford to neglect the consumption of goods and services. Physical survival being the essential first step, wealth creation in poor countries acquires a liberating teleology which gives to the economist who makes cost effective an irrigation scheme or proposes reforms that expand the supply of jobs the character of a modern missionary. Market capitalism enjoying an enviable track record, moreover, the freedom of exchange in growth-prioritising communities would appear to come with the historical endorsement that discovery processes linking up dispersed knowledge where property ownership is private have indeed faced up more satisfactorily to the constraint of scarcity than have the kings and the planners who have so often tried to put their intelligence before unguided search.

Economics as a science of niggardly rations has a long association with subsistence living standards and the market process that satisfies fundamental wants. The question must nonetheless be raised as to whether the circumstances of a richer society continue to warrant the time-hallowed emphasis on growth and productivity that made Adam Smith so keen to use economics to ward off the absolute deprivation that, in his perception, had robbed the common people in tradition-maximising China of comfort and of dignity alike: 'Any carrion, the carcase of a dead dog or cat, for example, though half putrid and stinking, is as welcome to them as the most wholesome food to the people of other countries.' (Smith, 1776:I, 81).

Smith, pointing to bodily needs in pre-capitalist China, was able to make himself the advocate of value-added and exchange. Galbraith, writing in prosperous America where so many goods, like the toaster which prints an inspirational message on each piece of toast (Galbraith, 1967:82), seemed to him 'of great frivolity' (Galbraith, 1958:140), took quite a different view of a science of scarcity stranded in a world of affluence: 'Obesity is now rather more a problem than malnutrition, and far more ingenuity now goes into the packaging of food than the producing of it . . . Similarly, the need for clothing is not pressing. We now design clothes for their aesthetic or exotic, but rarely for their protective, effect.' (Galbraith, 1960:22). Galbraith regards the economists' obsession with growth and markets, their failure to recognise the low-income elasticity of their mindset as a whole, as a regrettable instance of uncorrected obsolescence, a vestigial ideology which perpetuates past concerns when the circumstances to which they related have long since ceased to exist. Nowadays, Galbraith writes, 'even economists must agree with a social goal which accords the individual the opportunity of providing for all of his needs, not merely for a part of them.' (Galbraith, 1971:13). That in turn means a willingness to move on from the economics that was appropriate when absolute deprivation was the rule.

Lutz and Lux share with Galbraith the economist and Maslow the psychologist the perception that a failure to grow and mature is as unfortunate for a society as it is for a child that aspires to an unarrested development of self: 'The striving for more material goods is only rational so long as they are *needed*, but the continued wanting of goods is irrational behavior. It is here that we see the tragic irony of Rational Economic Man. The more he strives to conform to his own concept of rationality, by calculating the best way to increase his goods, the more he risks acting irrationally.' (Lutz and Lux, 1979:80). Children, over-indulged, are in danger of becoming trapped in the passive persona of the taker who knows only to react and absorb. Societies, economising on all save the shopper's gratifications, are no less in danger of achieving less by means of consuming more: 'Life in recent years has certainly taught us something about the pathology of *material* (lower need) affluence, of such outcomes as boredom, selfishness, feelings of eliteness, and of "deserved" superiority, of fixation at a low level of immaturity, of the destruction of brotherhood. Clearly, living the material or lower need life is not in itself satisfying for any length of time.' (Lutz and Lux, 1979:71). Lutz and Lux in the circumstances come down strongly in favour of a humanistic economics which puts the quality of human life above the quantity of inert consumables: 'Instead of the conventional emphasis on wealth and wants it focuses on development and needs.' (Lutz and Lux, 1979:23).

The economics of bodily comforts that is exemplified by Smith on wholesome food in China may be criticised on the grounds that the postulate of non-satiety is at variance with the diminishing utility of marginal consumables taken together as a class: 'Presumably, the more urgent things come first. This ... implies a declining urgency of need.' (Galbraith, 1958:145). Galbraith is convinced that more will not automatically, axiomatically, be ranked above less – but that the 'dependence effect' of supply-led demand successfully implants aspirations which *ex* manipulation would never have existed at all: 'We may say that the marginal utility of present aggregate output, ex advertising and salesmanship, is zero.' (Galbraith, 1958:154). It is Galbraith's message that commerce is creating its own validation, and that the higher needs – the not-for-sale needs – are being neglected and suppressed as a result of the gain-seeking goal function. Peter Pan is fixated at the lowest level of human want. He is stranded there, Galbraith would say, because of business-based brainwashers who produce the consumerhood that they can use.

Fromm is critical of over-developed materialism and of the psychological impoverishment with which he believes the consumer culture to be symbiotically linked. Economies of scale feed through to social patterning, passive conformity taking the place of active spontaneity. Political apathy becomes the conditioned response of the ground-down character, dominated into submission by inflexible organisation and unforgiving system. Imagination decays where it has so diminished a function: one consequence is the coincidence of mass literacy with mass media which supply a product that is trivial, debasing, voyeuristic, immoral and escapist. Self-love flourishes since want-creation by its very nature appeals to the narcissism of the monad who dines alone: the zero-sum character of the status symbol that is believed to buy esteem does little to strengthen the ties of relatedness or open ego's heart to the feelings of his fellows. Afraid of losing face even as he is greedy of advance, the consumer reaches compulsively for the latest model, 'lives for today' in his permissive attitude to the 'fun morality' of buying on credit, wastefully discards his obsolescent trinkets and gadgets in order not to stand out or look eccentric in an economy that unceasingly moves on. Struck by the status anxiety, the social separateness, the other-determined sense of self, the propensity to substitute possessiveness for a fully-rounded existence, Fromm is unprepared to identify the growth in the national product with an ongoing improvement in the satisfaction of innate and fundamental human needs. Generalising from indicators of destructiveness and self-destructiveness, what Fromm deduces is that the gratification of increasingly synthetic appetites may be nothing more than an exercise in diswelfare and even a short-cut to oblivion.

Fromm is critical of the pursuit of affluence as an end. Importantly, he is critical as well of the cost–benefit orientation that he believes to have made a contribution of its own to the terror of acquisition. He is in that sense as concerned about the market nexus as he is about the over-possessive culture of which it is a cause and an effect. A particular problem is the way in which, as he sees it, each person in an exchange society acquires the status of a marketable commodity, 'for sale' at a value that is set not by love and commitment but by supply and demand: 'Human qualities like friendliness, courtesy, kindness, are transformed into commodities, into assets of the "personality package", conducive to a higher price on the personality market. If the individual fails in a profitable investment of himself, he feels that *he* is a failure; if he succeeds, *he* is a success.' (Fromm, 1956:142). Shallowness is bound to be the rule in human relationships where each partner is evaluated not as a uniqueness to be respected but solely as a capital, a consumable, a means to an end: 'Love is often nothing but a favourable exchange between two people who get the most of what they can expect, considering their value on the personality market.' (Fromm, 1956:147).

Fromm takes the view that the salesman of self who shapes his identity in order to maximise his return and who derives his worth from his balance-sheet as a supplier of gratifications to others is likely to lose sight of every aspect of his character save those qualities that mark him out as a business asset: '*Things* have no self and men who have become things can have no self.' (Fromm, 1956:143). Abstract and objectified, fearful of rejection and dependent on others, malleable salesmen lose their name and their direction. To treat this repression of the hard core instead as the liberation of negotiated choice is, Fromm suggests, badly to confuse individual freedom with its antithesis in alienation, passivity and the childhood forever prolonged. Fromm writes that ethical judgement is itself the likely victim of disclosure stunted and selfness boxed in: 'Conscience exists only when man experiences himself as a man, not as a thing, as a commodity.' (Fromm, 1956:173). In saying this, he appears to be arguing that the market *per se* poses a threat to mental health which the economists and the utilitarians had regrettably failed to take into account.

Fromm in questioning the hegemony of possessive individualism makes two points about the one-dimensional culture. The first relates to need-satisfaction constricted into bodily appetite. The second concerns self-respect sold disproportionately by the approbation of others. Like Maslow, Fromm is convinced that man, not infinitely plastic, possesses an essence that is irreducibly a constant irrespective of the variance and the variability in the culture that surrounds it: 'Man's existential conflict produces certain psychic needs common to all men... I have called these psychic needs 'existential' because they are rooted in the very conditions of human existence. They are shared by all men, and their fulfilment is as necessary for man's remaining sane as the fulfilment of organic drives is necessary for his remaining alive.' (Fromm, 1973:226). Like Marx, Fromm is doubtful that man can fully become himself so long as self-definition through limitless commodification remains the primary objective in a dehumanised economic order.

Karl Marx criticised the capitalist system for giving man an inflated view of ownership and consumption as a value: 'Private property has made us so stupid and one-sided that an object is only *ours* when we have it – when it exists for us as capital, or when it is directly possessed, eaten, drunk, worn, inhabited, etc., – in short, when it is *used* by us.' (Marx, 1844c:139). Capitalism survives only because it continues to sell. Given the economic basis, Marx argued, the intellectual validation then follows predictably behind: 'The need for money is therefore the true need produced by the modern economic system, and it is the only need which the latter produces. The *quantity* of money becomes to an ever greater degree its sole *effective* quality.' (Marx, 1844c:147). The aggregated and the quantifiable become the indicators of success in a restless system where desiredness is forever bound up with expansion, acquisition and more-and-more.

Individuals in such a system draw the inference that because they can pay, therefore they are powerful: 'Thus, what I *am* and *am capable* of is by no means determined by my individuality. I *am* ugly, but I can buy for myself the most *beautiful* of women. Therefore I am not *ugly*, for the effect of *ugliness* – its deterrent power – is nullified by money.' (Marx, 1844c:167). Money for individuals in a capitalist system seems to possess the God-like capacity to bring all options within the choice-set. The reality, Marx maintains, is less attractive than the 'self-stupefaction', the 'illusory satisfaction', that is not so much the gratification of a need as its radical denial: 'The English gin shops are therefore the *symbolical representations* of private property.' (Marx, 1844c:153). The Irishman, living on the bare subsistence minimum at the height of the 'Hungry Forties' had good reason to associate commodity consumption with a better life procured: 'The Irishman no longer knows any need now but the need to *eat*.' (Marx, 1844c:149). For the rest of us, however, the link between things and needs becomes that much more tenuous.

The truth is the trade-off: 'The less you *are* ... the more you *have*.' (Marx, 1844c:150). The thought is a sobering one. The loss for the worker is the consequence of debasing toil, of repressive labour in which man the maker 'does not affirm himself but denies himself': 'As a result, therefore, man (the worker) only feels himself freely active in his animal functions – eating, drinking, procreating, or at most in his dwelling and in dressing up, etc.; and in his human functions he no longer feels himself to be anything but an animal.' (Marx, 1844c:110, 111). The capitalist too experiences a frustrating self-estrangement in that, insecure and vulnerable as the atomised competitor must always be, there is not so much deferred gratification as abandoned gratification in his mania for reinvestment: 'Accumulate, accumulate! That is Moses and the prophets! ... Therefore, save, save, *i.e.*, reconvert the greatest possible portion of surplus-value, or surplus-product into capital!' (Marx, 1867:595). The worker consumes but the human cost is 'misery, agony of toil, slavery, ignorance, brutality, mental degradation.' (Marx, 1867:645). The capitalist consumes but in eternal awareness that to give way to his human desires, to cut back on renunciation, asceticism and self-denial, is to gamble away his very status as a member of the bourgeois class. Neither the worker nor the capitalist has, in Marx's theory, any real opportunity to advance beyond the stage one pleasure-seeking of Maslow's hierarchy of need.

Market exchange as well as the taking-in compulsion plays an active part in distancing the individual from his need. Denied economic security by the reserve army of competitors, denied esteem and self-esteem by the perceived pointlessness of the function, denied the full unfolding of creative potential by the mental mutilation of the division of labour, the individual is further frustrated in his quest to become himself by a wall of prices that puts money between man and man: '*That which* mediates *my* life for me, also *mediates* the existence of *other people* for me. For me it is the *other* person.' (Marx, 1844c:166). Jack no longer sees Jill and Jill no longer sees Jack. What each sees instead is the mystification of the price tag, the reification of the commodity that (solely the product of human labour) seems to take on an identity independent of that of its father and mother.

Just as an atheist would call it false consciousness to impute to a Creator in Heaven the work that is performed on earth by man, so Marx calls it commodity fetishism to treat a price or a thing as anything other than a veil for Jack and Jill. Market exchange by its very nature sows intellectual confusion and makes the fact of inter-dependence that much more difficult to grasp. The alternative, clearly superior, is an economic order that does not have to rely on illusion: 'Assume *man* to be *man* and his relationship to the world to be a

human one: then you can exchange love only for love, trust for trust, etc.'
(Marx, 1844c:169). The transcendence of the pecuniary nexus is to the
Marxians the material prerequisite for extended need-satisfaction in the sense
of humanitarians like Maslow. Marx, like Fromm, is critical of a market order
in which man himself is made an object. Marx, like Fromm, is, however, less
forthcoming about the economics of the post-market society that he believes
would contribute so much to the satisfaction of need.

Maslow, Fromm and Marx are united in their perception that it is the task of
the economic system to acknowledge the validity of the full range of needs.
Sigmund Freud, dealing as a psychoanalyst with discrete individuals and not
with social wholes, was nonetheless in broad sympathy with the ideal of an
economic order that would assist his clients to overcome their frustrations.
More difficult to say is whether that economic order would be more capitalist
or less capitalist in the structure that it moulds to the constancy of need.

Freud's starting point is always the repression of desire. On the one hand
that repression can poison the body and entrap the spirit. Freud treated
unhappy patients who had come to him with neuroses that were the
unwelcome expression of the inability to act (Anna O's arm that went into
paralysis at the death-bed of a parent), of subconscious longings (the Oedipal
wish to murder the father and marry the mother), of long-suppressed memories
(a childhood seduction by a trusted adult). On the other hand that repression
can act as an inhibitor and a regulator that is the *sine qua non* for affluence in
the sense of Smith and co-existence in the sense of Hobbes: 'Civilization is
built upon a renunciation of instinct.' (Freud, 1930:97).

Repression is the precondition for economic growth. A simple example
would be the self-discipline that indolent creatures impose upon themselves
when they put work before play. A more complex illustration is the self-
control of the thwarted fornicator who withdraws his libidinous potency from
its non-economic outlet in order to devote his creative energies to material
achievement instead. Repression is also the precondition for peaceable
mutuality. Thanatos the death-instinct being as much a part of human nature
as Eros that is the champion of life, the minus-sum cruelty of 'a savage beast
to whom consideration towards his own kind is something alien' (Freud,
1930:112) is a *bellum* just around the corner in the absence of non-ego limits
to the satisfaction of the pleasure principle. Such limits are the consequence of
damming-up through education and guilt feelings inculcated through social
conditioning. Freud writes as follows about internalised ethics as a restriction
and a constraint: 'The cultural super-ego has developed its ideals and set up its
demands.' (Freud, 1930:142). It is a source of frustration which is conducive
to survival and solidarity, the basis for collective progress precisely because it
is a locus of self-punishment and self-deprivation.

The anxieties associated with infant sexuality, the sublimation of disruptive urges by means of the incest taboo, the purchase of the father's love (and, indeed, the approbation of a father-like God) that is conditional on merit and achievement, the non-rational imaginings to which the door will often be the interpretation of dreams – all are aspects of personality and its formation which no comprehensive account of need-satisfaction can afford to neglect. The welfareist craves security because of reassurance denied at an impressionable age. The male is dependent on creative employment since only the female can bring new life into being. The worker hates the capitalist because the boss is the adult's reminder of the childhood authority figure. In case after case, in other words, the relationship to the economy may, arguing in the language of Freud on compensation, be an expression of pressures and fantasies of which the presenting symptoms diagnosed by Maslow, Fromm and Marx are no more than the visible – the surface – emanations. This is not to invalidate the deep-seated distress felt by the unpromoted executive who thinks he has let his parents down, by the redundant employee who perceives his loss as a repeat rejection in an unstoppable series. What is important to remember, however, is that there can never be an economic system that deals directly with the neuroses born of a dysfunctional family, a private betrayal, the sense of loss or the fear of death.

Capitalism does not satisfy the psychological requirements of the unpromoted and the redundant. In other ways, however, it does provide an outlet for the aspirations of the discontented. Freud was especially interested in the direct link between toilet training and the economic psychology of parting with claims.

Parents educating babies provide positive reinforcement for successful defecation. Many adults for that reason associate spending with approval and affection. People will often spend more when they are feeling unloved. In the limit there is the spendthrift who spends his life buying parental reaffirmation through the elimination of an unwanted surplus.

Inevitably, however, there will be children whose first self-assertive act is to refuse to give up their stool. In their pleasure in the retention of excrement – an identification picked up by linguistic usages such as 'filthy lucre', 'stinking rich', 'throwing money down the drain', 'rolling in the stuff' – may be seen the origins of the financial constipation that underlies the accumulation of capital and the acquisition of assets as ends in themselves: 'We know that the gold which the devil gives his paramours turns into excrement after his departure, and the devil is certainly nothing else than the personification of the repressed unconscious instinctual life.' (Freud, 1908:174). Parents demanded the faeces and immediately disposed of them. The miser for his own part resists remembered pressures to become incontinent. A saver and not a spender, he has transferred his attention from excrement to collectables such as money that he is able to store. For all that he remains fixated at the anal stage by committing himself to retention, opposed to giving up.

Freud was convinced that there was a sexual dimension – 'anal eroticism' – in the infant's revolt, in the child's first-ever declaration of self-worth at the time of potty-training. Traces of that sexual dimension remain behind in the character of the retentive adult: consider the man who is unwilling to share his emotions, who treats money as a symbol of virility, who in extreme cases flees from women lest they drain him of his sexual and pecuniary potency. Freud would obviously see in the obstinacy and the stubbornness of the captain of industry, the parsimony and even the avarice of the Industrial Revolution's frugal bourgeois, the satisfaction of a human need that can only be regarded as an unintended outcome from the perspective of the capitalist economy.

The retentive character is attracted by the maximisation of the stock. Such a person is therefore careful and calculative as well. Punctual in his time-keeping, orderly in his approach to work, conscientious to the point of compulsiveness in his attention to detail, the character-type that emerges is nothing other than the *homo economicus* who is well-suited to the punctilious husbandry of time, money, and other scarce resources. Weber would explain the emergence of obsessive accounting and punctual execution in terms of ideals such as the Puritan Ethic. Marx would found predictable trustworthiness and regular performance on the Hobbesian jungle of competitive markets. Freud adds in the additional explanation of the body. Cleanliness and tidiness cast a giant shadow. Hygiene and hand-washing are all around.

9. The demand to supply

Jevons regarded consumption as the end, production as the veil of tears. In Eden there was want-satisfaction without the disutility of effort. East of Eden the fallen pair was cursed with the need to till the soil: 'With labour you shall win your food from it... You shall gain your bread by the sweat of your brow.' (*Genesis*, 3:17, 18). The Bible, like the utilitarians, gives the impression that God alone is in the business of creation without the constraint of scarcity. Adam and Eve are in a weaker position. Hungry, thirsty and cold, they associate pleasure with demand and see supply as an unpleasantness which it is in their self-interest to keep to the minimum.

Maslow is critical of a negative theory which treats supply not as an accumulation of good things but as a pain relieved: 'The desire or need presses toward its own elimination. Its only striving is toward cessation, toward getting rid of itself, toward a state of not wanting. Pushed to its logical extreme, we wind up with Freud's death-instinct.' (Maslow, 1962:29). Even God conceptualised his task as a closed-ended project enabling him on the seventh day to luxuriate in the state of rest. It is Maslow's contention that the six-day model of an irritant eliminated is too static to capture the eternal reaching out that is not the negation of a negation but rather the progressive fulfilment of a maturing promise: 'Satisfying deficiencies avoids illness; growth satisfactions produce positive health.' (Maslow, 1962:32). Demand is not followed by stasis. Instead it is followed by the pursuit of higher needs. One of those needs is supply.

Maslow writes as follows in support of the developmental vision that moves upwards from the foundation needs like nutrition to the higher needs like self-expression: 'Partly this intrinsic validity of living comes from the pleasurable-ness inherent in growing and being grown. But it also comes from the ability of healthy people to transform means-activity into end-experience, so that even instrumental activity is enjoyed as if it were end activity.' (Maslow, 1962:31). For Adam and Eve, basic appetites ungratified, it was too soon to think about self-actualisation when the rice bowl was empty and the river threatening to flood. East of Eden it was the bodily wants that piped the tune. Later on, however, it was activity itself that satisfied the newer and the higher need.

Alfred Marshall said as much. Criticising Jevons for putting passive consumption first, Marshall argued that activity is not just the source of goods and services but also an emancipating choice in itself: 'Work, in its best sense, the healthy energetic exercise of faculties, is the aim of life, is life itself.' (Marshall, 1873:115). Marshall believed that 'the vigorous exercise of faculties' (Marshall, 1873:112) enjoyed a high income elasticity of demand in a growing society in which needs had evolved beyond mere want-satisfaction alone: 'It is ... the desire for the exercise and development of activities, spreading through every rank of society, which leads not only to the pursuit of science, literature and art for their own sake, but to the rapidly increasing demand for the work of those who pursue them as professions.' (Marshall, 1890:75). Lower people, like lower animals, are ruled by their simplest wants. Later on, however, it is effort and self-expression, 'the desire for excellence for its own sake' (Marshall, 1890:75) and 'a proud interest in the glories of their art' (Marshall, 1873:116), that release men from the tyranny of satiability and the reactiveness of the taker's stance: 'Although it is man's wants in the earliest stages of his development that give rise to his activities, yet afterwards each new step upwards is to be regarded as the development of new activities giving rise to new wants, rather than of new wants giving rise to new activities.' (Marshall, 1890:76). As we evolve, so it becomes less and less true that consumption constitutes the scientific basis of economics. As we improve, in other words, so there is an inescapable shift at the margin in favour of the demand to supply.

It is that demand to create which is the subject of the present chapter. The discussion is divided into three parts. Section 1, Work and need, establishes the human essence that is released through economic production. Section 2, Intrinsic motivation, examines the unexpected economics of an action-theory in which the ends and the means converge. Section 3, The supply motive, explores the implications for profit rates of a revised vision in which the demand for self-esteem and creative achievement is to be ranked above the demand for goods and services satisfying wants that have long since lost their bite.

9.1   WORK AND NEED

The continuing emphasis on efficiency given scarcity is the basis of the neoclassical economics. The result is a legitimation of production and supply almost exclusively in terms of revealed preference and market price: 'The utilitarian economists make exchange value the central feature of their theories, rather than the conduciveness of industry to the community's material welfare.' (Veblen, 1899/1900:100). Not prepared to take price as the measure of welfare, Veblen, genetic, generative, dynamic, turned away from the Marshallian Cross to examine instead the cumulative transitions that progressively give form to the underlying teleology: 'The question of value is a question of the extent to which the given item of wealth forwards the end of Nature's unfolding process.' (Veblen, 1899/1900:49). The laws of nature, Veblen wrote, are evolutionary and purposive, adaptive and meliorative as well: 'The objective end of this propensity that determines the course of nature is human well-being.' (Veblen, 1899/1900:47). They are also an unambiguous vote in favour of the culture of serviceability that is the successor to the selfish era of self-seeking mastery.

Veblen, studying human nature, identified not just the destructive instinct that divided the community through competitive emulation but also a constructive endowment that led man to demonstrate his non-invidious sentiments 'chiefly and most consistently in some employment that goes to further the life of the group.' (Veblen, 1899:30). Fellowship and creativity, Veblen reported, were found together in the early stage of savage society. Temporarily eclipsed by the conspicuous consumption of the predatory class, they are bound eventually to reassert their primacy. The reason is human nature – since work is simply not to be reconciled with man's irreducible instincts which does not give him the chance to supply activity in which he sees some sense: 'He is an agent seeking in every act the accomplishment of some concrete, objective, impersonal end. By force of his being such an agent he is possessed of a taste for effective work, and a distaste for futile effort. He has a sense of the merit of serviceability or efficiency and of the demerit of futility, waste, or incapacity. This aptitude or propensity may be called the instinct of workmanship.' (Veblen, 1899:29). Man's welfare cannot be said to be at its maximum where he is being asked to cater to a jealous hedonism with which he cannot sympathise or where he is told to cut back on quality in order that a money-minded employer can steal a march on a rival. Assuming that economics is indeed about welfare and not a synonym for production *per se*, the frustration of the activities that would have allowed the worker to satisfy the full range of his needs can only be described as a perversion of the purpose of work. The worker has an inbred demand to supply. The profit-seeking system cannot afford to invest scarce resources in propensities that fulfil but do not pay their way.

Veblen finds in human nature an innate need to achieve self-determination through meaningful work. So does Marx, who sees productive activity as spontaneity, externalisation and the constitution of self: 'It is just in his work upon the objective world, therefore, that man first really proves himself to be a *species being*.' (Marx, 1844c:114). Man embodies himself in the material reality that he brings into being. It is in his nature to do so: 'An animal only produces what it immediately needs for itself or its young… Man produces even when he is free from physical need.' (Marx, 1844c:113). A creature that continues to produce even when the means to physical existence have been made secure is not simply a creature that suffers in order that it may consume. Instead it is a creator that is driven by an inner need to unfold his essence through the objectification of his uniqueness in a mirror with a face: 'All *objects* become for him the *objectification of himself... Man himself* becomes the object.' (Marx, 1844c:140). Such labour is not an economic means but rather an end and a confirmation that I am I.

In the humane economy it is – and 'What is life but activity?' (Marx, 1844c:111). In the capitalist economy it is not – since there the self-realisation of creativity is inverted into 'activity as suffering, strength as weakness, begetting as emasculating.' (Marx, 1844c:111). It is man's species-nature to reproduce himself in consciousness and in matter. The capitalist economy, Marx contends, converts that pride in self-revealing productiveness into a deep revulsion towards wage-slavery that denies the lump of labour the chance to soar into himself. The worker, in his work, 'does not affirm himself but denies himself, does not feel content but unhappy, does not develop freely his physical and mental energy but mortifies his body and ruins his mind.' (Marx, 1844c:110). Such work is not utility but disutility, 'not the satisfaction of a need' but 'merely a *means* to satisfy needs external to it.' (Marx, 1844c:111). It is no surprise that it is shunned whenever it can be avoided. Yet the urge to create is a core characteristic of the human condition. No one would question the validity of Veblen's 'parental bent' that is the source of self-reproduction through the procreation of descendants. No one, Marx would add, should question the validity of the need to create through work.

Capitalism, however, is the embodiment of just such a denial: 'Political economy knows the worker only as a working animal – as a beast reduced to the strictest bodily needs.' (Marx, 1844c:73). The consequence is an unfulfilling work function, orientated to productive efficiency and not to personal development. Long runs condemn the human appendage to the rhythm of the machine. The division of labour institutionalises the routine and repetitive monotony that Smith, like Marx, saw as a cause of 'mental mutilation' precisely because the operative who never faces a challenge will never develop the muscles that would prevent him from becoming 'as stupid and ignorant as it is possible for a human creature to become.' (Smith, 1776:II, 303, 308). Work makes men: 'The understandings of the greater part of men are necessarily formed by their ordinary employments.' (Smith, 1776:II, 302). Smith accepted the debasement as the price that had to be paid for the wealth of nations. Marx was more critical of any productive process that came between the free, conscious creator and the 'life-engendering life' (Marx, 1844c:113) that was *homo faber's* species need – and species right.

The *becoming* denied is to Marx not simply the consequence of techno- logical sophistication. It is also a socio-economic distortion, a man-made artificiality that is brought about by market allocation itself. The worker in the capitalist system is commodified into a thing, obliged to 'sell himself and his human identity' (Marx, 1844c:70) and to do so through a cold and faceless process that prices his human dignity by his productive potential, his value as a man by his value-added for another. The person becomes a product. Intimate expression becomes abstract labour for hire. The worker's relation to his own activity becomes the alienated one of commodity supply compensated for by cash: 'That which I am unable to do as a *man* ... I am able to do by means of *money*.' (Marx, 1844c:168). Such a nexus is socially divisive. Competition *per se* pits worker against worker, capitalist against capitalist: 'The only wheels which political economy sets in motion are *greed* and the war *amongst the greedy – competition.*' (Marx, 1844c:107). Besides that, it is the iron law of the profit-seeking economy that the reserve army should be offered the lowest-possible wage for the highest-attainable output. Exploited and over-worked in order to enrich the property-owning class, the labourer must feel as estranged from his capitalist as he is from his species-self when he contemplates the sacrifice of that which gives so much meaning to his life.

The worshipper puts himself at the disposal of God. The worker becomes the servant of capital accumulation. In the one case as in the other, a stranger may be said to be appropriating a part of the self – and the self may be said to be misunderstanding the nature of the confrontation that is in truth no more than a misinterpretation of a mirror image: 'The more man puts into God, the less he retains in himself. The worker puts his life into the object; but now his life no longer belongs to him but to the object ... Whatever the product of his labour is, he is not.' (Marx, 1844c:108). Just as there is a loss when a parent cannot recognise his child, so there is a loss when the creator only sees his product as something outside himself, separate and independent. Alienation through the work function itself, bondage to the illusion of the object and to the employer who owns the product – man the creator cannot be satisfying his needs as a producer where domination and dehumanisation build hostility, mystification and the loss of self into his economic affairs.

Marx doubted that private enterprise was capable of matching work to need. Believing productive efficiency to be purchased at the cost of spiritual development, he viewed with considerable scepticism the claim that rising welfare and rising living-standards were the same: 'The less you express your own life, the greater is your *alienated* life ... Everything which the political economist takes from you in life and in humanity, he replaces for you in *money* and in *wealth*.' (Marx, 1844c:150). Marx criticised the economics of capitalism for assigning pride of place to ownership and for neglecting the end-utilities that are synonymous with productive effort itself: 'Private property has made us so stupid and one-sided that an object is only *ours* when we have it – when it exists for us as capital, or when it is directly possessed, eaten, drunk, worn, inhabited, etc. – in short, when it is *used* by us.' (Marx, 1844c:139). Marx proposed a broader view that would bring in the privilege of production as well.

Human diversity complicates the matching of work to need. Clearly, if each person has an authentic self and no two persons have identical endowments, then an ego-releasing economy must come under considerable pressure to supply the work opportunities that individuals need in order fully to become themselves: 'A new discontent and restlessness will soon develop, unless the individual is doing what *he*, individually, is fitted for. A musician must make music, an artist must paint, a poet must write, if he is to be ultimately at peace with himself. What a man *can* be, he must be.' (Maslow, 1954:46). The self-actualising scenario, given faculties and talents that require so specific a channel, would seem to suggest that production be decided upon before consumption in order to ensure that potential left fallow does not become a locus of unacceptable distress.

Plato, anticipating Maslow, derived the division of labour from the dispersion of innate endowments: 'No two of us are born exactly alike. We have different natural aptitudes, which fit us for different jobs.' (Plato, c.375:118). Adam Smith, putting nurture above nature, reversed the chain of causality: 'The very different genius which appears to distinguish men of different professions, when grown up to maturity, is not upon many occasions so much the cause, as the effect of the division of labour.' (Smith, 1776:I, 19). Adam Smith argued that for the first six to eight years of their life at least, children tend to be 'very much alike' – but that, inevitably, the differences in their social exposure will separate them and shape them for different employments: 'The difference between the most dissimilar characters, between a philosopher and a common street porter, for example, seems to arise not so much from nature, as from habit, custom, and education.' (Smith, 1776:I, 19–20). Such plasticity gives some grounds for hope. Where natural propensities are at variance with the demand for skills, all too many street porters will have to seek work as philosophers which they find out of keeping with their true selves. Where nerves, brains and fingers can be conditioned and moulded, there the sensation of true essence denied will be that much less acute.

Work allows a creator with an essence to turn his personal uniqueness into an economic service. Aptitude aside, however, it is likely that the motor response will itself make a significant contribution to the satisfaction of human need. One model of man would emphasise his innate indolence, his 'sluggish existence', his 'listless inactivity' into which he would naturally lapse in the absence of God-given shocks such as the pressure of population on food:

'Necessity has been with great truth called the mother of invention. Some of the noblest exertions of the human mind have been set in motion by the necessity of satisfying the wants of the body... These stimulants could not be withdrawn from the mass of mankind without producing a general and fatal torpor, destructive of all the germs of future improvement.' (Malthus, 1798:202, 203, 204). Malthus, assessing the human essence in its state of nature, saw most crucially the sedentary lifestyle of the passive couch-potato, dependent on energy-saving technology to change the channels on his television: 'The savage would slumber for ever under his tree unless he were roused from his torpor by the cravings of hunger or the pinchings of cold.' (Malthus, 1798:203). An alternative view would, however, be that exercise itself can be a source of gratification. People undoubtedly demand some restful lethargy and some lazy days on the beach. Importantly, they also demand muscular exertion in the gym and mental stimulus in the theatre. The fact that they are willing to pay to secure the disruption of their psychic routine suggests that Hume was on the right track when he concluded that the truth was the mix: 'Human happiness, according to the most received notions, seems to consist in three ingredients; action, pleasure, and indolence... No one ingredient can be entirely wanting, without destroying, in some measure, the relish of the whole composition.' (Hume, 1752:21). Just as man seeks the substitution of leisure for labour when his income level allows him the Valhalla of comfort and feasting, so he also reveals a preference for disturbance and difficulty because the stagnation of equilibrium does not deliver the level of arousal that makes him feel enjoyably and purposively alert.

Keynes, recognising the challenge motive, drew attention to the large number of economic decisions which are the result not of profit-orientated calculation but of the non-rational need to be occupied, active and up-and-doing: 'Most, probably, of our decisions to do something positive, the full consequences of which will be drawn out over many days to come, can only be taken as a result of animal spirits – of a spontaneous urge to action rather than inaction, and not as the outcome of a weighted average of quantitative benefits multiplied by quantitative probabilities.' (Keynes, 1936:161). The entrepreneur in such a scenario is not simply an outcome-maximising machine. Instead he is a creature whose psychological restlessness impels him to take risks, to innovate, to explore novel breaches, to enter new industries because he knows the old ones too well. Arrival to him is boring, however lucrative the eternal repeat performance may happen to be. Initiative, on the other hand, gives him a sense of adventure that is not just another name for the frightened anxiety that ensures him his subsistence. Given the high incidence of investment decisions that emanate first and foremost from the need to keep busy, the economy, Keynes reflected, is far less likely to be self-equilibrating than it would be if material gain were to be the main motive that drives on the productive process.

Man, resisting the dullness of the *status quo*, craves change because the familiar rapidly loses its capacity to excite. The phenomenon, widely acknowledged in the case of consumption, lies at the heart of annual fashions that squander resources in a physical sense but also cater to the psychological dissatisfaction that is hungry for something new. People buy the tabloid press in order to consume the adrenelin rush of football extra-time, inventive criminality and film star sex scandals. People indulge in sequential infidelity in order to consume the thrill of the chase, the variety of fresh partners, the charades of imaginative concealment. People as consumers clearly treat change as a desideratum in itself that must not be confused with the endstate that is the result of the change. People as producers, it must be recognised, are no less keen to put some challenge and some excitement into their lives while at work.

That is why colleagues pick quarrels in order, overcoming difficulties, to enjoy the utility of conflict resolution. Business strategy, similarly, is a form of game-playing that satisfies the same need as sport or warfare. Competition, again, is valued because it makes the unexpectedness of the unpredictable into a resource that can be manipulated: 'After all, the matching of wits and skills is our main challenge, and other people's information, knowledge, experience, behavior, accomplishment, response to situations, solving of problems, and speculation about unresolved problems are our main sources of novelty.' (Scitovsky, 1976:83). More pay and more power are able to satisfy not least because they are a *more* and not simply a replication of the *same*: 'A rising income, therefore, may be worth much more than a high income, however high.' (Scitovsky, 1976:138). A rising income is refreshing not least because it is rising. The excitement is in the change. This is arguably one reason why the free enterprise system is seldom associated with zero-growth satiety or the asceticism of Zen. The need for excitement is a need like the need for food. Left to their own devices, men and women are most unlikely to opt out of a coping mechanism that they have come to welcome as a kind of play.

Marx, looking forward to the self-directing leaderlessness of post-scarcity communism, saw it as an economic order in which 'each can become accomplished in any branch he wishes': 'Society ... makes it possible for me to do one thing today and another tomorrow, to hunt in the morning, fish in the afternoon, rear cattle in the evening, criticise after dinner just as I have a mind, without ever becoming hunter, fisherman, shepherd or critic.' (Marx and Engels, 1845–46:53). Variety succeeds to constraint as work ceases to be narrow and over-specialised. Work itself, however, becomes not *less* but *more* important in an economy that takes activities as well as things as the needs that the process must meet.

Sombart, looking backward to the traditionalised productive system that antedated the means–ends profit-seeking of the commercial age, praised the craftsmanship of the guilds because it had made man and not gain the true measure of all: 'The work of production in the Middle Ages was a work for living, human beings, whose lives were devoted to it. Hence the laws governing it were thoroughly natural, comparable to the growth of a tree or the singing of a bird. Here, as in all things relating to production, the rule was *mensura omnium rerum homo.*' (Sombart, 1915:19–20).

Hobson, looking neither forward nor backward but at the conditions of labour in the present-day business culture found it at once 'an invasion and a degradation' of the worker's humanity, 'offering neither stimulus nor opportunity for a man to throw "himself" into his work. For the work only calls for a fragment of that "self" and always the same fragment. So it is true that not only is labour divided but the labourer.' (Hobson, 1914:87). Hobson, writing of the labourer, expressed the view that the calibre of the human input was being reduced through the de-humanisation of the producer at the place of work: 'A man who is not interested in his work, and does not recognise in it either beauty or utility, is degraded by that work ... It is manifest that, so far as his organic human nature is concerned, its unused portions are destined to idleness, atrophy, and decay.' (Hobson, 1914:87, 88). That decay is a threat not just to the operative's own self-respect and self-esteem but also to the nation's potential wealth and stock of usable resources. Meaningful work satisfies a human need. The denial of meaningful work cannot be expected to raise the sum total of material gratification.

9.2   INTRINSIC MOTIVATION

Activity that is extrinsically motivated, instrumental and means-to-an-end, is a response to non-ego demand. Performed not for its own sake but to reap a non-ego reward, it is not spontaneous learning and adaptation but passive compliance induced by the vision of punishment to be avoided, payment to be earned, praise to be won. It is the hard core of the economist's supply curve: 'Those, who have produced something for the lower price, will produce more for the higher price.' (Marshall, 1890:310). More leads to more and less leads to less. Drives, urges and emotions do not significantly threaten the rational norm that marries the market to money and not to the unfolding, the opening out, the actualisation of potential simply because it is there.

Activity that is motivated from without is mastery that varies in response to controls. Activity that is motivated from within is quite different in its thrust.

Treating the human being as organic development and not as mechanistic re-engineering, the theorist of growth and transformation concentrates on self-determination and agency in preference to the external energisers that fail to pick up the full range of choice. Activity that is motivated from within is defined as follows by Deci and Ryan: 'Intrinsic motivation is the innate, natural propensity to engage one's interests and exercise one's capacities, and in so doing, to seek and conquer optimal challenges. Such motivation emerges spontaneously from internal tendencies and can motivate behavior even without the aid of extrinsic rewards or environmental controls.' (Deci and Ryan, 1985:43). The arousal is innate and natural, the liberation of competence the positive step forward that Piaget had in mind when he wrote that 'the very nature of life is constantly to overtake itself.' (Piaget, 1971:362). The activity is not a knee-jerk reaction to stimulus. Rather, it is the product of consciousness and intentionality, interpretation and volition: 'To some extent, we assert, one's development is something that one does to satisfy one's needs, rather than something that just happens when structures inherently function.' (Deci and Ryan, 1985:115). Self-initiated and self-directed, intrinsic motivation must evidently be seen as human freedom both in the processes that are selected and in the outcomes that are the consequence of the expectations.

The model is not the conditioned reflex in the sense of Pavlov or Hebb. The dog performs a sanctioned activity in order to secure quiescence of appetite through the allocation of food. The rat avoids an electric wire in order to escape the pain of the shock. The dog and the rat have learned from past reinforcements the rewards that they can anticipate, the punishments that they should fear. Their associations of stimuli have been implanted in them from without. Intrinsic motivation, in contrast, is need-satisfaction that is not a passive reaction but instead an autonomous search.

Thus the mind, troubled by the incoherent and the incongruous, seeks to make sense of surprising recurrences even where no prize or payment provides an external – and a utilitarian – incentive to probe, to experiment and to explore. Adam Smith said that it was precisely this inbred curiosity, this fascination with the out-of-place that must be reconciled with the anticipated and the familiar, that constituted the core impetus for the scientist's investigations: 'Wonder, therefore, and not any expectation of advantage from its discoveries, is the first principle which prompts mankind to the study of Philosophy... They pursue this study for its own sake, as an original pleasure or good in itself, without regarding its tendency to procure them the means of many other pleasures.' (Smith, 1795:50). The mind has an innate need for tranquillity and composure. Confronted with the new and the singular, it explores causal sequences and tests for observable correlations in an attempt to impose order upon the uncertain and the unpredicted.

Veblen too made much of disinterested inquiry. This, like Smith, he derived from bewilderment and from man's 'idle curiosity.' (Veblen, 1906:10). Veblen traced the scientific impulse not to pragmatism and expediency but to the quest for knowledge needed to map the laws of cause and effect. He regarded the search to understand as a fundamental human drive, on a par with the instinct of self-preservation or the 'emulative or invidious comparison of persons'. (Veblen, 1899:29). Not useful so much as enjoyable, Veblen described the scientific imperative as being 'closely related to the aptitude for play observed both in man and in the lower animals.' (Veblen, 1906:10). Scientific investigation to Veblen has much in common with children's games.

Smith on 'Wonder' and Veblen on 'idle curiosity' recall Festinger's account of the 'cognitive dissonance' between fact and theory that, energised into aversive behaviour, stimulates people to re-discover or to re-explain primarily in order to reduce the psychological discomfort that they experience when confronted with a discrepancy that they feel impelled to resolve: 'Dissonance acts in the same way as a state of drive or need or tension. The presence of dissonance leads to action to reduce it just as, for example, the presence of hunger leads to action to reduce the hunger.' (Festinger, 1957:18). The reference to the reduction rather than the elimination of the incongruity is a reminder that, just as excessive uncertainty can be stressful, so excessive repetition can be a cause of nervous strain. It is in keeping with the theory of intrinsic motivation for people to alter their conduct or re-think their schemata in order to keep within acceptable limits the relationship between anticipation and feedback. It is equally in keeping with the theory of intrinsic motivation for people to open up new sources of disharmony in order to secure the need-satisfaction that accrues to the exercise of faculties and the extension of capacities. On the one hand the need for meaning, on the other the need for challenge – one inference that can be drawn is that neither disorientation nor equilibrium but rather moderate search accompanied by moderate coordination is the degree of cognitive dissonance that is most in keeping with the mixed portfolio, the balance of need.

People find fulfilment in the use of information and the application of skill. Deci writes that 'intrinsically motivated behavior is behavior which is motivated by one's need for feeling competent and self-determining.' (Deci, 1975:62). All human beings, he writes, bring with them this need to be on top of events when they interact with others and with their environment. An unintended outcome can be efficiency and achievement first and foremost because *to be* is also *to do*.

Human beings are born with a basic need for cognitive and creative self-expression. Their personal wellbeing, self-perceived, is enhanced by the opportunity to be resourceful in managing novelty, to become absorbed in constructive work, to produce changes in the world around them. They like to be stimulated, purposive and at the controls. They do not like to be helpless, inconsequential and swept along. Human beings also learn that success and excellence are visited with extrinsic rewards such as praise, recognition, approval, acceptance and, of course, money. However enjoyable the exploration, however hateful the toil, the non-ego payment will often be on offer from an outsider who thinks that performance warrants the compensation of the *quid pro quo.*

Energisation can be internal: the child who loves to practise the piano needs no other motivator than the activity itself. Energisation can be external: the child who hates mathematical proofs can be bribed with the promise of sweets. Energisation, moreover, can be *both* internal *and* external at once. It is in precisely this case that the related issues of over-compensation and crowding out cause such significant problems for the economics of incentives.

Over-compensation may be said to exist where the scientist gratified through curiosity and research is given a high salary as well. Alfred Marshall seems to be implying that just such a super-clearing price can survive in the market when, stating that creative work is 'the aim of life', 'life itself', he finds a philosopher's *Summum Bonum* in energetic activity as a mode of becoming: 'There has always been a substratum of agreement that social good lies mainly in that healthful exercise and development of faculties which yields happiness without pall, because it sustains self-respect and is sustained by hope.' (Marshall, 1897:310). As Talcott Parsons rightly observes, the Marshallian world-view is very much one of activity as its own justification, the payment for activity something of a functionless fifth wheel: 'On the whole Marshall saw the field of business enterprise as the principal opportunity for the exercise of what he considered the noblest traits of human character. The wealth acquired in the process was not the aim, but rather a by-product.' (Parsons, 1931:143). If a person is working because the work is making him himself, then, clearly, he cannot be said to require the supplementary motivator of a high salary purely in order to cue the effort that he is already ranking above inaction. While the consistent marginalist will stress that the high salary is the motivator for the *last* unit alone, the fact remains that the pay-packet is padded with a considerable amount of producer's surplus.

The upward-sloping supply curve is difficult to reconcile with the notion of disinterested devotion to activities. In that sense it is correct to say, with Parsons, that 'Marshall simply did not think through the implications of this result for a theory of real costs, when that term refers to sacrifices.' (Parsons, 1931:149). Nor are the implications entirely without ambiguity when the emphasis is placed exclusively upon extrinsic rewards. The reason is that social man, a part of a community, is dependent on non-ego outsiders for approval and not just for money. The esteem of his peers is a non-negligible net advantage accruing to the scientist who makes a breakthrough discovery or presents a well-received paper at a conference. The corporate chief executive values not just profits but 'high prestige for business activity' and 'a reputation for able leadership.' (Marshall, 1919:180, 633). Conspicuous successes such as these are well remunerated in money as well as approval. In receipt not of one but of two external rewards, the suspicion is real that they will be the beneficiaries of more prizes than are functionally necessary to retain them in the trade.

Over-compensation is one possibility in an economy where rewards can be both ego-determined and other-allocated. Crowding out is another. If a child who loves learning also achieves good marks in a test, will the external reward be complementary to the internal urge or will it cause the child, Festinger-like, to revise his perceptions to the detriment of his inner-directedness? If a child with no experience of music is told he will be punished for failing to practise, will the enforced compliance release a latent love or will it make the child so dependent on others' opinions as to cease his supply the moment that the threat is withdrawn? Questions such as these must clearly be addressed by experimental psychologists if sustained coexistence or, alternatively, a shift in the locus of causality is factually to be established.

The evidence that has been collected has a strong tendency to support the hypothesis that goals will be displaced and intrinsic motivation crowded out. Consider the finding of Kruglanski, Alon and Lewis, that 'when Israeli high school students were offered the valued reward of a tour through a university laboratory for working on a set of tasks, the students were less creative and exhibited poorer recall on these tasks, and they reported less enjoyment of the tasks than did students who were not promised the reward.' (Deci and Ryan, 1985:67). Consider the finding of Garbarino, that payment offered to peer-group tutors caused them to experience more pressure and more tension, to become less caring and less effective, than were their colleagues whose remuneration, internal, came in the form of self-esteem: 'Garbarino reported that the rewarded tutors were more demanding and more negative in their emotional tone than the nonrewarded tutors, and in turn that the students of the rewarded tutors learned less well and made more errors.' (Deci and Ryan, 1985:67). Consider the finding of McGraw and McCullers, that students paid to solve a puzzle had more difficulty with it than did control volunteers motivated exclusively by internal states – and that, in subsequent free-choice periods, 'those subjects who expected a reward were less likely to return to the uncompleted task than those subjects who did not. This led the authors to conclude that rewarding the performance of a task can lead to premature cognitive disengagement with the task.' (Deci and Ryan, 1985:68). Consider the finding of Kiesler and Sakamura, that persons paid to defend a cause in which they believe will (associating remuneration in their mind with action in which the mercenary holds no stake) experience a weakening in their attachment as a direct consequence of the bribe they are offered: 'Payments for espousing a belief-consonant position made subjects' beliefs more vulnerable to change during a subsequent period when they read an argument that was counter to their beliefs. In sum, it appears that when the expression of an attitude becomes instrumental to reward attainment, one's commitment to the attitude is weakened.' (Deci and Ryan, 1985:69). Assuming that these demonstrations of demotivation and alteration of motivation indeed confirm that reinforcement through additional motivation was far from being the case, the inference that must be drawn is that extrinsic rewards can actually limit people's freedom save to the extent that they rebel against the constraints by cutting back on task performance. While the minimum supplied for the maximum charged will presumably contribute something to their sense of being in charge, the reduction in effort consequent upon the shift from intrinsic motivation to the self-stigmatisation of the tool that serves another's purpose is unlikely to do very much to accelerate the rate of economic improvement.

Extrinsic rewards can undermine intrinsic motivation: interest and enjoyment become less, commitment and quality fall off. External rewards, importantly, are also capable of enhancing internal motivation: lessons are remembered longer, the quality of artwork is judged to improve. The apparent contradiction between the productive and the destructive tendencies is resolved by Deci when he decomposes the extrinsic acknowledgement into its two component strands: 'Every reward (including feedback) has two aspects, a controlling aspect and an informational aspect which provides the subject with information about his competence and self-determination. The relative salience of the two aspects determines which process will be operative.' (Deci, 1975:142). External reward can reinforce internal motivation even as it can weaken it. The outcome depends on whether the control or the information is the more prominent characteristic.

Where control is salient, empirical research suggests a negative relation-ship. Thus Patty and Safford, for example, were able to document a lower level of enjoyment where sample subjects were paid: 'Women who volunteered to give blood and expected the reward of free basketball tickets for doing so were significantly less positive toward blood donation than were women who gave blood without expecting the reward.' (Deci, 1975:149). Extrinsic rewards can be a threat to motivation and in that way to performance. Involvement in the activity is seen as instrumental, the reward as the principal reason for supplying effort. The locus of causality is believed to be situated outside the self. The self is believed to be the servant of another.

Where information confirming competence is the more conspicuous feature, there, in contrast, the relationship between felt self-determination and outside feedback can be a more positive one. Individuals offered success calibrators in verbal ('very good') or monetary form can experience a maintenance or even an increase in the level of their intrinsic motivation as a result of the resassurance that their efforts have borne fruit. Negative feedback can by the same token severely undermine their confidence: 'Negative feedback, whether given verbally by the experimenter or self-administered by the subject through failure at the intrinsically motivated task, caused a decrease in intrinsic motivation.' (Deci, 1975:147). Both women and men were subject to the same discouragement. Positive feedback, interestingly, affected them in different ways. Men were able to see rewards such as praise as conveying information. Women, however, perhaps because of socialisation into dependency and interpersonal skills, were more prone to see even information as a mode of control. Their intrinsic motivation is for that reason more susceptible to erosion as they gravitate into approval-seeking behaviour where a man would for longer treat achievement as an end in itself.

9.3   THE SUPPLY MOTIVE

The first section of this chapter was concerned with the satisfaction of human need through economic activity, the second with intrinsic motivation such as requires no external incentive. This third and final section examines the policy options that could cater for need through work and release latent energies that might otherwise be lost.

9.3.1   Need

Economics, if it is meaningfully to contribute to felt wellbeing, must take a view on the full range of human needs that the productive system must satisfy. No list is ever likely to be either exhaustive or uncontroversial. Nor is it easy to make distinctions, qualitative or quantitative, between needs which have differing degrees of urgency depending on the extent to which each has bygone-wise already been met. Ambiguities abound – freedom to T.H. Green is the opportunity to develop, to Milton Friedman the choice of outputs and inputs. Life-cycles confuse – the obsessions of the child may not be fully comparable with the values of the adult. The difficulties are real ones. Even so, a human-centred economics cannot decline to put forward a provisional list.

Thus the human being, following Maslow, may be said to have a need for safety and security, integration and belonging, esteem and self-esteem, creativity and self-actualisation. People need not just bodily gratifications but also the higher satisfactions of responsibility, relatedness and the chance to grow. Denied the satisfaction of those higher needs, they may compensate for their anxieties and disappointments by means of economic consumables that give them a short-lived 'high'. They may be acting *as if* maximising their utility from their limited choice-set. In respect of the extended psychological list, however, it is most unlikely that they are doing all that can be done to squeeze maximum welfare from a finite lifespan.

Assuming that *insecurity* is indeed a violation of need, there are courses of action that the individual can select in order to make himself feel subjectively better off. One of these is the market purchase of commercial insurance, of a smoke alarm, of a barking dog. Another is the choice of the 'job for life' in preference to better paid but more cyclical employment. In ways such as these capitalism itself can put on sale the conservative reassurance of a semi-predictable future. It is one of the attractions of an economic spectrum extending from the autonomous/aggressive to the sheltered/protected that it allows individuals to select the level of security as need-satisfaction that they themselves most want.

Sometimes, however, the market fails. The private sector does not insure against long-term unemployment or provide unrestricted cover for diagnosed illness. There is a reason for cradle-to-grave welfare that guarantees the social minimum of a robust safety net. The private sector, again, is handicapped by competition where rivals are too numerous to collude. Here the State can coordinate the dispersed, binding each equally by means of laws to restrict redundancies or to invest in safety harnesses. The State in such cases implements a standard of security that profit-seekers by themselves cannot unilaterally put in place.

Oligopolists employ price leadership and form cartels in order to promote reasonable security for the businesses and their staffs. Resale price maintenance and protective takeovers are used to ensure a non-adversarial life. The State falls back on tariffs and subsidies to preserve long-established industries and traditional communities. Licenses and permits are restricted to ensure that outsiders do not rock the boat or declare a price war against the settled. Both the profit-seekers and the social engineers, it is clear, are, in the mixed economy, in a position to deliver perceived security, even at the cost of productive efficiency foregone.

Integration is another need that, presumed to exist, must then be recognised and even met by a holistic economic order with a commitment to more than the material wants alone. Economic networks and workplace collegiality can be the cause and effect of those perceptions of cohesiveness, community, membership, belonging, citizenship, participation that make the individual see himself as a valued cooperator and a part of a whole. The need is the end: no one would reduce the Confucian concept of harmony or Shakespeare on the self-destructiveness of the stomach that demands its independence from the rest of the body to a simple stratagem for boosting the wealth of nations. Yet the need is even so a means. Consider the long-term trust that is built up through relational and repeated contracting (a world away from the evanescent anonymity of the spot once-for-all such as may be exemplified by car boot sales, fly-by-night pitches, door-to-door trading). Consider the labour force commitment that is the consequence of employers' care and consultation (an economic payoff to which the suppression of executive dining facilities, the introduction of *Mitbestimmung,* the compression of pay differentials irrespective of the short-run disincentives, may each be said to make a potential contribution). As Will Hutton writes, there can be dividend rationality in putting long-termism and solidarity above the price nexus that gives the free-rider no reason not to shirk: 'The key to productivity is not the wage system, but the system of human relations within an organisation.' (Hutton, 1995:253).

Precisely because performance provides an economic payoff, there are grounds for expecting the profit-seeking firm to invest resources in fostering a sense of integration. Thus it may eschew layoffs and wage cuts in the downswing lest it undermine loyalty by teaching its workforce that the input labour only sums up to hires and fires. It may promise lifetime employment such as, limiting turnover and mobility, also reduces the loss it would suffer if on-the-job training moved on to a business rival. It may provide occupational welfare through convalescent homes, generous pensions, long-service sabbaticals, first-in-last-out guarantees even for expensive older workers whose value to the firm has been undercut by efficient new technologies. Wanting to encourage attachment, the firm reduces information asymmetry through transparency and disclosure and presses for union involvement in promotions-rounds and staff evaluation. Wanting to discourage alienation, the firm rejects performance-related pay, individually-negotiated bonuses and fast-track promotion lest the unintended outcome of inquisitorial monitoring and perpetual supervision be division, resentment and leisure enjoyed at the place of work. Ronald Dore and others have attributed the high productivity of the Japanese business to the complementarity in the Japanese economy of consensus and responsibility at the input stage, unsentimental profit-seeking at the level of final output. Hutton is one of those who sees in the Japanese mix the nub of economic success: 'Competition is ferocious, but co-operation is extensive; the juxtaposition of apparently inconsistent forms of behaviour may strike those schooled in Anglo–American capitalism as irrational, but for the Japanese the tension actually enhances the strength of each.' (Hutton, 1995:269).

The mix of past-conditioned duties and gain-seeking markets is clearly a way of promoting felt integration without sacrificing the interests of the property owner. State intervention can codify that mix and make the discipline a general one. Thus progressive taxation on higher incomes, a minimum wage to raise up the low-paid, can contribute to the common culture that homogenises the rich with the poor. Comprehensive education and a National Health Service can generate a sense of oneness that makes the worker less likely to envy the boss. A tripartite Incomes Board can settle wage claims in the light of the national consensus. Macroeconomic management, ensuring full employment, can block off the short-sighted temptation to offer a subsistence wage because of a reserve army prepared to undercut the insider incumbents. What the State does in cases such as these is to threaten 'free' markets in the short run in order to promote better-performing markets once labour has become persuaded that no person is being treated as a commodity, as a thing to be used.

Esteem is a further need in the sense of Maslow that must be satisfied by an economic system committed to a mix of ends. People want to be approved of, to feel welcome, to be appreciated, to be loved. They also want to be in a position to live at ease with themselves. It is the contention of the Maslow-type economist that the need for respect and self-respect must be made a topic in social economics and not left to the curative care of individual psychology alone.

Priced economic relationships are a source of status in a market order where trade is a measure of merit. The problem is that a hierarchical allocation of recognition and prestige is bound to leave some worth stigmatised, some self-worth in the shade. Persons opposed to the social distance that condemns the also-rans to the self-definition of the failure often therefore call for the levelling down of prizes such as wealth (the nation-building function of inheritance duties and the capital gains tax) and of power (collective bargaining, plant-level co-determination). They will call in addition for the levelling up of entry-level opportunities (human capital formation through local polytechnics, apprenticeships, day-release, grants) and of high-profile outcomes (affirmative action, quota schemes, credential-blind recruitment). Economic institutions in ways such as these can seek to cocoon the fragile self from the school-like grades awarded by self-appointed judges in the shopping centre or while waiting for the bus.

One answer to the problem of esteem not accorded, self-esteem put at risk, is for people to build their identity on firmer foundations than economic roles and the lace-curtain busybodies. Comparisons are a recipe for anxiety, not least because no person can come first in every race. Riesman's 'other-directedness' dumbs searching autonomy into the frightened passivity of

Adorno's 'authoritarian personality'. One answer in such circumstances would therefore be to return the need for esteem and self-esteem to the psychologist (teaching realistic adaptations) and the clergyman (preaching 'love they neighbour' - *and thyself*) without asking the market economy to take on board a need that it has neither the capacity nor the obligation to satisfy. Another answer to the problem of esteem and self-esteem would, however, be the economy itself, and the mix.

Thus the private sector contributes to the supply of esteem both through economic growth (often the antidote to the felt exclusion of absolute deprivation) and through mass consumption (the standardisation produced by long production-runs making it more difficult to distinguish high-earners from low-earners than it was in the days when the king wore a crown and the banker wore a bowler hat). The higher average propensity of the rich to save means that absolute differences will not fully be put on view. The embourgeoisement of work culture means that more and more of the lower paid will look and act in some measure like their social superiors. Common television programmes, High Street copies of couture originals, the social cement of sport and the 'Top Ten', are not a way of saying that the debate about distributive justice has definitively come to an end. What they might signal is simply that, thanks to the private sector, human dignity and mutual acceptance have become more general; and that, for great numbers of people, esteem in a richer society is likely to be equal enough.

The State sector too has a contribution to make to a 'positive sense of self' (Doyal and Gough, 1991:199). The 'right to a job' is at once the guarantee of a role: desperate unhappiness and sometimes suicide can result where prolonged unemployment deprives the individual of a sense of participation in socially meaningful activity. Generous income maintenance gives the low-paid, the unemployable, the retired, a foothold in social as well as physical survival: children from deprived backgrounds are empowered to buy a football and are not shut out from school excursions. A national curriculum teaches that no one should be ashamed of his race and includes role-models from the minority cultures. Emphasising that the *Leitkultur* must be broad enough to bring out the best in all, the State is held by its supporters to be in a position to include the unesteemed in a going concern.

Self-actualisation in the sense of Maslow means that the growth of persons and not the growth of things comes to be man's most urgent necessity: 'Human life will never be understood unless its highest aspirations are taken into account. Growth, self-actualization, the striving toward health, the quest for identity and autonomy, the yearning for excellence (and other ways of phrasing the striving "upward") must by now be accepted beyond question as a widespread and perhaps universal human tendency.' (Maslow,

1954:xii–xiii). People need to make themselves. Making things is one of the ways in which they seize that option.

People have a need to be creative. Meaningful work provides an outlet for self-expression through economic embodiment. Workaholics and Weberian Calvinists treat office hours as the means to the end of self-respect earned through assiduity and diligence. Personal growth through work is, in contrast, the perspective that physiological exhilaration, aesthetic manipulation, the skilful use of tools, the imaginative use of intelligence are all ways in which supply can release vital strengths that might otherwise be dammed up. The process *per se* and not just the finished product can be made a source of pleasure. The process becomes a utility, an economic resource that the self is eager to consume.

Veblen believed that the practical expedients of 'efficiency and economy, proficiency, creative work and technological mastery of facts' were in truth their own reward: 'Efficient use of the means at hand and adequate management of the resources available for the purposes of life is itself an end of endeavour, and accomplishment of this kind is a source of gratification.' (Veblen, 1914:31-2, 33). History speaks with a single voice on the economic serviceability of the 'idle' propensity where 'no utilitarian aim enters in its habitual exercise': 'The instinct of workmanship brought the life of mankind from the brute to the human plane, and in all the later growth of culture it has never ceased to pervade the works of man.' (Veblen, 1914:37, 88). That is why the business era, committed as it is to pecuniary principles, is such a threat to humanity's survival as God the Father, as Mother Earth – as an instinctive producer that does not count the cost.

Veblen looked to the engineers, the craftsmen, the efficiency-minded for the social revolution that would topple the hegemony of salesmanship at the cost of potential: 'In their struggle against the cultural effects of the machine process ... business principles cannot win in the long run.' (Veblen, 1904:375). Veblen, like Marx, was too eager to predict the collapse of the system under the weight of its presumed inner contradictions. He also underestimated the capacity of the mixed economy to supply the outlet which he sought.

Such an outlet obtains where workers agree to a lower rate of pay because the job satisfaction of craftsmanship without routinisation is made a part of the package. An illustration would be an organisation that relies on small-scale production, employs intermediate technology, rejects de-skilling, resists mechanisation. Even if the cost per unit were to rise, so, it could be argued, would the self-fulfilment of the creator whose personal aspirations were put before the GNP. Nor, as Schumacher stresses, is there any necessary reason why a 'Buddhist economics' of moderation and the middle way should inevitably lead to a diminution in productivity: 'Development does not start with goods; it starts with people and their education, organization and discipline. Without these three, all resources remain latent, untapped, potential.' (Schumacher, 1973:159). Need-satisfaction for that reason can also be the cause of an improvement in quantity or quality or both. People are at once the end and the means. Concerned about materialistic values, Schumacher is in no doubt that 'small is beautiful' can deliver economic as well as personal gains: 'People are the primary and ultimate source of any wealth whatsoever. If they are left out, if they are pushed around by self-styled experts and high-handed planners, then nothing can ever yield real fruit.' (Schumacher, 1973:160).

Self-actualisation presupposes work that does not stultify the intelligence. It also presupposes a sense of involvement, a sense of purposiveness in the context of community. Taking *Gemeinschaft* to be the locality, the firm could promote peaceful symbiosis by hiring local labour, producing for local needs, integrating its transactions into the local skein of social networks that makes each the guardian of his neighbour's rectitude. Taking *Gemeinschaft* to be the business itself, the organisation could transcend the capital–labour divide by evolving into a cooperative, owned and operated from within. Robert Owen, J.S. Mill, the Ricardian socialist Thompson, the French utopian Fourier, are only some of the thinkers who have believed that social harmony would be improved if the employees, calling themselves proprietors, were to hire capital (via loans and bonds) rather than being hired themselves by a moneyed class outside. The proposal for producer cooperatives can be amplified with sub-clauses intended still further to make the organisation into a community. There can be a constricted wage dispersion lest excessive inequality stand in the way of brotherhood. There can be a limitation of size (Fourier restricted the *phalanstère* to 400 families) in order that the members should become personally acquainted. There can be the bottom-up election of managers (a world away from the *national*isation in which one bureaucracy simply replaces another). In ways such as these the labour-managed firm could, conceptually speaking, reduce the detachment that manifests itself in sub-Stakhanovite nine-to-five-ism. It has, of course, done so only infrequently. If the labour-owned firm is genuinely both fulfilling and competitive, then it is hard to say why such enterprises have so seldom been demanded by the rank-and-file, been established, been successful.

Even if worker ownership is not the highest-ranked means to the end of self-actualisation, industrial democracy, formal and informal, is likely to have an unlocking function as a means of making self-holders feel active and integrated, not merely points on an organisational chart. Even work that is boring in itself can *become* interesting if the participants feel consulted and involved. Elton Mayo's pioneering interviews at the Hawthorne Works of the

Western Electric Company documented, as early as 1927–32, that *morale* and economics go hand in hand.

The Western Electric Company had already found that productivity rose when the light level was increased. They had also found that a decrease in the light level was capable of producing the same result. Allowing for other work-related variables such as scheduling, Mayo and his Harvard colleagues established that *any* change (perceived or not to be an improvement) tended to raise productivity; but that the operative variable was the element of consultation that made each change a topic in collaboration and not coercion. Good human relations, Mayo concluded, was good business as well: 'The larger and more complex the institution, the more dependent is it upon the whole-hearted co-operation of every member of the group.' (Mayo, 1949:62).

Stability, respect and belonging, human needs in themselves, are also inputs into the people-centred workplace that Mayo found to be productive both of efficiency and job satisfaction. The group, he stated, is a home, a refuge, a source of mutual support: 'For all of us the feeling of security and certainty derives almost always from assured membership of a group. If this is lost, no monetary gain, no job guarantee, can be sufficient compensation.' (Mayo, 1949:67). The group should evidently not change too rapidly lest this, threatening comradeship, make the worker isolated, empty, anxious and afraid, 'more difficult both to fellow workers and to supervisor.' (Mayo, 1949:67). The tribalism, the them-and-us collegiality, is a reason why workers sometimes resist upgrading to a different group with different companions; why throughput can be boosted by professional pride and the 'desire to stand well with the team' (Mayo, 1949:99) – and why democracy at work can be significantly improved by banding workers into smaller groups, each with some discretion over the rules by which it is bound. Self-actualisation is promoted by power. The small group offers clear opportunities for power to be shared and the individual to become involved.

The private sector will have no absolute resistance to the need for self-actualisation. Profit-seekers will find their way to job rotation, union directors, devolution to teams, grass-roots initiative, quality-control circles, where the consequence of these policies is higher productivity, fewer quits, less absenteeism, an improved quality of output, a lowered cost of supervision. The private sector can do much for self-actualisation; but there is even so a role for the State. Subsidisation can encourage lifetime education that upgrades the unskilled into jobs that exercise the mind. Unions can be required to decide strikes on the democratic principle of one person, one vote. Firms can be required to facilitate buy-outs where in-house stakeholders put their rights above those of absentee shareholders. In ways such as these, in short, the mixed economy can bring about a degree of self-actualisation that would be recognised as market failure in the absence of the State.

9.3.2   Intrinsic Motivation

Some tasks are inherently so unpleasant that extrinsic rewards like money or applause are essential if they are to be done at all: 'This is similar to that attitude toward life which values it less for its own sake than because one goes to Heaven at the end of it.' (Maslow, 1962:31). Other tasks are further removed from the pure instrumentality of the economist's supply curve. It was suggested in Section 9.2 that much of productive work satisfies the human need to be competent, to bring about a desired outcome, to be self-determining and engaged. If the economic problem is truly the constraint of scarce resources, then self-reinforcing activity is clearly a wealth-producing asset that should not be allowed to go to waste.

The private sector has an economic stake in human development. Research subjects asked for their voluntary cooperation have been seen to solve a problem more rapidly than research subjects rewarded for the same task. Research subjects paid to lose weight do less housework in general and are more likely to regain the weight once the payments end. The private sector, aware of empirical evidence such as this, has a profit-seeker's stake in ensuring that maximal efficiency should be squeezed from all the intrinsic motivation that it is able to harness.

Insight and insider knowledge, for one thing, can be made into paying inputs by promising the operative a range of discretion within an agreed-upon job description. An example would be an investigative journalist. Such a reporter is likely to be demotivated by surveillance, prescription, over-management and the time-clock. An appeal to professional pride will often deliver the better story. Trusted rather than monitored, the journalist is likely to be remotivated by the chance to use his initiative, to think laterally, to stretch his skills to the full without the feeling that only a narrow and rigid response will be in keeping with his contract of service.

The quality of workmanship can itself be a high-return characteristic. An example would be the handwoven carpets of the Middle East that Deci describes so evocatively in the following words: 'It has been said that modern rugs seem to come from the *hands* of the weavers, whereas the older rugs seem to have come from the *hearts* of the workers.' (Deci, 1978:175). It is the consumer of rugs who in the last analysis will decide the fate of the craftsmen. Should heritage and skill be valued economic attributes, the weaver and his rugs will be demand-led and in the money. The consumer is king. Thus would capitalism itself stave off automation and the robot. Business itself would protect the aesthetic self-confirmation of the creator who knows best.

The private sector knows that *morale* and attachment can make the worker a better-paying investment. That is why prudent profit-seekers, taking the longer view, will often find it rational to phase out irritants like piece rates, sales commissions, clocking on, bonuses, fines and suspensions in favour of variety, teamwork, responsibility, Internet home-working, maternity breaks, power-sharing, profit-sharing, and company housing. Treating people as subjects, not objects, is a moral act in itself. Appealing as it does to intrinsic motivation, it is likely to raise consumer welfare and competitive market share as well.

The private sector will often have a money-maximising incentive to make work into play. Sometimes it will not; and then it might be the role of the State to defend the non-commercial part of felt wellbeing. Tax holidays can reward firms which over-equip staff with general computer skills. Regulations can specify that annual appraisals be presented as counselling and not as fault-finding. Public ownership can be the last sanction for a bad employer whose sole interest is perceived to be gain: 'When the situation implies that one's behavior is for someone else's purposes rather than for one's own, the situation is likely to be experienced as more controlling.' (Deci and Ryan, 1985:96). In the case of supply as in the case of demand, a mix of motives can evidently be encouraged by a mix of market and State.

10. Organisational order

Organisations are made up of people and hark back to the past. The business firm is no exception to the rule that a machine has no goal function of its own but that a human group is a thicket of interests and alliances, recollections and routines. The neoclassical approach has been to abstract from the 'who-talks-to-whom-how-often-about-what' (Simon, 1965:xx) in order to treat the firm as if an inanimate entity, a black box, a production function with no more than a profit-maximising purpose. The behavioural approach, on the other hand, has made its focus the thicket and its *explicandum* the sociological and psychological baggage that men and women bring with them when they go to work. The answers may in the end be the same – in that economic suppliers must willy-nilly decide on price and quantity and do so through markets always to some extent competitive. The questions, importantly, must always be different – since the neoclassical economist reifies the business into a legalism in itself whereas the institutional economist insists that the firm is no more than what its members do. Organisations are made up of people and hark back to the past. Rather than being surprised that the production process because of interaction and convention can never be fully rational, the observer ought to be grateful that there is evolution in the organisation at all.

Organisations are made up of people and hark back to the past. This chapter considers the ways in which shared lives and inherited conventions impose order upon the industrial structure in a manner, neither impersonal nor anonymous, which is a valuable complement to the market-mediated coordination of the supply-and-demand price. There is more to free enterprise capitalism than the timeless Walrasian auctioneer. The three sections of this chapter consider three dimensions of the institutional binding that makes the real-world business firm react as it does.

Section 1, X-efficiency, is variations on a theme made famous by Leibenstein, that productivity is a function not just of land, labour and capital but of inducement, preference and attitude as well: 'There is more to the determination of output than the obviously observable inputs. The nature of the management, the environment in which it operates, and the incentives employed are significant.' (Leibenstein, 1966:87). Alongside the plots, the bodies and the plant, there is, in other words, the residual that is outlook which accounts for so much of the variance, the expansion – and the waste.

Section 2, Organisational memory, takes up the historical practices that are embedded in the life of the group. Initially it is the task of business routines to optimise outcomes in such a way as to ensure the survival and success of the team. Later on, familiar servants who have done their job well, they will acquire a status of their own that makes them resistant to further maximisation lest it prove a threat to established procedures. Past heuristics become present-day parameters, as Hodgson explains: 'While a favourable adaptation may occur in relation to a given environmental situation, and the first few adaptations may be favourable for the units concerned, the accumulation of such adaptations may alter the environment itself, and the eventual result may be that the same adaptation no longer yields beneficial results for any individual unit.' (Hodgson, 1999:180). The gain is the stability. The cost is the reluctance to explore.

Section 3, The network as social capital, shows that much of economic action is routed through the personal relationships of identifiable partners who over time have built up reliable knowledge of one another. Social networks situate the competitive process within an ongoing matrix of favours, faces and reputations: 'Causation resides in the intersection of relations.' (Burt, 1993:96). Sometimes, Burt says, that matrix will be the only game in town: 'Trust is critical precisely because competition is imperfect. The question is not whether to trust, but who to trust. In a perfectly competitive arena, you can trust the system to provide a fair return on your investments. In the imperfectly competitive arena, you have only your personal contacts.' (Burt, 1993:72). Absent the institutional economy, Burt is saying, not a great deal would remain of supply and demand.

10.1   X-EFFICIENCY

Allocative efficiency relates to the welfare economics of resource use where the aim is to maximise the satisfaction derived from a limited endowment and where market prices are taken to be the most dependable signals. The competitive mechanism is seen as the source of the Paretian benefit. The single producer is treated as a passive atom that is directed by gravity into its best-possible equilibrium.

X-efficiency relates not to endowment and exchange but to the internal constraints that influence the achievement of the productive potential. The firm is only exceptionally an owner-operator trading without staff. The firm in almost every case is a varying set of paid agents legally responsible to the property holder who in title remains the principal. There is no reason to expect that the motives of the salaried will coincide with the interests of the profit-seeking; and thence the probability of shortfall. The result of the separation of ownership from execution is likely to be slack and slippage, a failure to minimise costs and an indifference to new opportunities. That shortfall, measured as 'the degree to which actual output is less than maximum output (for given inputs)' (Leibenstein, 1976:95), is an indicator of economic underperformance that Harvey Leibenstein has termed x-inefficiency.

The reason for the shortfall, Leibenstein writes, is not incorrect pricing but rather the man-made choice spectrum that is a characteristic of the layered organisation: 'The standard theory of production treats human and nonhuman inputs almost symmetrically, or essentially symmetrically. My theory drops this approach.' (Leibenstein, 1976:95). The standard theory of the factors of production treats the employment of staff as if it were the installation of plant. Leibenstein prefers to make a clear distinction – since people have consciousness and, unlike objects, a will of their own: 'In most work contexts individuals pursue their own motives as well as the interests of the firm. Usually, they try to work out a compromise between the two sets of interests.' (Leibenstein, 1976:257). Leibenstein concludes that supervisors 'cannot fully control firm members': 'All individuals have some scope for individual interpretations of their jobs.' (Leibenstein, 1976:255). It is expressly because of that freedom that underperformance as seen from the perspective of the principal might remain a feature even of a market economy. Efficiency-maximising behaviour, Leibenstein believes, is only likely in a one-person business trading in the situational determinism of perfect competition. All else is likely to prove a shortfall from the scarcity-textbook's grace.

Machines and land can be purchased outright. Human labour, save where slavery exists, can never be more than rented. It is rented on the terms set out in a contract of service – and it is in the nature of any such agreement that it will always be incomplete and underspecified: 'Once we focus on the internal workings of the organization we will see that formal employment contracts, or what may be interpreted as such contracts, are almost trivial in helping to explain how people behave in work contexts. The presumed formal contract cannot by itself tell us what it is that we want to know about intraorganizational behavior.' (Leibenstein, 1987:4).

The formal contract, legally binding though it is, will be brief. It will set out the hours of work and give a general description of what the job will entail. It will not include any mention of effort, alertness, willingness to share sensitive information, tolerance of co-workers' resentments where new conventions are put to a vote. Occupational roles are always in some measure self-defined. Monitored indicators are only a sampling of overall contribution. Continuous change means open-ended adaptation. The formal contract, rationally crafted but also brief, is no match for the simple truism that not every aspect of every job is susceptible to unambiguous codification in advance. The result is a margin of employee discretion, of autonomy, of flexibility that makes the organisational hierarchy into a penumbra of imprecision and uncertainty. It is in that intra-firm penumbra that Leibenstein's 'x' may be said to dwell.

Leibenstein recognises that it is only individuals and never organisations that can formulate a preference. His focus is therefore the discrete utility-maximiser who, within the goalposts of contract and structure, has considerable freedom to adjust the APQT components which influence the distance travelled in the direction of the productive frontier.

A in the sense of Leibenstein refers to the choice of activity: the employee is given outline information and instruction about his duties but is obliged to use his judgement and initiative to flesh out his tasks. P is pace: while hours spent in attendance may be prescribed and enforced, the speed and rhythm of throughput are subject to variation, and so are the informal breaks for chats and friendships. Q is quality: care, accuracy, concentration, trustworthiness are all parts of the input package but also characteristics that are almost as difficult to circumscribe in a job description as the undertaking of love and commitment in the marriage vows. T is time, both its total and its patterning: even if the schedule is fixed, employees at the margin can come slightly late, leave slightly early, volunteer for overtime, under-exploit their holiday allowance. The employer can try to pre-set the APQT package in line with his profit and output objectives. Try as he might, his staff (and not just the self-employed) will *de facto* operate within a decision-making band.

Individuals experiment with different APQTs. They search through trial and error to isolate the combination that best satisfies their personal goal-function – to some the idleness of a quiet life, to others the industriousness that leads to an early promotion. Their *ex ante* determination to succeed recalls the neoclassical theory of utility if not the neoclassical theory of profit upon which the prediction of allocative efficiency must crucially depend. Even so, the theory of APQT is unmistakably *social* in the institutional sense of Chapters 2 and 3.

In respect of social embeddedness, individuals make choices but they do so in public. Informal sanctions affect the relative attractiveness of alternative APQTs (and are more likely to reinforce the group norm than they are to reward sub-standard or super-normal contribution). Approbation as a motivating agency can give a focus to guesstimates and games (and can in that way provide a lead in 'prisoner's dilemma' type situations which shifts the balance away both from radical uncertainty and from material inducement). Much work in any case is a team undertaking (the implication being that all members must work with roughly the same intensity in order that their operations dovetail and their supplying be made consistent). Employment, like Hell, is other people. Embeddedness to that extent makes utility-seeking individuals the servants of an interpersonal consensus.

As with people, so with the past. In respect of social conventions, individuals make choices but they do so with a memory. Traditional practices provide epistemological anchoring in a dynamic economy. They can also be non-rational and suboptimal where circumstances move on and rules of thumb do not. Standard procedures reduce the psychological and decision-making costs of change. They can also mean that a new opportunity is passed up because the perceived discrepancy is resistant to the customary prescription. Unquestioned conventions perpetuate compromises between intra-organisational coalitions and protect the inertia of hard-won tit-for-tat. They can also legitimate the default choice of non-action because the stability loss of reopened search is perceived to be too high a price. Above all, the heuristic exists and the past is handed on: 'Thus, the early period in the life of an organization may turn out to be extremely important in determining how efficient its operations are, since it is in the early period that some critical precedents will be established.' (Leibenstein, 1987:68). Choices are made but they are made in a context. The new employee who asks 'How are things done around here?' is in effect situating his APQT in a matrix of recurrences and norms which were already predetermining and precommitting when history was a lad.

Leibenstein's APQT is unmistakably *social* in the dual sense of people and past. The two strands, needless to say, are closely connected. People are past: the self is habituated into patterns of emulation and cooperation as a result of learning that took place in a group. The past is people: salience only coordinates if it is a common property in the sense that office hours are only efficient hours because all offices conform to the well-recognised repetition. People and past are closely connected. That in itself is a reason why Simon's satisficing so frequently takes on the character of premature capitulation: 'No individual will necessarily move to the superior option, since it is not a superior option unless everyone else also moves.' (Leibenstein, 1987:73). What all can do, each will consider a prohibitive burden: 'The gain for any individual in shifting is likely to be less than the cost of attempting to persuade everyone to move away from the current convention and adopt a new one. Hence, existing nonoptimal conventions can persist.' (Leibenstein, 1987:72).

They can persist because there is no incentive for one individual to take the lead unless all individuals simultaneously commit themselves to the task of reform. Thus might the large group end up with a *status quo* that its members fail to acknowledge as the best conceivable. Each is constrained by all in his choice of the APQT. That APQT need not be the bundle that any single actor, calculating in isolation, would himself have made his own first choice. Alongside the efficiency slippage which reduces the goal-attainment of the organisation there is evidently a utility slippage which strands even the rational somewhat short of their home.

Leibenstein's theory seeks to identify the impact on the successful exploitation of scarce resources of decisions made *within* the firm. Leibenstein is convinced that the empirical evidence on the comparative experience of countries with similar stocks of knowledge, capital–labour ratios, propensities and capacities to save bears out his belief that the x is if anything more significant than the *allocative*: 'Productivity studies after World War II established that differences in physical capital explain very little of the differences in productivity. I suggest that the main differences can be explained by the motivations of firm's members during their work, by the motivational atmosphere they find on the job, and on the type of interactions and influences toward work and production that people have on each other as well as the attitudes they bring to the work context. These factors are probably the most significant ones in explaining differences in productivity in the same industry and between countries at roughly similar stages of development.' (Leibenstein, 1976:270). The theory, Leibenstein argues, is firmly rooted in the facts. It points directly to the ubiquity of shortfall.

Discretion, it could be argued, can enhance productivity rather than impair it. Stress, boredom and irritation are less where detailed over-supervision gives way to a climate of trust: 'Non-preset schemes make working life tolerable.' (Leibenstein, 1976:102). Also, specialist knowledge being unequally distributed, freedom and devolution may be the precondition for timely intervention. Completeness of contracts in an uncertain world could actually create the inefficiency that Leibenstein would attribute to autonomy. Working to rule can plunge a firm into chaos.

Leibenstein is aware that employees pursing their own utilities need not be doing so at the expense of business profits. Overall, however, he tends to believe, with Adam Smith, that bureaucrats are less likely than capitalists to squeeze the maximum gain from their undertaking's constrained potential. Assuming that the nation has made up its mind to reduce the slippage that occurs within the hierarchy, several policy inferences then suggest themselves to raise the x-efficiency of the organisation with a staff.

The first policy inference relates to attachment. Leibenstein stresses that managers have to *produce* the motivation upon which they depend: 'It is as important to production as steel or nails or raw materials or energy.' (Leibenstein, 1976:257). He also recognises that money *per se* is not enough to buy trustworthiness, loyalty or commitment: 'Motivation is not a purchasable input in the marketplace.' (Leibenstein, 1976:257). Where the necessary input is not fully marketable, there resources must be invested in the creation of a workplace culture favourable to responsibility and quality control. The Hawthorne studies showed how output could be raised through an improvement in labour relations. It is a message that will be greeted with approval by all advocates of worker identification who believe that developments like rounded job functions, employee consultation, corporate pride, the revival of the work ethic, promotion from the shop floor, the Japanese-style implicit contract for life – 'Mutual fulfilment of expectations can be achieved over long periods' (Leibenstein, 1987:218) – can do much to bring the APQT of the agents more closely into line with the goals of the principals.

The second policy inference relates to restructuring. Smaller work groups paid bonuses as a team are less likely to be adversarial and more likely to be productive. Frequent rotation challenges unthinking conservatism and breaks up self-perpetuating interest groups that are refractory to new signals. Flattened pyramids reduce the number of layers through which scarce information must be filtered. Communication and explanation make the worker aware of the way in which his job serves a purpose. Franchises and de-mergers return control to hands-on entrepreneurs. People cannot be compelled to duplicate the best practice that is spelled out by their boss: 'All jobs have to be interpreted to a greater or lesser degree.' (Leibenstein, 1976:256). What the option of restructuring does suggest is, however, that there is much that can be done through policy to cut out the fat.

The third policy inference relates to competition. Rivalry by itself does not push business firms to their productive limits: 'Organizations do not necessarily have to be efficient. Even the survival of an economic enterprise does not depend on efficiency in an absolute sense. At most, all that matters is the *relative* efficiency of firms *vis-à-vis* each other.' (Leibenstein, 1987:4). Rivalry among firms with the same level of internal slack does little by itself to maximise output per unit of input. Rivalry among firms under pressure to under-cut is a more effective stimulus to the minimisation of cost. Sheltering mechanisms like protective tariffs, predatory monopolies, oligopolistic cartels, nationalised industry might in the circumstances all be subjected to careful scrutiny by legislators convinced that policy instruments like free international trade, anti-trust legislation, fair trade regulations, privatisation of bureaucracies are more likely than not to spur managers through competition to monitor and re-design, to take risks and to make themselves unpopular. Market competition to that extent can challenge x-inefficiency in a manner that is quite separate from the allocative benefit so frequently cited by the liberal neoclassical in its support.

Leibenstein's economics suggests that much motivation is interpersonal and many institutions are lagged. As with the non-existence of a unique equilibrium in Cournot's theory of duopoly, as with the endemic fuzziness which prevents Simon's satisficing from settling at a single-valued maximum, so perfect rationality in the Leibenstein-like organisation simply cannot be taken on trust. Leibenstein, aware of the indeterminacy, sees no way to eliminate it. X-inefficiency is what x-inefficiency does. A residual that the allocative economics cannot explain, it is effectively the control loss that occurs when the principal–principal trade of the butcher, the brewer and the baker gives way to the agent–agent dealings of the butcher's boy, the barmaid and the shop assistant on the till. In that sense Leibenstein's 'organizational theory of the firm' (Leibenstein, 1987:vii) is by its very nature no theory at all.

Leibenstein makes a clear distinction between resource use within the hierarchy and resource use that crosses the market. Not all economists are prepared to acknowledge a conceptual divide. As Alchian and Demsetz observe: 'Telling an employee to type this letter rather than to file that document is like my telling a grocer to sell me this brand of tuna rather than that brand of bread.' (Alchian and Demsetz, 1972:120). The business corporation, in the view of Alchian and Demsetz, is fundamentally a network of agreed-upon contracts, only superficially a structure of power-based relationships. The firm, they write, has 'no power of fiat, no authority, no discretionary action any different in the slightest degree from ordinary market contracting between any two people.' (Alchian and Demsetz, 1972:119). Management in such a perspective simply means the negotiation of agreements on terms acceptable to all parties, to the residual claimants and to the suppliers of labour alike.

The model is not the Marxian *bellum* where the capitalist hires and fires and the passive worker does what he is told. Denying that the exchange nexus is necessarily an unequal one, Alchian and Demsetz replace the socialist vision of authoritarian directive with the catallactic 'not from benevolence' of the mutually acceptable *quid pro quo*. Each party making both a purchase and a sale, the essence of the capital–labour relationship is the market (even *within* the hierarchy) that James Buchanan describes in general terms in the following assessment of economics as governance and conflict resolution: 'Economics comes closer to being a "science of contract" than a "science of choice"... The maximizer must be replaced by the arbitrator, the outsider who tries to work out compromises among conflicting claims.' (Buchanan, 1977:242). Applied to the theory of the organisation, what this means is a symmetry of command. The employee commands the employer to pay the wage. The employer commands the employee to do the job. The employee can quit. The employer can dismiss. To the contractarian, there is no real difference in the status of the two.

Leibenstein would not question the existence of the contract. What he would question is the preciseness of the specification. The contract in the sense of Alchian and Demsetz sets out the broad parameters. The Leibenstein thesis is that those parameters carry no prediction of productive-potential maximisation at work.

Yet a contract is a bargain; and no rational individual intendedly enters into an agreement unless he has a reasonable expectation of securing value in exchange. The worker, unmetered, supplies some idleness and spares some effort. The entrepreneur, far-sighted, shades the wage in anticipation of the shortfall. Talking macroeconomic growth, the nation probably does lose out on the goods and services that could have been squeezed from the same scarce endowment. Talking microeconomic satisfaction, the welfare implications are less clear. The worker buys the under-performance that he desires. The entrepreneur pays no more than the marginal product is worth. Internal markets and finely-targeted contracts would increase the transparency of the swap. Even so, the exchange posture can without doubt be read into the commitment invested in work. Looked at through the window of revealed preference, x-inefficiency then becomes not inefficiency in any recognisable sense but rather a utility to be bought and sold.

10.2   ORGANISATIONAL MEMORY

Individuals have aptitudes, personalities and human capital. Organisations have heuristics, conventions and operational precedents. Individuals joining organisations have got to find out the 'common codes of communication and coordinated search procedures' (Teece et al., 1994:15) which situate their job function in time and space. Individuals joining organisations have got to go back to school: 'Business learning involves organizational rather than individual skills. While individual skills are of relevance, their value depends on their employment in particular organizational settings.' (Teece et al., 1994:15).

Individual skills like cost-accounting have an economic value. That economic value will normally be realised, however, only in an organisational setting that has its own ways of processing knowledge and of linking together a plethora of activities. The learning resides in the structure and cannot be transmitted, as objective facts would be, by means of formal lessons. Instructors and manuals lack the overview to guide the novice through the diffuse world of the unteachable and the unspoken: 'Many of the factors which make machinery and jobs idiosyncratic, such as the sounds and smells of equipment, are extremely difficult to describe.' (Doeringer and Priore, 1971:17). Written records would not repay the cost of investment. Osmosis in any case hands on the know-how. There is, in the real-world firm, no alternative for the entrant who wants to learn but to 'recognise that knowing and doing are inseparable' (Hodgson, 1989:577) and to participate actively in the ongoing practices of the group: 'Because of the complexity of such behavior, knowledge embedded in routines cannot be fully captured in codified form. That is, it has a tacit dimension that often cannot be readily articulated. Hence, it is the routines themselves, and the ability of management to call upon the organization to perform them, that represents an enterprise's essential capability.' (Teece et al., 1994:15).

Individuals joining organisations ask their co-workers and their managers for explicit guidance. Very often their request is met with the incomprehension – 'We can know more than we can tell' (Polanyi, 1967:4) – of Michael Polanyi's bicycle-rider when asked to put into words how he does what to him has become an unthinking reflex. Words do not provide the way in to the sequences and the complementarities, the actions and reactions, that make each organisation quintessentially itself. No single teacher can explain what is going on. That is why individuals joining organisations are compelled to educate themselves even as they perform their job. They play about with the computer. They observe the short cuts that co-workers employ. They discover that the upstairs printer is seldom in use. In the end the curriculum emerges *ex post* as a result of physical proximity and hands-on learning: 'The knowledge possessed by a firm's personnel tends to increase automatically with experience.' (Penrose, 1959:76).

The organisation is people and it is in people alone that collective practices are stored. The life in common, Penrose emphasises, is the business firm's finely-targeted source of skills: 'An administrative group is something more than a collection of individuals; it is a collection of individuals who have had experience in working together.' (Penrose, 1959:46). The life in common inculcates the hidden and passes on the amorphous. To that extent it is capable of raising economic productivity as a direct consequence of the information that it releases: 'When men have become used to working in a particular firm or with a particular group of other men, they become individually and as a group more valuable to the firm in that the services they can render are enhanced by their knowledge of their fellow-workers, of the methods of the firm, and the best way of doing things in the particular set of circumstances in which they are working.' (Penrose, 1959:52). The context has a pay-off. Knowing what *we* do raises our value as a team.

Penrose uses history-dominated constructions like 'have had experience' and 'have become used' to describe the learning process of the cogs that join the wheel. Time in that sense is an economic variable for the obvious reason that it takes time for non-ego patterns to become entrenched in personal performance. Yet there is a further sense in which time is of relevance to learning. This relates to the fact that the wheel had a recognisable identity even before the new generation of cogs moved in to join an already-working unit. Past people shape present practices. That is what learning through observing, imitating and exercising is all about.

Routines are blueprints, Nelson and Winter write, that the done-and-dusty have left behind: 'We claim that organizations *remember by doing*.' (Nelson and Winter, 1982:99). Individuals keep alive an embodied skill such as a foreign language not by filing it but by using it. Collectivities, Nelson and Winter say, are no different when they encode their cognitive dimension not in instruction books and written records but in the signals and referents that are the substance of the replicated, the remembered response.

The past is like a free good, a public good. The present can draw upon it and does not have to pay. Yet the past is also an elusive asset, a fragmented stock. Even top management cannot claim that it has situated every turning on its map of the whole. It is in the nature of labour divided that each person knows his own work function but not that of his cooperating workmates. A market in the economics of Hayek is one way of reconciling the uncoordinated. Organisational memory made a part of corporate culture is another. The remembered response ensures at least that ego's information will be complementary to alter's understanding. It cannot be otherwise in a past-driven organisation which looks to inherited systematisation for the reproduction of its order: 'To view organizational memory as reducible to individual member memories is to overlook, or undervalue, the linking of those individual memories by shared experiences in the past, experiences that have established the extremely detailed and specific communication system that underlies routine performance.' (Nelson and Winter, 1982:105).

The past is conservative at the level of the image. Established schemata spotlight relevant characteristics and cause other stimuli to be marginalised as insignificant: 'No firm ever perceives the complete range of services available from any resource, because the range of services recognized is for the most part confined by the management's existing ideas as to possible combinations.' (Penrose, 1959:86). The past is conservative too at the level of phenomena – since pictures in the mind lead to real-world purchases and new resources, once in place, become a material constraint with a cumulative causality of their own. Fixed plant means that the output mix is not infinitely malleable: 'The selection of the relevant product-markets is necessarily determined by the "inherited" resources of the firm – the productive services it already has.' (Penrose, 1959:82). Past executives predetermine future specialisations: 'The plans put into effect by past management limit the rate at which newly hired personnel can gain the requisite experience.' (Penrose, 1959:47). Edith Penrose as an economist was familiar with the neoclassical case for letting bygones be forever bygone since sunk costs can no longer be converted into objects of choice. As a member of the public, she like the rest of us had heard that there was no point in 'crying over spilt milk', that the past was 'water under the bridge', that 'what's done cannot be undone', that Lot and Orpheus had made the fatal mistake of looking back. As a realist, however, Penrose was able to see that the past is a part of the present and that business life is only exceptionally a *tabula rasa*. In common with the present, the future too will reflect the irreversibilities and the conventionalities of an earlier era when existing decision-makers were themselves not yet in post.

Path dependence means that a route once selected is not easy to re-contract: 'The local nature of enterprise learning significantly restricts what firms can do. Their future activities are highly dependent on what they have done in the past.' (Teece et al., 1994:16). Thus is change ensnared by momentum and creative destruction dispatched down a single, marked trail: 'Physically desirable resources are purchased in the market for their known services; but as soon as they become part of a firm the range of services they are capable of yielding starts to change. The services that resources will yield depend on the capacities of the men using them, but the development of the capacities of men is partly shaped by the resources men deal with.' (Penrose, 1959:78). The process is two-way, the effect is reciprocal – and the past is a part of the present that the future will have to accept as a *fait accompli*.

It is one thing to acknowledge the existence of a ratchet of precedent. It is quite another thing to assess the contribution that conservative order makes to economic efficiency. The pluses and the minuses can be listed and described. The thrust of the balance, more difficult, will be as provisional as time and place.

The principal cost is the threat to innovation and novelty. Existing interpretations frame new thoughts – gaps, discrepancies and openings might not be noticed where people do not see beyond their conditioned range. Realised investments discourage major disruptions – shocks put at risk the continuity and may lead to the unwelcome scrapping of assets and skills. Firm-specific lock-ins and non-transferable 'how-tos' reduce the likelihood that labour will be mobile – people who do well in a given team know that their value on the outside market will be significantly less. The dialogue with the past insulates in-house traditions from economic pressures that would break the mould. The consequence can be a self-reproducing set-up in which the date-stamped and the non-portable might stand in the way of upgrading and new horizons.

Successful entrepreneurship presupposes an outlet for imagination, ingenuity, vision, ambition, audacity, initiative, versatility, flexibility, a willingness to experiment with the intuitively sensed and a shrewd alertness to what might catch on. It is by no means certain that the memory-heavy organisation will be quick enough off the mark to provide a forum for restless search; or will have the internal elasticity to shape an unknown future in the organisation's self-selected image. The most optimistic scenario from the perspective of a society that values change is therefore the possibility that *ab initio* entrants will leap into the breach left by existing firms who maximise not profits but their fidelity to fixed customs. The least optimistic scenario is that economies of size will be enough to make even under-utilisation non-contestable, the entrepreneurial competitor no match for the head start of scale.

The principal cost of intra-organisational routine is a reluctance to dream. The principal benefit is the quick response. Calculation is time-consuming and the future is unknowable. A rule remembered at least assists the dweller in the whirlwind to adapt to circumstances that are never fully understood.

Uncertainty and unknowledge, the unexpected and the unanticipated are not imperfections in the mechanism but rather the hard core of what the market *is*. Models of equilibrium in the comparative statics text give the impression that free enterprise inputs a careful processing of the raw data of experience and outputs maximised efficiency as if guided by an omniscient mind. The economy in flux has, however, far too little information about what the unforeseeable will bring to permit a rational choice from incomplete data-sets that remain still to be revealed and written down. Where the 'best' cannot be chosen because it cannot be known, at least a rule from the past can serve as a fixed point from which to start.

Thus, since 'maximum' profit is *ex ante* as unrecognisable as the face of God, an aspiration level in the sense of Simon or an *average* cost mark-up in the sense of Hall and Hitch might be the best targeted and the least expensive way of deciding the business firm's prices and quantities. Imitation of an established leader is a rule durable which prevents negative-sum price wars and promotes product development through the mimicry of success. Extrapolation of future out-turns from proven strategies is a demonstration that re-ordering in line with ordering is expected to protect *status quo* survival standards that market participants believe to be the best deal they can secure. What is called 'rational' expectations could itself be called 'lagged' expectations. The historical *tâtonnement* took place in the past. We today are 'rational' quite specifically because we live off the intellectual capital that was a gift.

An economy of time and effort will result whenever an organisation opts for a pre-programmed rhythm, a familiar code: 'A typist who can rattle off "through" without a thought is likely to have to slow down and pay attention to type "hguorht", or even "ughthro".' (Nelson and Winter, 1982:75). Business success often presupposes an instantaneous reply. Even an imperfect script or an unthinking knee-jerk can be the more economical option where discovery costs and implementation lags would price out of consideration the disembedded scientist's *optimum optimorum*.

Organisational memory can be good business in the processing of things. Routines and heuristics can be of no less value where they coordinate people's interests and defuse the conflicts to which bureaucratic politics so frequently gives rise. Things do what they are told. People sulk and feud and go on strike.

Any rule that keeps people peaceably non-Hobbesian must make a worthwhile contribution to the maintenance of organisational order.

It is an important characteristic of the behavioural approach to the firm that it takes the ends of the group to be no more than the ends of the human beings who make up the group: 'Firms as such do not actually *have* objectives.' (Nelson and Winter, 1982:58). Once it is recognised that there need not be some single-minded maximand like the rational pursuit of long-term profit, it becomes more difficult to evaluate the goal attainment of the team. Some members will press for returns and dividends, others for job satisfaction and product development, still others for sales maximisation and the prestige of growth. The very choice of the corporate purpose becomes an exercise in negotiation and social exchange within the group. The constituencies are disparate, the goal functions divergent – but still the past is able to impose a truce: 'As a result of organizational precedents, objectives exhibit much greater stability than would typify a pure bargaining situation. The "accidents" of organizational genealogy tend to be perpetuated.' (Cyert and March, 1963:34). A mix of motives is ground out by the arbiter of tradition. The alternative could have been a civil war.

Peace is in the gift of precedent. So is the perception that the equilibrium is an equitable one. Groups over time develop rigid conventions. The rigidity of those institutions gives them the status of legitimate 'ought-to-bes' that should be respected: 'When employment is stable, the same workers come into regular and repeated contact with each other. The result is the formation of social groups or communities within the internal labor market. Communities of this type – in a workplace or any other social setting – tend to generate a set of unwritten rules governing the actions of their members and the relationship between members and outsiders. Eventually, these rules assume an ethical or quasi-ethical aura.' (Doeringer and Priore, 1971: 23). Unwritten rules indicate what is '*just* cause for dismissal', what is a '*fair* day's work', what is '*equal* pay'. Any threat to those rules is a threat to the peace which is the consequence of precedent which is in the gift of time.

The benefit is peace. With the peace comes the rent of self-advancement – 'payments to members of the coalition in excess of what is required to maintain the organization' – that Cyert and March have termed 'organizational slack'. (Cyert and March, 1963:36). Such slack may be a fair price to pay for the cushion of agreement. Particularly is this so since, contracts being under-specified and monitoring never complete, an organisation that is divided is vulnerable to the slippages and the defections that impose a cost of under-performance of their own. Mutual trust is more likely in an organisation that breeds confidence through its rules than in one which stumbles piecemeal from the *ad hoc* to the *ad hominem*.

Listing the costs and describing the benefits, what is clear from the discussion of conservatism as economics is that adaptation will seldom be perfect nor adjustment smooth and instantaneous. Repeated and glaring discrepancies can unleash a feedback mechanism that results in a revision of the conceptual framework. So can ferocious competition such as threatens the very survival of conspicuous laggards who make labour and not capital the non-negotiable fixed factor. In the penumbra of ambiguity where the good-enough is ranked above the best-conceivable, however, different levels of average cost and return to capital can co-exist in a single industry effectively because organisational cultures differ and different people want different things.

Friedman and Alchian look to natural selection and entry and exit to weed out businesses that pay profits below the norm. Nelson and Winter, on the other hand, believe that 'nonoptimal rules may survive in selection equilibrium'. (Nelson and Winter, 1982:154). Nelson and Winter, referring both to intentions and to endstates, ultimately reject the notion 'that economic actors are rational in the sense that they optimize.' (Nelson and Winter, 1982:8). In its place they put a mix of the current response to fresh stimuli and the fixed cost that is the heuristic. It is that mix of the new with the old that Teece and his colleagues have in mind when they write as follows about the firm: 'Where it can go will ... be a function of where it has been.' (Teece et al., 1994:17).

Organisational rules transmit information through time: 'These routines play the role that genes play in biological evolutionary theory.' (Nelson and Winter, 1982:14). Family resemblance, changing only slowly, is a symbol of the lineage and its identity. Business reproduction, organisational memory would suggest, is subject to the same Marshallian gradualism of *natura non facit saltum.*

An important inference would be that the rate of growth of the firm must forever be braked by the capacity of the going concern to school new blood in the unique practices of a one-off context: 'Individuals with experience within a given group cannot be hired from outside the group, and it takes time for them to acquire the requisite experience... The experience they gain from working within the firm and with each other enables them to provide services that are uniquely valuable for the operation of the particular group with which they are associated.' (Penrose, 1959:46, 47). The whole alone is in possession of the unwritten syllabus and the lore that the newcomer has to acquire. The assimilation of new hires can evidently proceed no faster than the capacity of in-house mentoring and learning by doing to make clear to new arrivals 'the shapes into which new pieces will have to be fitted.' (Marris, 1998:64).

Robin Marris warns that the pace of recruitment can be too rapid – the limiting case being 'an organization attempting to expand at an infinite rate, whose members, their average length of service being infinitesimal, would not even know each others' names.' (Marris, 1998:65). Like Edith Penrose, he sees the economic inputs as being more than land, labour and capital, the production function as going beyond technology and research and development. The diseconomy of size, Marris believes, is not to be confused with the entirely separate diseconomy of *speed*. Growth *per se* has a cost.

Demand can be created through marketing. Diversification is a response to market saturation. Investment can be funded by loans and new issues. Management can be expanded since the overview is embodied in the routines. Arguments such as these suggest that there is no physical limit to the size of the firm. The pace of change is more of a problem. Teaching and learning is not a once-for-all exogeneity but rather an internal process. Moving too fast, the danger is real of 'such disorganization that the firm will be unable to compete efficiently in the market.' (Penrose, 1959:47). Organisational memory is protective of organisational order. In a disequilibrium world, the past may be the only equilibrium that can be found.

10.3   THE NETWORK AS SOCIAL CAPITAL

Robert Putnam sees interlocking relationships and background ethics as a capital asset with an economic return: 'By analogy with notions of physical capital and human capital – tools and training that enhance individual productivity – "social capital" refers to features of social organization such as networks, norms, and social trust that facilitate coordination and cooperation for mutual benefit.' (Putnam, 1995:67). Social capital is an amalgam of mutual support and communicated self-restraint: 'The greater the density of associational membership in a society, the more trusting its citizens. Trust and engagement are two facets of the same underlying factor – social capital.' (Putnam, 1995:73). As we join our golf clubs, our book discussion societies, our neighbourhood action groups, so we build up an asset in reciprocation, personal knowledge and the experience of working together. It is a decapitalisation of our common wealth to go bowling alone.

Social capital in Putnam's definition has two separate facets. Networks relate to matter. Norms and trust relate to mind. Both sets of institutions impose order on the organisation and on the macro-society of which it is a part. There is more to the reconciliation of expectations than the price mechanism alone.

The network is people: not atomised and anonymous but familiar and face-to-face, it is in the nature of time-hallowed connections that link friends and colleagues, contacts and neighbours, regular suppliers and blood-bound kinsmen that social and physical proximity spreads the word about individuals and puts a name to a role. The network is past: the community built up gradually through the snowballing of loyalties, piece-by-piece contracting culminating in the non-calculative rubber stamp of the long-term validation, history is at the heart of the ongoing structures and overlapping matrices that make the collectivity into a beehive of interpersonal debts. The network is situation and location, repeated interaction and self-fulfilling expectation. It is infinitely preferable to the stern Leviathan that is, Robert Putnam contends, the next-best substitute for mutual assistance, proudly volunteered: 'In the absence of solidarity and self-discipline, hierarchy and force provide the only alternative to anarchy.' (Putnam, 1993:112).

Putnam, studying Italy, found that the public order depended less on the police in regions where hiking groups and bird-watching societies were strong than in areas where sports clubs and political parties were weak and unembedded. The Catholic Church, partly because it treats its worshippers as passive supplicants, partly because its commanding hierarchy distances itself from civic involvement, he found to be an alienating influence that made little contribution to the stock of social capital: 'In Italy, at least, the most devout church-goers are the least civic-minded... Good government in Italy is a by-product of singing groups and soccer clubs, not prayer.' (Putnam, 1993:175-6). Theatre-going societies and mutual aid associations, non-Church and non-authoritarian, had a more positive impact upon that bedrock of deliberate and concerted participation that is the *sine qua non* for liberty and democracy: 'The more civic the context, the better the government.' (Putnam, 1993:182). Amoral individualists who opted out of their institutional affiliations were more likely to end up with the police State instead.

Jane Jacobs, studying the great American cities, was equally persuaded that order without tyranny is unlikely or impossible where personal involvement is minimal and personal trust is weak: 'The public peace ... is not kept primarily by the police, necessary as police are. It is kept primarily by an intricate, almost unconscious, network of voluntary controls and standards among the people themselves, and enforced by the people themselves.' (Jacobs, 1961:41). The public peace is kept by the *de facto* surveillance of parks that are well frequented rather than lonely, by neighbours who throng shops and cafés – 'There are plenty of eyes on the street' (Jacobs, 1961:64) – and look out of windows. Cars are less easily stolen, children can play out of doors in greater safety, because the locals, 'in *the course of carrying on their other pursuits*' (Jacobs, 1961:92), mount an uncoordinated watch that is none the less effective for being undirected. Town planning that avoids an artificial separation of business zones from residential districts would clearly do much to enable a concentrated population to deliver a level of law enforcement that the after-hours ghost town can never enjoy: 'Such places are jungles. No number of police can enforce civilization where the normal, casual enforce-ment of it has broken down.' (Jacobs, 1961:41).

Geographical proximity makes a contribution to the overlapping, the inter-locking, the interleaving upon which the social peace depends. Social proximity makes a similar contribution: consider the cheek-by-jowl attachment of people who have a long-term involvement in a birds-of-a-feather interest group or the bush-telegraph grapevine that makes a self-contained community of the latent lobby to restrict road building in rural areas. Whether it exists in physical or in social space, however, the crucial point about the informal network is that it causes its members to take actions which do more than simply advance their personal and private interests.

The stable network, Jane Jacobs writes, is an emotive *Gemeinschaft* where 'internal continuity' is the cause and effect of 'a feeling for the public identity of people, a web of public respect and trust, and a resource in time of personal or neighbourhood need. The absence of this trust is a disaster to a city street. Its cultivation cannot be institutionalized. And, above all, *it implies no private commitments.*' (Jacobs, 1961:67, 142). Neither as small-scale as the family nor as macro-sociological as Titmuss's nation, Jane Jacobs clearly believes that the cross-linked network unthreatened by excessive turnover brings out an altruism in human nature that irresponsible mobility could irrevocably erode.

Jacobs, studying the great American cities, revealed a strong sympathy with people who stay put and public policies that bring work to the long-settled. Her vision is a conservative one, workmates added to school friends added to co-religionists in a thick weave of relationships which gives only exceptional isolates the freedom to be unkindly or closed. Her vision, importantly, is not just an ideal but, to her, the precondition for the public peace: 'If self-government in the place is to work, underlying any float of population must be a continuity of people who have forged neighbourhood networks. These networks are a city's irreplaceable social capital. Whenever the capital is lost, from whatever cause, the income from it disappears, never to return until and unless new capital is slowly and chancily accumulated.' (Jacobs, 1961:148). The passage has a certain historical significance. It contains the first-ever use in print of the term 'social capital'.

Social capital has two separate facets. The first is non-ego networks. The second is the subjectivity of norms and trust.

Francis Fukuyama, like Durkheim, Polanyi and Hirsch, is convinced that the market order is embedded in a pre-existent stock of non-market rules: 'Few human beings enter into economic exchange without bringing with them a host of previously existing social norms that strongly influence their willingness and ability to co-operate.' (Fukuyama, 1997:94). It is that stock of institutions in the mind that Fukuyama treats as the core of social capital: 'Social capital can be defined simply as the existence of a certain set of informal values or norms shared among members of a group that permit co-operation among them.' (Fukuyama, 1997:4).

The rules are more than surface icing on the cake of commerce. Values or norms *permit* co-operation among the members of a group. Institutions in the mind make something possible which the Enlightenment utopia of rationality and exchange is incapable by itself of cementing into place: 'Without the transcendental sanctions posed by religion, without the irrational attachments, loyalties and duties borne out of culture and historical tradition, modern societies would come apart at the seams.' (Fukuyama, 1997:8). The *bellum* is just round the corner. It is social capital that prevents flimsy social order from unravelling into war.

Market capitalism is dependent on the moral consensus for the legitimation of its core constructs – individual rights, the autonomy of choice, the gratification of wants, independence, self-reliance, the law of contract. Ranging more widely, the devolved order would be prohibitively expensive without background social virtues like reliability, honesty, integrity, the commitment to obligation, the abstention from predation. Indices of a society coming apart at the seams would be petty litigation, political corruption, tax evasion, mindless parenting, casual shoplifting, violent crime. Indicators of a society in which inherited social capital remains in good repair would, in contrast, be unlittered streets, high voter turnout, reciprocation of stranger gifts, perceived connectedness – and participation in social networks, neither markets nor hierarchies, that are built around 'a moral relationship of trust': 'A network is a group of individual agents that share *informal* norms or values beyond those necessary for ordinary market transactions.' (Fukuyama, 1997:67). The network, Fukuyama believes, harnesses personal relationships to perpetuate the culture of custom. Like Bible reading, it draws upon the past to hand on the conventions of the future.

Some networks can make themselves the conduit for norms and trust because all of the members know each other in their personal capacity. The nuclear family is such a network. Other networks are weaker, thinner, more diffuse, less face-to-face. Immigrants from the same Chinese village fall into this category. Some networks (the members, for example, of a professional association) will have a legal status. Other networks will be as casual as the friends of friends at a sequence of receptions or the usual participants in a squash tournament at work. The networks differ in strength and scope. Unifying them is nonetheless the fact that each *de facto* is a custodian of attitudes and orientations. To the extent that values or norms become externalities to the wider society – to the extent, say, that mutual trust spills over from the bowling club into blood donation for the nation as a whole – to that extent the institutions in the mind may be said to be a social capital and not a social dyscapital that does not good but harm.

Putnam, studying Italy, found that social capital had been conducive to material improvement: 'Historically, ... norms and networks of civic engagement have fostered economic growth, not inhibited it. This effect continues today.' (Putnam, 1993:176). Good morals, at least in Italy, meant good money as well. Business is uncertain: regular partners with a reputation to uphold open the door to mutually beneficial exchanges that would not be possible in the absence of tried-and-tested expectations built up through intertemporal and interpersonal links. Business is expensive: networks and norms reduce the transaction costs of search and sift, of collecting and processing a plethora of information, of negotiating and renegotiating a sequence of formal contracts. Considering the uncertainty, considering the expense, there is an intuitive appeal in Putnam's interpretation of the historical record: 'Networks of organized reciprocity and civic solidarity, far from being an epiphenomenon of socioeconomic modernization, were a precondition for it.' (Putnam, 1995:66).

La Porta and his colleagues made a similar discovery. The World Values Survey asks 1000 randomly selected individuals in 40 countries about their attitudes and their conduct. La Porta, Lopez-de-Silanes, Schleifer and Vishny studied the answers on the preparedness to trust and reached the following conclusion: 'The effects of trust on performance are both statistically significant and quantitatively large. Holding per capita GNP constant, a standard deviation increase in trust raises judicial efficiency by 0.7, the anticorruption score by 0.3, bureaucratic quality by 0.3, and tax compliance by 0.3 of a standard deviation.' (La Porta et al., 1997:315). Civic participation improved. Infant mortality fell. The growth rate went up. Both the private and the public sector derived a significant benefit from the socially-efficient outcomes that were the result of frequent interaction and structured interdependence.

The contribution of webs of interdependence was acknowledged by Alfred Marshall when he argued that external economies accrue because the steel industry is geographically concentrated in Sheffield or Solingen, the printing industry localised in Fleet Street and Paternoster Square. New technology is transformed word-of-mouth into a non-exclusive resource: 'Each man profits by the ideas of his neighbours: he is stimulated by contact with those who are interested in his own pursuit to make new experiments.' (Marshall, 1879:53). The development of skills is in the air: 'Where large masses of people are working at the same kind of trade, they educate one another.' (Marshall, 1879:53). Quality is protected by insider knowledge and the fast feedback of the well-informed spectator: 'Good work is rightly appreciated, inventions and improvements in machinery, in processes and the general organization of the business have their merits promptly discussed.' (Marshall, 1890:225). The network is the same trade in the same place. The benefits to the wealth of nations are tips, training and a good standard of service.

The concentration of activity – of finance on Wall Street, of computing in Silicon Valley, of theatres in the West End – means that an undergrowth of specialist subcontractors, lenders and educational institutions develops to service the local need. This secondary network offers additional scope for informal communication. A valuable contribution will be made by trade associations and local chambers of commerce. An evening lecture is a two-edged sword: while one entrepreneur derives a benefit from the early warning, so, at the same time, do the rivals over whom the profit-maximiser must steal a march. The cocktail hour afterwards is more obviously a positive sum game: strangers become acquaintances, common interests bond, and dishonesty thereafter will be more visible and shaming.

Personal knowledge is an important filter in the market for labour. There social capital frequently takes on a screening function which the economics of human capital would be unwise to play down as subjective and biased. Friends, relatives, earlier migrants, the 'old boy net', current workmates reduce the cost of getting a job. Internal labour markets offer rewards for enthusiasm and cheerfulness as well as for speed and quantity. An employer, able to rely on a reference within the trade, can spare himself the overhead of employment agencies and aptitude tests. Paper certificates never amplify the Cambridge First with the caveat 'but his face didn't fit'. Human multipliers and wild knock-ons have the advantage that they fill the market gap: 'Social networks allow trust to become transitive and spread: I trust you, because I trust her and she assures me that she trusts you.' (Putnam, 1993:169).

Granovetter found that 'who you know' was a vital element in diffusing knowledge of job opportunities beyond the confines of the organisation that wants to expand. Empirical evidence from the United States suggests that 20 per cent of jobs are secured through formal mechanisms (newspaper advertisements, employment agencies, university careers offices) but that at least 56 per cent are mediated through personal acquaintances external to the firm (Granovetter, 1974:11). Granovetter was struck by the impact on economic success of the randomness of social mixing: 'Job-finding behavior is more than a rational economic process – it is heavily embedded in other social processes that closely constrain and determine its course and results.' (Granovetter, 1974:39). What organisations do is what people do. What people do is very often what they do as parts of surrounding webs.

Looking on the bright side, workers with contacts had access to a high-quality job description that extended to the muddle-headedness of the boss and the rumours of retrenchments. Such workers stayed longer and reported higher job-satisfaction: 'The more satisfied individuals are in their jobs, the more likely they are to have found them through contacts.' (Granovetter, 1974:14–15). Looking on the more sombre side, top jobs are gossiped about by top people whereas the excluded, the ethnic and the disadvantaged only talk among themselves: 'In particular groups, finding jobs through contacts may be one's best option... Yet the jobs found may still be of poor quality by general standards if this is all the group can provide. You cannot get blood from a stone.' (Granovetter, 1974:150–51). Access to the organisation depends to a surprising extent on lunching with the right contact at the right time. Luck is necessary but it is made sufficient only by the situation. Optimality in the labour market is not guaranteed. That, however, does not detract from the 'what is' importance of personal knowledge as an argument in the dynamics of information-flows.

As with labour, so with finance. Social capital is economically efficient where a credit-seeker has no property to pledge as collateral but does have social connections and a gain-seeker's stake in a good name preserved. A lender clearly enjoys some protection from the uncertainties of moral hazard and adverse selection where a mutual acquaintance is able to vouch for the applicant. Some claims are entirely fiduciary. The money substitute of trade credit is entirely dependent on personal information and intuitive confidence. In countries where the national currency is only reluctantly held, adequate liquidity itself may wait upon adequate visibility.

Veblen was clear as to what this would mean. In earlier productive systems, he wrote, customary standards of fairness and workmanship were protected because 'the personal contact between the producer and his customer was somewhat close and lasting': 'Under these circumstances the factor of personal esteem and disesteem had a considerable play in controlling the purveyors of goods and services.' (Veblen, 1904:52). In modern conditions the process takes on an 'impersonal character' and 'sentimental considerations of human kindness or irritation or of honesty' give way to a 'temperate and sagacious calculation of profit and loss' that charges all the traffic will bear: 'One can with an easier conscience and with less of a sense of meanness take advantage of the necessities of people whom one knows of only as an indiscriminate aggregate of consumers.' (Veblen, 1904:53). Honesty is the best policy if the customer is repeat business and if the Jacobs-like street would be outraged at any hint of sharp practice. Short-changing, under-filling, altering the date stamps, re-clocking the log book are, Veblen's argument would suggest, much more likely where it is the law and not the networks and norms that police the economic contract.

The theory of perfect competition explains market efficiency in terms of anonymous units, homogeneous and atomised. The theory of social capital, focussing on collaboration and communication, adopts a different perspective. It maintains that it is personal trust and historical ties that give people the will to do their best. As Penrose puts it, referring specifically to the firm: 'Extensive planning requires the co-operation of many individuals who have confidence in each other, and this, in general, requires knowledge of each other.' (Penrose, 1959:47).

Networks such as the firm inculcate a respect for others and a resistance to opportunistic short-termism. A civil servant refuses a bribe because dereliction of duty would mean the loss of his friends. New immigrants set up rotating credit associations to pool their capital. Settlers on the American frontier get involved in harvester-sharing and log-rolling. The attitudinal conditioning can be the cause of third-party spillovers: a stranger waiting at a bus stop is gifted the information that the No. 11 does not run on Sunday without the expectation that he will supply a return-favour in exchange. The thicket of civil society can serve to keep at bay an unwelcome Leviathan: never omniscient or costless, sometimes not even-handed or effective, the State might be perceived as so oppressive, so tyrannical, that neighbourly assistance becomes an attractive alternative to powerlessness and neglect. Social capital, it is clear, can make a contribution to the social fabric. It can do so in areas where the economic market might not be able to compete.

Social capital can be an asset. It can also be a liability. All capital is exposed to depreciation and obsolescence. A machine when it wears out is replaced by a better vintage. Friends and family are more difficult to scrap. There is an ever-present danger that old allegiances and alliances will be retained even where human or physical capital has become the more efficient, the less-expensive choice. Social capital in such a case can be a liability rather than an asset in effect because self-reproducing loyalties are an investment in ossification such as retards the adaptation to change. As Francis Fukuyama warns: 'Bonds of social reciprocity that facilitated production in the earlier time period become obstacles to production later.' (Fukuyama, 1997:7). Emotion and closeness becloud the judgement. They make it more difficult to switch and upgrade.

Collaboration leads to trust. Trust leads to collaboration. Networks reinforce attitudes. Attitudes reinforce networks. The circular flow of ongoing relationships is an institutional fact. One consequence of the stability in the social capital might be a tendency for the market price to signal information other than that which relates to demand and supply. Where there obtains not a single price in a single market but rather a variety of prices even for a commodity that is basically the same, many economists would say that the price mechanism was not properly fulfilling the allocative function that is its own.

At least it would be the lesson of rational choice that the liability of ingrained practices will be contained within an upper and a lower limit. Recurrent dealings with the same seller eliminate the cost of shopping around – the buyer is rational to pay a bit more for the convenience. Recurrent dealings with the same buyer keep down the burden of advertising and salesmanship – the seller is rational to take a bit less for the privilege. Rational choice, clearly, is in a position to map out potential boundaries and to signpost the limits to abuse. Search will reopen and exit perhaps result should one partner seek to travel free on the customs and contacts that were accumulated in the past. Within the penumbra of accommodation, however, it will be the lesson of rational choice that the partners will find it economical to appease their monopolist, their monopsonist, with a concession towards the price that he demands.

Rational choice will influence the boundaries. Non-rational choice, even so, will widen further the bands. The endowment effect, the fear of the unknown, the commitment to tradition, the stigma of desertion – frictions such as these can cause the trader to resign himself to the conventions that he knows rather than to search out the market-clearing price that will cost him too much. It is not easy to drop a greengrocer with whom one plays cricket or to refuse a loan to the vicar with whom one used to hunt. The tolerance is not unlimited; but still the penumbra is wider than the marketed magnitudes alone would suggest.

Alfred Marshall, writing of pricing 'when trade is slack', advised that 'general opinion' condemns the undercutter and that no sensitive man would want to be the focus for 'odium.' (Marshall, 1890:299, 312, 380). Prices could be reduced to the average variable cost and the glut of commodities auctioned away at a stroke. Instead there is a price-stickiness and an over-supply of fresh fish that the fishermen will not sell. Odium is, however, a terrible thing, and a municipal fish market an intensely public place. Mechanical solidarity succeeds to organic solidarity and the remembered reference-price becomes the symbol that binds. The market in such circumstances clearly does not move in line with relative scarcities despite the fact that the price-takers are so numerous as to be natural candidates for the leadership of the invisible hand.

Social capital can stand in the way of allocative efficiency where the market is a competitive one. Even more is it likely to do so where the size of the club is small. Oligopolistic rivalries are kept within manageable limits by industry-wide associations and established price leadership; by investment banks with an equity position in each of the prominent players; by an interchange of board members that coordinates the business forecasts; by joint ventures and research and development protocols that undermine the operational independence of the legally separate entities. Networks such as these cause social relations to acquire a supremacy over market relations which, however beneficial to live-and-let-live within the industry, need not make the contribution to economic performance that the members of the community most want to see.

The selection of the mutually-beneficial strategy may occur in the course of a tournament that has a past (a history of repeated iterations) and a future (an expectation of infinite rounds). The number of players is limited; information about their track record is available; the future is not very much discounted. The public in such a game can win a welfare surplus: consider the case where the recognisable principals decide to end escalating promotion of their respective brands rather than fight for market share through arms race deadweight. The public, unfortunately, can also score a welfare loss: this would be the result where a gain-minded cartel put up the price of a necessity in order to hold the desperate community for ransom. The defector who cheats by supplying beyond his quota is likely here to be seen as a public benefactor. Bad morals are likely here to be regarded as the high-road to the public interest.

The cartel illustrates a micro–macro tradeoff. It is not the only instance where the objectives of the micro-group might be at variance with the well-being of the macro-society of which each boundedness is a part. Trust within the clan can mean the exclusion of meritocrats who happen also to be outsiders. Honour among thieves affords protection to a criminal conspiracy. Ethnic self-definition breeds racial intolerance. And there is politics. Interest groups show a stronger preference for redistributing wealth than for increasing it. Writing of these 'distributional coalitions', Mancur Olson has objected that they put him in mind of 'wrestlers struggling over the contents of a china shop': 'On balance, special-interest organizations and collusions reduce efficiency and aggregate income in the societies in which they operate and make political life more divisive.' (Olson, 1982:44, 74). Looked at in that light, norms, networks and collective action can be a serious embarrassment to a society that has set its sights on information technology, living standards and even-handed democratic governance.

Interest groups, Olson warns, press for legislation which favours their own narrow partiality at the cost of the growth and productivity of the nation as a whole. The ancient ties vanished with the collapse of Fascism in Germany and Japan: an economic miracle was the consequence of the freedom, the atomism and the competition that the devastation of war bestowed upon the countries that had lost. Collective associations emerged unscathed from the pro-market reforms of post-Communist Russia – and the result was at once progress held back, pricing that did not clear, and widespread dissatisfaction with the capitalism that never was: 'The scelerotic devolution of the system of extraction that Stalin had established left the formerly communist countries with large enterprises that were much better at insider lobbying than at producing.' (Olson, 2000:170). The market by itself was not enough. Market-contrary regulation had also to go.

Gorbachev failed to kick-start the dynamism of enterprise because he failed to take on the micro-groups that were standing in the way of the generalisation of prosperity. Deng in China, Olson contends, was much more successful since Mao had already blasted into pebbles the giant boulders that had long been obstructing the route: 'The encompassing interest of Deng, the new pragmatic autocrat, prevailed, largely because the cultural revolution had destroyed the narrowly entrenched interests with a stake in the status quo.' (Olson, 2000:167).

Bad institutions can make a rich country poor. Good institutions, fortunately, can have the opposite effect. Thus it is that Olson encourages the poor countries to 'wise up' and abandon the belief that individual rationality plus factor endowments are all that they will need for catch-up development and the narrowing of the gap: 'The bargains needed to create efficient societies are not, in fact, made... The great differences in the wealth of nations are mainly due to differences in the quality of their institutions and economic policies.' (Olson, 1996:19, 21). The government in the country falling further behind would do well to invest impartially in the macro-society by phasing out the special-interest legislation which is blocking the way to the productive frontier.

Social capital is clearly not an unmixed blessing. The family business can be a locus of nepotism and in-breeding. Cliques within organisations can mean favouritism and patronage. Multiple loyalties can subvert and circumvent the formal structures. Multiple networks can be wasteful and unintegrated. And there is interest-group politics in the sense of Mancur Olson. Observations such as these would suggest not organisational order but organisational randomness, organisational asymmetry and organisational under-performance. Free marketeers would in the circumstances call not for more social capital but for more individualism, more discretion, more transactions that cross the market frontier. A less hasty conclusion would be that social capital is sometimes a liability but sometimes an asset – and that in any case the thing is there.

The thing is there – but is it *capital*? Networks and attitudes undeniably have an effect on the economic order. The question is whether the metaphor of capital is an appropriate one to capture the essence of that effect. The structures and mental states last more than a single period. They deliver a return that is spaced out over time. That much recalls the formation and durability of physical plant. Conspicuous differences nonetheless suggest that the match of concepts need not be a perfect one; and perhaps even that the comparison is too loose to be of real value.

Physical capital is targeted on return: no one buys a bottling plant for its intrinsic utility. Social investment, on the other hand, involves enjoyable contacts and self-defining behaviour patterns. The root of 'social' is *socius*, the Latin word not for asset but for friend. Something that is its own reward is difficult to lump together with something that is exclusively the means to a future income stream.

Motivation is relevant. Foregone consumption, 'deliberate sacrifice in the present for future benefit', is the means–ends *agendum* of the machine; whereas 'the essence of social networks is that they are built up for reasons other than their economic value to the participants.' (Arrow, 2000:4). People do not normally select their marriage partner on the basis of the business contacts promised by the clan. People join a tennis club for tennis and not soley for the free-and-easy exchange of insider tips. People protect their reputation because of internalised norms, half-forgotten parental pressures, a tyrannical superego that sees trustworthiness as much more than the present value of the discounted pay-offs. In some cases there is no alternative to the capital: doctors who do not join the British Medical Association do not have the right to practise their trade. If the means is the end and if convention or law sets bounds to the freedom of choice, the parallel with physical capital, purposively created after conscious deliberation, becomes a less convincing one. Of course there are people who set out to marry into a dynasty or to build up a good name as an earning asset. Far more numerous, however, are those people who are happy for their social capital to evolve non-intendedly as the by-product of their other activities. Even if the function resembles that of physical capital, the motive may well be very different indeed.

There is also an asymmetry concerning depreciation. Some anthropocentric infrastructure undoubtedly gets used up over time: witness the experience of printers and typesetters when desktop publishing broke into their closed circle. Some contacts and practices, on the other hand, must be constantly renewed if they are not to lose their force: 'Social capital does not wear out with use but rather with disuse.' (Ostrom, 2000: 179). A friend not cultivated is less likely to respect mutual commitments. Handshake contracts infrequently concluded are less likely to be treated as binding. Physical capital wears out. Tacit knowledge, however, is strengthened in the field; while reciprocity and good faith are self-reinforcing if made a part of the way of life.

Social capital, moreover, is difficult to measure. A production line is visible. Common understanding is unseen. It is not clear how to quantify overlapping allegiances or to calibrate the strength of emotions and affects. It is not clear how to put a value on learning experiences with downstream externalities in unrelated situations. It is not clear whether the focus should be the stock or the flow or in what units the calculation should be conducted. Especially problematic is the estimation of a social capital that is simultaneously an asset to a micro-group and a liability to the nation as a whole. The political 'machine', the Mafia, *guanxi* in Chinese communities, *blat* and the *nomenklatura* in the old Soviet Union, coteries and cronyism in much of South-East Asia – all of these networks of favours for friends are of considerable benefit to the persons directly affected but rent-seeking at the macro-level nonetheless. It is not clear whether to include the crude roster with a plus sign, the misallocation and the cynicism with a minus sign; or whether to drop altogether the attempt to measure an intangible that may be impossible to pin down.

Indicators can be found. An objective index might be newspaper readership, attendance at parent–teacher meetings, subscribers to football clubs and cultural associations. A subjective index could be attitudinal surveys of perceived trust, of confident belonging. Neither approach is entirely convincing. Neither measure resolves the chicken-and-egg problem of whether the affiliation was the cause or the effect of the wish to get involved. Neither is an obvious statistic that can be tracked with economic performance for the purpose of testing whether groups affect growth. Neither identifies unexploited substitutions at the margin or homes in on the optimal proportions between physical, human and social forms of capital. Measures can be found. Whether they are as meaningful as the measures of plant must be a good deal less clear.

Further problems arise because of the nature of the market. Physical capital has a sale price and a re-sale value. Social capital is difficult or impossible to alienate for reward. The buyer does not know how much to pay for a diffuseness that cannot be articulated. The seller appreciates that his Methodism generates diligence and sobriety from which non-contributors cannot cost-effectively be excluded. The public-good property is a disincentive to profit-seeking entrepreneurs who have might otherwise have wanted to make an investment. An under-supply of social capital is likely, logically speaking, to be the direct consequence of the ease of access.

In any case there is the State. Social capital, far more than physical, is at the crossroads of public policy. Determined to ban unions lest they foment conflict, to put State welfare in the place of charity and kin, to mix ethnic groups in integrated housing estates, what the government might unintentionally do is to create dependency on the public sector on the one hand, to crowd out private agencies of socialisation on the other. The government could, of course, concentrate on policy interventions that had the opposite effect. It could prime the pump of civil society through decentralisation and grass-roots funding. It could subsidise home ownership to reduce defection from neighbourhood-specific networks. It could eliminate the taxation of mobile phones and e-mail link-ups in order to price in the virtual village at the expense of television watching, anti-social and with-drawn. It could shape the course of future history, plotted out and not predetermined, through the delegation of local issues to the local communities that must live out the trial and error. Assuming that the effective utilisation of physical capital presupposes a minimal commitment of social capital as well, any attempt by the State to reinforce the complements of teamwork and fairness would represent in effect the public provision of social embeddedness that the market sector by itself is unable to match. The private sector normally supplies its physical capital without the intervention of the State. Social capital, however, is different. Perhaps it is so different as to suggest that the metaphor be left as a first approximation and confined to the figure of speech.

Robert Putnam records as one of the lessons of Third World development the survival of a vacuum in the area of institutional design: 'It is easier to build a road than to build an organization to maintain that road.' (Putnam, 1993:10). This chapter has drawn attention to three aspects of that organisational order: x-efficiency, organisational memory and social capital. Each of them is an integral part of supply and demand. Each of them makes a contribution to a market *process* that only in exceptional circumstances will settle into a price-mediated equilibrium.

The market is the process. The process includes the institutions. There is more to free enterprise capitalism than the timeless Walrasian auctioneer. It was a discovery that the post-Communist societies of Eastern Europe had to make for themselves: 'These ex-communist countries are advised to move to a market economy, and their leaders wish to do so, but without the appropriate institutions no market economy of any significance is possible. If we knew more about our own economy, we would be in a better position to advise them.' (Coase, 1992:714). Coase feels that the big issues have been obscured by a 'blackboard economics' that has cut itself off from its real-world base. He calls for 'a detailed knowledge of the actual economic system' (Coase, 1992:714) in order to put people and past back in again.

11. Organisational cost

Organisations, North writes, stand between the past which remembers and the future which creates: 'Organizations and their entrepreneurs engage in purposive activity and in that role are the agents of, and shape the direction of, institutional change.' (North, 1990:73). Organisations are bureaucracies that have acquired a patina of establishment. Entrepreneurs are revolutionaries who implement a deviation from the path. Precisely because the organisation is embedded in a constitutional settlement, there are limits to the leadership that the entrepreneur can legitimately exercise. Memory and precedent impose order upon the productive system. People and past keep even the entrepreneur in line.

Shared lives and inherited rules have an impact upon the administration of economic activity. Expense does so as well: 'If information and enforcement were costless, it would be hard to envision a significant role for organizations. But they are not.' (North, 1990:73). Sequential contracting relies upon demand and supply to price goods and services each time anew. The approach is sensitive, flexible, in touch – but it also puts a strain on scarce economic resources. Sometimes that drain will not be so much of a deterrent as to price out the free-market option of unit choices made consistent through the mechanism of exchange. Sometimes, however, the overhead of the *tâtonnement* will exceed the opportunity cost of the structured plan; and then the reliance upon command and hierarchy will prove the more economical choice in a way that it would not were information and enforcement to be a free good and not a deadweight loss.

Organisational order was the subject of the previous chapter. It argued that the matrix of dialogue, neither impersonal nor anonymous, is a valuable complement to the orchestration of price. The present chapter is closer to neoclassical cost, less willing to emulate the anthropologist's openness to interaction and memory. The first section, Entrepreneurs and bureaucrats, examines the two personality types that make the organisational sector *de facto* into an economic mix. The second section, Contract and command, shows that transaction costs, in the business-minded assessment of Ronald Coase, can leave decentralised buying-in a less competitive choice than in-house delivery. The third section, Markets and hierarchies, explores the ways in which Oliver Williamson has extended the theories of dynamic and allocative efficiency to incorporate the cost-effectiveness of institutional alternatives and the pricing-in of plan.

11.1 ENTREPRENEURS AND BUREAUCRATS

Dynamic capitalism is unceasing transformation because of the arbitrage and the initiative of the entrepreneurial function. Schumpeter's 'perennial gale of creative destruction' (Schumpeter, 1942:84) is the route not to the allocative equilibrium of the Walrasian price-vector and the Edgeworth box but to process and progress, to change without end. Schumpeter says that 'the entrepreneurial function is ... the vehicle of continual reorganisation of the economic system.' (Schumpeter, 1911:155–6). Entrepreneurship, Schumpeter insists, is about newness – 'the new commodity, the new technology, the new source of supply, the new type of organization.' (Schumpeter, 1942:84). It is not about the filial loyalty of 'precedents without number' (Schumpeter, 1911:80) that passes on the gift of history without looking it cost-effectively in the mouth: 'Carrying out a new plan and acting according to a customary one are things as different as making a road and walking along it.' (Schumpeter, 1911:85).

Entrepreneurship is about making a new road rather than following an established track. It is about profiting from uncertainty in the sense of Frank Knight and about spotting the unnoticed in the sense of Israel Kirzner. It is the spillover benefit to the growth-minded community of 'daring and powerful constructive genius' (Marshall, 1919:833n) in possession of the character traits, Alfred Marshall insisted, upon which the wealth of the nation depends – 'discretion', 'energy', 'alert apprehension' (Marshall, 1919:240), 'sympathy, imagination, strength and tact' (Marshall, 1919:855), 'judgement, prudence, enterprise, and fortitude' (Marshall, 1919:355), 'courage ... in taking selected risks.' (Marshall, 1919:651). An anxious fear of loss, an obsession with peace and order, a reluctance to question, a sensitivity to criticism, a refusal to confront are none of them character traits that appear on Marshall's list.

The entrepreneur attempts novel combinations of inputs; is innovative in his sources of supply; takes new initiatives in his methods of production and his administrative arrangements. The entrepreneur is quick to seize new opportunities before his rivals, wide-awake and success-minded, snatch away the gambles and make them pay off. The entrepreneur is aggressive in his marketing strategies; is unafraid to trust his own judgement; is creative and independent in his preference for disruption over conformity. Material incentives and social approbation will do much to make the most of such entrepreneurial endowments as a nation can command. Even so, the instincts, the aptitudes and the propensities are likely always to be in inelastic supply.

Economic exchange gives the entrepreneur a dedicated battlefield in which he can test his intuitions against the hunches of his competitors. Economic exchange is itself dependent on across-the-board alertness. Without the consumer who 'shops around', without the retailer who knows what other retailers are doing, the price mechanism would, becoming random, lose the rationality that makes it efficient. The individual buyer, the individual seller, is each revealing something of the entrepreneurial when he launches himself into the discovery process of economics. The same may be true of the individual bureaucrat as well.

Entrepreneurs are adventurers who value the challenge as well as the reward. Bureaucrats are constitutionalists who take their charter from their office. The ideal types are opposite poles. What counts most for the entrepreneur is blazing the trail. What counts most for the bureaucrat is not risk-taking but fitting in.

Max Weber, developing the ideal types, believed that the right answers could be economically ground out through a wisely-structured hierarchy of roles, subordination of functions and division of expertise. He was in no doubt that an intelligently-designed organisation could be highly effective as a problem-solving machine. Non-traditional (unlike the family, the feudal system, the Medieval guilds), directed towards explicit, unambiguously-specified goals, expected to attain those goals efficiently, with the greatest economy in the use of scarce resources, the ideal-typical bureaucracy, he believed, was *zweckrational* through and through: 'The purely bureaucratic type of administrative organization ... is, from a purely technical point of view, capable of attaining the highest degree of efficiency and is in this sense formally the most rational known means of carrying out imperative control over human beings. It is superior to any other form in precision, in stability, in the stringency of its discipline, and in its reliability. It thus makes possible a particularly high degree of calculability of results.' (Weber, 1947:337).

The bureaucracy, as Weber saw it, is a multi-period normative code, stable, impersonal and neutral. These institutions define the roles of the revolving-door incumbents, none of them able to own his own function or to make his job his private capital. Recruitment and promotion within the organisation become a reflection of merit, qualifications, technical training, demonstrated capability. Assessment is objective, minutes are kept in files, areas of juris-diction are scientifically defined. The result is a structure of specialisations designed to perform well. If it did not perform well, it would be rationally re-designed.

Weber was convinced that the formal hierarchy promised machine-like precision. He would have had little sympathy with the Leibenstein-like notion that people, not depersonalised cogs in the wheel but sentient beings, sentimental, spontaneous, solidaristic, would want or be able to subvert the organisational chart in the manner to which Boulding draws attention in his imputation of two-way interaction between the role and the personality: 'The cellular units of organization are not men, but, as it were, parts of men, men acting in a certain role... The individual, however, never merely passively fits a role. He reorganizes the role itself through the operation of his own peculiar images. When a square peg is fitted into a round role it is true that the peg becomes rounder, but it is also true that the role becomes squarer.' (Boulding, 1956:27, 60). Images, mutually modified through communication, then acquire a dynamic force which gives the Weberian cog the opportunity not simply to execute the orders he receives from above but also to act as an entrepreneur in the management of his life.

Morally speaking, the rescue of the soul from the status of the robot must be a good thing. In terms of allocation and growth, however, the de-alienation may well impose on the community an unwanted tax. *De facto* leadership returned from the generals in Whitehall to the cannon-fodder in the trenches, the possibility must be recognised that the organisation will adapt to its internal environment even as its members seek to maximise the throughput that Weber expected from the evolution of rational command. Just as the formal decision-makers will be adapting to the constraints of competition, finance and market share, so the Weberian interchangeable parts will be adapting to the values, expectations and priorities of men and women who are ashamed to be cut down into things.

In the limit, as Cyert and March observe, 'it makes only slightly more sense to say that the goal of a business organization is to maximize profit than to say that its goal is to maximize the salary of Sam Smith, Assistant to the Janitor.' (Cyert and March, 1963:30). In the real world, as every property owner must hope, external pressures will ensure that the proprietor's interests will not be completely displaced by bottom-up's objectives. Still, however, the balance-sheet of the organisation is unlikely to indicate the genuine efficiency-maximum that the convinced Weberian would be led to expect. The reason is entrepreneurship – the entrepreneurship of organisational cogs with their own view of APQT and the determination to proceed strategically in order to stamp their individuality on the job.

Entrepreneurship exists at the lower levels of organisation. Crucially and conspicuously, it also exists at the top. Weber made clear that at the apex of rational authority there is always a leader whose appointment reflects charismatic and non-technical characteristics even more than the ability to squeeze into his predecessor's invariant job description: 'At the top of a bureaucratic organization, there is necessarily an element which is at least not purely bureaucratic.' (Weber, 1947:335). The non-rationality itself can be a rational choice. The organisation must move swiftly if it is to be successful in exploiting new openings or in neutralising unwelcome surprises. The quality that is required at the helm is not in the circumstances bureaucratic replication so much as the flair and imagination of the natural entrepreneur.

Flair and imagination are the complements to precedent and institution. Whether the mixed *organisational* economy will indeed throw up enough of the entrepreneurship to turn the bureaucratisation to its best advantage is more problematic. Weber expressed fears about the routinisation of charisma into visionless administration which the pessimistic Schumpeter was able to endorse: 'Can capitalism survive? No. I do not think it can.' (Schumpeter, 1942:61). More pressing than any threat from the Marxian proletariat, Schumpeter believed, is the immobilisation of initiative within an organisation that Werner Sombart captured so eloquently in the following description of El Dorado found and then lost again: 'In our own day capitalism must suffer wreck because of the increasingly bureaucratic character of all our undertakings ... It is clear enough that in a huge business run on a bureaucratic basis, where economic rationalism no less than the spirit of enterprise is a mechanical process, there is no room for the capitalist spirit ... And when the capitalist spirit has lost its power of expansion, what then? ... Possibly it may be the Twilight of the Gods and the gold will have to be restored to the caverns of the Rhine.' (Sombart, 1915:359). And no one wants that.

11.2   CONTRACT AND COMMAND

The firm is not a market. It is a republic. Employees agree to a contract in order to join the club. Once inside the organisation, they accept that subsequent decisions will follow the political pattern of command.

Neoclassical economics models the purchases and sales that cross the frontier between separate entities. At least as many choices, however, are made by the parliaments and the lawmakers who sit in the offices and the committee rooms of the firm. Neoclassical economics models contract and exchange. Political economics models command and power. Both pricing and debating are relevant to an understanding of productive and allocative processes in a mixed organisational economy where markets and republics come together in the theory of the firm.

Not every organisation is a firm. The capitalist conglomerate is a firm. So is the nationalised corporation, the independent school, the worker-owned cooperative. The household, on the other hand, is not a firm. Nor is the tribe, the Sunday football-side that no one owns, the self-employed producer who trades solely in his business: 'The possibility of a single person acting as a firm is excluded... A firm is an organization always made up of two or more people.' (Hodgson, 1999:238). Not every organisation is a firm. The definition of a firm is a restrictive one. The firm, it makes clear, is effectively four things at once.

First, the firm is a bundle of property rights held by a single owner, a group of partners or a mass of shareholders. The existence of those titles gives the firm a distinctive status in law. Where the firm is incorporated, the uniqueness of its property base will become even more transparent. Not just a production function but an autonomous trader, the business where incorporated will have a signature and an identity of its own. The firm will then be legally entitled to demand input, to supply output, to make binding contracts without the express consent of the capitalists who own the rights.

Second, the firm is a planning unit, a unified structure, a coherent chain of command made one not through exchange but through management. Edith Penrose describes it as 'a collection of productive resources the disposal of which between different uses and over time is determined by administrative decision.' (Penrose, 1959:24). The administrative framework is crucial. The boundaries of the firm, Penrose writes, are in essence the limits that enclose its areas of 'administrative coordination' and of 'authoritative communication.' (Penrose, 1959:xi).

Penrose ascribes to the firm the 'economic function' of 'acquiring and organizing human and other resources in order profitably to supply goods and services to the market.' (Penrose, 1959:xi). By 'market' is meant the *external* market: 'True markets rarely, if ever, exist within firms.' (Hodgson, 1999:237). Where a firm introduces an internal market, what it calls a market is not really an economic market at all. Business divisions, because they have no legal independence, cannot sell on their property rights or disappear into bankruptcy. In-house dealings, discrete and not continuous, use accounting values, corporate rules and profit targets as a substitute for supply and demand. Intra-firm trades lack the same-side competition, the contestability of entry, the escape clause of exit that identify price allocation as a rational process. What this confirms is that the firm is a planning unit. It buys and sells in markets outside. Within the walls, however, it is a republic that is ruled by command.

Third, the firm is a productive enterprise that makes a value-adding contribution to the supply of goods and services. Hodgson appeals to common usage when he states that a group of proprietors who rent out their machinery and their factory buildings to a group of managers are not normally what is known as a firm. It is the managers who play the active part in production and sale. The asset owners do no more than passively lend the economic potential that it will be for others to develop: 'They would simply be the providers of the capital goods. The team of managers and their employees would constitute the firm. The management team would own that which is produced in the factory. Their contractual role as owners of the product makes this team the firm, not the owners of the capital goods.' (Hodgson, 1999:237). The firm is a network of relationships. It is a network of relationships with the express mission of adding to supply.

Fourth, the firm is embedded in its culture and a part of the past. Even a new firm will be integrated into a system of antecedent laws and strong conventions which enforce the nexus of contract and legitimate the hierarchy of command. Time passing, the firm will solidify into a durable structure with its own routines, corporate culture, organisational memory, uncodified communication. New people learn the established ways. Markets are spot and transient. Firms have historical continuity and expected longevity on their side.

The firm is a political unit that makes possible the freedom of exchange. The firm offers bureaucratic rationality in the sense of Weber. The market offers entrepreneurial rationality in the sense of Smith. Each one of the institutional alternatives has its economic benefits but also its economic costs. Ronald Coase in 1937 was among the first to demonstrate that market economics itself could be used to specify the most economical mix.

Winner-loser logic suggests that there ought not to be a middle-ground compromise at all. The typical question raised by an ideologue with a first-past-the-post expectation – the terms 'market' and 'firm' can be reversed to invert the *a priori* poles – would be the following: 'Why, if by organizing one can eliminate certain costs and in fact reduce the cost of production, are there any market transactions at all? Why is not all production carried on by one big firm?' (Coase, 1937:42–3). The integrated business plans and does not haggle: 'The distinguishing mark of the firm is the supersession of the price mechanism.' (Coase, 1937:36). Lenin had proposed that the nation be run as if one giant firm. Stalin had institutionalised the norm of allocation by authority in his Five Year Plans. Prolonged unemployment in Britain had led to a loss of confidence in the *laissez-faire* mechanism. Winner-loser logic was in the air when Coase published his path-breaking paper on 'The Nature of the Firm' in 1937. The parallel between the capitalist corporation and the collectivist ministry cannot have failed to escape his attention.

Winner-loser logic was in the air; but that does not mean that extreme positions had ended pragmatic speculation on the merits of a mix. Keynes in *The General Theory* in 1936 showed that the State could regulate even if it did not own. Macmillan in *The Middle Way* in 1938 proposed a centre-ground conservatism of welfarist compassion and the streamlining of industry. Dickinson, Lange, Hall and Lerner demonstrated the need for price flexibility even in a socialist economy. The theories aside, there were also the facts. The evolution of capitalism had not meant the triumph of either market or hierarchy but rather the continuing survival of both. Coase was intrigued by the persistence of the mixed organisational order. Writing exclusively as an economist and not at all as an ideologue, he sought to use Marshall's analytical construct of substitution at the margin to prove that there can be optimisation and rationality in an equilibrium balance that many of his contemporaries would have dismissed as a weak-willed historical compromise.

Coase uses neoclassical economics to explain the nature of the institutional mix. Invoking competition between allocational alternatives in the same way as other microeconomists would employ competition to show which businesses do best, he says that it is in the nature of the gain-seeking system to gravitate to the mix which delivers the most economical outcome: 'A firm will tend to expand until the costs of organizing an extra transaction within the firm become equal to the costs of carrying out the same transaction by means of an exchange on the open market or the costs of organizing in another firm.' (Coase, 1937:44). If organisation stops short of the equality point, the economy will be incurring avoidable burdens through relying too heavily on prices and contracts. If organisation swells out beyond the equality point, the economy will be in a position to make a welfare gain through cutting back on command and turning actively to the outside market instead.

The rule is the familiar one of maximising efficiency by means of a comparison with the next-best opportunity foregone: 'The limit to the size of the firm is set where its costs of organizing a transaction become equal to the cost of carrying it out through the market.' (Coase, 1988:7). Coase knows that no one can make a categorical pronouncement on the final mix that comparative statics will bring into being. Unable to address directly the composition of the optimum, the best-possible answer can only be a procedural question on gravity and the marginal cost: 'The question always is, Will it pay to bring an extra exchange transaction under the organizing authority?' (Coase, 1937:55). The question remains the same. The mix itself will vary in time and space.

The success indicator is the value of production: 'When an economist is comparing alternative social arrangements, the proper procedure is to compare the total social product yielded by these different arrangements.' (Coase, 1960:34). The value of production will be at its maximum where no allocative slippage can be eliminated through a further shifting of resources from one institutional alternative to the other.

The option of exchange is often treated as a free good. Coase as an economist is critical of this practice. Employing phrases like 'the costs of using the price mechanism' (Coase, 1937:53), 'the cost of market transactions' (Coase, 1960:114) and even 'marketing costs' (Coase, 1937:53; 1960:114), he stresses that the decision to trust to independence and trade is also a decision to bear the associated costs: 'In order to carry out a market transaction, it is necessary to discover who it is that one wishes to deal with, to inform people that one wishes to deal and on what terms, to conduct negotiations leading up to a bargain, to draw up the contract, to undertake the inspection needed to make sure that the terms of the contract are being observed, and so on.' (Coase, 1960:114). The game of exchange is evidently not a free good. On the contrary: no one can play who does not buy an entry ticket or pay his user charge.

The cost of supply is made up not just of production economies alone but also of the dealing costs which must be incurred if the good is successfully to be converted into cash. Searches must be conducted in order to identify appropriate trading partners and find out the direction of underlying market trends. Information must be made available in order to arouse interest in the product and its perceived properties. Decision-making and bargaining must take place in order to bring into being the mutually-acceptable prices that without the process of negotiation would have no Walras-like existence of their own. Concords must be monitored and agreements enforced in order to protect the buyers and the sellers from the sharp practices of ruthless cream-skimmers who put the immediacy of the 'quick buck' above the possibility of future business. Non-production costs such as these can represent a significant proportion of the total cost of supply. Beyond some point, cost-calculators will say, the internalisation of the burdens within the framework of a single hierarchy can well become the more competitive choice.

Information is less of a stumbling block where no division is itself an independent profit-seeker. The hierarchy saves the search through the prescription of internal supply chains. It guarantees sufficient interest in each of its services by means of its corporate plan. Promises made in-house are likely to be less costly to secure. Policing will be easier since collaborators will be less tempted to keep secret their costings. In these ways and in others, it is clear, the organisation can have an absolute advantage over more expensive exchange. Even the State (by levying a sales tax on tradables but not on intra-firm transactions) can provide an economic incentive for a cost-conscious business to move from decentralisation to authority.

Yet organisation too has its costs. As the structure grows in size, as its activities become spatially more dispersed and sectorally more differentiated, so the organiser or leader will move into a realm of diminishing returns, increasing costs. That diminution in effectiveness cannot be explained in terms of a single-product upward-sloping supply curve: the firm has the freedom to diversify into a lower-cost line of business instead. It can only be explained in terms of the supervisory overhead spreading itself too thin. This is a limit to the growth of the firm and a reason why the price-mechanism has not completely been swept aside: 'As each producer expands he becomes less efficient; the additional costs of organizing extra transactions increase.' (Coase, 1937:44). Even so, no equilibrium can be expected to last forever. Improvements in electronic communication in particular are likely to have a significant effect on the supply price of organisation and thence on the relative cost of exchange.

Coase takes as his subject the institutional mix. He approaches this mix using the familiar microeconomic constructs of performance and opportunity cost: 'To have an efficient economic system it is necessary not only to have markets but also areas of planning within organizations of the appropriate size. What this mix should be we find as a result of competition.' (Coase, 1992:716). The vision represents an imaginative application of marginal cost and marginal benefit. We rely on the invisible hand to identify the limits of the invisible hand. We rely on market economics to define the scope of organisation and hierarchy: 'The main reason why it is profitable to establish a firm would seem to be that there is a cost of using the price mechanism.' (Coase, 1937:38).

Coase is using the market to explain the non-market. It is supplementary costs like conflict-resolution and the inspection of standards, he says, which account for the pricing out of price: 'Their existence implies that methods of coordination alternative to the market, which are themselves costly and in various ways imperfect, may nonetheless be preferable to relying on the pricing mechanism, the only method of coordination normally analyzed by economists.' (Coase, 1992:715). Coase is right to criticise economists for neglecting the option of non-price allocation. Curiously, however, the main criticism that many will make of his own institutionalism is that he too will not look beyond the boundaries of relative cost and relative benefit when he seeks to explain why it is that the option of price is sometimes competed into second place.

Coase believes that his market for markets has predictive power on its side. Decentralisation and organisation gravitate into equilibrium roles which survival given rivalry will have identified for them. Positive in the sense that it explains, there is also an optimiser's 'ought-to-be' that legitimises the selection of the most appropriate tool: 'Economic policy consists of choosing those legal rules, procedures, and administrative structures which will maximize the value of production.' (Coase, 1988:28). Competition among alternatives is a valued procedure. Maximum output is the reason why it is valued. The evolution of institutions is here being flattened into purchase and sale. The criticism that many will make is that there is more than the butcher, the brewer and the baker to the modelling of contract and command.

Property rights are a prism and an *explicandum*. Coase treats them as an exogeneity and a fact of life. Coase, starting from here, takes efficiency to be single-valued. Samuels and Medema, starting from circularity, see efficiency instead as a range of possibilities linked to a range of distributions. If the level of costs determines the convection of rights, they say, then so too does the pattern of rights determine the level of costs: 'Wealth maximization itself is necessarily always conducted and calculated in terms of some price structure which is in turn a function of its corresponding rights structure... There is no unique wealth maximization... Different rights assignments imply different cost registrations on the market and therefore different wealth maximizations.' (Samuels and Medema, 1998:171). Present prices and costs are not independent of past entitlements and endowments. Coase starts from here. The history of head starts does not.

Coase in his 1960 paper on 'The Problem of Social Cost' shows a conspicuous lack of curiosity about the pre-period allocation of rights. All he says is that the confectioner and the doctor have arrived at a point where they know that their interests are in conflict: 'The real question that has to be decided is, Should A be allowed to harm B or should B be allowed to harm A?' (Coase, 1960:96). A choice must be made; and Coase shows ('the Coase Theorem') that the requisite internalisation can be brought about through private bargaining. The problem is that the negotiations do not take place in a virgin forest. People and past have come to stay. They significantly limit the freedom of the present day to maximise its gains by means of voluntary choice.

Property rights must be assigned *before* the trade of titles can commence. The initial distribution clearly impacts upon the Pareto optimality that will emerge and the established interests that will be the decisive ones. An existing patent over-compensates a monopoly windfall. A slave-owner insists that his lawful investment warrants a fair return. The assignments were made in the past. The institutions, however, influence the bargains that are made in the present. The rules have history and not rationality on their side. Once in place, however, they develop the habit of looking after their own.

That is why there is a certain irony in Coase's conclusion on the statutes, the precedents and the courts: 'The legal system will have a profound effect on the working of the economic system and may in certain respects be said to control it.' (Coase, 1992:717–18). What Coase says is, of course, true: the rules are good if only because lawlessness is bad. Yet there is an irony, and it relates to optimality. The past has left the present with a *status quo* that it is expensive and inconvenient to put right. Pressure groups and marginal constituencies restrict the ability of the legislature to do what is maximising for the whole. The costs of litigation introduce both discontinuity and asymmetry into judge-made law. The costs of enforcement mean that not every infraction will be followed up and corrected. Thence the irony. The legal system has a profound effect. Yet it might not be the effect that would do the most to increase felt wellbeing within the nation.

A calm surface hides the turbulence beneath. It is easy to assume that Coase's 'cost of market transaction' is a straightforward invitation to compare known numbers in order to spotlight the most economical value. The truth is that Coase's 'cost', subtle, confusing and profoundly ambiguous, is a concept that may be interpreted in no less than three distinctive ways. Not one of those interpretations lends itself to precise quantification in a real-world setting.

The first meaning relates to the ink costs and the shoe-leather costs incurred in the physical acts of bargaining, contracting, coordinating and monitoring. It is this meaning to which the accountant will point when he says that he knows how to operationalise Coase. The difficulty is that no closed-ended list can ever be drawn up. Deciding what to include and what to exclude is not a cookery-book procedure. Falsifiable testing of transaction-related hypotheses will for that reason seldom be conclusive.

The second meaning, focusing not on inputs but on outcomes, has to do with the 'shortfall from what could have been achieved if institutions worked perfectly.' (Goldberg, 1985:400). Goldberg says that this disparity 'better captures Coase's intent' (Goldberg, 1985:399) than does a simple adding-up of the eggs that make up the omelette. Coase's 'cost', Goldberg believes, is best interpreted as a failure to do that which in retrospect would have been maximising, a failure to avoid wastage through making the appropriate adaptation. Coase himself well captures the sense of cost as shortfall when he speaks of 'the loss through the waste of resources' that is caused by the entrepreneur who makes 'mistakes', by the businessman who does not 'place the factors of production in the uses where their value is greatest.' (Coase, 1937:43, 45). Under-achievement imposes a cost. The measurement of performance below potential is nonetheless not a task that will confidently be undertaken save by a statistician who thinks he can find precise data on all the 'if onlys' that could have been fact.

The third meaning of Coase's 'cost of market transaction' picks up the ubiquity of unknowledge in a decision-making environment where much in the present is the unsupported guess and nothing of the future is as yet in view. It cannot be easy to add up an open-ended cost-set already in existence or to avoid a mistake because of a miscalculation of potential. It must be many times more difficult to estimate a transaction overhead that is trapped between the 'don't know' of an under-informed present and the 'haven't a clue' of Shackle's history-to-come. Be that as it may, unknowledge is undeniably at the heart of the third meaning that can be attributed to Coase's 'cost'. As Hodgson writes: 'It is clear that transaction costs as a category are not meaningful without some concept of true or radical uncertainty.' (Hodgson, 1999:207). It is clear to Hodgson. It is clear to Coase.

Coase's use of comparative statics make it appear that his theory is one of known magnitudes. A careful examination of his work reveals that there is in fact as much of disequilibrium as of equilibrium in his understanding of cost. The mix of Marshall and Shackle gives his economics a high degree of sophistication. It is in the nature of uncertainty, however, that it is resistant to precise quantification in a real-world setting.

Coase is alert to uncertainty. Writing of business, he assigns to the 'entrepreneur-co-ordinator, who directs production' (Coase, 1937:35–6) a range of undefinable functions that no bureaucrat will have the sensing skills to be able to carry out. The entrepreneur must discover a good partner and form an opinion on a reasonable price. He must disseminate information so that latent desires can be converted into effective demand. He must decide when to terminate search, to cease negotiation and to make the contract. Describing these functions, Coase is describing the treacle of unknowledge as well: 'It seems improbable that a firm would emerge without the existence of uncertainty.' (Coase, 1937:40).

The contract itself is a grey area of indeterminacy. Referring to the hire of labour (but, implicitly, to land rented and capital borrowed as well), Coase draws attention to the shadow–land of multiple outcomes: 'The contract is one whereby the factor, for a certain remuneration ... agrees to obey the directions of an entrepreneur *within certain limits*.' (Coase, 1937:39). The contract comes first. The job description evolves over time: 'The service which is being provided is expressed in general terms, the exact details being left until a later date.' (Coase, 1937:40). Indeterminacy at the market stage means discretion within the organisation. Both contract and command, it would appear, must proceed in an environment where the facts are created as the agreement unfolds.

Coase is critical of Pigou for assuming a knowledge to which he had no right to pretend. Coase says that it is virtually impossible in the absence of market-determined values for the policy-maker, using taxes and subsidies, to equate private and social cost in the sense of *The Economics of Welfare*: 'Such tax proposals are the stuff that dreams are made of.' (Coase, 1988:185). Coase in his political economy is critical of utopian interventionists who make policy recommendations on the basis of net costs and benefits that they cannot know. Unknowledge exists at the level of the State. The State should not take on duties that it cannot perform.

Coase, approaching transaction cost in the third of its three senses, reminds the Pigovians that social engineers, however well-intentioned, have no crystal ball that would protect their interventionism from the unplanned-for, the unexpected and the unforeseen. The problem is that Coase, approaching transaction cost in the first of its three senses, is himself prepared to employ the textbook let-us-assume of adequate information when he calls for rational choice in the mix of contract and command. The following, on the respective pay-offs to market and State, gives the clear impression of a Coase who is as confident as a Pigou that the economist as a calculator has the facts he requires to make a cost-effective contribution: 'The Coase Theorem ... does not imply, when transaction costs are positive, that government actions (such as government operation, regulation, or taxation, including subsidies) could not produce a better result than relying on negotiations between individuals in the market. Whether this would be so could be discovered not by studying imaginary governments but what real governments actually do. My conclusion: let us study the world of positive transaction costs.' (Coase, 1992:717).

Let us study it – if we can find it. Coase, approaching transaction cost in the first of its three senses, evidently believes that we can. Just as Pigou would expect the economist to assist in internalising the neighbourhood spillovers of the smoking chimney, so Coase would expect the economist to advise on the most economical set of corrective institutions. Pushing back the choice from the decision made *within* a framework to the decision made *about* a framework does not, however, lighten the darkness of unknowledge that led Coase, approaching transaction cost in the third of its three senses, to describe the Pigovian proposals as 'the stuff that dreams are made of'. Samuels and Medema rightly recognise that Coase cannot have it both ways: 'It would seem that the Coasean approach is no less a dream than the Pigovian, and on the same grounds. No one can ever *know* all the costs and benefits knowledge of which is required by Coase's approach.' (Samuels and Medema, 1998:174).

Coase wants to use market economics to define the non-market sector: he makes the value-judgement that market logic is the meta-rule that should be used first. Coase looks at the history of State regulation and knows precisely what the numbers reveal: the State, he says, 'has commonly made matters worse'. (Coase, 1988:26). Both in his methodology and in his assessment he shows a bias for the voluntary order. An alternative perspective would, however, be that the State has made matters better and not worse. The reason is that the State, like any organisation, may have a decisive ability to reduce the transaction costs that would immobilise the private sector in inaction. Coase relies on dyadic instances like the cowman and the farmer to show that bargaining can deliver a mutually-satisfactory compromise. Many conflicts of interest arise, however, where the size of the group is large.

Dixit and Olson emphasise that free-riding and non-excludability can mean that the public good is under-provided in large groups since rational volunteers will have no convincing incentive to do their share: 'The Coase Theorem often leads to absurd conclusions because it does not take account of the way that an increase in the number who must participate in the internalization of an externality or the provision of a public good makes it difficult or impossible for Coaseian bargaining to achieve Pareto efficiency.' (Dixit and Olson, 2000:312). In large groups, the trading solution might not be enough. Abstracting, perhaps prematurely, from the interpersonal pressures of organisational memory and social capital, Dixit and Olson decide that success in such groups is not guaranteed 'if they rely soley on voluntary participation choices of individuals. Successful provision of public goods, or internalization of externalities in large groups, usually requires some form of coercion.' (Dixit and Olson, 2000:316).

Coercion is here another name for democracy. The bargaining solution is a two-stage progression. First, looking ahead, we as voters decide in complete freedom to select leaders to conduct future negotiations on our behalf. Second, in-period, we as citizens accept the discipline of the rules even if opportunistic conduct is subsequently revealed to have the higher pay-off. Constitutionalism here means that consent is given in advance. What it does not mean is that the doctor and the confectioner solve their own incompatibilities in their own distinctive manner. The politicians get involved, bargains are bundled, and the outcome might not be the same as the cost–benefit first choice of the unique individuals themselves. That is the down-side. The up-side is that decisions get made and a solution emerges.

Whether the centralised scenario is more costly or less costly than the Coasean trade is not clear. It is essentially an empirical question. Coase says that the State in the past 'has commonly made matters worse'. The future may be different. We simply cannot be sure until we have added up the results.

Frank Knight sees the firm as a shock-absorber in a dynamic world of discovery and disturbance: 'When uncertainty is present ... the task of deciding what to do and how to do it takes the ascendancy over that of execution... Centralization of this deciding and controlling function is imperative.' (Knight, 1921:268). Entrepreneurship requires the support of a bureaucracy when choices are hedged about with unknowledge. Decentralised bargaining grinds out no market clearing price where business people lack the knowledge to make an informed judgement. Knight explained the failure of the organisation to dissolve into sequential contracts in terms of the superior ability of the structure to cope with the void of the future. His justification of command clearly has no place for comparative statics or the equilibrium state.

Knight makes uncertainty a necessary condition for the existence of the firm. Langlois detects a similar emphasis on self-insurance through banding in the cost-theory of Coase: 'Coase's explanation for the emergence of the firm is ultimately a *coordination* one. The firm is an institution that lowers the costs of qualitative coordination in a world of uncertainty, where by *coordination* I mean the process of aligning the knowledge and expectations of the parties who need to cooperate in production, and by *qualitative* coordination I mean coordination involving the transmission of information beyond price and quantity.' (Langlois, 1998:6). Just as the market is a discovery process to the Hayekian, so to the Coasean is the firm.

An uncertain future is undeniably a Coasean reason for the internalisation of foresight and planning in a unified decision-making structure. Hodgson, sympathetic as he is to theories of disequilibrium states, is still not convinced that the necessary condition is also a sufficient one: 'What has to be shown ... is that some kind of economy of information costs can be obtained by organizing the agents together under an institutional umbrella.' (Hodgson, 1999:205). It has to be shown that an institutional umbrella is genuinely more economical than would be sequential horse-trading and re-drafting. It has also to be shown 'why such an institution should be a firm, and not merely an association of producer-traders who pool relevant information.' (Hodgson, 1999:205). The firm is one port in the storm of uncertainty. Hodgson's point is that it is not the only port; and that an either/or approach to contract and command does wrong to ignore the intermediate points that dot the institutional map.

Thus search could become the province of specialist market-researchers bought in on piece-rate to advise. Bargaining and risk-assessment could be dealt with through the *ad hoc* employment of *pro rata* consultants. Policing and enforcement overheads could be cut by information-pooling and computerised credit ratings. If economies of scale in the containment of unknowledge point to integration within the firm, then they could just as easily point to independence and contract.

Coase, writing as he does as follows, would have no *a priori* objection to any form of contracting that paid its way: 'We can imagine a system where all advice or knowledge was bought as required.' (Coase, 1937:50). What he also believes is that transaction costs have a tendency to promote the development of the organisational response. This section, not denying the truism that rational profit-maximisers will opt for economic institutions that rationally maximise their profits, takes issue with the confidence that underlies his expectation. Uncertainty being the most uncertain of animals, there is simply no way of knowing at which point on the institutional map a cost-conscious economy will ultimately choose to dwell.

Where knowledge is incomplete, the decision-maker will often fall back on the conventional routine. Learned, familiar, taken for granted, difficult to change, the established rule is at once an economy in the use of limited computational capacity and a constraint on the freedom of the present-day to start from here.

Coase on cost is a theory of calculation, minimisation and continuing comparison. The heuristic, on the other hand, makes rationality bounded and filters current values through quasi-permanent practices. History takes over. The past decides.

Memory inhibits the fresh response at the level of the individual's choice. The ongoing and the conservative have a similar impact upon efficiency and adaptation at the level of the group. Coase, concentrating on costs, benefits, margins and payoffs, sees no need to explore the sense in which learning, capacity and productivity are themselves the consequence and not just the cause of organisational affiliation. The previous chapter on Organisational order made a somewhat stronger case for context-dependent analysis, for people and past.

Tacit knowledge in such a way of looking at things is embedded in existing patterns and firm-specific experiences. Not susceptible to verbalisation, the creature of interaction and situation, the endogeneity is difficult to quantify but an element in cheapness and costliness nonetheless. Organisational memory integrates information and coordinates reactions despite the fact that each unit is in possession of a small fraction only of the organisation's knowledge-stock. Much that is tacitly known is only known at all because of the 'ands' that knit the dyadic relationships into a skein.

The organisation, moreover, is feeling and attachment. Land and capital do not look to fellow inputs for confirmation and affirmation. Labour is more temperamental. People in some organisations feel bound to their company by strong ties of loyalty, commitment, trust and belonging. People in other organisations treat APQT as a game to be played against the boss. People in some organisations strive and shirk as parts of a dense network, informal but strong. People in other organisations have been revolved, rotated and re-defined to such an extent that they have the distance of strangers at work. Each organisation, in short, is a culture *sui generis*, with its own internal dynamic and its own process of evolution. Coase studies allocative efficiency as between his two polar types. Generalisations, however, conceal; and people are a problem. The fact is that there is no representative organisation.

Organisational memory and embodied interaction are a reminder that path-dependence and learned reactions have an impact on the new choices that the established unit can make. One transaction more through contract, one transaction less through command, is a Coasean trade-off for the *ab initio* undertaker on which the bureaucracy already in possession of a constitution will find it difficult to act. Coase compares institutions on the basis of their relative costs. Fukuyama finds in institutions the stamp of patterns and customs. Coase is speaking as Coase and not as Fukuyama when he says: 'It makes little sense for economists to discuss the process of exchange without specifying the institutional setting within which the trading takes place, since this affects the incentives to produce and the costs of transacting.' (Coase, 1992:718). To Coase the choice of institutions is the choice of transaction costs. To Fukuyama it is a broader choice.

Coase can envisage a society in which the coordination of the numberless atoms is ensured entirely by means of markets and not at all by command: then 'society becomes not an organization but an organism' (Coase, 1937:34) and automaticity does all. In a world of zero transaction costs – admittedly, 'a very unrealistic assumption' (Coase, 1960:114) – the firm would wither away and economic articulation would be the costless gift of the invisible hand.

It is Coase's belief that firms exist because transactions have costs. A different view would be that they have scale economies in the productive use of technology. A compromise would be that it is the sum of the production costs *plus* the transaction costs that sway the economic balance in favour of organisation or of exchange. Since the volume of production has a direct influence on the volume of the transactions that have to be costed, it makes good sense for the two sets of costs to be treated as mutually determining. It makes little sense for the firm to be reduced to legal title alone or for the output that it produces to be impounded within the *ceteris paribus*.

Besides that, the level of cost, influenced by and influencing the size of the organisation, has a feedback effect on the market structure. Prices respond flexibly where firms are small perfect competitors. Prices can be more rigid where firms have power. An oligopolistic industry with a convention of price leadership or a practice of respecting the kink will be better modelled by live-and-let-live than in terms of the cost-minimisation on which passive perfect competitors will predictably converge. Coasean cost comparison in such a case picks up not just scale but also the dominance that that size makes possible. Whatever such a comparison may mean, it will certainly not be an optimum in the sense of Coase.

11.3   MARKETS AND HIERARCHIES

Institutions like the firm, Oliver Williamson writes, 'have the main purpose and effect of economizing on transaction costs.' (Williamson, 1975:1). Textbook economics explains the rise – and size – of the business organisation in terms of economies and diseconomies in the average cost of production. In Williamson's economics the focus shifts to the transaction overheads that make possible the market economy. Transaction costs are the equivalent in the economics of unit exchanges versus centralised corporations of frictions impeding gravitation in the classical physics. They are the sand that grinds against the balance when supply and demand become too expensive and hierarchy emerges as the more economical choice.

Ronald Coase as an economist was able to use the gain-seeking logic of costs and benefits to refute the inevitability thesis of organisational thinkers like Marx, Weber and Schumpeter. Prophets of size such as these believed that the small transactor would be left behind by a process of concentration and rationalisation that Galbraith, describing the American anti-trust laws as 'a charade' (Galbraith, 1967:202) – 'It is evidently not so practical to indict a whole economy' (Galbraith, 1952:65) – clearly takes to be a law of structural evolution: 'Large tasks require large organizations. That is how it is.' (Galbraith: 1977:277). Coase adopts a position that is more open-ended, less confident. Most fundamentally of all, he explains the size of the structure in terms of transactions and not at all in terms of production. His window on the world is that of Oliver Williamson as well.

Fixed costs, technical indivisibilities and increasing returns, Williamson says, are 'rarely decisive': 'Transactional considerations, not technology, are typically decisive in determining which mode of organization will obtain in what circumstances and why.' (Williamson, 1975:2, 248). The cost of transacting, Williamson is convinced, will throw into relief the most economical mix. That is why he, like Coase, is prepared to let economic analysis speak for itself. Smith had a preference for wealth-enhancing exchange and Marx believed monopoly capitalism to be inefficient and unjust. Williamson, on the other hand, makes much of his contention that a 'relatively calculative orientation to economic organization' (Williamson, 1985:xiii) is unlikely to have an *ex ante* ideological slant: 'The approach is comparatively value-free – it is biased neither for nor against unfettered market modes of organization.' (Williamson, 1975:253).

Just as markets can fail, so can hierarchies: 'Organizational failure is a symmetrical term meant to apply to market and nonmarket organizations alike.' (Williamson, 1975:20). Williamson, as Coase had done before him, seeks to show that, in institutional equilibrium, the unavoidable imperfections will be at their economic minimum: 'Remediable frictions ... associated with one mode of organization' will be 'attenuated by shifting the transaction, or a related set of transactions, to an alternative mode.' (Williamson, 1975:20). The consequence will be an economic optimum where there will be no way of economising further on the transaction costs that form the focus of Williamson's institutional comparisons.

Decentralised exchange allocates more efficiently than does planning by command where all relevant information is encoded into the costlessly-revealed signals of the auctioneer's price. The problem in the real world is that unknowledge so often impedes or even prevents the reaping of the rational economiser's gains from trade. Williamson, like Coase an uneasy mix of the maximiser and the satisficer, has no doubt what this fall from transparency must mean for the second-best economics of costly search: 'The organizational imperative that emerges in such circumstances is this: *Organize transactions so as to economize on bounded rationality while simultaneously safeguarding them against the hazards of opportunism.*' (Williamson, 1985:32). Economising on transaction costs thus becomes co-terminous with economising on that little that we know.

Herbert Simon is the theorist who more than any other has explored the fallen economics of decision-makers limited neurophysiologically and linguistically in their ability to receive, process, store and retrieve information without omission and without misapprehension. People are not lightning calculators. Their cognition is not the equal of the evidence. The future is uncertain and unpredictable. Rationality, in other words, is bounded – and thence the need for hierarchy in the place of sale: 'It is only because individual human beings are limited in knowledge, foresight, skill, and time that organizations are useful instruments for the achievement of human purpose.' (Simon, 1957:199).

Internal organisation, Williamson writes, can coordinate more cost-effectively than will market contracting since the psychological limits to calculation and cognition drive a wedge between the ideal and the attainable: 'If, in consideration of these limits, it is very costly or impossible to identify future contingencies and specify, *ex ante*, appropriate adaptations thereto, long-term contracts may be supplanted by internal organization. Recourse to the latter permits adaptations to uncertainty to be accomplished by administrative processes in a sequential fashion. Thus, rather than attempt to anticipate all possible contingencies from the outset, the future is permitted to unfold.' (Williamson, 1975:9). Inadequate statistics stand in the way of supply and demand. The integrated bureaucracy in the circumstances promises the faster entrepreneurial response to decision-making in the dark.

No contract can ever be comprehensively specified in advance. Administration will have a recognisable advantage over trade in precisely those circumstances 'under which complex contingent claims contracts will be costly to write, execute, and enforce': 'Faced with such difficulties, and considering the risks that simple (or incomplete) contingent claims contracts pose, the firm may decide to bypass the market and resort to hierarchical modes of organization.' (Williamson, 1975:9). The transfer of transactions from exchange to structure imposes economic costs of its own which every student of Smith on unintended upgrading or Hayek on unguided adaptation will be quick to decry as opportunities foregone. Given unknowledge, however, the internalisation of decision-trees in a non-market hierarchy might nonetheless be the least-cost compromise in a situation where the ideal is regrettably not a paying proposition.

The contracting parties could possess an identical endowment of radical unknowledge. Given the division of labour and the premium on specialisation, so equitable an equal start cannot be assumed to obtain. Where information is asymmetrically distributed, Williamson states, where the imbalance known as 'information impactedness' (Williamson, 1975:31) is seen to exist, there the threat is real that dishonesty and mistrust will make the conclusion of a mutually-satisfactory contract so costly as altogether to price it out of the choice-set: 'Because the party buying the information can establish its accuracy only at great cost, possibly only by collecting the original data itself, the exchange fails to go through.' (Williamson, 1975:16). Rational actors are tempted in the real world by 'opportunism', by 'a lack of candor or honesty in transactions', by 'self-interest seeking with guile.' (Williamson, 1975:9). Rational actors are led to make false promises, to use threats, to conceal information, to distort data – to behave opportunistically, in other words, rather than relying on the lubricant of trust. The substitution of organisation for exchange is in such a situation nothing other than a mutual defence pact that unites potential Hobbesians under the banner of a common cause.

If the discrete profit-seekers were to become dependable collaborators, the abuse of power through selective disclosure would cease to be a cause for concern: 'If ... rivals were not given to being opportunistic, the risk of strategic distortion would vanish and the (organizationally efficient) specialization of information could proceed.' (Williamson, 1975:17). Buying-in makes economic sense so long as the trading partners give each other a Kantian's guarantee. Hierarchy waxes and the market wanes as soon as the suppliers are seen to cut back on quality and the buyers fail to honour their cheques. Williamson expresses the opinion that opportunistic duplicity is less likely to be an impediment to communication where fellow team-mates have no separate claim on the profits of the whole. Not denying the reality of salaried staff's self-interest, he takes the view that empire-building and concealment of failure are as nothing compared to the opportunism that exists across the paid-for *quid pro quo*.

The 'bounded rationality' problem is one of simple access to the facts that are needed: 'The reason why outsiders are not on a parity with insiders is usually because outsiders lack firm-specific, task-specific, or transaction-specific experience.' (Williamson, 1975:31). The 'opportunism' problem relates not so much to the simple quantity of information as to its strategic deployment. In a market the premium is on concealed, not revealed preference. In an organisation, Williamson argues, there is no intra-firm incentive to seek appropriable rents at the expense of identifiable sub-groups reporting to the same apex authority.

Internal organisation is more easily audited than is anonymous exchange. Continuous relationships facilitate the settlement of disputes without expensive recourse to expert witnesses and courts of law. Acrimonious bargaining is avoided since inter-departmental transfers are charged at cost or not charged at all. Organisation is also the cause of a beneficial upgrading in attitudinal capital. Hierarchy has the advantage over the market that, providing an outlet for non-rational, non-commercial sentiments in the sense of Maslow, it releases the latent social assets of trust, trustworthiness and the willingness to cooperate that can make a significant economic contribution to the performance of the collectivity: 'Associational benefits can accrue to peer groups through increased productivity among members of the group who feel a sense of responsibility to do their fair share as members of the group but, left to their own devices, would slack off.' (Williamson, 1975:44). Market-clearing motivation evidently leaves untapped a valuable part of the commitment to supply.

Felt involvement reduces the temptation to ride free on the inputs of altruists. It makes less urgent the non-productive deadweights of metering, monitoring, written records. It also delivers 'a more satisfying trading atmosphere' (Williamson, 1975:40) which, an antidote to malingering, is also a consumer good and an end in itself. Some people, of course, will nonetheless prefer an interest-based nexus and will perform more effectively in the amorality of exchange. Williamson's approach, strictly comparative, is capable of explaining the existence – and the co-existence – both of hierarchy that mobilises involvement and of market that appeals to the self. Williamson gives no unequivocal endorsement to either mode of economic articulation. The failure, the success, depends exclusively on the relative values of the transaction costs.

People and past are subordinate to current calculation in Williamson's institutional economics. Implicit more frequently than explicit, they are even so undeniable elements in his balance-sheet. Williamson, like Coase, falls back on costs and benefits to explain the equilibrium that evolves: 'Transaction cost economics is akin to orthodoxy in its insistence that economizing is central to economic organization.' (Williamson, 1985:xii). Conservative conventions and tried-and-tested precedents are economic costs and benefits like any others.

In the market as well as the hierarchy time remembered plays a role: consider the business assets of reputation and of network, both of which bend back the economic incentive to defection and deceit. Williamson nonetheless relates 'efficient codes' and reiterated adaptations most commonly to the stable organisation. Such replication 'economizes on bounded rationality. Complex events are summarized in an informal way by using what may be an idiosyncratic language.' (Williamson, 1975:25). Recurrence, even inertia, is here at once a source of guidance and a bulwark against abuse.

A merger between discrete enterprises can in that sense standardise practices to an extent that one-shot contracting can never match. Internal organisation 'promotes convergent expectations, serving in this way to attenuate uncertainties that are generated when interdependent parties make independent decisions with respect to changing market circumstances.' (Williamson, 1975:4). While business rivals are seen to offer each other some protection against unreconciled production plans (the function of the oligopolistic cartel or the price-leadership arrangement), the argument is that a unified organisation is even better placed to evaluate its future in the light of its past.

Where the verdict is positive, and where no offsetting costs are incurred, 'a shift from market to hierarchy will promote efficient adaptation.' (Williamson, 1975:26). The opposite assessment would suggest the opposite prediction. Williamson writes: 'Organizational variety arises primarily in the service of transaction cost economizing.' (Williamson, 1985:387). There is little more to his rational choice than that.

People and past are subordinate to current calculation. It is a valid criticism of Williamson's institutional economics that they are under-represented relative to the advantage-seeking maximisation that transaction theory shares with the neoclassical mainstream.

Williamson makes possessive catallactics the bedrock of his economic sociology: 'In the beginning there were markets.' (Williamson, 1975:20; 1985:87). The social economist is more sceptical about the baseline without a hinterland in which there was nothing but the contract: 'There can be no such beginning as the market itself involves socially generated procedures and norms. The market is not a "state of nature" as Williamson implies, but a social institution.' (Hodgson, 1988:206). The economist, Hodgson is saying, is wrong to begin his exposition with the market when exchange itself is embedded in rules and conventions, loyalties and networks, traditions and routines that form no part of the in-period purchase.

There is more to the economic process than the cost–benefit calculus of the isolated one-off. Property rights are taken to be legitimate because of a non-rational belief that lawful entitlements cannot be called into question. Enforcement presupposes the consensual acceptance of a protective agency (normally the democratic State) with a monopoly of force. Existing structures have a first-mover's experience. Powerful networks have a cumulative momentum of their own. Historical survivals, as illustrated by the sub-optimal QWERTY keyboard, need not be ideally suited to present-day conditions to be able to see off the challenge from a lower-cost new rule. Economising in Williamson's theory means no more than economising at the margin. A fuller account would include the inherited and the embodied that make the *best possible* into the *best attainable* now that we have already started our journey and have to go on from here.

The economising stance is itself a social fact. Even the gain-seeking mindset is a topic in social conservatism. Machiavelli and Hobbes, free-ridership and selfish individualism are, in some measure at least, a function of soil and climate.

Williamson's theory presupposes the alertness of the entrepreneur and not the character-capital of the bureaucrat. It is not for that reason entirely even-handed as between markets and hierarchies. Human behaviour in organisations is qualitatively different from human interaction across the exchanges. The inter-temporal stability of the lasting interdependencies tends to breed and perpetuate a higher density of adhesion and trust than can be expected in the evanescence of the passing-stranger swap. Economists like Williamson, as Hodgson observes, are therefore too quick to assume the same short-term calculativeness in the organisation that they would expect in the trade: 'Following in the tradition of individualistic social scientists, Williamson puts forward a model of individual human nature ("opportunism") and recklessly assumes that this applies equally to the market and the firm. No recognition is made of the effect of the institutional environment in moulding actions and beliefs.' (Hodgson, 1988:211).

Markets and organisations need not be the home to the same set of character traits. Transaction cost theorists (partly for purposes of exposition, more probably because they expect the real world to gravitate into the bargaining mode) show a preference for market logic which may not capture the fullness of the organisational experience. Even the business firm can be something other than a passive mechanism for the comparison of costs and benefits. Even the institutional mix can be something other than the equilibrium efficiencies of the minimising imperative.

Transaction thinkers set out their alternative to the textbook vacuum of frictionless optimality. They make clear that their focus is the non-production cost of doing business that, as North explains, the neoclassical tradition one-sidedly takes to be zero: 'The net gains from exchange are the gross gains, which are the standard gains in neoclassical theory and in the international trade model, minus the costs of measuring and policing the agreement and minus the losses that result because policing is not perfect.' (North, 1990:31). North as an economic historian goes further still. Not only does he set out his hypothesis, he quantifies the burdens. North calculated in 1990 that transaction costs in the American economy accounted for 45 per cent of total value-added. They had amounted to only 25 per cent a century before. (North, 1990:28).

North would say that the hypotheses can be tested. More sceptical thinkers would be less confident. The problem, as was discussed with reference to Coase, is the nebulous nature of the costs involved. Precision is difficult where the boundaries themselves are a matter for debate.

At the microeconomic level it would presumably make sense to include the production-facilitating costs (including the time costs) of collecting information, negotiating agreements, monitoring compliance, counting up deviation. At the national level there are the overheads of trademarks and warranties, auditors and accountants, banking and insurance, police services and law courts. The specification can be as narrow as the time-and-motion study or the recourse to arbitration. It can also be as open-ended as the risk premium automatically added against default or the precautionary resistance to lock-in specialisation, 'a form of insurance when the costs and uncertainties of transacting are high.' (North, 1990:34). The list can be as literal as supervision and measurement, transport costs and retraining costs: the best-attainable price, the median quality-standard, are endstates that depend on time spent in queues and expensive newspapers bought to find out about conditions. The list can also be as imaginative as hostage-taking through interlocking shareholdings, distorted communication when expanding bureaucracies require additional strata, and even the government as the guarantor of property rights and stable prices: 'One cannot have the productivity of a modern high income society with political anarchy.' (North, 1990:35). Precision is difficult where lists can vary. Testing becomes tautologous where virtually any supporting cost can be called a transaction cost for the purposes of an investigation into the core hypothesis of growth-rates retarded and productive potential slipping into the sand.

It is easy to say, with North, that there is a cost: 'The more resources that must be devoted to transacting to assure cooperative outcomes, the more diluted are the gains from trade of the neoclassical model.' (North, 1990:58). It is much more difficult to quantify that cost in the real world. Most difficult of all is the task of tracking the evolution when institutions mutate and different services are demanded. Once the shopper had to internalise the cost of sorting and grading his fruit. Nowadays the supermarket invests the time and effort to classify the qualities. Once repeat dealing and community values gave the trader a personalised heuristic. Nowadays there is third-party enforcement because codes and networks are threatened by mobility and anonymity. Things change. History moves on. Of course there is a marginal cost. The point is that there is a marginal benefit as well. Different lifestyles demand different overheads. Different means different. It is singularly recalcitrant to the calculus of more or less.

12. Conclusion

The subject of this book has been the mixed economy. No book on demand and supply can have a different subject.

The economy, first and foremost, is a mix of individual choices and collective values. Only the sensing self can, methodologically speaking, put into words and deeds the nature of the non-standard sensation. Only discrete Ego can reveal the preference; but still it can be peer groups and reference groups, overlapping expectations and community consensus, that embed his choice in a fabric of which he is but a thread. Sometimes the purchase or sale will be as autonomous and private as Jack Spratt's wish to eat no fat, Jill Spratt's decision to dress only in green. Sometimes it will be as socialised as interdependent consumption-sets, emulated and replicated, as public as interdependent work–patterns, convergent and shared. Sometimes the origin will be the irreducible and the unique. Sometimes the origin will be sanctioned conformity and mutual reinforcement. Always, however, the truth will be the mix.

The economy, moreover, is a mix of the remembered and the current, of inherited conventions and innovative reactions. History hands on templates and teaches the as-yet-unborn the customs and adaptations that the long-since-forgotten once found functional for their survival. Whirling challenge, on the other hand, compels perpetual search to an extent that even the most acculturated of conservative constitutionalists will find difficult to ignore. Trust and cooperativeness are time-dominated traits which reduce the incidence of deceitful opportunism even in faceless and anonymous deals. Market competition, on the other hand, puts a premium on winning which prices away the time and effort that can be invested in economic chivalry, Good Samaritanism, the Categorical Imperative and intrinsically-motivated activity. The past provides the precedents, the mindsets, the multiperiod precommitments, the rules of the game. The present contributes the upsets, the surprises, the novelties and the disequilibria that, shocking economic actors out of their reassuring inertia, compel them to swim with a tide that has altered its course.

On the one hand there is the non-ego force of the tried-and-tested, protective of track records and resistant to change. On the other hand there is the non-ego force of gain-seeking rivalry, a locus of uncertainty and a reason to move fast. On the one hand there is the familiar heuristic which has performed tolerably well, the established routine that situates, satisfices, locates and identifies. On the other hand there is the possessive adventurer's restless determination to acquire more, to acquire better, to acquire different precisely because non-satiety is an axiom to which the scarcity-minded maximiser can easily relate. Torn between the pull of fitting in and the push of setting out, the individual can be in no doubt that the determinism which drives him on but also holds him back is not a single but a double constraint. The truth, in other words, is the mix.

The economy, again, is a mix of exchange and authority, of one-off market contracts and long-lived organisational hierarchies. Negotiating outside the unified set of property rights the entrepreneur will have an absolute advantage in alertness and initiative that the bureaucrat will not have been socialised to match. Adapting within a handed-on structure in possession of an organisational memory the relative capacities to succeed and thrive are likely to be reversed. A capitalist economy which channels its creative destruction through planning structures with a logic of their own is in that sense a multi-axial environment which breeds and expects contradictory characteristics from Janus-faced ground-breakers who also perpetuate and preserve.

As the agents of competing corporations the executives and the administrators must be imaginative and decisive, resolute in haggling and economical with the truth. As salaried collaborators, however, who derive satisfaction from the teamwork life in common, the same individuals will know that a higher pay-off accrues to integration than may be expected from dynamism where the interactions are repeated and evaluation is diffuse. On the one hand the managers and the technocrats are expected to mobilise their leaderliness and their acumen in the service of the shareholders' profits. On the other hand they are led by their own gains and losses to utilise the discretionary power conferred by skeleton contracts for the attainment of behavioural objectives like job satisfaction, prestige, security, promotion, pay, fringe benefits and the inculcation of the ingrained. On the one hand the business looks outward to the market. On the other hand the business looks inward to its staff. The truth, in other words, is the mix.

The economy, finally, is a mix of market and State, decentralisation and command, economics and politics. Allocative and dynamic efficiency are normally taken to presuppose the instrumental rationality and the pecuniary self-interest that are disciplined and encouraged by the economic determinism of the competitive process. Coordination through price-signalling and ambition released by the invisible hand are wealth-related arguments for a *laissez-faire* government that knows enough not to kill the golden goose.

Reality, however, is less confident than mathematics about the predictive power of a single-valued solution.

Impulse buying and reference points, loss aversion and an abbreviated discounting period, repeat business because of a minimax fear of the new, all call into question the vision of the price-mechanism as the impersonal optimiser of value for money. Empathy and compassion, the gift relationship and the prick of conscience, levelling down because of a loser's antipathy to stigma, all suggest a distribution of productive resources other than that which would have maximised the growth-rate through profits and parsimony. Stasis, anxiety, envy, altruism, involvement and concern are not easy to reconcile with a defence of freedom that appeals to the endstate of national wealth. Emotion combined with reason is a mix. It may not, however, be the mix that makes the greatest-possible contribution to the alleviation of material need.

Where there is a productive shortcoming, it might be to direction and not to automaticity that the community will turn for the correction of the market failure. Law enforcement is the precondition for the rule of contract. Externalities could be contained by means of regulations and standards. Taxes and subsidies could align the private with the social cost. Job quotas and comprehensive schooling could spread the net of the common culture. Public goods could be provided free where social consensus gives the mandate. Even competition needs a home. A State that takes the broader view might be in a position to add a brick to that home.

On the one hand separate decisions are reconciled into an undesigned matrix through the impersonality of the auction. On the other hand consistency is combined with the Social Welfare Function by a pragmatic polity that makes the market no more than one means among many. On the one hand the 'I'. On the other hand the 'We' – or the 'They'. Whatever the precise spot balance between the individual and the State, the fact is that exchange and authority are always to be found in a compound. Economising is not the whole of economics. The truth, in other words, is the mix.

Bibliography

Ackerman, F. (1997), 'Consumed in Theory: Alternative Perspectives on the Economics of Consumption', *Journal of Economic Issues*, Vol. 31, pp. 651-64

Alchian, A.A. and Demsetz, H. (1972), 'Production, Information Costs, and Economic Organization', *American Economic Review*, Vol. 62, in H. Demsetz, *Ownership, Control, and the Firm* (Oxford: Blackwell, 1988)

Argyle, M. (1987), *The Psychology of Happiness* (London: Routledge)

Arrow, K.J. (1972), 'Gifts and Exchanges', *Philosophy and Public Affairs*, Vol. 1, pp. 343-62

Arrow, K.J. (2000), 'Observations on Social Capital', in P. Dasgupta and I. Serageldin, eds, *Social Capital: A Multifaceted Perspective* (Washington, D.C.: The World Bank), pp. 3-5

Asch, S.E. (1952), *Social Psychology* (Oxford: Oxford University Press, 1987)

Axelrod, R. (1986), 'An Evolutionary Approach to Norms', *American Political Science Review*, Vol. 80, pp. 1095-1111

Baudrillard, J. (1988), *Selected Writings*, ed. by M. Poster (Stanford: Stanford University Press)

Baumol, W.J. (1975), 'Business Responsibility and Economic Behavior', in E.S. Phelps, ed., *Altruism, Morality, and Economic Theory* (New York: Russell Sage Foundation), pp. 45-56

Baxter, J.L. (1988), *Social and Psychological Foundations of Economic Analysis* (Brighton: Wheatsheaf)

Becker, G.S. (1976), *The Economic Approach to Human Behavior* (Chicago: University of Chicago Press)

Becker, G.S. (1981), 'Altruism in the Family and Selfishness in the Market Place', *Economica*, Vol. 48, pp. 1-15

Becker, G.S. (1993), 'The Economic Way of Looking at Life' (Nobel Lecture), *Journal of Political Economy*, Vol. 101, in *Accounting for Tastes*, infra, pp. 139-161

Becker, G.S. (1996), *Accounting for Tastes* (Cambridge, Mass.: Harvard University Press)

Becker, G.S., Grossman, M. and Murphy, K.M. (1994), 'An Empirical Analysis of Cigarette Addiction', *American Economic Review*, Vol. 84, in Becker, *Accounting for Tastes*, supra, pp. 85-117

Becker, G.S. and Murphy, K.M. (1988), 'A Theory of Rational Addiction', *Journal of Political Economy*, Vol. 96, in Becker, *Accounting for Tastes*, supra, pp. 50–76

Blau, P.M. (1964), *Exchange and Power in Social Life* (New York: John Wiley and Sons)

Bocock, R. (1993), *Consumption* (London: Routledge)

Boland, L.A. (1979), 'Knowledge and the Role of Institutions in Economic Theory', *Journal of Economic Issues*, Vol. 13, reprinted in G.M. Hodgson, ed., *The Economics of Institutions* (Aldershot: Edward Elgar, 1993), pp. 314–29

Boulding, K.E. (1956), *The Image* (Ann Arbor: University of Michigan Press)

Boulding, K.E. (1973), 'Toward the Development of a Cultural Economics', in L. Schneider and C.M. Bonjean, eds, *The Idea of Culture in the Social Sciences* (Cambridge: Cambridge University Press), pp. 47–64

Boulding, K.E. (1981), *A Preface to Grants Economics: The Economy of Love and Fear* (New York: Praeger)

Bourdieu, P. (1984), *Distinction*, tr. by R. Nice (London: Routledge and Kegan Paul)

Buchanan, J.M. (1975), *The Limits of Liberty* (Chicago: University of Chicago Press)

Buchanan, J.M. (1977), *Freedom in Constitutional Contract* (College Station: Texas A. and M. University Press)

Buchanan, J.M. (1986), *Liberty, Market and State* (Brighton: Wheatsheaf)

Buchanan, J.M. and Tullock, G. (1962), *The Calculus of Consent* (Ann Arbor: University of Michigan Press)

Burt, R.S. (1993), 'The Social Structure of Competition', in R. Swedberg, ed., *Explorations in Economic Sociology* (New York: Russell Sage Foundation), pp. 65–103

Choi, Young Back (1993), *Paradigms and Conventions* (Ann Arbor: University of Michigan Press)

Coase, R.H. (1937), 'The Nature of the Firm', *Economica*, n.s., Vol. 4, in his *The Firm, the Market, and the Law*, infra, pp. 33–55

Coase, R.H. (1960), 'The Problem of Social Cost', *Journal of Law and Economics*, Vol. 3, in *The Firm, the Market, and the Law*, infra, pp. 95–156

Coase, R.H. (1988), *The Firm, the Market, and the Law* (Chicago: University of Chicago Press)

Coase, R.H. (1992), 'The Institutional Structure of Production' (Nobel Lecture), *American Economic Review*, Vol. 82, pp. 713–19

Collard, D. (1978), *Altruism and Economy* (Oxford: Martin Robertson)

Commons, J.R. (1934), *Institutional Economics* (New York: Macmillan)

Commons, J.R. (1950), *The Economics of Collective Action* (New York: Macmillan)

Conlisk, J. (1996), 'Why Bounded Rationality?', *Journal of Economic Literature*, Vol. 34, pp. 669–700

Cooley, C.H. (1902), *Human Nature and the Social Order*, revised edn (New York: Scribners, 1922)

Crosland, C.A.R. (1949), 'The Way Towards More Socialist Equality', *The Tribune*, 19 August, pp. 10–11

Crosland, C.A.R. (1956), *The Future of Socialism*, revised ed. (London: Jonathan Cape, 1964)

Csikszentmihalyi, M. and Rochberg-Halton, E. (1981), *The Meaning of Things: Domestic Symbols and the Self* (Cambridge: Cambridge University Press)

Culyer, A.J. (1976), *Need and the National Health Service* (London: Martin Robertson)

Cyert, R.M. and March, J.G. (1963), *A Behavioral Theory of the Firm* (Englewood Cliffs: Prentice-Hall)

Deci, E.L. (1975), *Intrinsic Motivation* (New York: Plenum Press)

Deci, E.L. (1978), 'Applications of Research on the Effects of Rewards', in M.R. Lepper and D. Greene, eds, *The Hidden Costs of Reward* (Hillsdale, N.J.: Lawrence Erlbaum Associates), pp. 193–203

Deci, E.L. and Ryan, R.M. (1985), *Intrinsic Motivation and Self-Determination in Human Behavior* (New York: Plenum Press)

Dixit, A. and Olson, M. (2000), 'Does Voluntary Participation Undermine The Coase Theorem?', *Journal of Public Economics*, Vol. 76, pp. 309–35

Doeringer, P.B. and Priore, M.J. (1971), *Internal Labor Markets and Manpower Analysis* (Lexington, MA: D.C.Heath)

Douglas, M. (1982), *In The Active Voice* (London: Routledge and Kegan Paul)

Douglas, M. (1987), *How Institutions Think* (London: Routledge and Kegan Paul)

Douglas, M. and Baron Isherwood, (1979), *The World of Goods* (London: Allen Lane)

Doyal, L. and Gough, I. (1991), *A Theory of Human Need* (London: Macmillan)

Duesenberry, J.S. (1949), *Income, Saving and the Theory of Consumer Behavior* (Cambridge, MA: Harvard University Press)

Durkheim, E. (1895), *The Rules of Sociological Method*, tr. by S.A. Solovay and J.H. Mueller (New York: The Free Press, 1938)

Durkheim, E. (1897), *Suicide* tr. by J.A. Spaulding and G. Simpson (London: Routledge and Kegan Paul, 1952)

Durkheim, E. (1912), *The Elementary Forms of the Religious Life*, tr. by J.W. Swain (London: George Allen and Unwin, 1915)

Durkheim, E. (1925), *Moral Education*, tr. by E.K. Wilson and H. Schnurer (New York: The Free Press, 1961)

Durkheim, E. (1928), *Socialism and Saint Simon*, tr. by C. Sattler (London: Routledge and Kegan Paul, 1959)

Earl, P. (1986), *Lifestyle Economics* (Brighton: Wheatsheaf Books)

Easterlin, R.A. (1974), 'Does Economic Growth Improve the Human Lot? Some Empirical Evidence', in P.A. David and M.W. Reder, eds, *Nations and Households in Economic Growth* (New York: Academic Press)

Easterlin, R.A. (1995), 'Will raising the incomes of all increase the happiness of all?', *Journal of Economic Behavior and Organization*, Vol. 27, pp. 35–47

Edgeworth, F.Y. (1881), *Mathematical Psychics* (London: C. Kegan Paul)

Elster, J. (1989), 'Social Norms and Economic Theory', *Journal of Economic Perspectives*, Vol. 3, reprinted in G.M. Hodgson (ed.), *The Economics of Institutions* (Aldershot: Edward Elgar, 1993), pp. 261–279

Etzioni, A. (1988), *The Moral Dimension* (New York: The Free Press)

Fernandez de la Mora, G. (1987), *Egalitarian Envy* (New York: Paragon House)

Festinger, L. (1954), 'A Theory of Social Comparison Processes', *Human Relations*, Vol. 7, in H.H. Hyman and E. Singer, eds, *Readings in Reference Group Theory and Research* (New York: The Free Press, 1968), pp. 123–46

Festinger, L. (1957), *A Theory of Cognitive Dissonance* (London: Tavistock Publications, 1962)

Frank, R.H. (1999), *Luxury Fever* (New York: The Free Press)

Frank R.H. and Cook, P.J. (1995), *The Winner-Take-All Society* (New York: The Free Press)

Freud, S. (1908), 'Character and Anal Erotism', tr. by J. Strachey in *The Complete Psychological Works of Sigmund Freud*, Vol. IX (London: Hogarth Press, 1959), pp. 167–75

Freud, S. (1930), *Civilization and Its Discontents*, tr. by J. Strachey in *The Complete Psychological Works of Sigmund Freud*, Vol. XXI (London: Hogarth Press, 1961), pp. 57–145

Friedman, M. (1957), *A Theory of the Consumption Function* (Princeton: Princeton University Press)

Friedman, M. (1962), *Capitalism and Freedom* (Chicago: University of Chicago Press)

Fromm, E. (1956), *The Sane Society* (London: Routledge and Kegan Paul)

Fromm, E. (1973), *The Anatomy of Human Destructiveness* (New York: Holt, Rinehart and Winston)

Fromm, E. (1976), *To Have or To Be?* (London: Abacus, 1979)

Fukuyama, F. (1992), *The End of History and the Last Man* (London: Hamish Hamilton)

Fukuyama, F. (1997), *The End of Order* (London: Social Market Foundation)

Furnham, A. and Argyle, M. (1998), *The Psychology of Money* (London: Routledge)

Galbraith, J.K. (1952), *American Capitalism*, revised edn (Harmondsworth: Penguin Books, 1967)

Galbraith, J.K. (1958), *The Affluent Society*, 2nd edn (Harmondsworth: Penguin Books, 1970)

Galbraith, J.K. (1960), *The Liberal Hour* (Harmondsworth: Penguin Books, 1963)

Galbraith, J.K. (1967), *The New Industrial State*, 2nd edn (Harmondsworth: Penguin Books, 1974)

Galbraith, J.K. (1969), *How to Control the Military* (Garden City: Doubleday and Company)

Galbraith, J.K. (1971), *Economics, Peace and Laughter* (Harmondsworth: Penguin Books, 1975)

Galbraith, J.K. (1977), *The Age of Uncertainty*, (London: British Broadcasting Corporation and André Deutsch)

Gauthier, D. (1986), *Morals by Agreement* (Oxford: Clarendon Press)

Goffman, E. (1959), *The Presentation of Self in Everyday Life* (Harmondsworth: Penguin Books, 1971)

Goldberg, V.P. (1985), 'Production Functions, Transaction Costs and the New Institutionalism', in G.R. Feiwel, ed., *Issues in Contemporary Microeconomics and Welfare* (London: Macmillan), pp. 395–402

Granovetter, M. (1974), *Getting a Job*, 2nd edn (Chicago: University of Chicago Press, 1995)

Granovetter, M. (1992), 'Economic Institutions as Social Constructions: A Framework for Analysis', *Acta Sociologica*, Vol. 35, reprinted in R. Swedberg, ed., *Economic Sociology* (Cheltenham: Edward Elgar, 1996), pp. 269–77

Hamilton, W.H. (1932), 'Institution', in E.R.A. Seligman and A. Johnson, eds, *The Encyclopedia of Social Sciences*, reprinted in G.M. Hodgson, ed., *The Economics of Institutions*, supra, pp. 3–8

Hansmann, H. (1989), 'The Economics and Ethics of Markets for Human Organs', *Journal of Health Politics, Policy and Law*, Vol. 14, pp. 57–85

Hayek, F.A. (1949), *Individualism and Economic Order* (London: Routledge and Kegan Paul)

Hayek, F.A. (1960), *The Constitution of Liberty* (London: Routledge and Kegan Paul)

Hayek, F.A. (1973), *Law, Legislation and Liberty*, Vol. I: *Rules and Order* (London: Routledge and Kegan Paul)

Hayek, F.A. (1975), *Law, Legislation and Liberty*, Vol. II: *The Mirage of Social Justice* (London: Routledge and Kegan Paul)

Hayek, F.A. (1979), *Law, Legislation and Liberty*, Vol. III: *The Political Order of a Free People* (London: Routledge and Kegan Paul)

Hayek, F.A. (1988), *The Fatal Conceit* (London: Routledge and Kegan Paul)

Heiner, R.A. (1983), 'The Origin of Predictable Behavior', *American Economic Review*, Vol. 73, pp. 560-95

Hirsch, F. (1977), *Social Limits to Growth* (London: Routledge and Kegan Paul)

Hirshleifer, J. (1985), 'The Expanding Domain of Economics', *American Economic Review*, Vol. 75, Supplement, pp. 53-68

Hobson, J.A. (1914), *Work and Wealth*, 2nd edn (London: George Allen and Unwin, 1933)

Hodgson, G.M. (1988), *Economics and Institutions* (Cambridge: Polity Press)

Hodgson, G.M. (1989), 'Institutional Rigidities and Economic Growth', *Cambridge Journal of Economics*, Vol. 13, in G.M. Hodgson, ed., *The Economics of Institutions* (Aldershot: Edward Elgar, 1993), pp. 570-592

Hodgson, G.M. (1993), *Economics and Evolution* (Cambridge: Polity Press)

Hodgson, G.M. (1999), *Evolution and Institutions* (Cheltenham: Edward Elgar)

Hoffman, M.L. (1981), 'Is Altruism Part of Human Nature?', *Journal of Personality and Social Psychology*, Vol. 40, pp. 121-37

Hume, D. (1739/40), *A Treatise of Human Nature* (London: Longmans, Green and Co., 1898)

Hume, D. (1752), *Political Discourses*, in E. Rotwein, ed., *David Hume: Writings on Economics* (London: Nelson, 1955)

Hutton, W. (1995), *The State We're In* (London: Jonathan Cape)

Jacobs, J. (1961), *The Death and Life of Great American Cities* (Harmondsworth: Penguin Books, 1964)

Jevons, W.S. (1871), *The Theory of Political Economy*, ed. by R.D.C. Black (Harmondsworth: Penguin Books, 1970)

Jevons, W.S. (1882), *The State in Relation to Labour*, 4th edn (London: Macmillan, 1910)

Johnson, D.B. (1982), 'The Free-Rider Principle, the Charity Market and the Economics of Blood', *British Journal of Social Psychology*, Vol. 21, pp. 93-106

Kahneman, D. (1994), 'New Challenges to the Rationality Assumption', *Journal of Institutional and Theoretical Economics*, Vol. 150, pp. 18-36

Kahneman, D., Knetsch, J.L. and Thaler, R.H. (1986), 'Fairness and the Assumptions of Economics', *Journal of Business*, Vol. 59, pp. 285-300

Kahneman, D. and Tversky, A. (1979), 'Prospect Theory: An Analysis of Decision Under Risk', *Econometrica*, Vol. 47, pp. 263-91

Kant, I. (1785), *Groundwork of the Metaphysic of Morals*, tr. by H.J. Paton, in H.J. Paton, ed., *The Moral Law* (London: Hutchinson University Library, 1961)

Kasper, W. and Streit, M.E. (1998), *Institutional Economics* (Cheltenham: Edward Elgar)

Katona, G. (1951), *Psychological Analysis of Economic Behavior* (New York: McGraw-Hill)

Katona, G. (1964), *The Mass Consumption Society* (New York: McGraw-Hill)

Keynes, J.M. (1930), 'Economic Possibilities for Our Grandchildren', in *The Collected Writings of John Maynard Keynes*, Vol. IX: *Essays in Persuasion* (London: Macmillan, 1972), pp. 321–32

Keynes, J.M. (1936), 'The General Theory of Employment, Interest and Money', in *The Collected Writings of John Maynard Keynes*, Vol. VIII (London: Macmillan, 1973)

Keynes, J.M. (1937), 'The General Theory of Employment', *Quarterly Journal of Economics*, Vol. 51, in *The Collected Writings of John Maynard Keynes*, Vol. XIV (London: Macmillan, 1973), pp. 109–23

Knight, F.H. (1921), *Risk, Uncertainty and Profit* (Boston: Houghton Mifflin)

Knight, F.H. (1935), *The Ethics of Competition and Other Essays* (Freeport: Books for Libraries Press, 1969)

Kropotkin, P. (1902), *Mutual Aid* (London: William Heinemann)

Kuran, T. (1995), *Private Truths, Public Lies* (Cambridge, Mass.: Harvard University Press)

Lancaster, K.J. (1966a), 'A New Approach to Consumer Theory', *Journal of Political Economy*, Vol. 74, in *Modern Consumer Theory* (Aldershot: Edward Elgar, 1991), pp. 11–43

Lancaster, K.J. (1966b), 'Change and Innovation in the Technology of Consumption', *American Economic Review*, Vol. 56, in *Modern Consumer Theory*, supra, pp. 44–9

Lancaster, K.J. (1975), 'Socially Optimal Product Differentiation', *American Economic Review*, Vol. 65, in *Modern Consumer Theory*, supra, pp. 155–80

Langlois, R.N. (1998), 'Transaction Costs, Production Costs, and the Passage of Time', in S.G. Medema, ed., *Coasean Economics: Law and Economics and the New Institutional Economics* (Boston: Kluwer Academic), pp. 1–21

La Porta, R., Lopez-de-Silanes, F., Schleifer, A. and Vishny, R.W. (1997), 'Trust in Large Organizations', *American Economic Review (Papers and Proceedings)*, Vol. 87, in P. Dasgupta and I. Serageldin (eds), *Social Capital: A Multifaceted Perspective* (Washington, D.C.: The World Bank, 2000), pp. 310–21

Leibenstein, H. (1950), 'Bandwagon, Snob, and Veblen Effects in the Theory of Consumers' Demand', *Quarterly Journal of Economics*, Vol. 54, in *Beyond Economic Man*, infra, pp. 48-67

Leibenstein, H. (1966), 'X-Efficiency versus Allocative Efficiency', *American Economic Review*, Vol. 56, in *Beyond Economic Man*, infra, pp. 29-47

Leibenstein, H. (1976), *Beyond Economic Man* (Cambridge, Mass.: Harvard University Press)

Leibenstein, H. (1987), *Inside the Firm: The Inefficiencies of Hierarchy* (Cambridge, Mass.: Harvard University Press)

Lindblom, C.E. (1982), 'The Market as Prison', *Journal of Politics*, Vol. 44, pp. 324-36

Loasby, B. (1976), *Choice, Complexity and Ignorance* (Cambridge: Cambridge University Press)

Locke, J. (1690), *An Essay Concerning the True Original, Extent and End of Civil Government (Second Treatise on Civil Government)*, ed. by P. Laslett (Cambridge: Cambridge University Press, 1960)

Loewenstein, G. and Adler, D. (1995), 'A Bias in the Prediction of Tastes', *Economic Journal*, Vol. 105, pp. 929-37

Loewenstein, G. and Prelec, D. (1992), 'Anomalies in Intertemporal Choice: Evidence and an Interpretation', *Quarterly Journal of Economics*, Vol. 107, pp. 573-97

Löwe, A. (1935), *Economics and Sociology: A Plea for Co-operation in the Social Sciences* (London: George Allen and Unwin)

Lutz, M.A. and Lux, K. (1979), *The Challenge of Humanistic Economics* (Menlo Park, CA.: Benjamin/Cummings)

Lutz, M.A. and Lux, K. (1988), *Humanistic Economics: The New Challenge* (New York: The Bootstrap Press)

Malinowski, B. (1922), *Argonauts of the Western Pacific* (London: Routledge and Kegan Paul)

Malthus, T.R. (1798), *An Essay on the Principle of Population*, ed. by A. Flew (Harmondsworth: Penguin, 1970)

Marris, R. (1998), *Managerial Capitalism in Retrospect* (London: Macmillan)

Marshall, A. (1873), 'The Future of the Working Classes', in A.C. Pigou, ed., *Memorials of Alfred Marshall* (New York: Augustus M. Kelley, 1966), pp. 101-18

Marshall, A. (1879), *The Elements of Industry*, 2nd edn (London: Macmillan, 1881)

Marshall, A. (1890), *Principles of Economics*, 8th edn (1920) (London: Macmillan, 1949)

Marshall, A. (1897), 'The Old Generation of Economists and the New', *Quarterly Journal of Economics*, Vol. 12, in A.C. Pigou, ed., *Memorials of Alfred Marshall* (New York: Augustus M. Kelley, 1966), pp. 295-311

Marshall, A. (1919), *Industry and Trade*, 4th edn (London: Macmillan, 1923)

Marx, K. (1842), *Wage-Labour and Capital*, in *Karl Marx: Selected Works*, Vol. I (London: Lawrence and Wishart, 1942)

Marx, K. (1844a), 'Critique of the Hegelian Philosophy of Law', in T.B. Bottomore and M. Rubel, eds, *Karl Marx: Selected Writings in Sociology and Social Philosophy* (Harmondsworth: Penguin Books, 1963)

Marx, K. (1844b), 'Contribution to the Critique of Hegel's Philosophy of Right. Introduction', in *Karl Marx: Early Writings*, ed. by T.B. Bottomore (London: G.A. Watts, 1963)

Marx, K. (1844c), *Economic and Philosophic Manuscripts of 1844*, tr. by M. Milligan (London: Lawrence and Wishart, 1973)

Marx, K. (1867), *Capital*, Vol. I (Moscow: Foreign Languages Publishing House, 1961)

Marx, K. (1875), *Critique of the Gotha Programme*, in *Karl Marx: Selected Works*, Vol. II (London: Lawrence and Wishart, 1942), pp. 505–601

Marx, K. and Engels, F. (1845-6), *The German Ideology*, Part I, ed. by C.J. Arthur (London: Lawrence and Wishart, 1970)

Maslow, A.H. (1954), *Motivation and Personality*, 2nd edn (New York: Harper and Row, 1970)

Maslow, A.H. (1962), *Toward a Psychology of Being*, 2nd edn (Princeton: Van Nostrand, 1968)

Matthews, R.C.O. (1981), 'Morality, Competition and Efficiency', *The Manchester School*, Vol. 49, pp. 289–309

Mauss, M. (1950), *The Gift*, tr. by W.D. Halls (London: Routledge, 1990)

Mayo, E. (1949), *The Social Problems of an Industrial Civilization* (London: Routledge and Kegan Paul)

Menger, C. (1871), *Principles of Economics*, tr. by J. Dingwall and B.F. Hoselitz (New York: New York University Press, 1976)

Menger, C. (1883), *Investigations into the Method of the Social Sciences with Special Reference to Economics*, tr. by F.J. Nock (New York: New York University Press, 1985)

Mill, J.S. (1848), *Principles of Political Economy*, 9th edn, ed. by W.J. Ashley (London: Longmans, Green and Co., 1909)

Mill, J.S. (1859), *On Liberty*, ed. by G. Himmelfarb (Harmondsworth: Penguin Books, 1974)

Mill, J.S. (1861), *Utilitarianism*, in *John Stuart Mill: Collected Works*, Vol. X: *Essays on Ethics, Religion and Society* (Toronto: University of Toronto Press, 1969), pp. 203–59

Mises, L. von (1949), *Human Action*, 3rd edn (Chicago: Contemporary Books, 1966)

Nagel, T. (1970), *The Possibility of Altruism* (Oxford: Clarendon Press)

Nelson, R.R. and Winter, S.G. (1982), *An Evolutionary Theory of Economic Change* (Cambridge, Mass.: Harvard University Press)

Nisbet, R.A. (1968), *Tradition and Revolt* (New York: Random House)

North, D.C. (1990), *Institutions, Institutional Change and Economic Performance* (Cambridge: Cambridge University Press)

Oakeshott, M. (1956), 'On Being Conservative', in *Rationalism in Politics* (London: Methuen, 1962)

Olson, M. (1965), *The Logic of Collective Action* (Cambridge, Mass.: Harvard University Press)

Olson, M. (1982), *The Rise and Decline of Nations* (New Haven: Yale University Press)

Olson, M. (1996), 'Big Bills Left on the Sidewalk: Why Some Nations are Rich, and Others Poor', *Journal of Economic Perspectives*, Vol. 10, pp. 3–24

Olson, M. (2000), *Power and Prosperity: Outgrowing Communist and Capitalist Dictatorships* (New York: Basic Books)

Ostrom, E. (1990), *Governing the Commons: The Evolution of Institutions for Collective Action* (Cambridge: Cambridge University Press)

Ostrom, E. (2000), 'Social capital: a fad or a fundamental concept?', in P. Dasgupta and I. Serageldin, eds, *Social Capital: A Multifaceted Perspective* (Washington, D.C.: The World Bank), pp. 172–214

Oswald, A.J. (1997), 'Happiness and Economic Performance', *Economic Journal*, Vol. 107, pp. 1815–31

Parsons, T. (1931), 'Wants and Activities in Marshall', *Quarterly Journal of Economics*, Vol. 46, in *Structure of Social Action* (1937) (New York: The Free Press, 1968), pp. 129–77

Parsons, T. and Smelser, N.J. (1956), *Economy and Society* (London: Routledge and Kegan Paul)

Penrose, E. (1959), *The Theory of the Growth of the Firm*, 3rd edn (Oxford: Oxford University Press, 1995)

Piaget, J. (1971), *Biology and Knowledge* (Chicago: University of Chicago Press)

Plato (c.375), *The Republic*, tr. by D. Lee (Harmondsworth: Penguin, 1974)

Polanyi, M. (1967), *The Tacit Dimension* (London: Routledge and Kegan Paul)

Putnam, R.D. (1993), *Making Democracy Work* (Princeton: Princeton University Press)

Putnam, R.D. (1995), 'Bowling Alone: America's Declining Social Capital', *Journal of Democracy*, Vol. 6, pp. 65–78

Rabin, M. (1998), 'Psychology and Economics', *Journal of Economic Literature*, Vol. 36, pp. 11–46

Rawls, J. (1971), *A Theory of Justice* (Oxford: Clarendon Press, 1972)

Roberts, R.D. and Wolkoff, M.J. (1988), 'Improving the Quality and Quantity of Whole Blood Supply: Limits to Voluntary Arrangements', *Journal of Health Politics, Policy and Law*, Vol. 13, pp. 167–78

Runciman, W.G. (1966), *Relative Deprivation and Social Justice* (London: Routledge and Kegan Paul)

Sahlins, M.D. (1968), 'Notes on the Original Affluent Society', in R.B. Lee and I. DeVore, eds, *Man the Hunter* (Chicago: Aldine), pp. 85–9

Sahlins, M.D. (1972), *Stone Age Economics* (London: Tavistock)

Sahlins, M.D. (1976), *Culture and Practical Reason* (Chicago: University of Chicago Press)

Samuels, W.J. and Medema, S.G. (1998), 'Ronald Coase on Economic Policy Analysis: Framework and Implications', in S.G. Medema, ed., *Coasean Economics: Law and Economics and the New Institutional Economics* (Boston: Kluwer Academic), pp. 161–83

Sartre, J.P. (1946), *In Camera (Huis Clos)*, tr. by S. Gilbert (London: Hamish Hamilton)

Schlicht, E. (1998), *On Custom in the Economy* (Oxford: Oxford University Press)

Schoeck, H. (1969), *Envy*, tr. by M. Glenny and B. Ross (London: Secker and Warburg)

Schotter, A. (1981), *The Economic Theory of Social Institutions* (Cambridge: Cambridge University Press)

Schumacher, E.F. (1973), *Small is Beautiful* (London: Abacus, 1974)

Schumpeter, J.A. (1911), *The Theory of Economic Development*, tr. by R.Opie (New York: Oxford University Press, 1961)

Schumpeter, J.A. (1942), *Capitalism, Socialism and Democracy*, 5th edn (London: George Allen and Unwin, 1976)

Schumpeter, J.A. (1954), *History of Economic Analysis* (London: George Allen and Unwin)

Schwartz, B. (1967), 'The Social Psychology of the Gift', *American Journal of Sociology*, Vol. 73, pp. 1–11

Scitovsky, T. (1976), *The Joyless Economy* (London: Oxford University Press)

Sen, A. (1977), 'Rational Fools: A Critique of the Behavioural Foundations of Economic Theory', *Philosophy and Public Affairs*, Vol. 6, in *Choice, Welfare and Measurement* (Oxford: Basil Blackwell, 1982), pp. 84–106

Shackle, G.L.S. (1967), *The Years of High Theory* (Cambridge: Cambridge University Press)

Shackle, G.L.S. (1972), *Epistemics and Economics* (Cambridge: Cambridge University Press)

Simon, H.A. (1957), *Models of Man* (New York: Wiley)

Simon, H.A. (1959), 'Theories of Decision-Making in Economics and Behavioral Science', *American Economic Review*, Vol. 49, pp. 253–83

Simon, H.A. (1965), *Administrative Behavior*, 2nd edn (Glencoe: The Free Press)

Simon, H.A. (1979), 'Rational Decision Making in Business Organizations', *American Economic Review*, Vol. 69, pp. 493–513

Smith, A. (1759), *The Theory of Moral Sentiments*, 6th edn (New York: Augustus M. Kelley, 1966)

Smith, A. (1763), *Lectures on Justice, Police, Revenue and Arms*, ed. by E. Cannan (Oxford: Clarendon Press, 1896)

Smith, A. (1776), *The Wealth of Nations*, ed. by E. Cannan (London: Methuen, 1961)

Smith, A. (1795), 'The History of Astronomy', in *Essays on Philosophical Subjects*, reprinted in J.R. Lindgren, ed., *The Early Writings of Adam Smith* (New York: Augustus M. Kelley, 1967)

Sombart, W. (1915), *The Quintessence of Capitalism*, tr. by M. Epstein (London: T. Fisher Unwin)

Stigler, G.J. and Becker, G.S. (1977), 'De Gustibus Non Est Disputandum', *American Economic Review*, Vol. 67, in Becker, *Accounting for Tastes* supra, pp. 24–49

Tawney, R.H. (1933), 'The Study of Economic History', in J.M. Winter, ed., *History and Society: Essays by R.H. Tawney* (London: Routledge and Kegan Paul, 1978)

Teece, D.J., Rumelt, R., Dosi, G. and Winter, S.G. (1994), 'Understanding Corporate Coherence: Theory and Evidence', *Journal of Economic Behavior and Organization,* Vol. 23, pp. 1–30

Thaler, R.H. (1980), 'Toward a Positive Theory of Consumer Choice', *Journal of Economic Behavior and Organization*, Vol. 1, pp. 39–60

Titmuss, R.M. (1970), *The Gift Relationship* (Harmondsworth: Penguin Books, 1973)

Townsend, P. (1979), *Poverty in the United Kingdom* (Harmondsworth: Penguin Books)

Tversky, A. and Kahneman, D. (1974), 'Judgement under Uncertainty: Heuristics and Biases', *Science*, Vol. 185, in D. Kahneman, P. Slovic and A. Tversky, eds, *Judgement Under Uncertainty: Heuristics and Biases* (Cambridge: Cambridge University Press, 1982)

Tversky, A. and Kahneman, D. (1981), 'The Framing of Decisions and the Psychology of Choice', *Science*, Vol. 211, pp. 453–8

Vanberg, V.J. (1986), 'Spontaneous Market Order and Social Rules: A Critical Examination of F.A. Hayek's Theory of Cultural Evolution', *Economics and Philosophy*, Vol. 2, in Vanberg, *Rules and Choice in Economics*, infra, pp. 77–94

Vanberg, V.J. (1994), *Rules and Choice in Economics* (London: Routledge)

Vanberg, V.J. and Buchanan, J.M. (1989), 'Interests and Theories in Constitutional Choice', *Journal of Theoretical Politics*, Vol. 1, in Vanberg, *Rules and Choice in Economics*, supra, pp. 167–77

Veblen, T. (1899), *The Theory of the Leisure Class* (London: George Allen and Unwin, 1970)

Veblen, T. (1899/1900), 'The Preconceptions of Economic Science', *Quarterly Journal of Economics*, Vols 13 and 14, in W.C. Mitchell, ed., *What Veblen Taught* (New York: The Viking Press, 1936)

Veblen, T.B. (1904), *The Theory of Business Enterprise* (Clifton, N.J.: Augustus M. Kelley, 1975)

Veblen, T. (1906), 'The Place of Science in Modern Civilization', *American Journal of Sociology*, Vol. 11, in W.C. Mitchell, ed., *What Veblen Taught*, supra.

Veblen, T.B. (1914), *The Instinct of Workmanship* (New York: Augustus M. Kelley, 1964)

Veblen, T. (1919), *The Place of Science in Modern Civilisation and Other Essays* (London: Routledge/Thoemmes Press, 1994)

Veenhoven, R. (1993), *Happiness in Nations* (Rotterdam: Erasmus University)

Wallas, G. (1921), *Our Social Heritage* (London: George Allen and Unwin)

Weber, M. (1947), *The Theory of Social and Economic Organization*, tr. by A.M. Henderson and T. Parsons (New York: The Free Press)

Williamson, O.E. (1975), *Markets and Hierarchies* (New York: The Free Press)

Williamson, O.E. (1985), *The Economic Institutions of Capitalism* (New York: The Free Press)

Wilson, E.O. (1975), *Sociobiology: The New Synthesis* (Cambridge, Mass.: Belknap Press)

Winter, J.M. and Joslin, D.M. (1972), eds, *R.H. Tawney's Commonplace Book* (Cambridge: Cambridge University Press)

Wolf, C. (1970), 'The Present Value of the Past', *Journal of Political Economy*, Vol. 78, pp. 783–92

Wright, D. (1971), *The Psychology of Moral Behaviour* (Harmondsworth: Penguin Books)

Wrong, D.H. (1961), 'The Oversocialized Conception of Man in Modern Sociology', *American Sociological Review*, Vol. 26, pp. 183–93

Index

absolute status 69–71
Ackerman, F. 75
adaptation 14–15
addiction 83–6
Adler, D. 52, 53
administrative coordination 229
affluence *see* wealth
AGIL schema (adaptation, goal
　　attainment, integration, latency)
　　14–15
Alchian, A.A. 202
alienation 175
allocation 3
altruism 2, 95–118, 119
　gift relationship 101–8
　gifts and groups 108–18
　and self-interest 96–101, 104–6
　politics of benevolence 134–9
anal eroticism 169–70
anthropocentric economics 142, 162–70
APQT (activity, pace, quality, time)
　　198–9
Argyle, M. 3, 143
Arrow, K.J. 104, 221
Asch, S.E. 24, 108
attachment 200–1
authority 51–2
Axelrod, R. 42

bargaining, Coaseian 237–8
Baudrillard, J. 67, 89
Baumol, W.J. 137
Baxter, J.L. 3
Bay of Pigs landing 1961 63
Becker, G.S. 4, 5, 10, 16, 99
　addiction 83, 84–6
benevolence *see* altruism
bias, cognitive 49–59, 64
Bible, the 101–2, 123, 130, 171
Blau, P.M. 16, 99
Bocock, R. 159

Boland, L.A. 44
blood
　donations 100, 104, 113–14, 138, 139
　market for 116–17
Boulding, K.E. 12–13, 30, 97, 112–13,
　　227
bounded rationality 45–9, 64, 243
Bourdieu, P. 78–9
Brazil 146
Buchanan, J.M. 32, 38, 96, 123–4, 161,
　　202
　constitutions 39
　uncertainty 40
bureaucrats 225–8
Burke, E. 30
Burt, R.S. 196

cadaveric organs 117
capitalism 166–8
　hierarchy of needs 159–60
　work and need 174–6
　see also market
cartels 219
Catholic Church 211
change 177–8
characteristics approach to commodities
　　87–9
China 163, 219–20
Choi, Young Back 128
choice
　choices and consequences 57–9
　constitutions and choices 38–43
　freedom of 65–6, 87–94
　individual choice 10, 18–22, 250
　kaleidoscope of 87–91
class 78
Coase, R.H. 223
　transaction costs 230–41 *passim*
coercion, democratic 137, 238
cognitive bias 49–59, 64
cognitive dissonance 181